AF291480

NIGHTMARE

ON ONE SHEET

Korero Press Ltd,
157 Mornington Road, London, E11 3DT, UK

www.koreropress.com

First published in 2023 © Korero Press Ltd

ISBN-13: 9781912740239

Book Design by Belle Piec and Yak El-Droubie

A CIP catalogue record for this book is available from the British Library

Printed in China

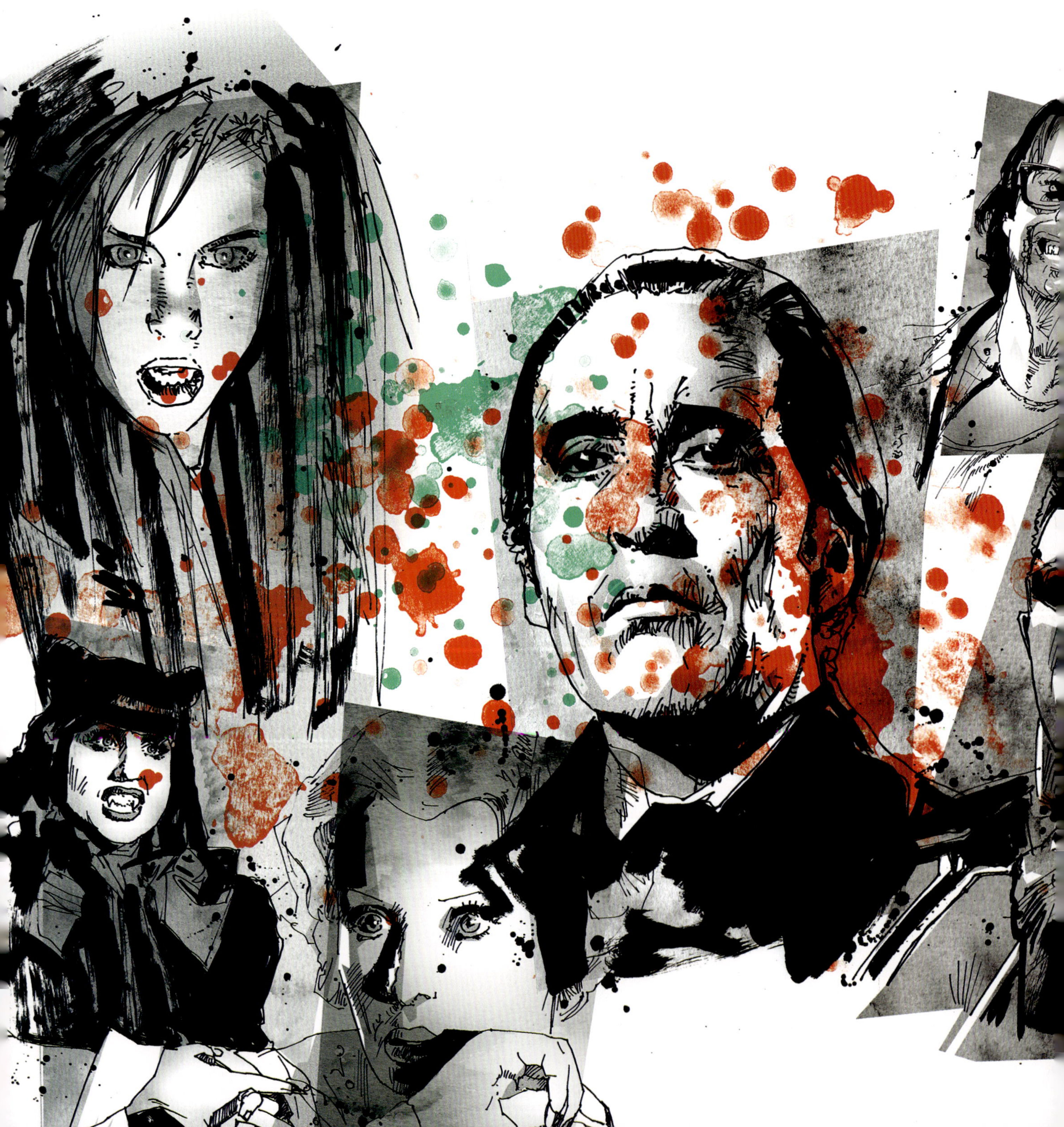

NIGHTMARE
ON ONE SHEET
THE HORROR ART OF GRAHAM HUMPHREYS

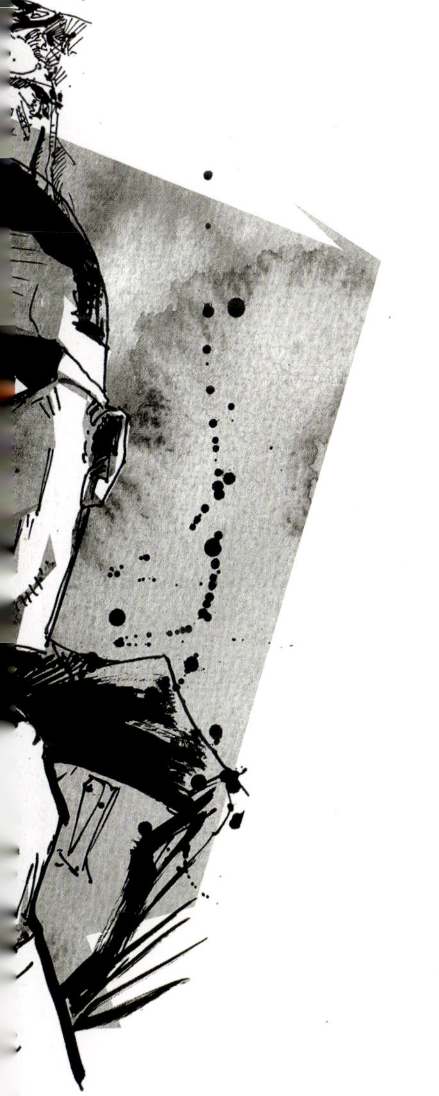

KORERO
PRESS

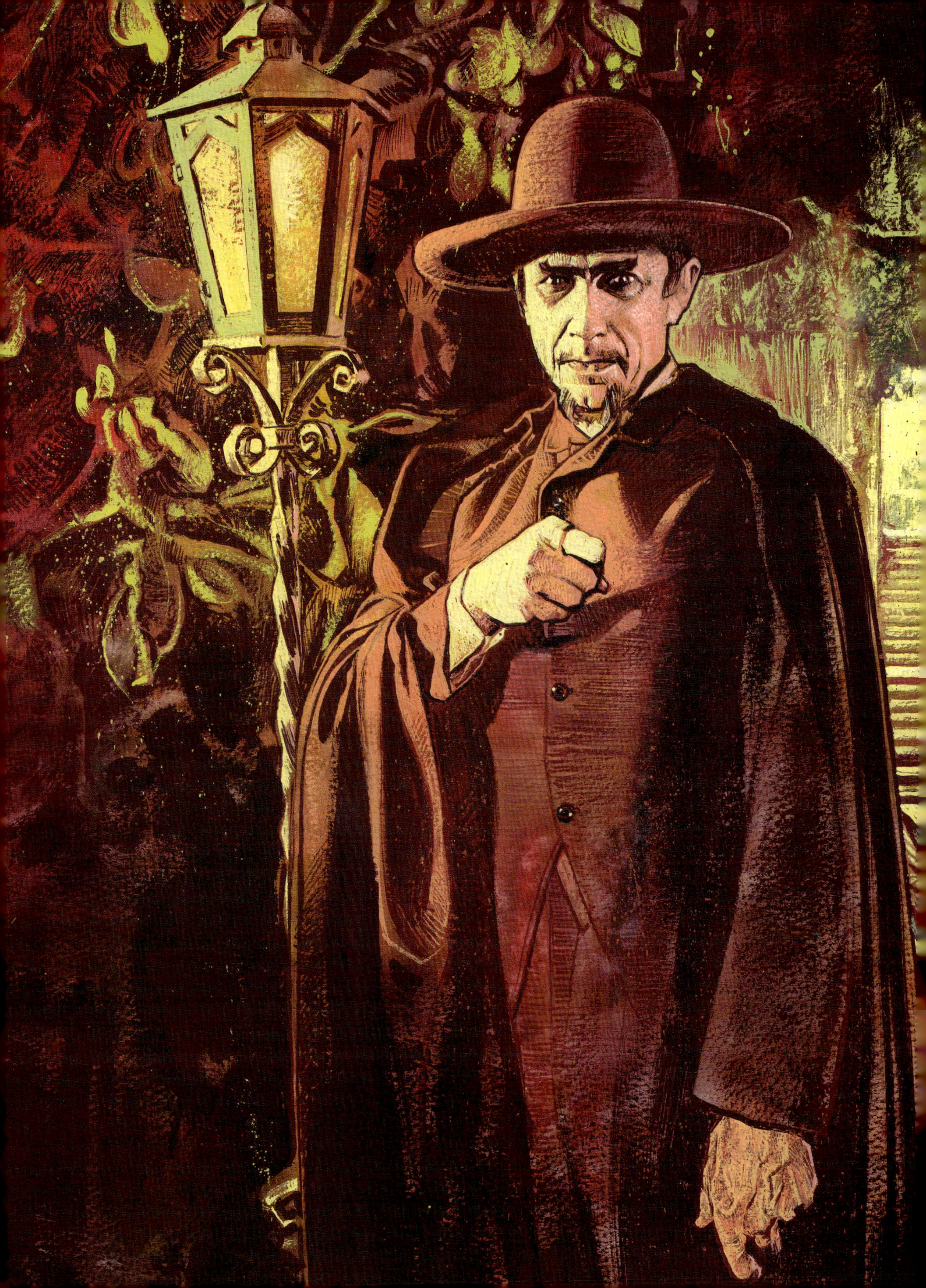

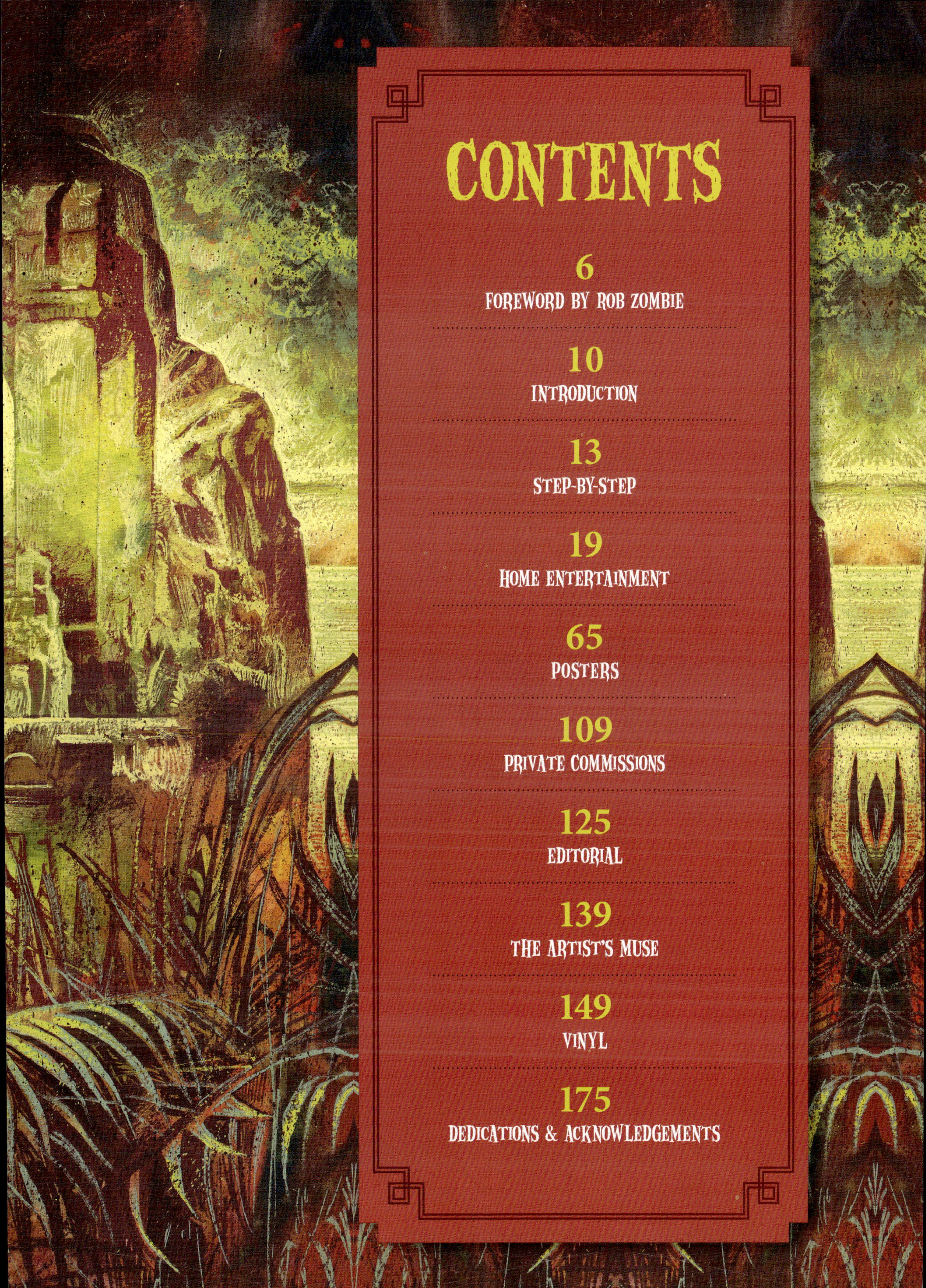

CONTENTS

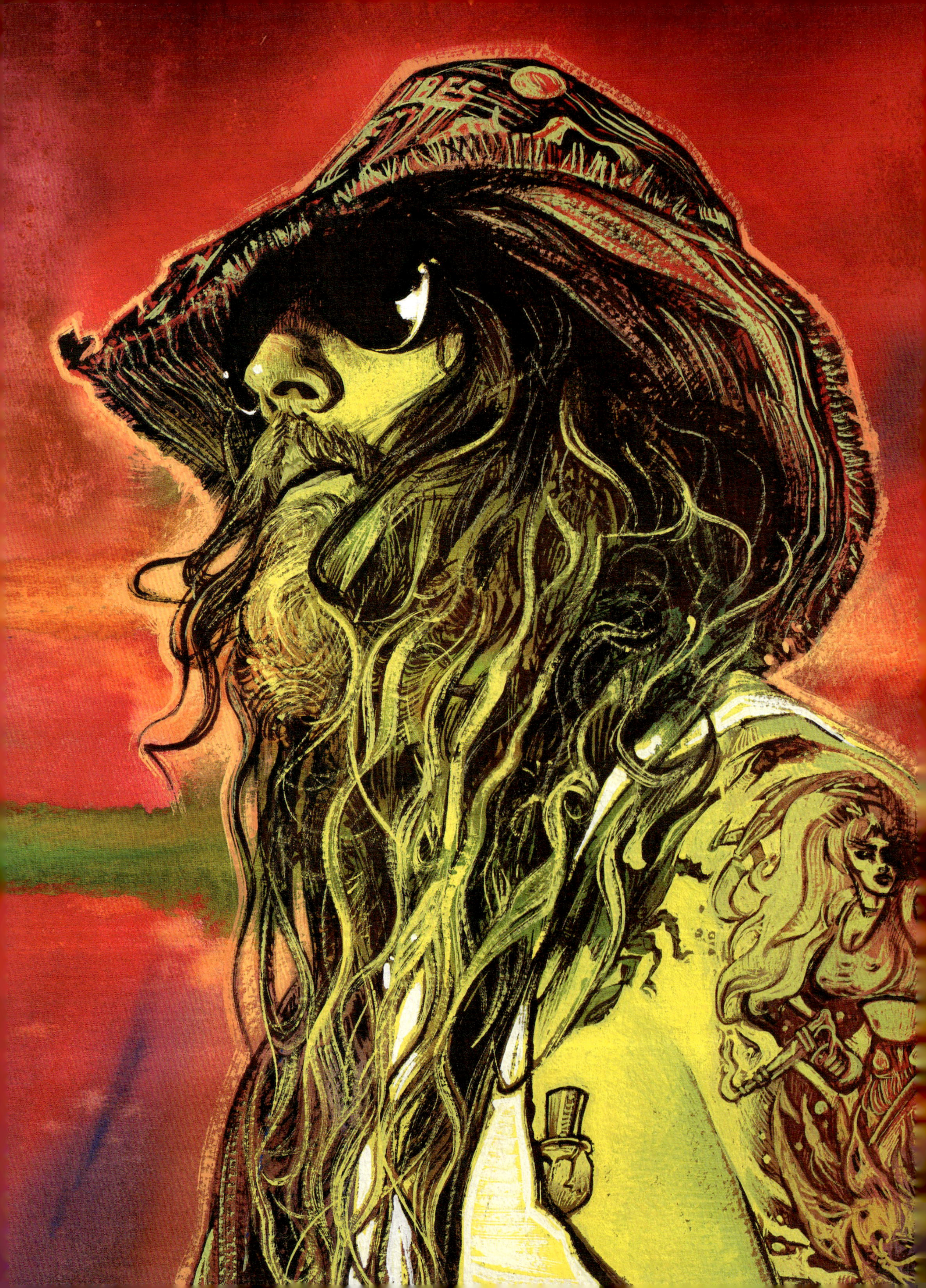

FOREWORD

L et's discuss the art of horror or monster art, or whatever… call it what you like. It's hard to explain the importance of this subject to the new generation of monster fans. In these days of overly Photoshopped images plastered on one sheets and DVD covers, what's the point of spending countless hours toiling over a hand-painted image? Seems like a lot of work.

Well, I'll tell you the reason. It's art… and art takes time. Even if you recognize the reference photo used by the artist to create his masterpiece, there's still something extra that elevates it to another level. Once a human hand puts a pen or brush to paper, magic happens! The strokes of colour form into something otherworldly. It goes beyond what a mere photo can convey to the viewer.

The artist breathes new life into the image, even though sometimes it's an image you've seen a million times. For instance, take a photo of Lon Chaney from *The Phantom of the Opera* – an amazing actor in an iconic role in a classic film. A black and white photo from the film is certainly incredible to see, but it's not quite alive. Now put that same photo in the hands of a master artist, and bam! — the phantom lives again!

We older monster fans remember a time when the painted poster sucked us into a movie like a tractor beam. Granted, many a time the poster was way, way better than the actual film, but somehow we didn't care. I'd say that Reynold Brown is the man most responsible for making lousy movies seem amazing. A few examples being *Monster on the Campus*, *Attack of the 50 Foot Woman*, *The Amazing Colossal Man*, *Attack of the Puppet People*… and so on.

Then you had monster magazines. So many artists brought our favourite creatures to life on those glorious covers, but the king of the eye-catching cover image was, without a doubt, Basil Gogos. Starting in 1960 with the screaming face of Vincent Price in *The Pit and the Pendulum*, our dear Basil blazed a trail of mind-blowingly psychedelic *Famous Monsters of Filmland* covers that still take our breath away. The way he could take a black and white fiend like Karloff's Frankenstein monster and explode him with colour, yet somehow stay true to the original, is a baffling wonder.

Back then, in a time before you could access any movie, any time, anywhere, these covers were all we had. Sure, inside the magazine were photos from the actual films, but they were low quality on cheap paper. It was the cover painting that brought the *Famous Monsters of Filmland* to life in our little minds.

LEFT: *Rob Zombie* (2021), Waxwork Records; logo element.

The series of classic horror soundtrack releases *Rob Zombie Presents* required a portrait in the same style as the covers. A black and white photo was selected as my reference for the art, with the instruction to interpret it with my own colours.

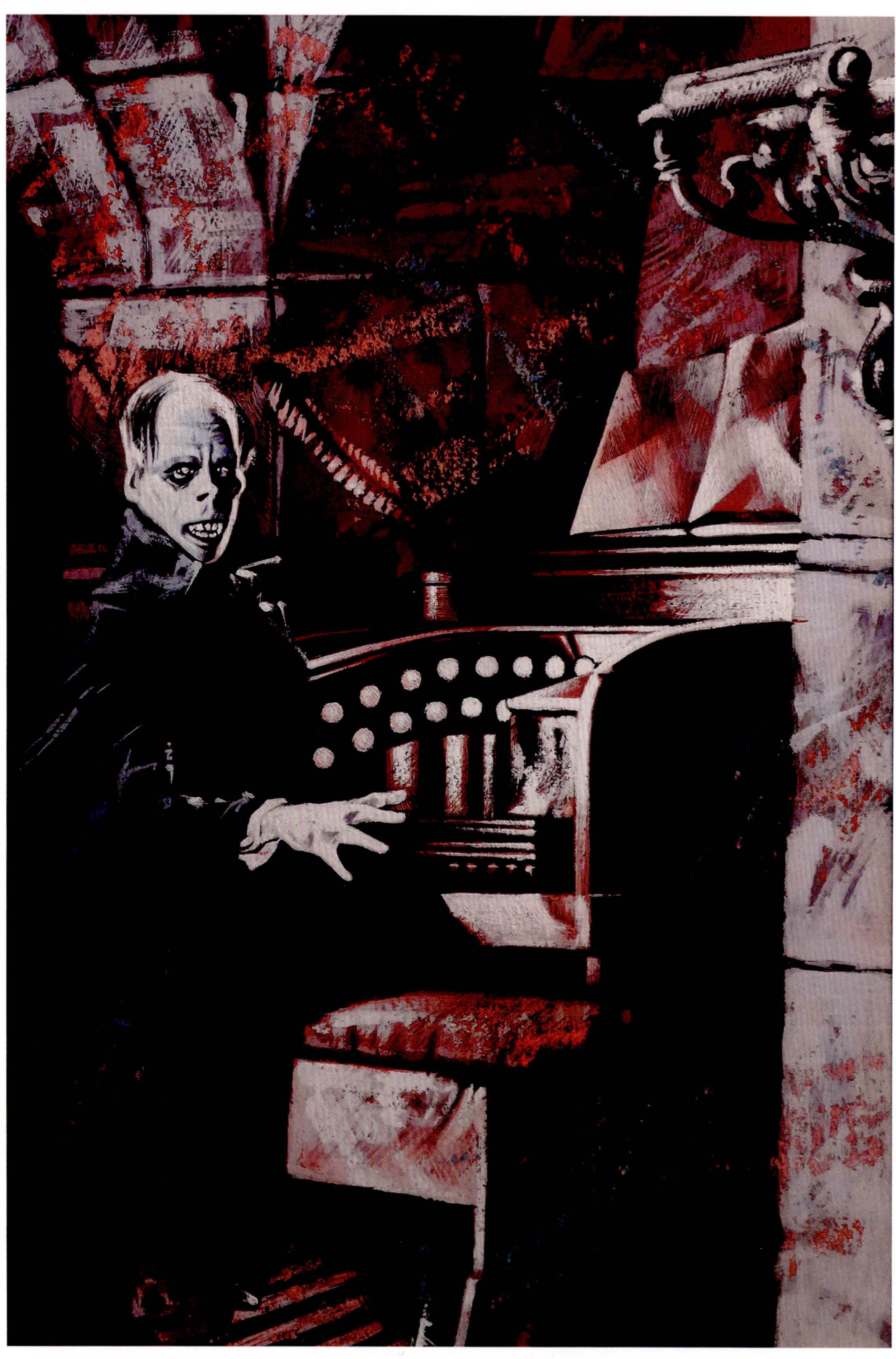

But personally, I believe the first painted images that really grabbed me were the James Bama box art for the Aurora models kits. Man, those things just flew off the shelf into our clammy little hands. I'm sure you felt the same disappointment that I did when I compared my crummy paint job on the model with the incredible box art. Anyway, my point is that there's a rich tradition of excellent monster art. Something I hope never dies — and it won't as long as we have cats like Graham Humphreys on the scene.

Graham is a master at bringing a film to life in a two-dimensional space. Take a gander at his work… the images literally jump off the page, whether it's Christopher Lee or Bruce Campbell, the result is equally remarkable. The aspect of his work I admire the most is his ability to really capture the subject's vibe. It's not just that he's a master craftsman and can nail the likeness… it's something more. His images seem to breathe the same air as the actual people he represents.

So, it goes without saying that when I was looking for an artist to bring the *Rob Zombie Presents* soundtracks to life, I knew exactly who to go to. Thanks to Graham, *White Zombie*, *Spider Baby*, and *The Last Man on Earth* live again!

And of course, *The Munsters*. Who better to bring the new gang from Mockingbird Lane into the now? The Munsters never looked so good.

So, in closing, I'll say… support your local monster artist!

ROB ZOMBIE
Hollywood, California

OPPOSITE: *The Phantom of the Opera* (1980); artist's folio sample.

In the year that I left art college, I was experimenting with techniques that can be recognised in my earliest commercial work, most notably the quad poster for *The Evil Dead* (see page 140).

This painting measures little more than 18 x 13 cm and is painted on illustration board, with a scratched gouache surface over a base of scribbled oil pastel. This was a technique I'd abandoned by 1984, as I was aware that the surface became fragile where the water-based gouache was placed over the repelling oil pastel.

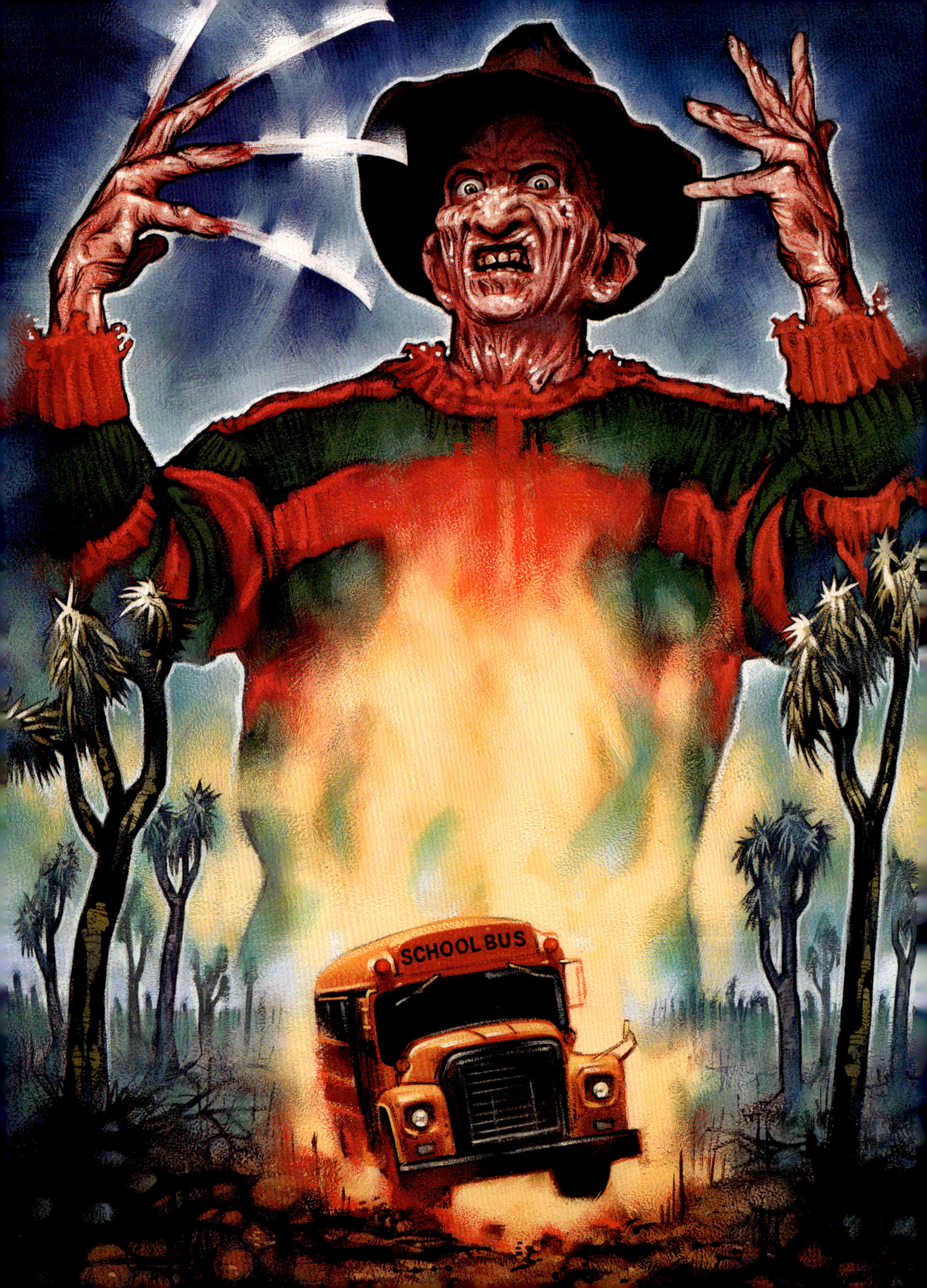
SCHOOL BUS

INTRODUCTION

I t was with great pride that in 2019 I was able to present a collection of my commissioned work in a volume called *Hung, Drawn and Executed*. The book included a number of older paintings, to provide some additional context for the nature of my work — for instance, vintage VHS cover art that eventually led to commissions for new Blu-ray cover art.

Since submitting the images for *Hung, Drawn and Executed*, I've amassed a further body of work, justifying the publication of this new volume, *A Nightmare on One Sheet*. The terrible pun in its title aside, I felt a reference to the earlier part of my career would prove relevant in the new book, too — context is everything — so a couple of vintage paintings have been included. However, this collection is mostly the output from the latter half of 2019 and the two years of Covid pandemic lockdowns that followed. Although I'd previously worked from a London West End office space, I found myself obliged to work from home — back in the very same corner of a room where I'd worked 35 years earlier: in Tooting, South London. With little else to occupy my time, my work became more focused, and I feel that I produced some of my best art during those Covid-ravaged years. By its very nature, my output is the product of a solitary profession.

During the pandemic, with so many people confined to their homes — some furloughed from work or on reduced hours — home entertainment really came into its own. Whilst streaming is a favoured way for many of us to see new products (and revisit old favourites), physical media still has value for collectors, myself included. Therefore, printed products are still manufactured, requiring packaging that helps market the item and add aesthetic appeal. In my work, these have included specialist Blu-ray editions, new vinyl soundtrack releases, and limited edition books. Additionally, private commissions have allowed me to explore new ways of presenting cult favourites with new artwork unfettered by commercial restraint.

It's a challenge to re-present a beloved classic with a dedicated global fan base that doesn't disappoint expectations. All my work, indeed that of any commercial artist, is delivered with a subjectivity that might not necessarily connect with the spectator. It's a risk taken not only by the artist but also by the commissioning client. A level of mutual trust needs to exist to maintain a good working relationship. Ultimately, it's the feedback from customers that decides what's worked and what hasn't. The artist must meet an

OPPOSITE: *Freddy's Revenge* (1986); photograph of the original artwork, artist's archive.

In my poster for the first sequel to the original *A Nightmare On Elm Street*, I've referenced the opening scenes. I felt that the surrealism perfectly captured the central dream theme. As my poster for the original film celebrated the night and the limited palettes of moonlight, this poster is saturated with sunlight and lurid primary colours. And while the image of "Freddy" was a shadow in the original poster, here he is a star!

additional challenge to retain the integrity of instinct and experience that bolsters the confidence in our ability to make the best decisions when creating images, which will also give space for the personal expression that makes any work unique to that person. It's how we view films, filtered through the layers of our personal experiences and situations. At best, I hope to empathise and connect to a shared understanding and mutual respect for the genre.

In dealing with the global challenges of a pandemic, and with all the political fallout from "normality" subverted, the horror genre seems to provide a natural outlet for insecurity and fear, offering a cathartic balm for troubled times. It's possible to map the history of the last century by the genre films that responded to upheaval and instability, from the early Universal horror films born out of the horrors of World War I, the mutant insect monsters spawned by the new Atomic age, the blood horror in reaction to the fear of Aids in the 1980s, to the home invasion and eco horrors of more recent years. I'm fascinated by the context of past cinema (including "straight to video" horror films!) and the political epoch in which films were generated, and as a result, try to bring texture to my work that reflects something of the time.

I'm often asked where my ideas come from (the choice of imagery, compositions, and colour). Whilst most of the images are the result of viewings and a psychological distillation process, I've often found that my compositions are formed in dreams, literally a complete artwork formulated in the moment before I wake. In trusting my instincts, I need only to try and reproduce this apparition as accurately as possible. All the work results from my life experience — the places I've seen, the people I know, and the upheavals we all share. It's informed by the books, the films, and the people that inspire and stimulate. My work isn't revolutionary, and I've no illusions about its place in the world; it's a drop in a vast ocean. But if it tickles a fancy or makes someone pick up a pencil and make some marks, then I feel very fortunate.

As I did in *Hung, Drawn and Executed* I've included here a step-by-step re-creation of a commercial job, to demonstrate the techniques and thought processes behind a typical commission. I hope it provides a valuable insight into this solitary profession.

GRAHAM HUMPHREYS
London, England

STEP-BY-STEP

The images in this chapter illustrate how one of my commissions typically evolves from beginning to end. Although every commission has its own challenges and requirements, the physical process remains mostly the same.

In this instance, the commission was for the 4K release of *Cannibal Holocaust*, a 1980 Italian found footage film directed by Ruggero Deodato. The film is not without considerable controversy; in 1984 it was banned in the UK under the Video Recordings Act, a response to the tabloid sensationalism that coined the term "video nasty". The Act named 72 titles unsuitable for public viewing, and *Cannibal Holocaust* was among them. The issues with the film weren't centred around any fictionalised depiction of cannibalism but with the actual footage of animal cruelty (mostly excised from subsequent releases). A serious viewing of the film reveals that the narrative horror unfolds with the intervention of a young film crew who purposefully

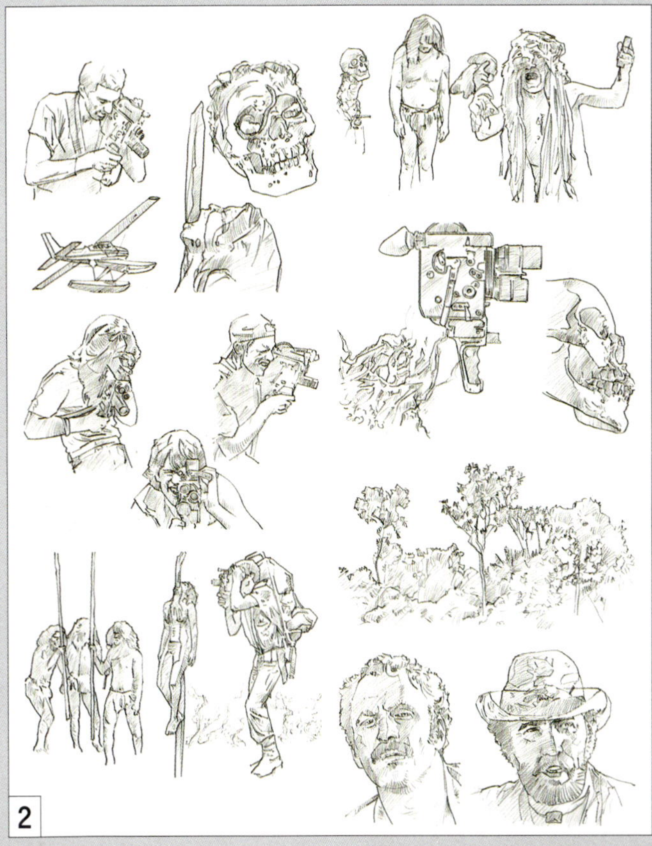

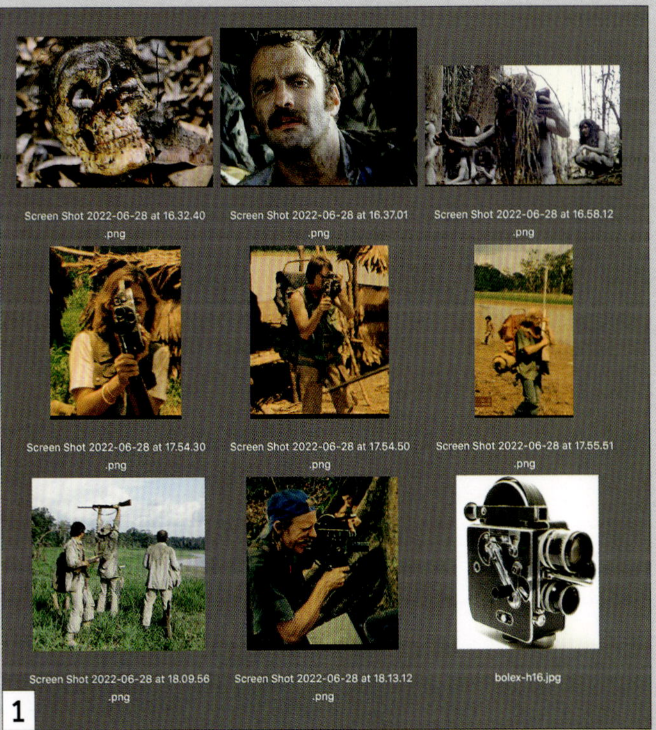

provoke violent scenarios to generate sensational content. Naturally, things go horribly wrong. The film is often cited as the precursor to the contemporary found footage genre. It certainly feels prescient in the new world of greed-driven influencers, tabloid click-bait, and conspiracy theorists.

I watch a film at least three times: first to understand the content and context, second to identify the key scenes that will form the basis of my composition, and third to take screen grabs (or actual photographs of the screen when software doesn't allow). Covering all bases with an initial collection of 50–100 shots, I can then decide which images work best as reference material. Where material doesn't exist in the film, I can supplement the reference with sourced images and my own photography. My final options include sourced images of a camera to match those used in the film (1).

I then make tracings of the key elements (2). Tracing is essential to guarantee the most accurate representation, and it saves time — all jobs are constrained by their

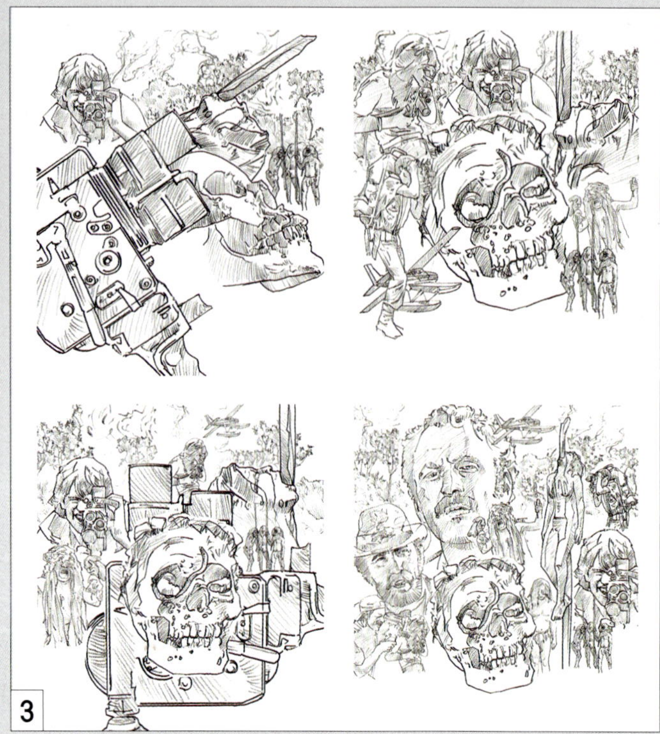

3

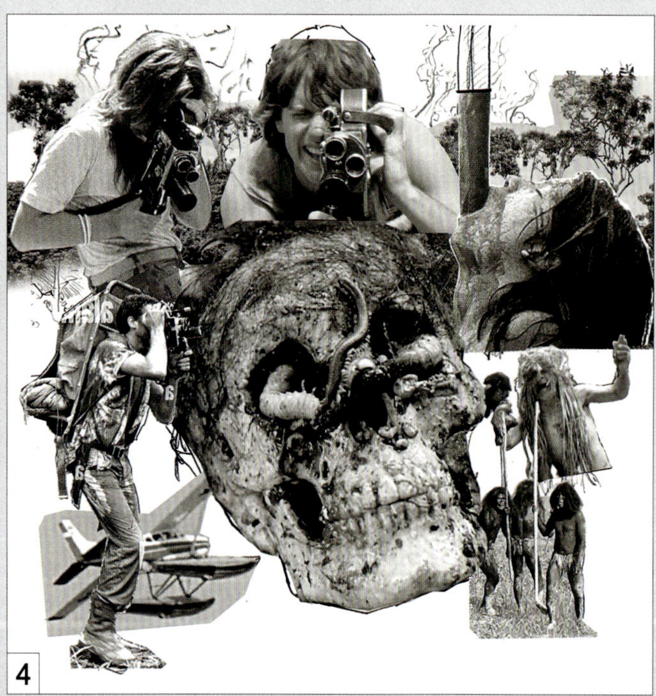

4

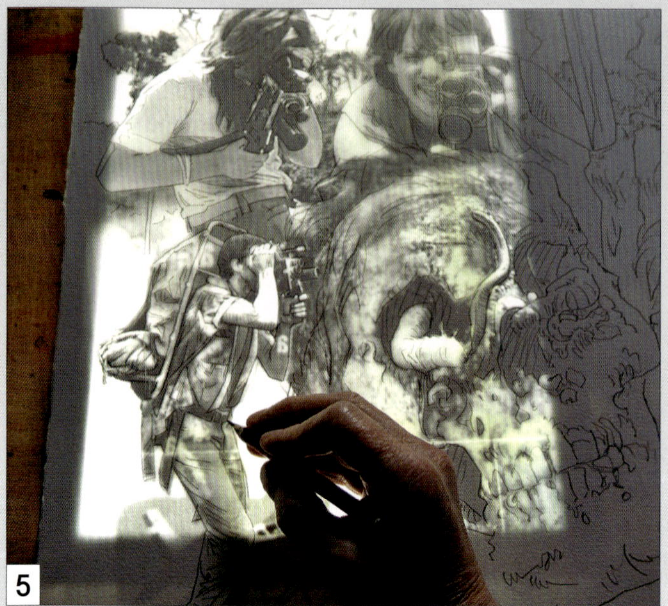

5

layout will suffice, but I'll usually offer between three and seven versions, depending on the scope of the subject. Here, four compositions were emailed to the client, who selected the one top right as their preference (3).

With the composition decided, to create the best reference for my painting, in Photoshop, I lay the photographic source material over my sketch to ensure that my final art remains positioned as the client has approved it (4–5). The image is then traced in pencil onto my preferred paint surface. I use Bockingford Watercolor Paper NOT 190 gsm/90lb. It's thin enough to allow tracing but substantial enough to deal with the punishing paintwork. The paper is taped to a wooden board so that it will dry flat when the wash is applied (6).

budget and deadline. The elements are then scanned into Photoshop. Being mindful that a title, certificate, and distributor logo need to be accommodated within the layout, I construct options for the client, shifting the emphasis between characters and elements to take the final art in various directions. On rare occasions, one

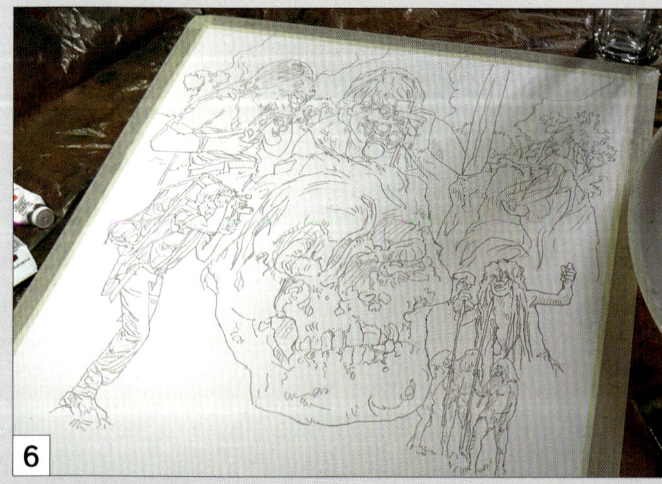

6

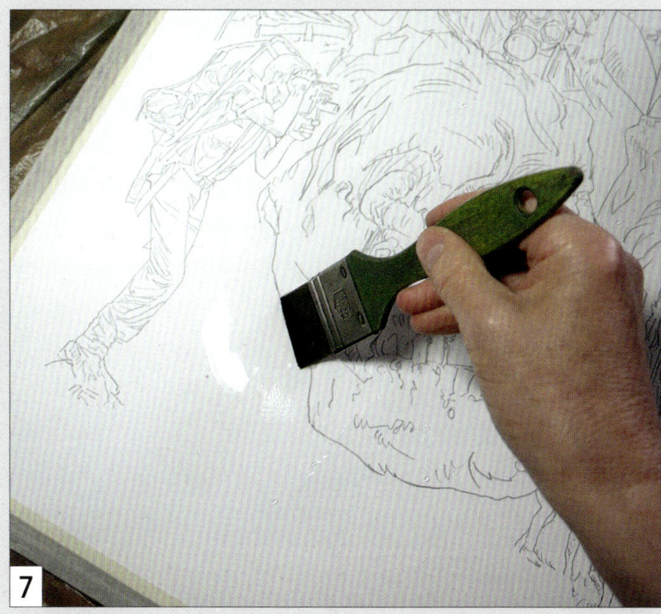

7

All my work is painted with Designers Gouache. I use a limited selection of colours from which I mix everything. I can mix them to give a smooth flow for detail or use a thicker mix for "dry brush" techniques. The paint dries fast but can be reconstituted, allowing for transparent washes and opaque blocking.

When I apply the wash, I first wet the paper (7). This is done swiftly so the paper doesn't get sodden and buckle too severely. The paint is applied while the surface is

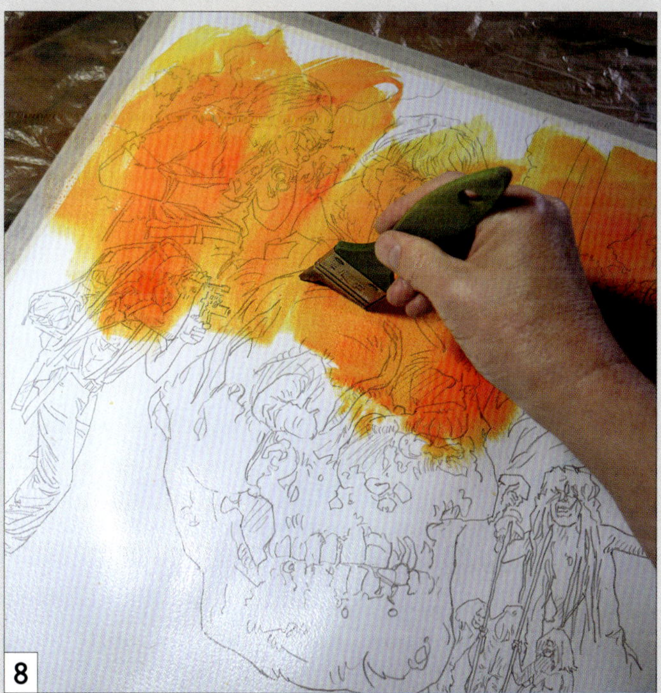

8

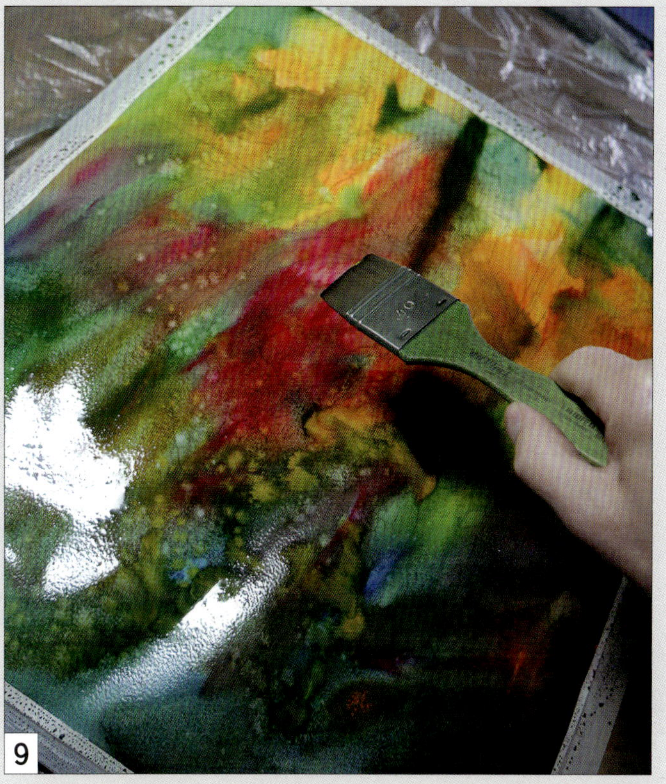

9

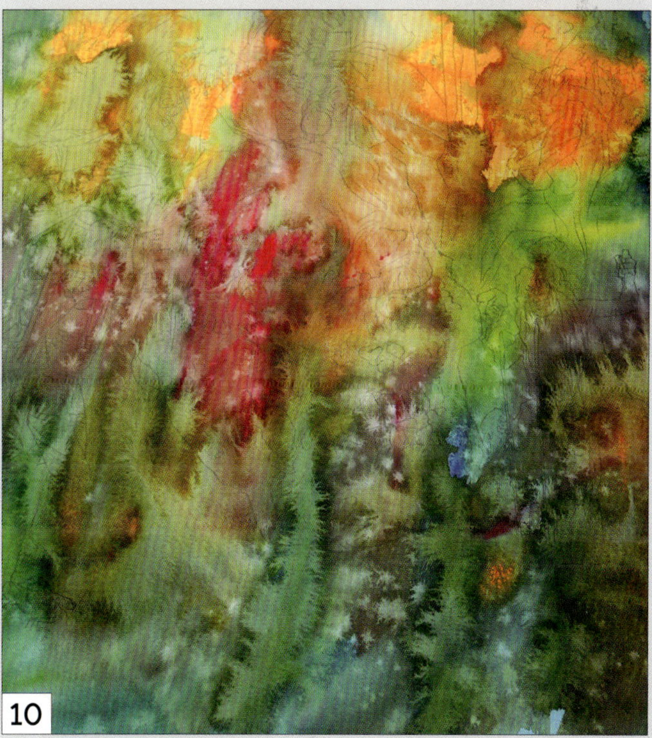

10

still wet (8), and the colour theme is built with a few targetted splashes to add texture and random paint effects (9). When dry, the pencil guides are still visible beneath the wash (10).

The image is picked out in a darker colour, much like the drawing process, creating an even ground upon which to build the paint layers (11). The elements are defined, with constant reference to my photographic source material (12). I balance the colours and attempt to give a visual coherence to the many parts (13).

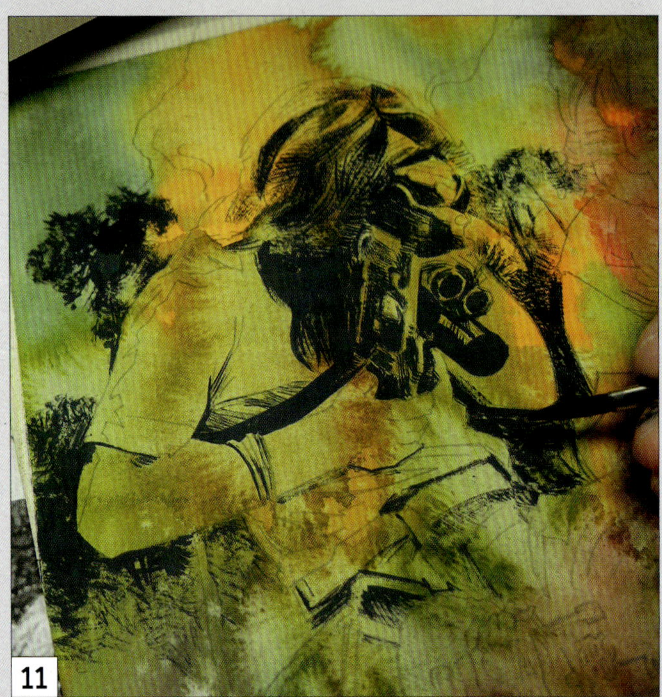

11

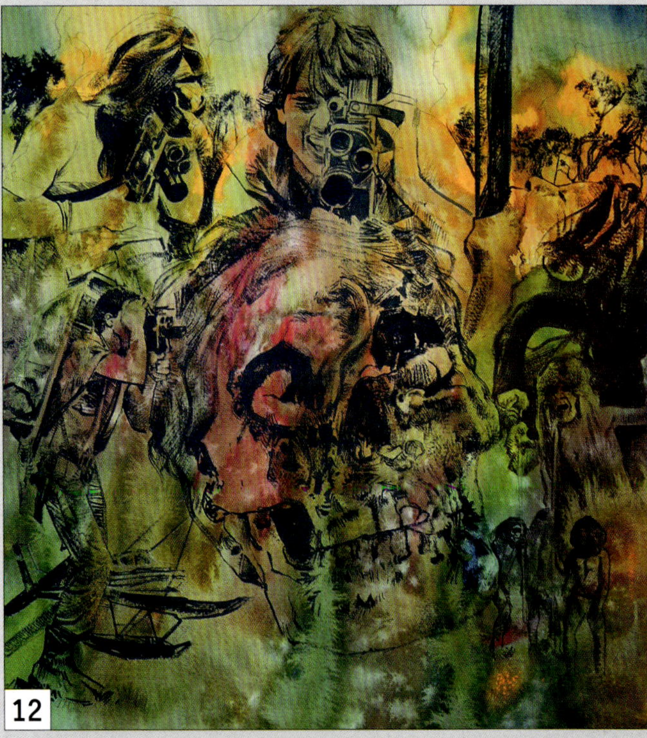

12

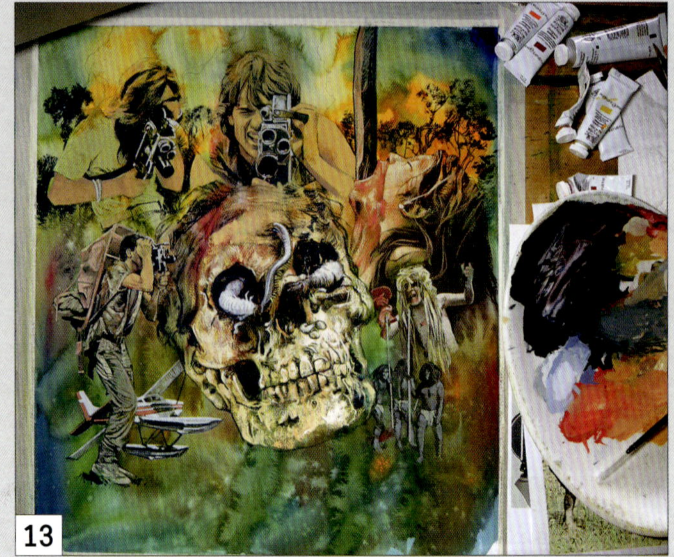

13

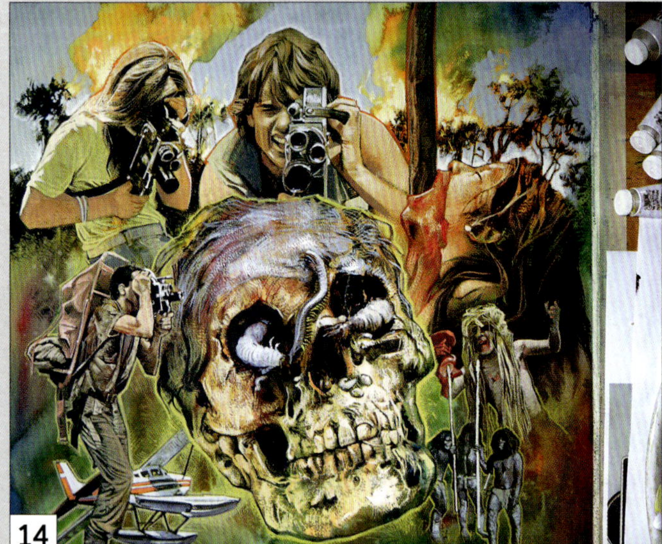

14

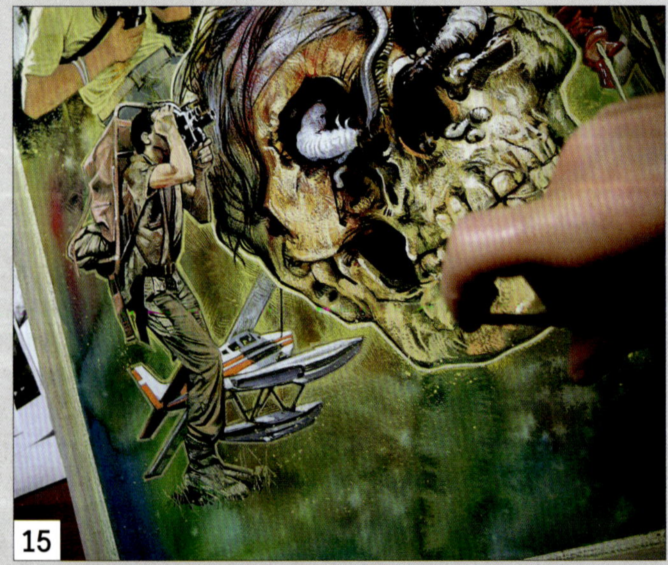

15

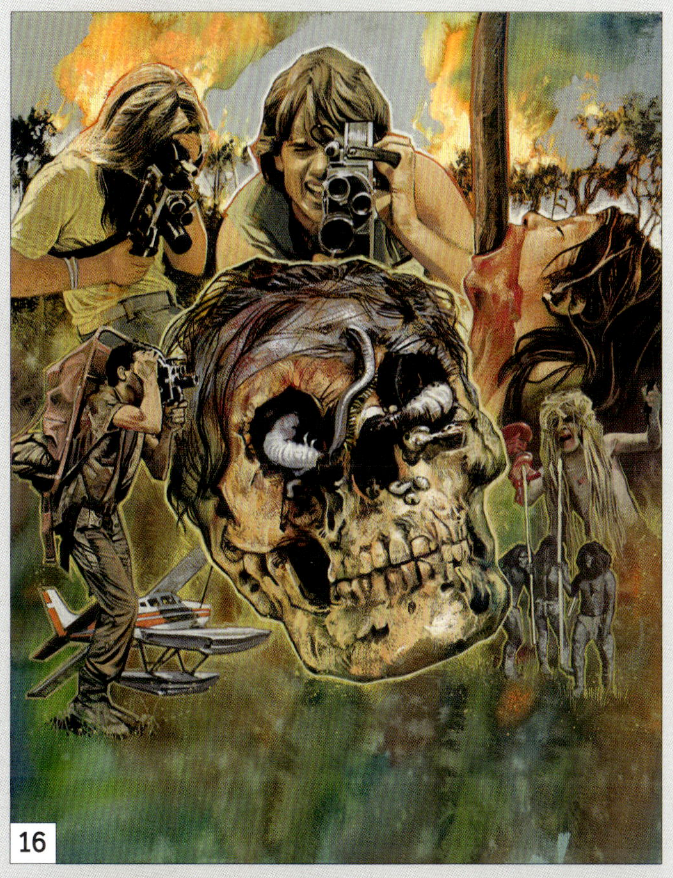

16

As I reach the final stages, I let my eye roam around the art, identifying the areas that might need more focus (14). Knowing when to stop is key; it's a painting, not a photo, and hyperrealism isn't the aim.

The additional texture is added using a carefully targeted splatter technique (15); the paint has to be just the right consistency, and the colour has to be carefully considered. Several mixes might be used across the overall image. The final touches are added before the final scan for digital delivery (16). The title is added on a digital layer (so it can be moved or changed). You can see the crop lines on the final file (17). Bleed is essential for printed items, to avoid a white edge when trimming the paper. The digital file is delivered to the client, and a mock-up of the final product is generated by the client for pre-sales (18).

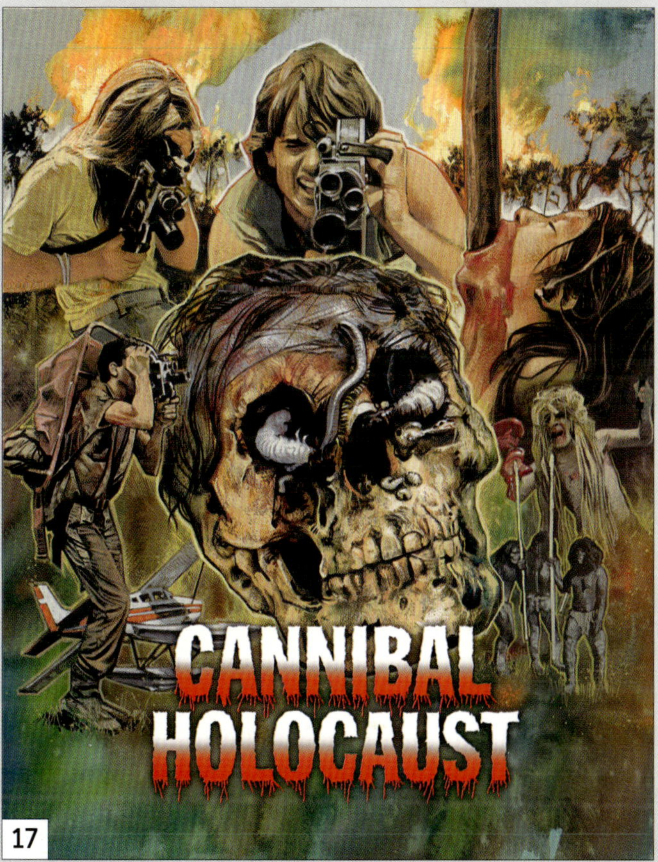

17

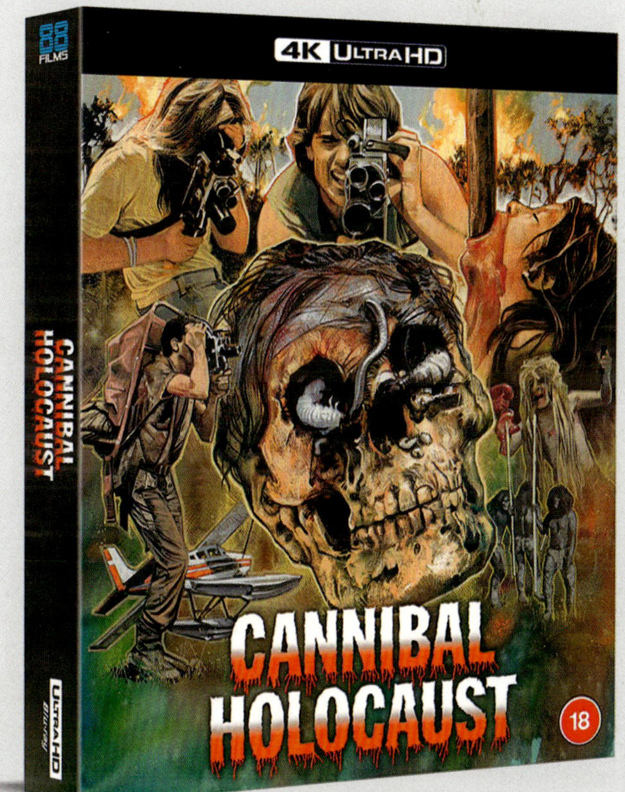

18

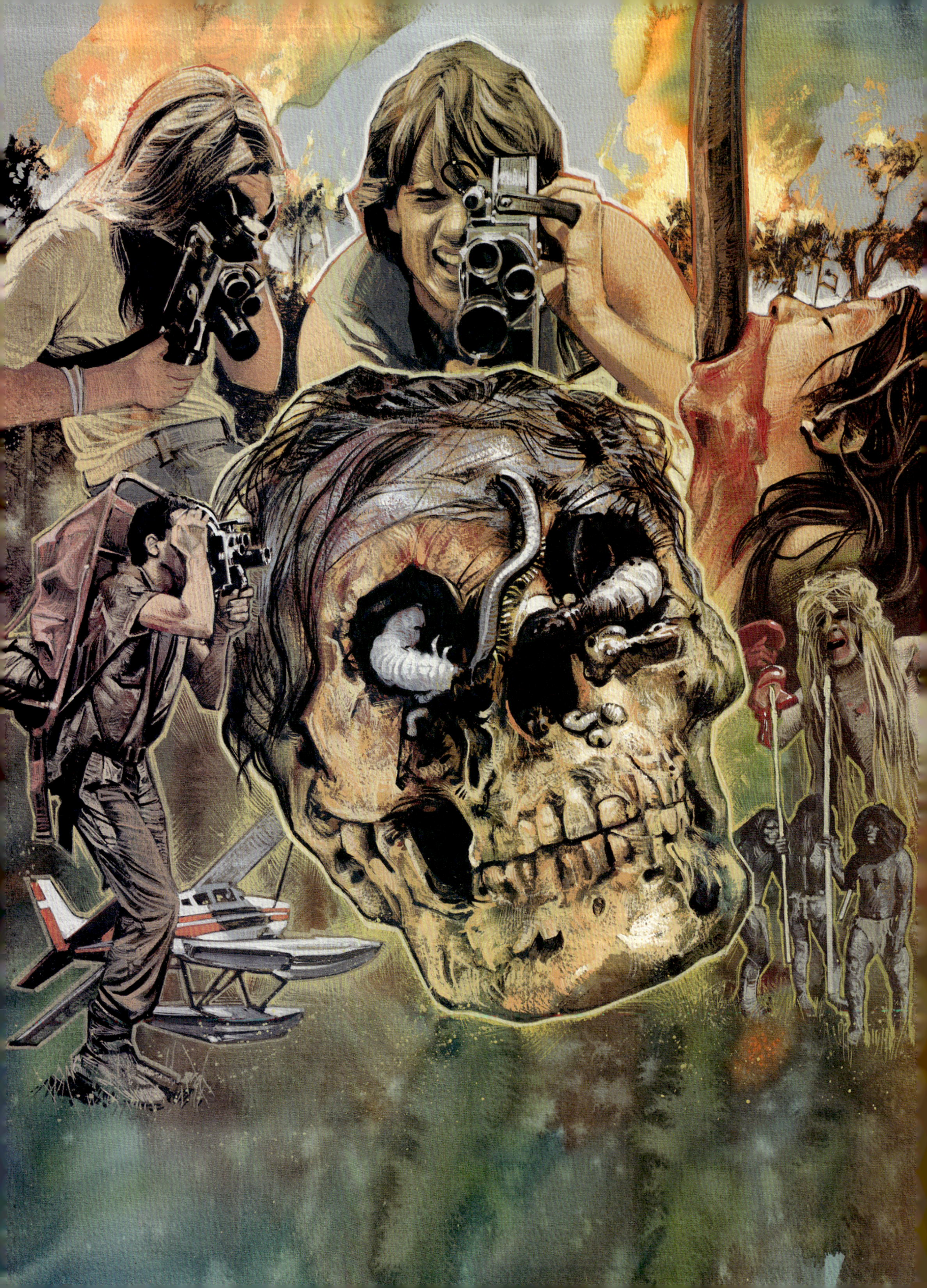

HOME ENTERTAINMENT

Once the bedrock of my career, the humble VHS cover evolved into DVD, then Blu-ray. The objective remained the same: to scream an idealised presentation of the content from the shelves and advertisements using whatever means might ensnare. The trick was always to be true to the film: not to lie, but to embellish and deliver the promise of satisfaction. As back catalogues are exhumed and many forgotten films rise from the grave, these paintings are designed to breathe new life into reissues. But sometimes they're fresh meat to be packaged for a customer who knows their "special stuff" well.

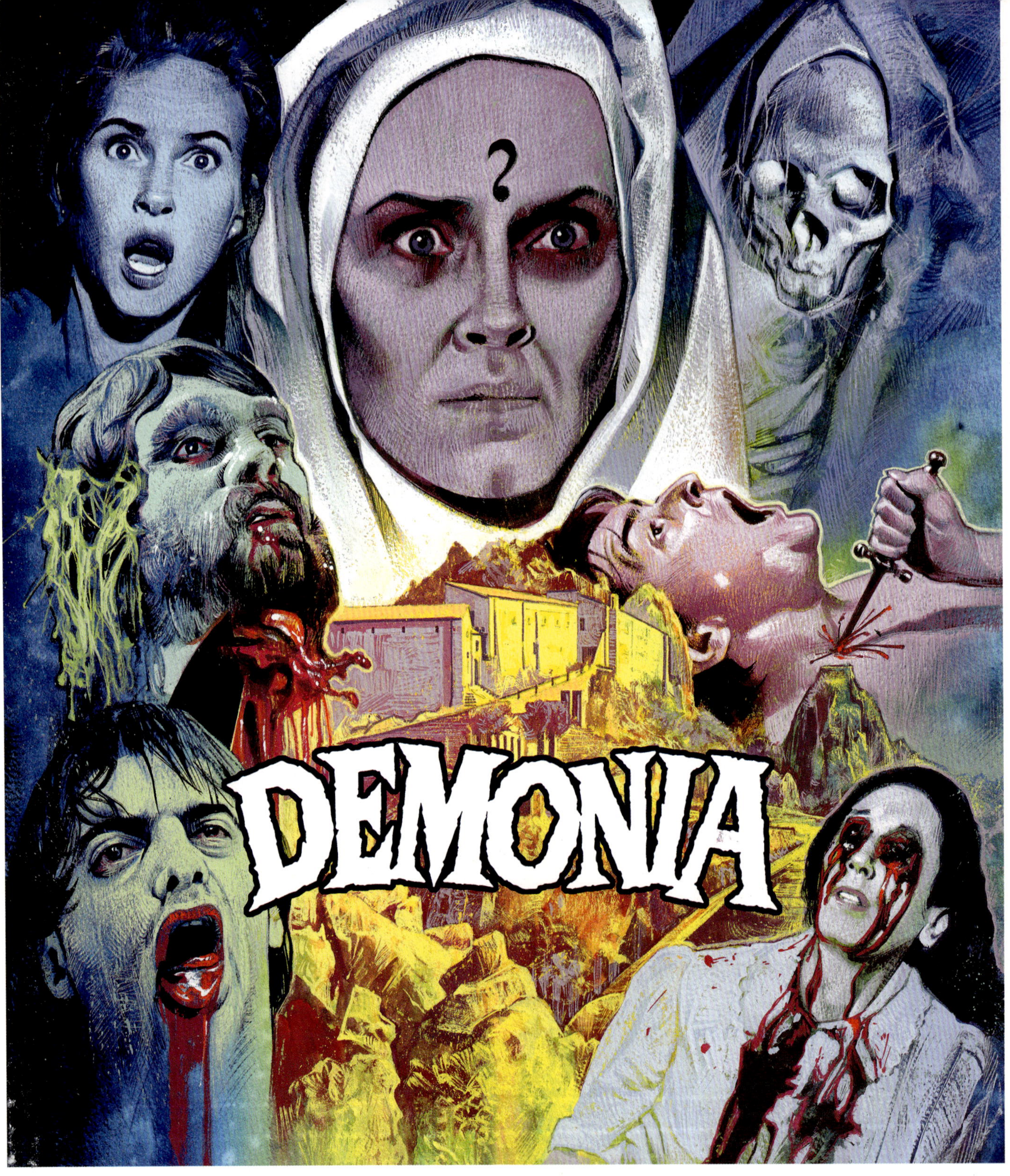

ABOVE AND RIGHT: *Demonia* (2022), Arrow Films; Blu-ray packaging.

The initial commission became two: a box cover and a booklet cover. Additionally, I was asked to create the form of the packaging, adding extra elements to enhance the layout. The package opens up in the form of a cross. The original image is the more complex version, depicting various moments. I loved the look of the location and made it my central image. I was determined to avoid the usual horror palettes and try something more psychedelic. Yellow is a colour I rarely use, but it felt right for this image. The package cover is inspired by the film's climax, in which a coven of murderous nuns is crucified and then burned, with only their charred skeletons remaining. I used one of my small collections of real human skulls for reference. The use of yellow is repeated.

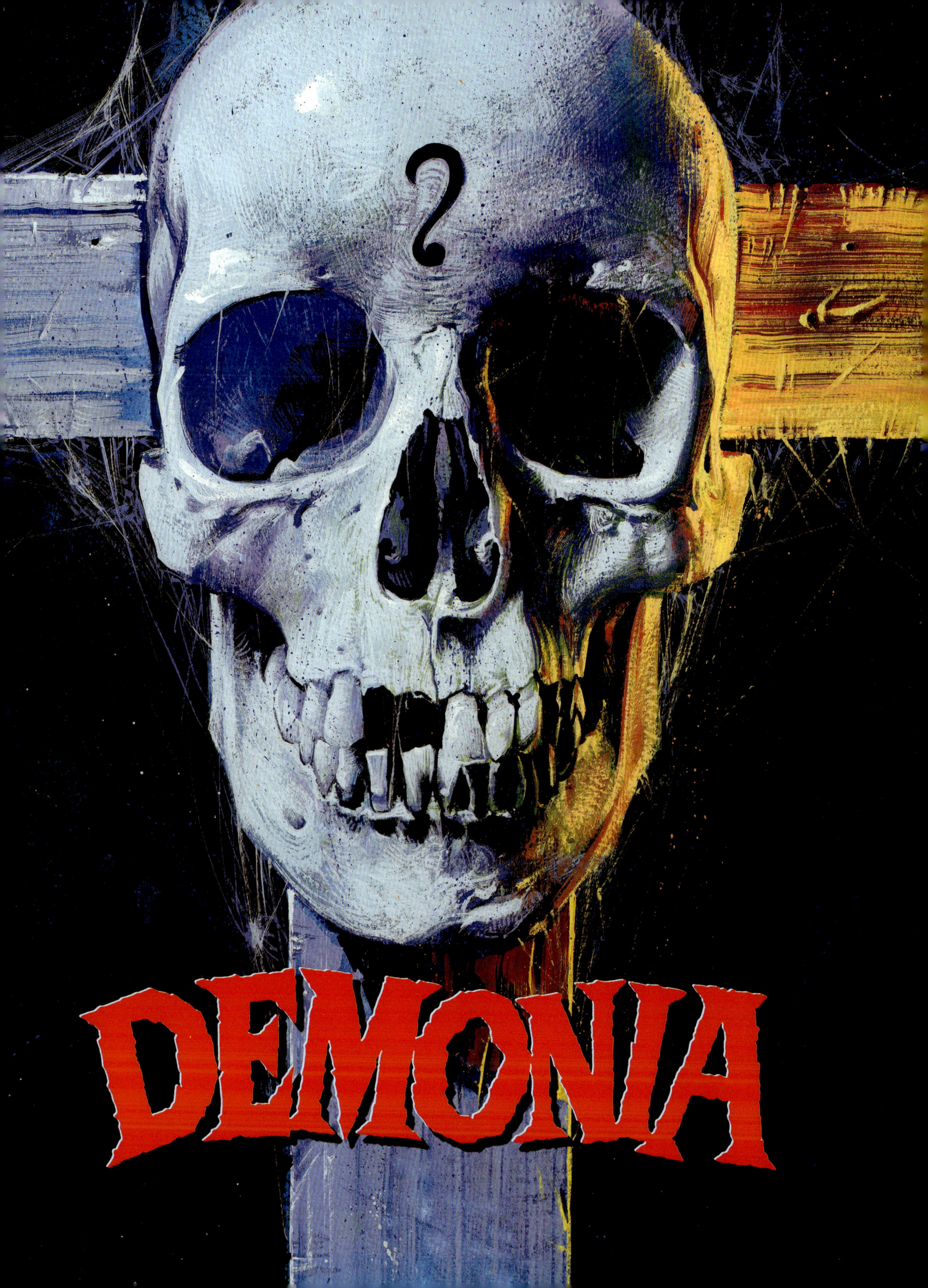
DEMONIA

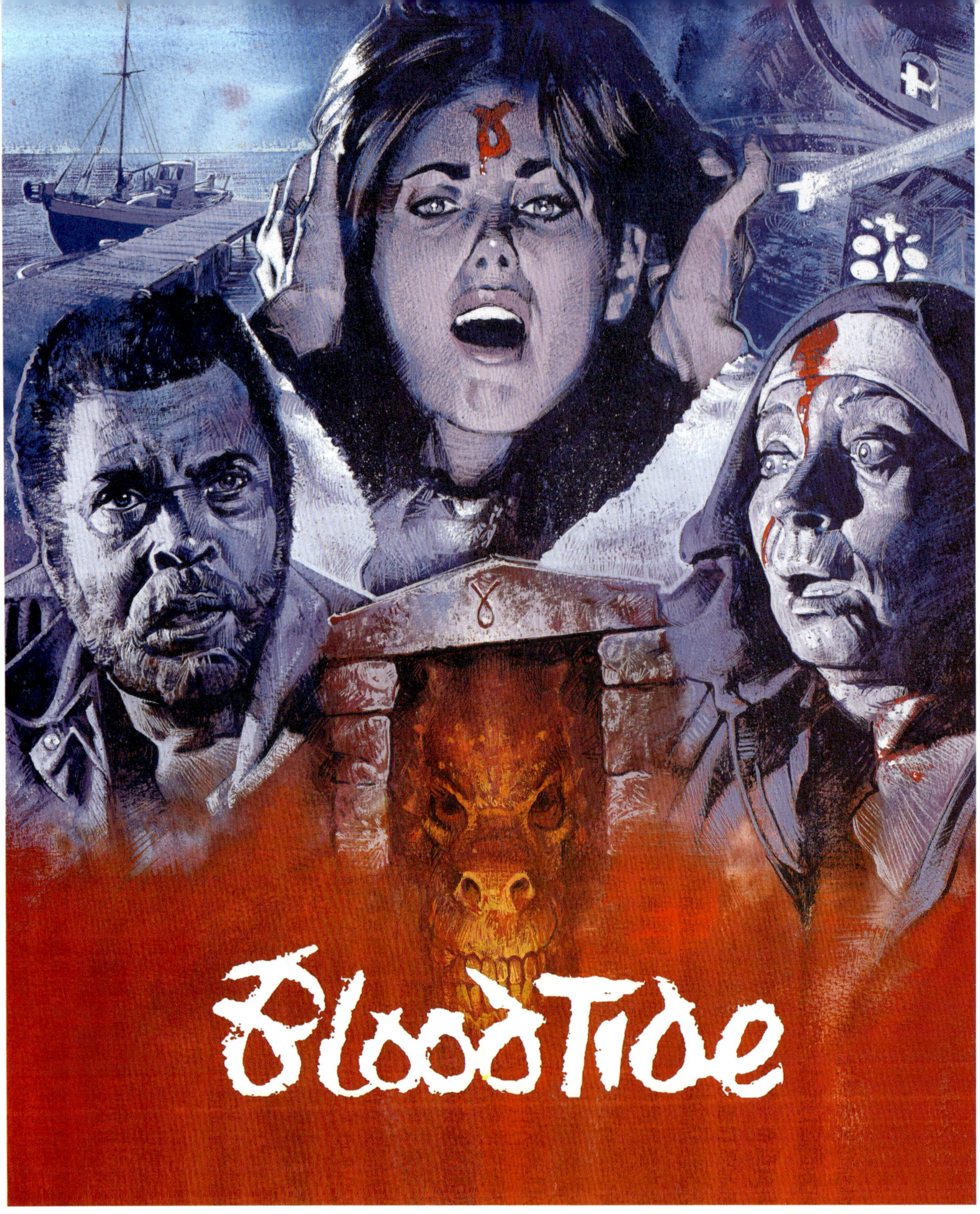

ABOVE: *Blood Tide* (2020), Arrow Films; Blu-ray cover.

This is part of the Nico Mastorakis library. Its cast features James Earl Jones, who I remembered from *Exorcist II: The Heretic*, and for this reason, I gave him a prominent part in the composition. The monster within the movie isn't very convincing and is rarely glimpsed, and that's the way it appears in the painting!

RIGHT: *Bloodstone* (2020), Arrow Films; Blu-ray cover.

Part of the Nico Mastorakis collection. I wanted to reflect the colourful locations (the film was shot in India) by adopting the look of a Bollywood poster. The villain is played by actor Christopher Neame, who played the villain in Hammer's *Dracula AD 72*. For my own selfish reason, I wanted him central to the image!

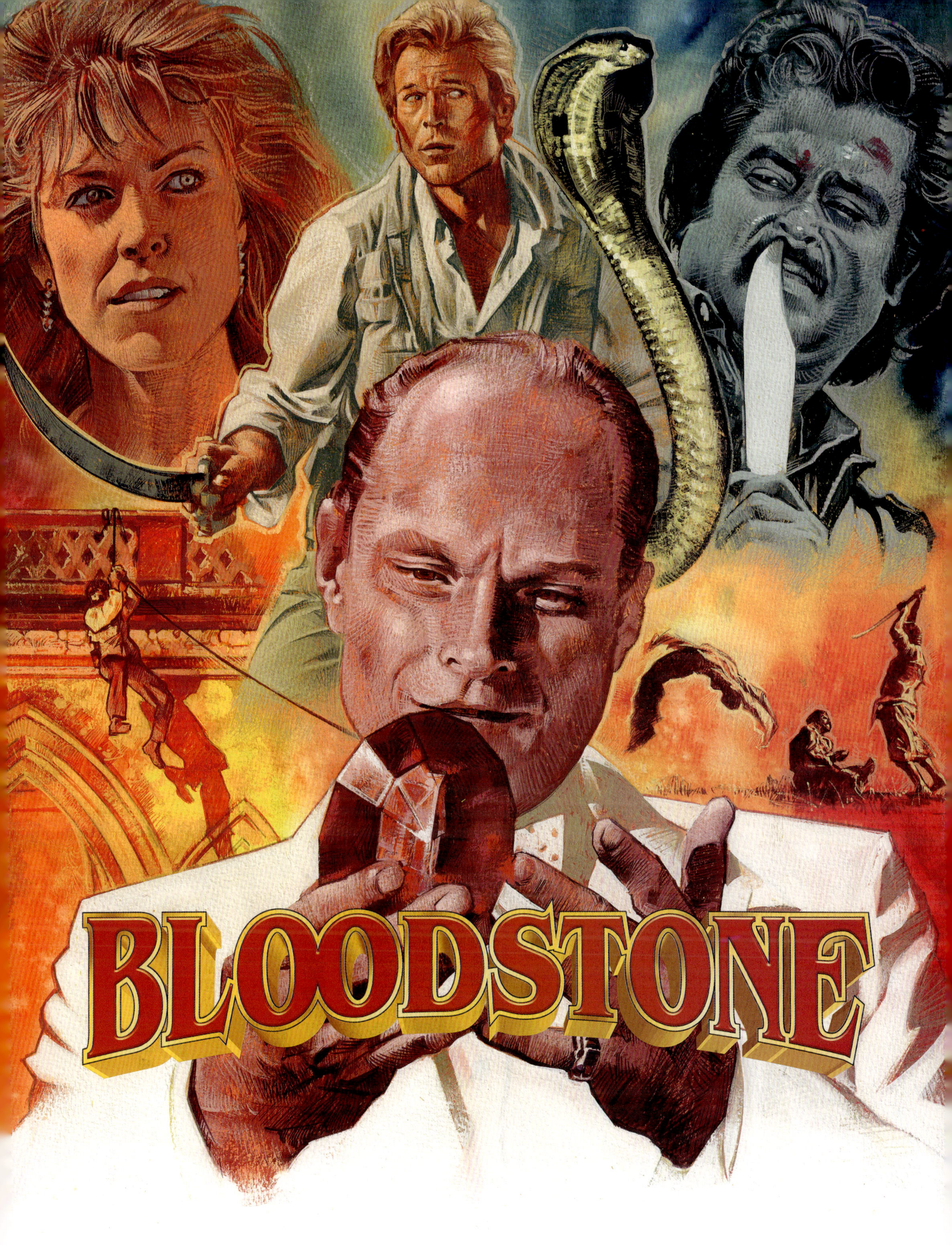
BLOODSTONE

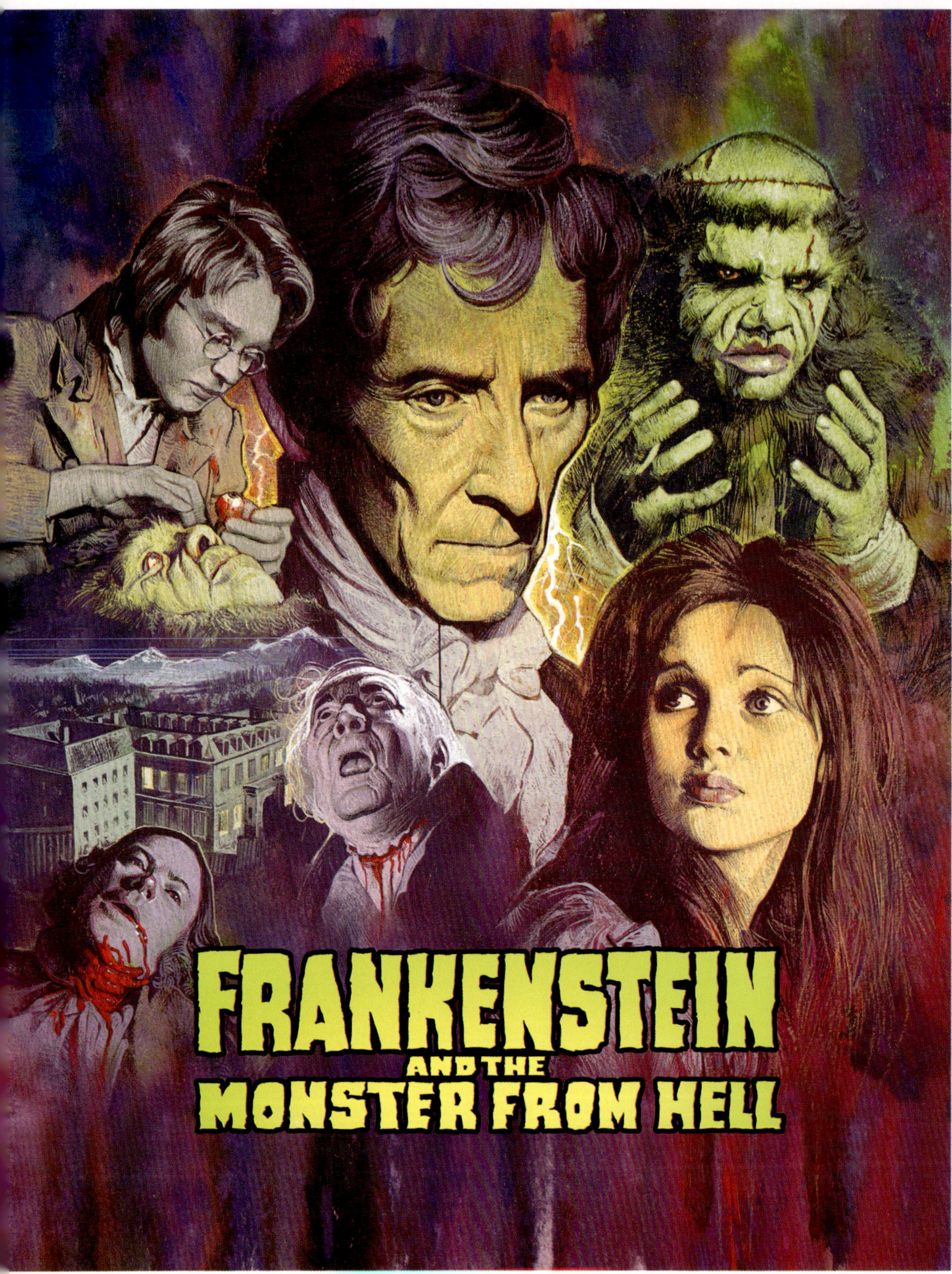

LEFT: *Frankenstein and the Monster from Hell* (2020), Second Sight; Blu-ray cover.

One of my top 10 Hammer horror films, this final entry into the Hammer Frankenstein cycle has only more recently been reappraised with affection. Peter Cushing is particularly gaunt in this film (the actor was apparently not in the best of health at the time), but nevertheless he cuts a striking presence. I looked to some of the period Belgian posters promoting Hammer horror films for my colour inspiration, hoping to capture something of the essence. Madeline Smith deserved prominence; this, she has said, was the first Hammer role that focussed on her face!

RIGHT: Jess Franco's *Count Dracula* (2023), 88 Films; Blu-ray cover.

Christopher Lee is best known for his performances of the vampire Count in the series of films made by Hammer (beginning with *Dracula* in 1958 and ending with *The Satanic Rites of Dracula* in 1973). In 1970, he played Dracula in this film directed by Spaniard Jesús Franco. Although it follows Bram Stoker's novel within the constraints of the budget, its clear deviations from the source material make it a loose adaptation. However, the moustache reinstates a detail missing in the Hammer films. In representing the film, I chose to concentrate on the Gothic elements without attempting to portray all the additional named talent (among them Herbert Lom and Soledad Miranda). I focussed on the power triangle of Christopher Lee's "Count Dracula", Maria Rohm's "Mina Murray", and Klaus Kinski's "Renfield". The sparse background is intended to convey the empty loneliness of Dracula's existence.

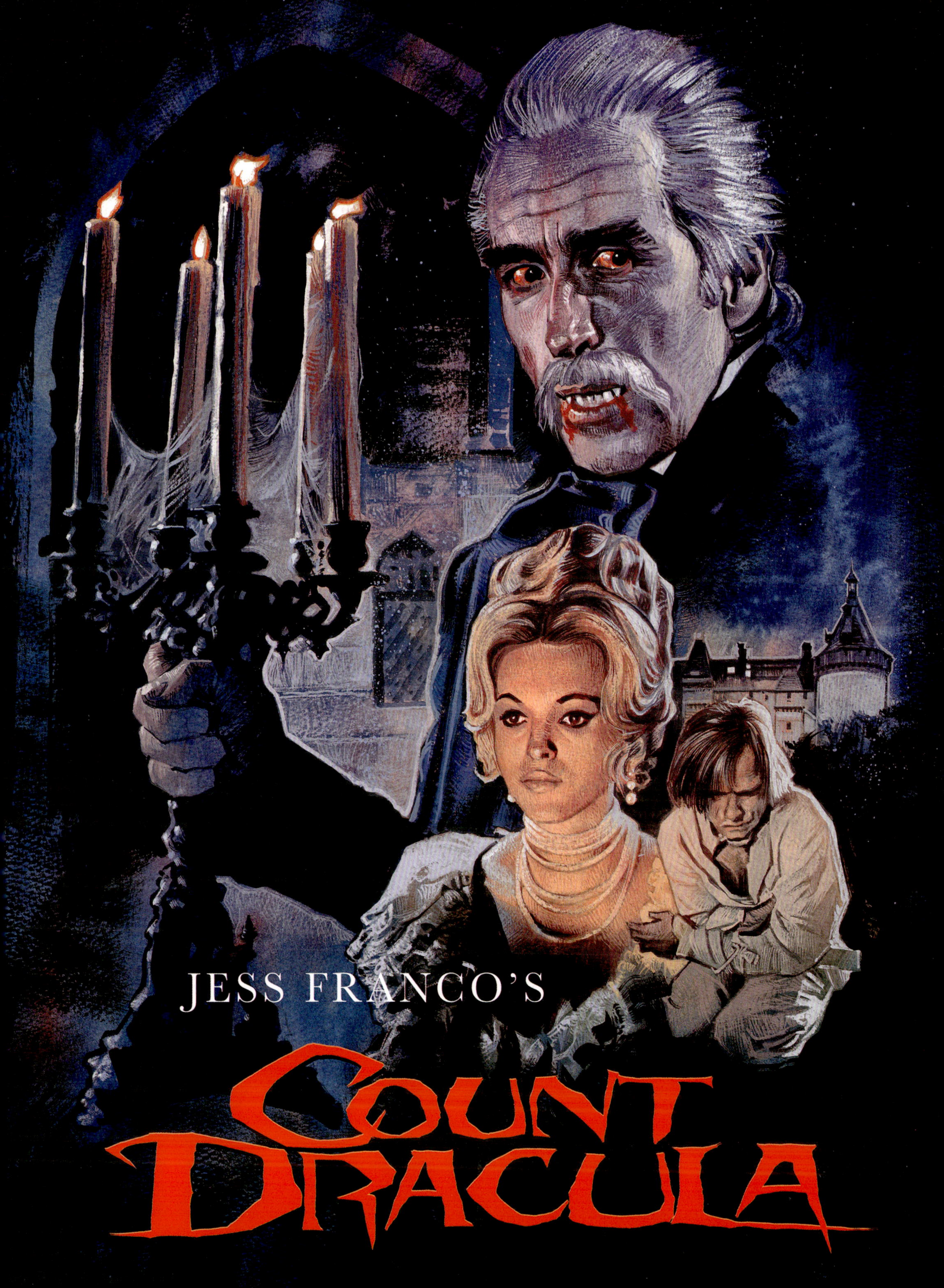
JESS FRANCO'S
COUNT DRACULA

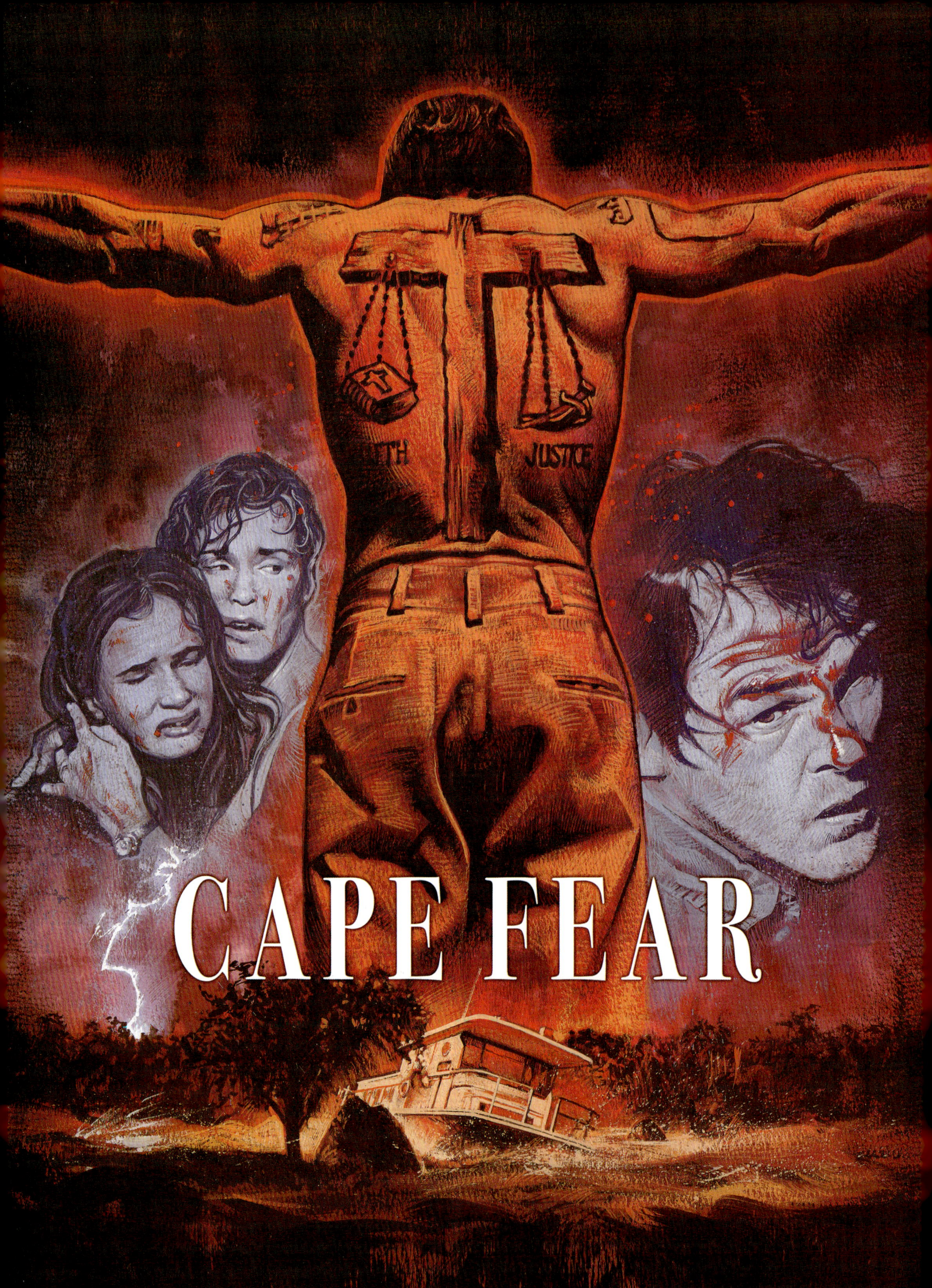

TH
JUSTICE
CAPE FEAR

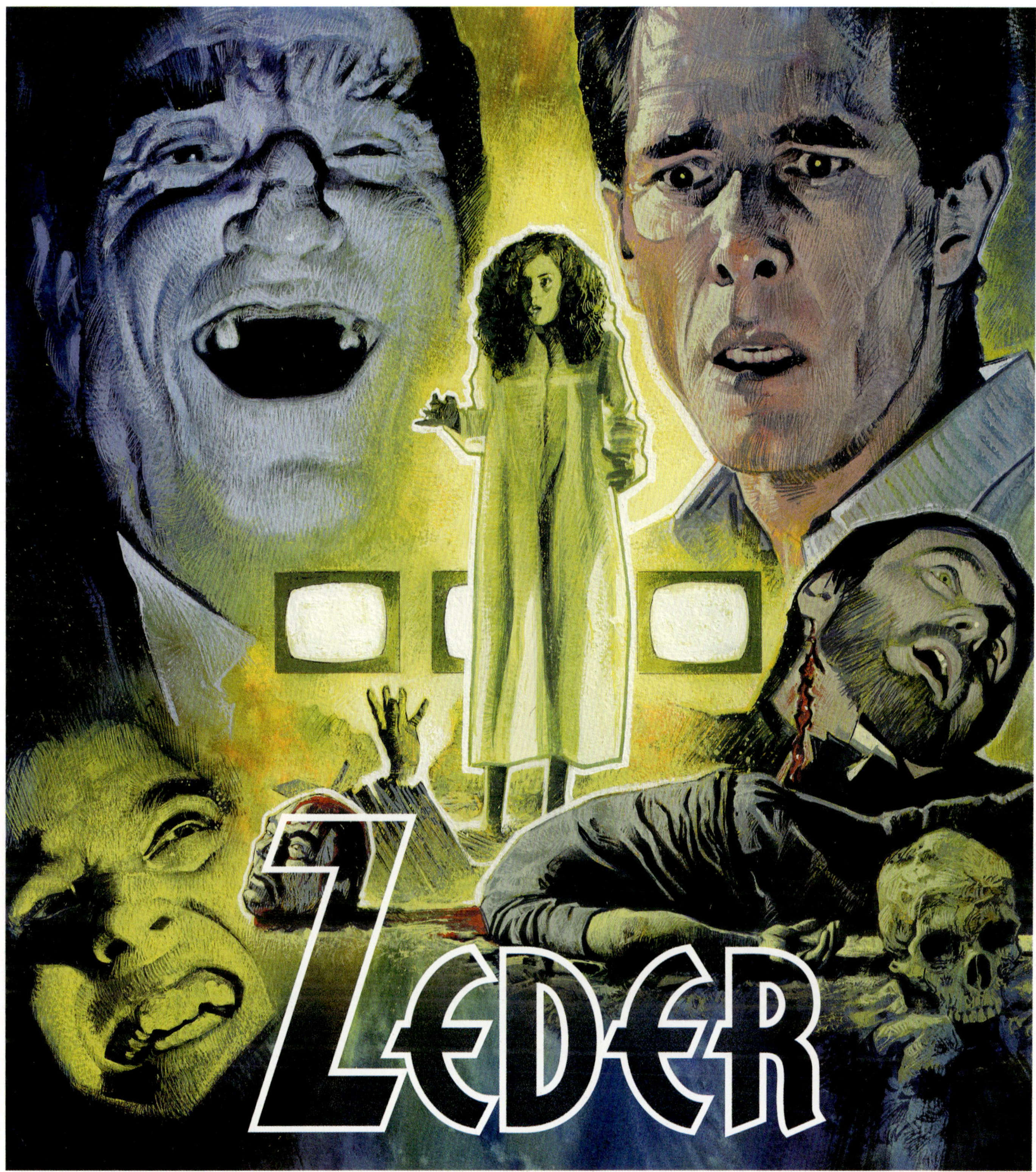

LEFT: *Cape Fear* (2020), Fabulous Films; Blu-ray cover.

This budget release required a different approach to the film. Although Robert De Niro's face appeared prominently in some of my initial concepts, I thought it would be more interesting to suggest the character's presence rather than the actor himself, playing on his religious fixation. I wanted the family to be obvious victims of this sociopathic entity, pushing the image firmly into the horror genre. The intense reds and blues against the black are intended to suggest a dark subversion of the US flag.

ABOVE: *Zeder* (2022), 88 Films; Blu-ray cover.

With so many mixed and confusing elements, it was difficult to pin down a direction for this layout. The plot crossed the sci-fi and horror genres, so I tried to signify both. The sinister, toothless face was too good to omit, but the actor Gabriele Lavia, who had featured in at least two of genre master Dario Argento's most-watched films, was an important inclusion. The aim was to keep the narrative a mystery but to include a blend of technology, horror, and enough imagery to suggest the purchase would be worthwhile.

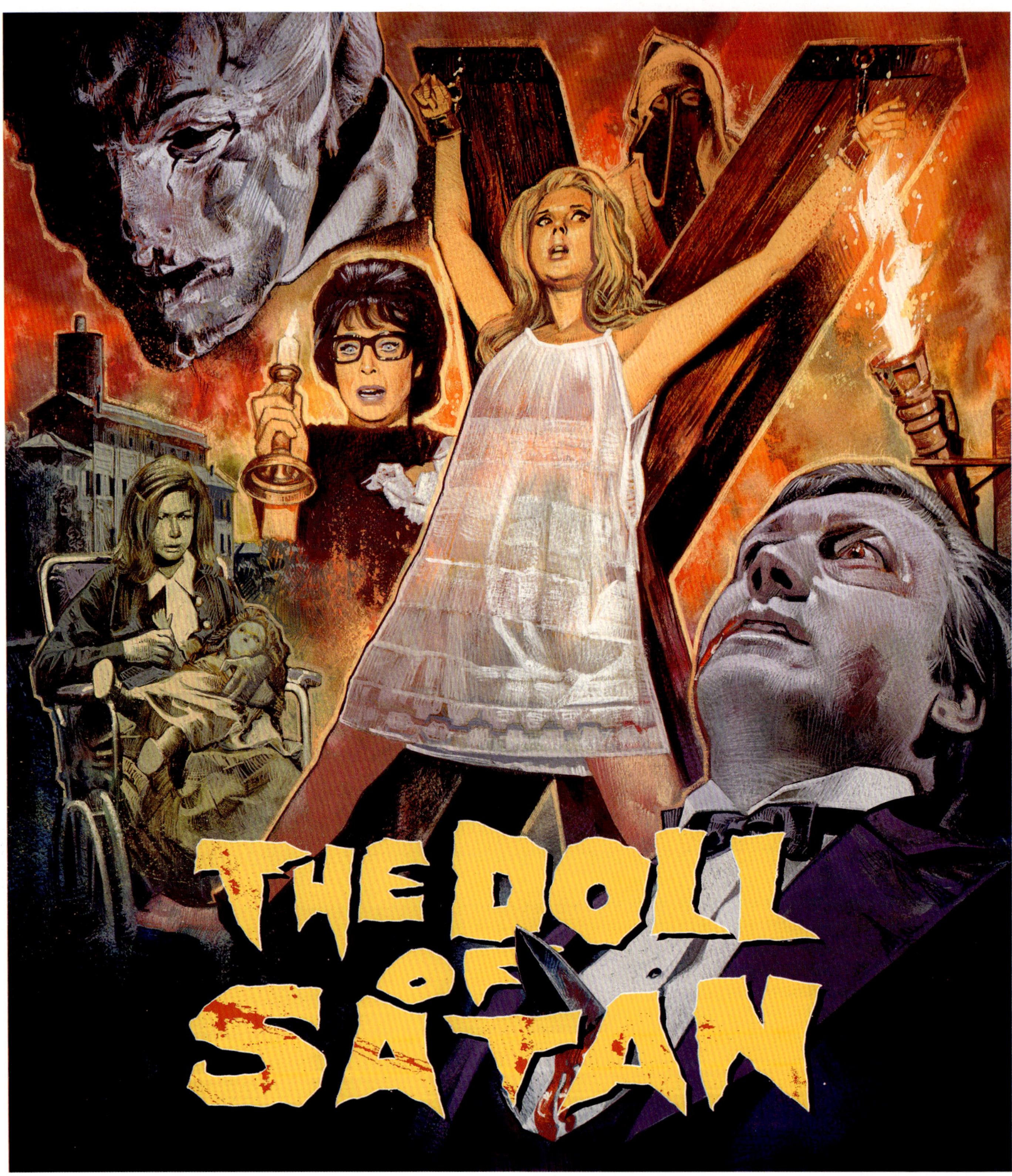

The image of the female lead, tied to the X-cross, was an already familiar element in previous posters for the film, but as a strong central image, the client requested that I retain it as the focus. In retrospect, I wish I'd made the mask in the top left corner larger, but I was determined to add the extra imagery to build the range of characters.

Another curiosity from director Nico Mastorakis. Because I'd already worked on some Mastorakis titles for the same client, it was logical that this should follow. The addition of a "tech" element was requested. Indeed, it's central to the story but not something easily rendered in paint. So, although I tried to keep the palette suggestive of electronics, I had to resort to Illustrator and Photoshop to complete the "tech" elements.

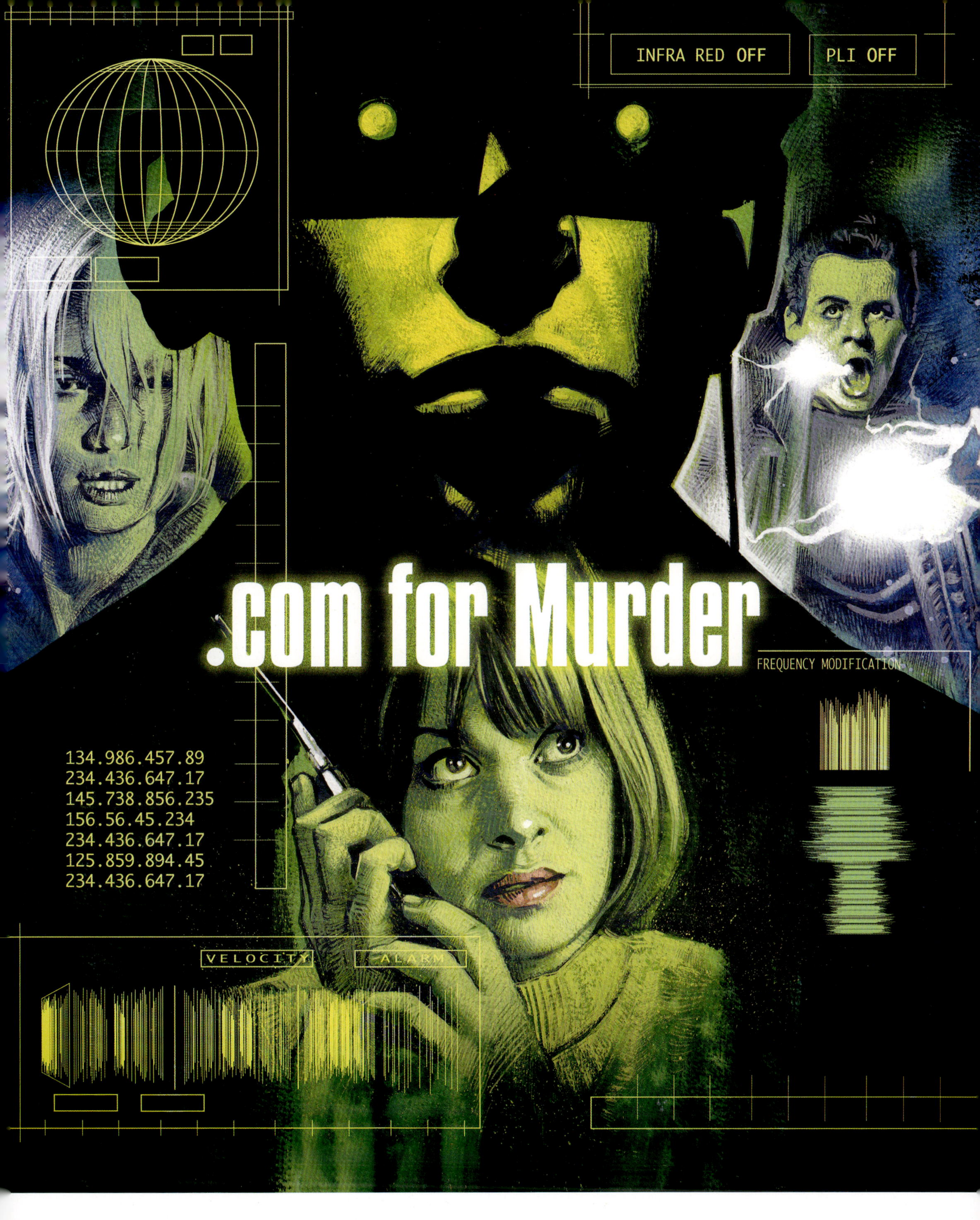
INFRA RED OFF
PLI OFF
.com for Murder
FREQUENCY MODIFICATION
134.986.457.89
234.436.647.17
145.738.856.235
156.56.45.234
234.436.647.17
125.859.894.45
234.436.647.17
VELOCITY
ALARM

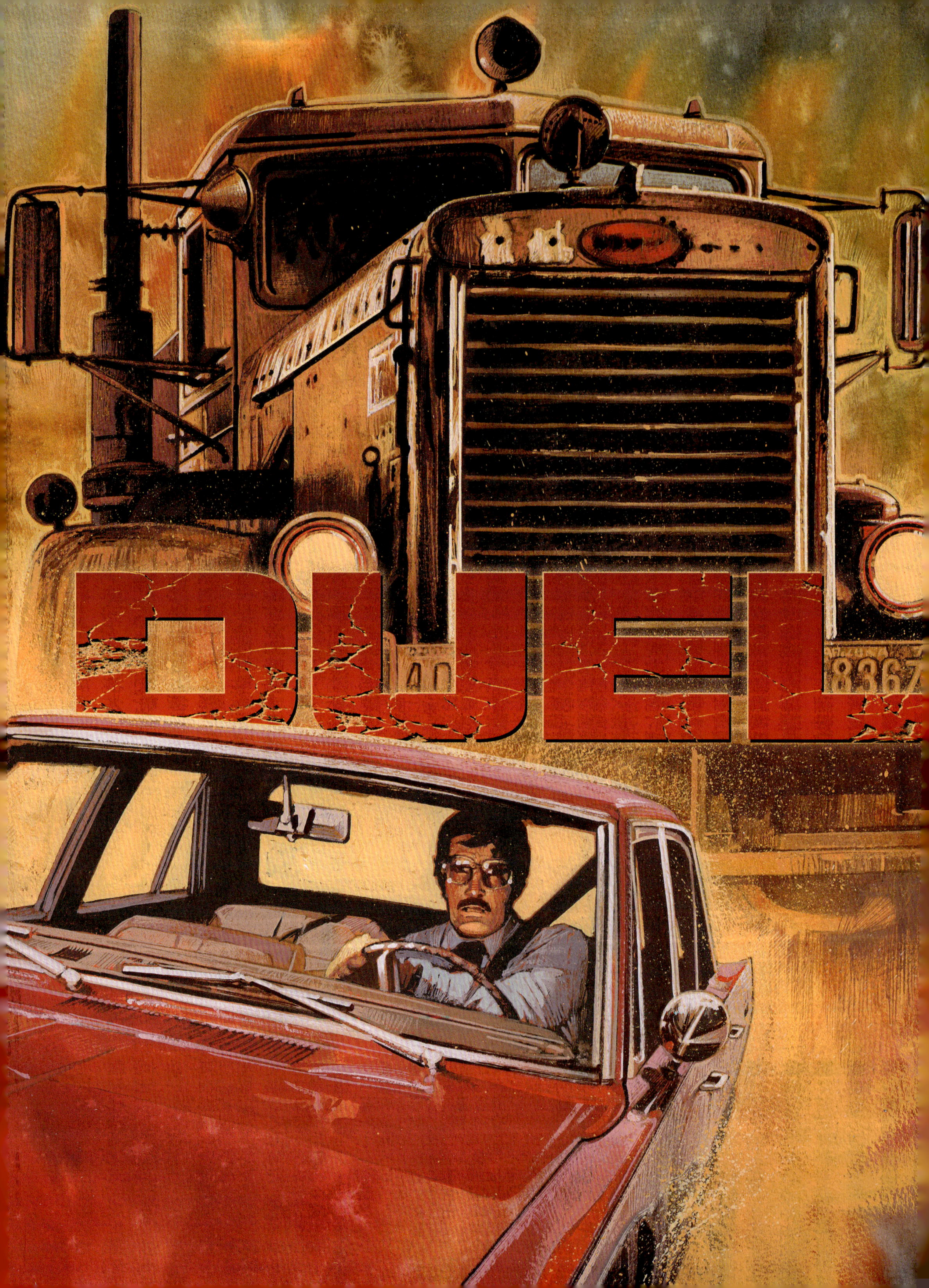
DUEL
40
8867

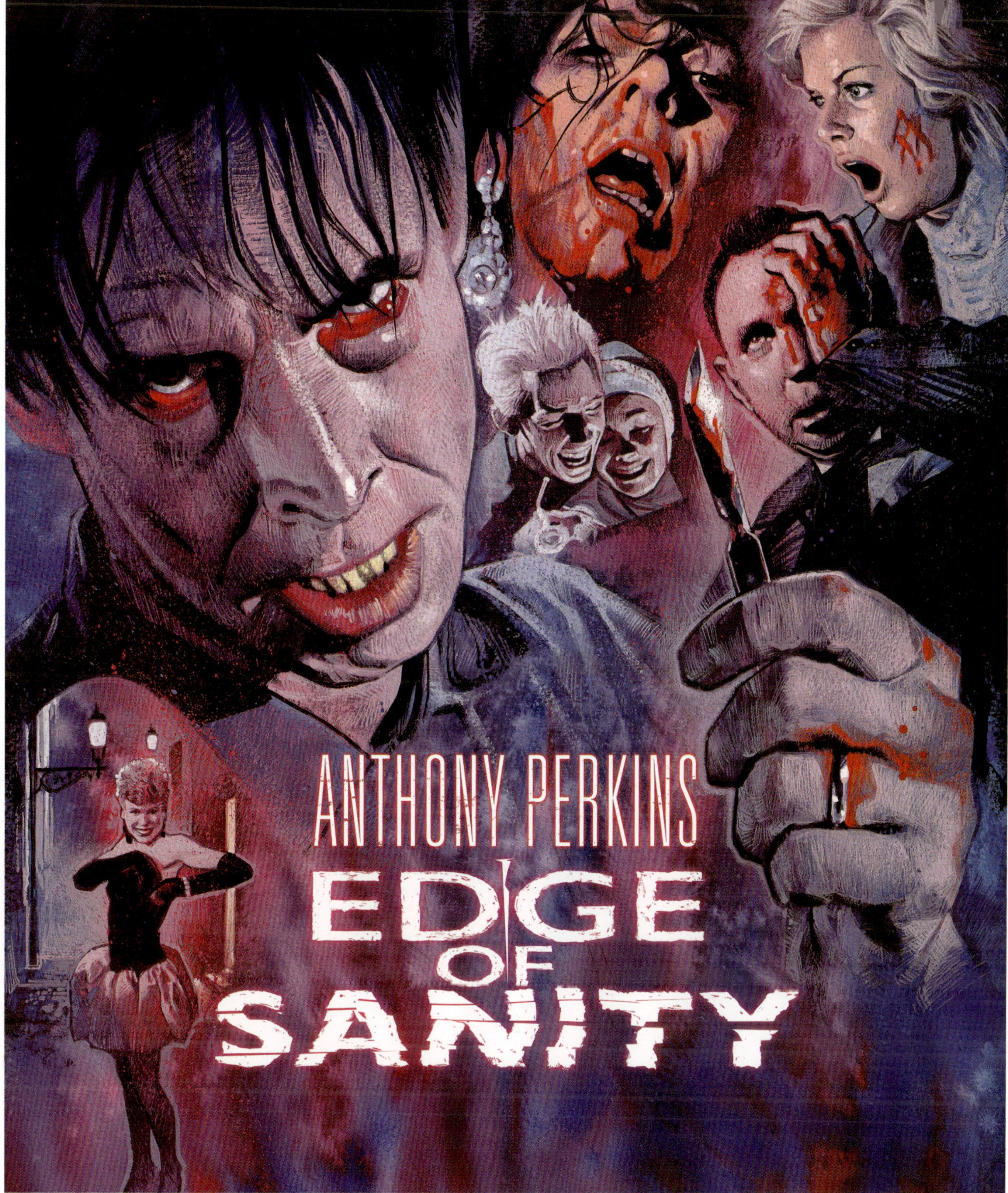

LEFT: *Duel* (2021), Fabulous Films; Blu-ray cover.

Although it's not horror in the traditional sense, there's a suggestion of the supernatural in the "man vs faceless monster" narrative. In *Duel*, the "monster" is a metal Behemoth that dwarfs the increasingly unhinged victim. Although I submitted compositions that added further visual interest, my client preferred the bare-bones approach.

ABOVE: *Edge Of Sanity* (2022), Arrow Films; Blu-ray cover.

A curious hybrid of costume drama set at the turn of the 20th century and Jack the Ripper meets Jekyll and Hyde, with the bonus of detail and styling that screamed 1980s – the big hair, the "Boy" branding, and the New Romantic meets fetish wear… However, with plenty to draw from, the colours were intended to evoke the shocking pinks of the '80s. The US distributor requested that all reds became brown to make it less "bloody" (which seemed a little odd for a culture in which gun crime is ubiquitous). This is the intended "bloody" version.

When I was growing up in the 1960s and '70s, my father owned cinemas, and from an early age, I collected movie posters. At that time, most of them were painted; this style had been going on since the silent era. I developed an appreciation for artwork — and the artists who painted them — because of these seminal images.

My favourite poster of all time is the American B-style for *The Fearless Vampire Killers* (1967), featuring the realistic upper portion of Sharon Tate in a bubble bath about to be bitten by a vampire played by Ferdy Mayne (the artist's identity has been debated but never proven). The lower portion was a caricature, created by the great Frank Frazetta, of Sharon Tate, Roman Polanski, and Jack MacGowran fleeing the snowy castle in a coffin/bobsled with all the vampires nipping at their heels. (Uncharacteristically, Frazetta "signed" this artwork by carving his initials, "F.F.", into the side of the coffin.) This amusing chase scene — in the mode of Frazetta's similar poster artwork for *What's New Pussycat?* — still haunts me to this day and is the loving inspiration for the cover of my recent book, *I Was A Teenage Monster Hunter!* illustrated by Dan Gallagher.

When the trend for photographic poster designs started to catch on in the 1970s and 1980s, I was horrified. I clung to the lavish holdouts like Richard Amsel's *Raiders of the Lost Ark* and the posters of Bob Peak and others. In 1982, at age 25, I became head of marketing at United Artists Classics and, later, Spectrafilm, where I won *Hollywood Reporter* Key Art Awards for designing posters for Fassbinder's *Veronika Voss* and Verhoeven's *The Fourth Man*. I hired my dear late pal Vincent Topazio to paint those posters in the old-fashioned way and they were positively stunning — far more attractive than the generic, lackluster photographic posters of the era.

In 2000, I directed *Elvira's Haunted Hills*, a spoof of the Vincent Price/Edgar Allan Poe/Roger Corman movies of the 1960s. I designed the poster to be an homage to the key art of *The Pit and the Pendulum*, and we recruited the great cheesecake artist Olivia De Berardinis to paint the exquisite imagery.

By then, however, my taste in poster design was considered passé by the new generation of Hollywood marketeers. Balderdash.

As the decades ticked by, the art form became as rare as the dodo bird. But, Monster Kids like us held on to the nostalgic yearning for classically painted key art. And very wise marketing folks at some of the Blu-ray companies like Shout! Factory and others (who were bona fide Monster Kids themselves) resurrected the idea and applied it to exclusive new cover art for Blu-ray packaging and occasionally, limited-edition posters.

There's has also been a wave of "mondo-posters", basically "fan art" tributes to movies old and new, featuring original, classically painted designs that evoke the era when painted posters were in fashion.

I, for one, am a huge proponent and fan of this return to form. And Graham Humphreys is at the forefront of this renaissance, with his deliriously wicked watercolour masterpieces that whiplash our attention. His style is as instantly recognizable as that of Frazetta, Amsel, Peak, and other forefathers of a bygone era. Thanks to Graham and his peers, the genre is en vogue all over again.

SAM IRVIN,
Los Angeles, California

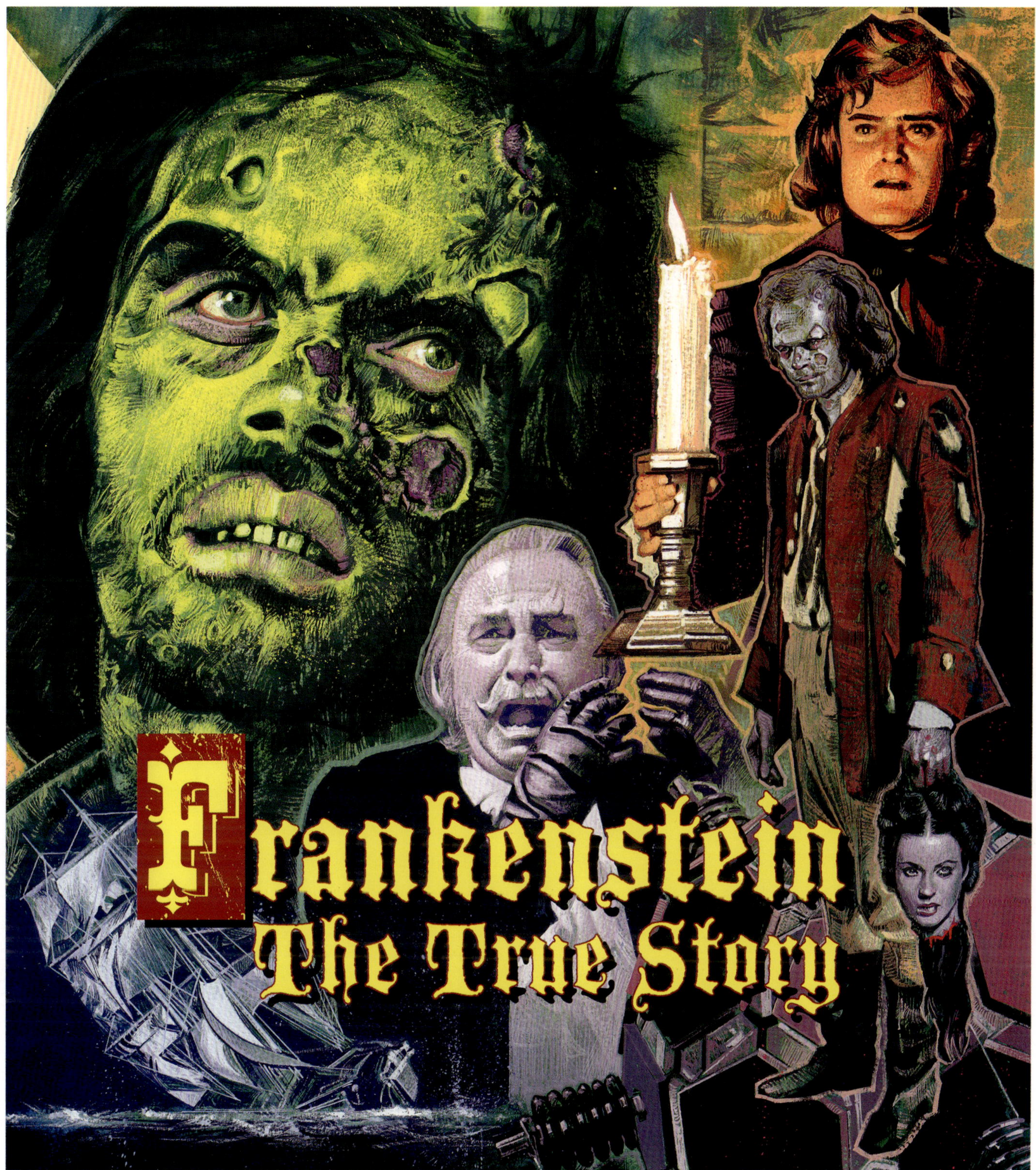

ABOVE: *Frankenstein: The True Story* (2022), Fabulous Films; Blu-ray cover.

This was made for TV in two parts (1973) and later edited as a single movie; I remember seeing it at the impressionable age of 13, knowing that it was something that would stay with me throughout my life. One particular scene gave me nightmares for months! Beautiful production design and a thrilling cast made the film very special. I chose to give my image the full Hammer horror treatment, faking the green monster's face (the tones are natural in the film) and adding some of the fear and savagery that propels the narrative. I paid particular attention to how the characters are positioned and posed; the dynamics within the film are powerful and unexpected.

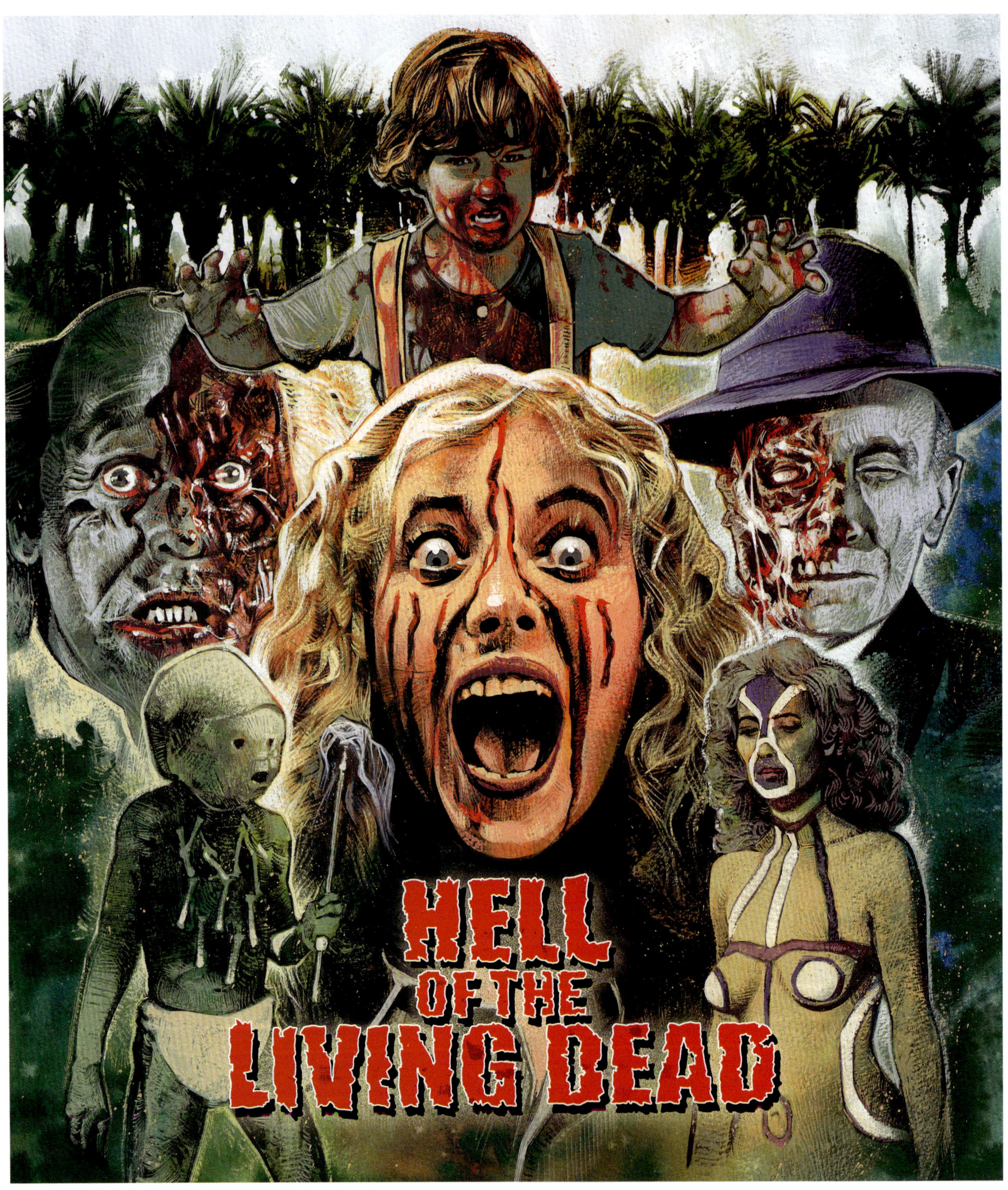

ABOVE: *Hell of the Living Dead* (2022), 88 Films; Blu-ray cover.

I was familiar with images from this film but hadn't actually seen it until the commission presented itself. I opted for the zombie characters that are the fan favourites — and the fantastically wide-eyed reaction of the actor. Zombie children occupy a space in several genre films, creating a discomfort around the need to nurture and protect a child

and the obvious threat of a lethal eating machine. So, of course, the kid had to go right at the top! The curious jungle sequences appeared to swerve into the territory of the cannibal genre, which was popular at the time (1980), but it seemed to add another level of interest to the image.

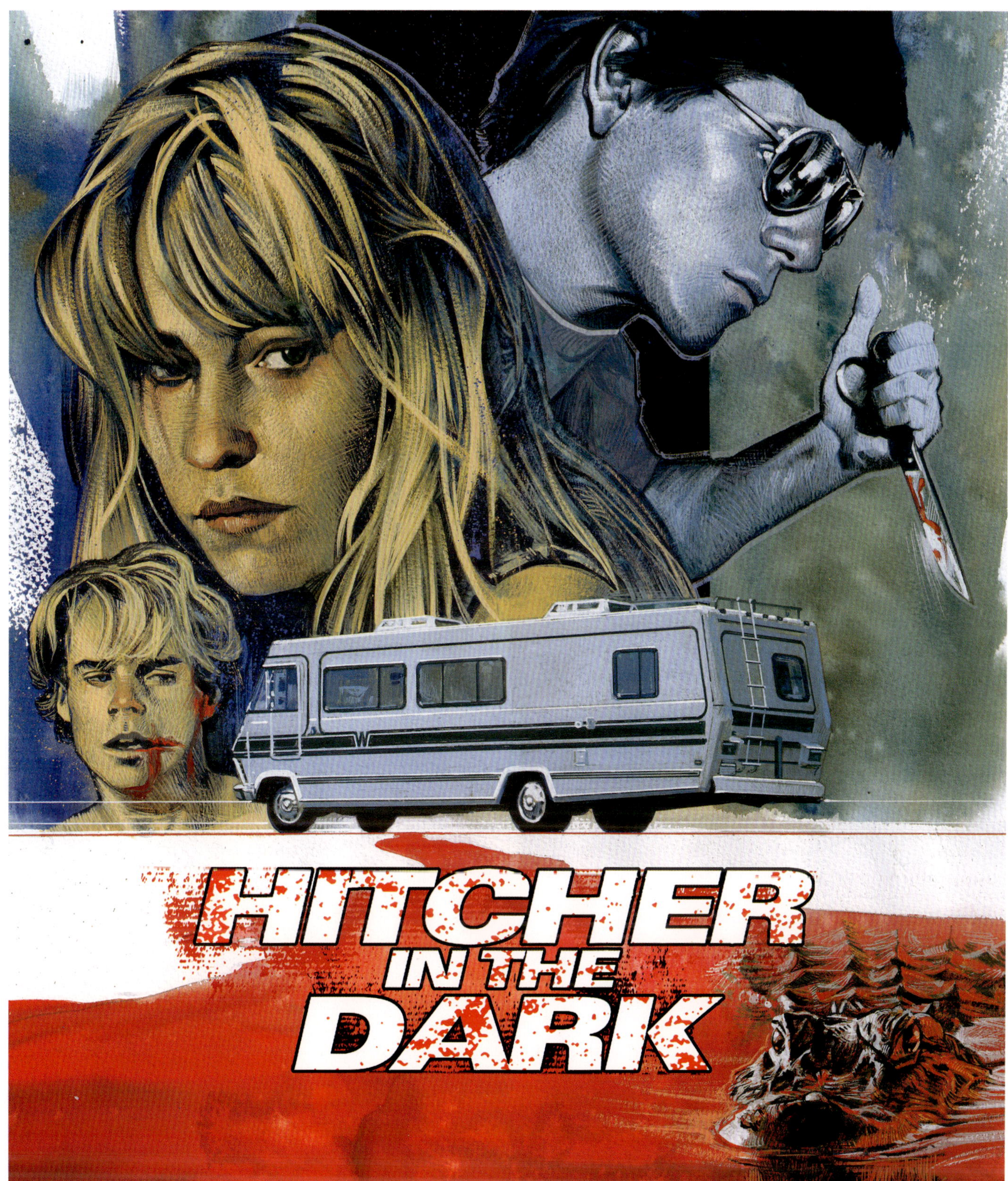

ABOVE: *Hitcher in the Dark* (2022), 88 Films; Blu-ray cover.

Despite the title, little of the film seems to take place in the dark. As the trailer is the focus of the crimes, it provides the best option around which to build the character composition. Keeping a white background ensured that the trail of blood emanating from the trailer would create a stark graphic. Although the alligator isn't central to the plot (but appears in a key scene), it felt like an interesting way to visually expand on a simple premise.

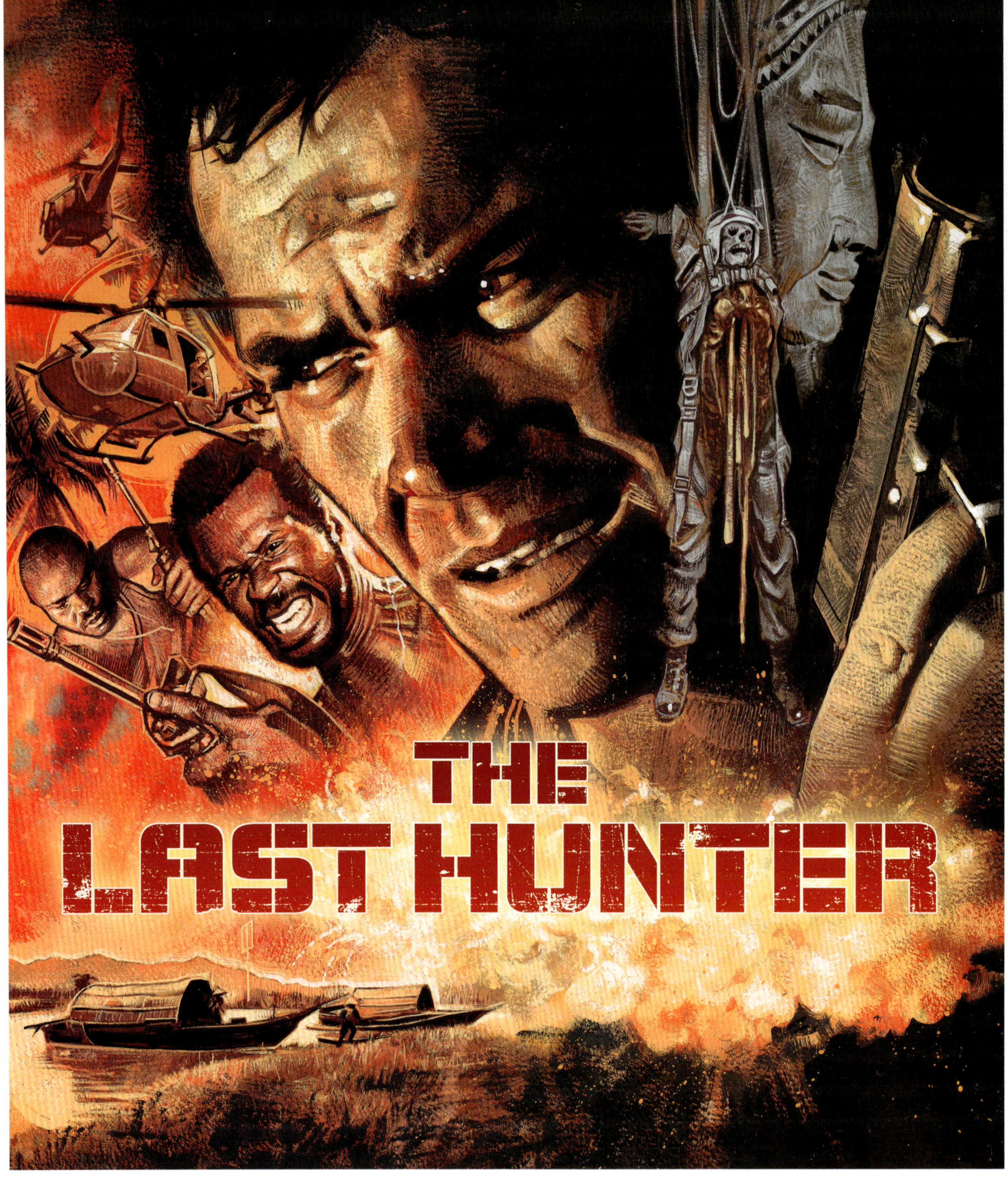

ABOVE: *The Last Hunter* (2022), Treasured Films Ltd; Blu-ray cover.

The first release on a new label. My client was keen to re-create the energy of the 1980s video boom. The subject matter is clearly a shadow of *Apocalypse Now*, almost a budget remake. Actor David Warbeck takes centre stage, as his inclusion defines the era for many video fans. I searched for additional elements to add interest and arrived at the parachute corpse and temple statue. My viewing copy wasn't crisp, and it was a struggle to make use of blurred references. A common issue with any commission is when the original material pre-dates digital technology, and the restored version isn't available in its final form.

RIGHT: *House of the Long Shadows* (2022), Fabulous Films; Blu-ray cover.

Clearly written as a vehicle for its horror royalty cast, the portraiture was the primary consideration here. Beyond that was a setting (the house) and the narrative-driven inclusion of the bloodied typewriter, with the skeletal hand portending death. Because of how the film is lit and framed, it was difficult to harvest good facial references, but it was essential to show a variety of expressions that might best capture the range of the characters and their demeanours.

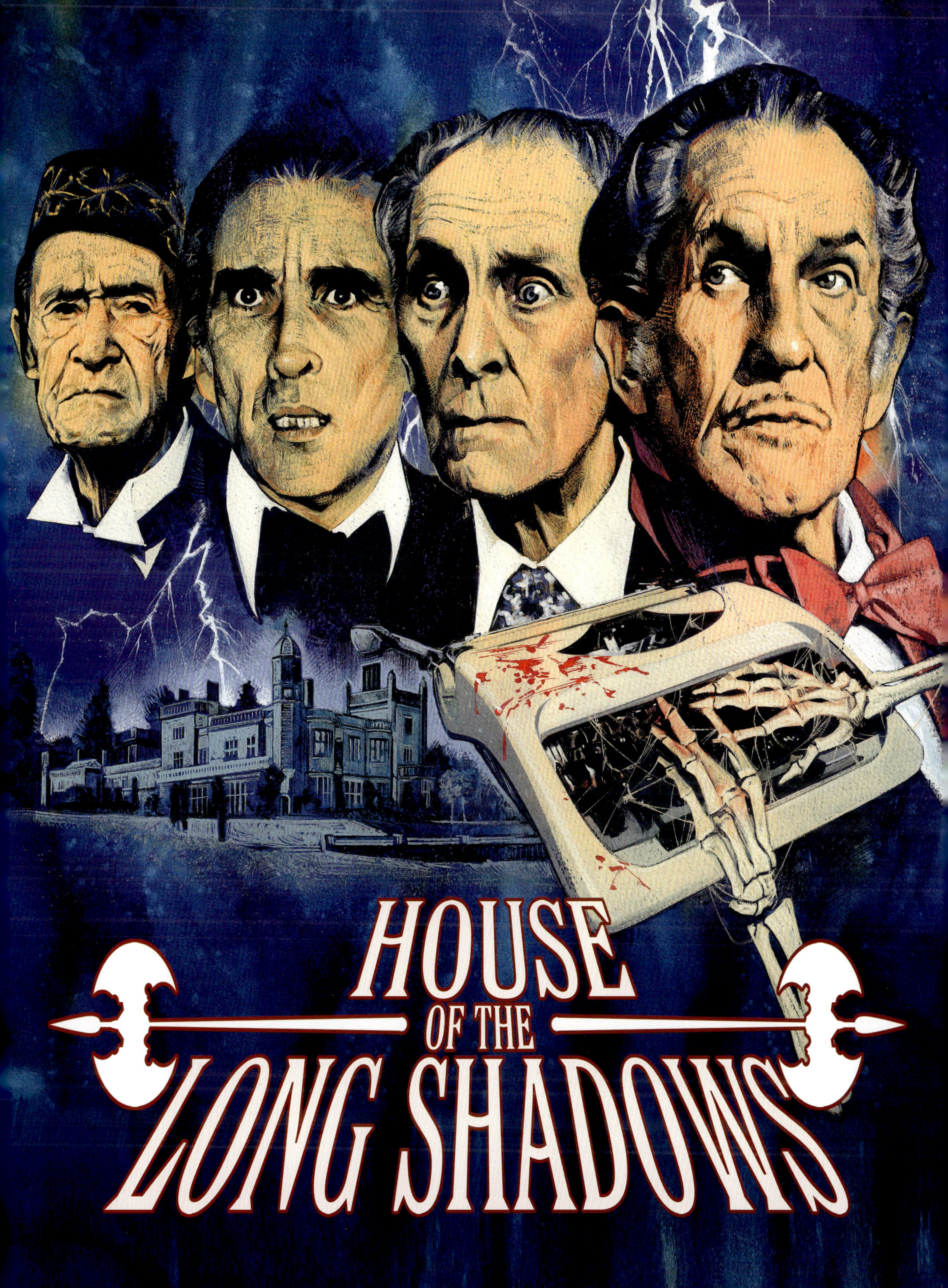

HOUSE
OF THE
LONG SHADOWS

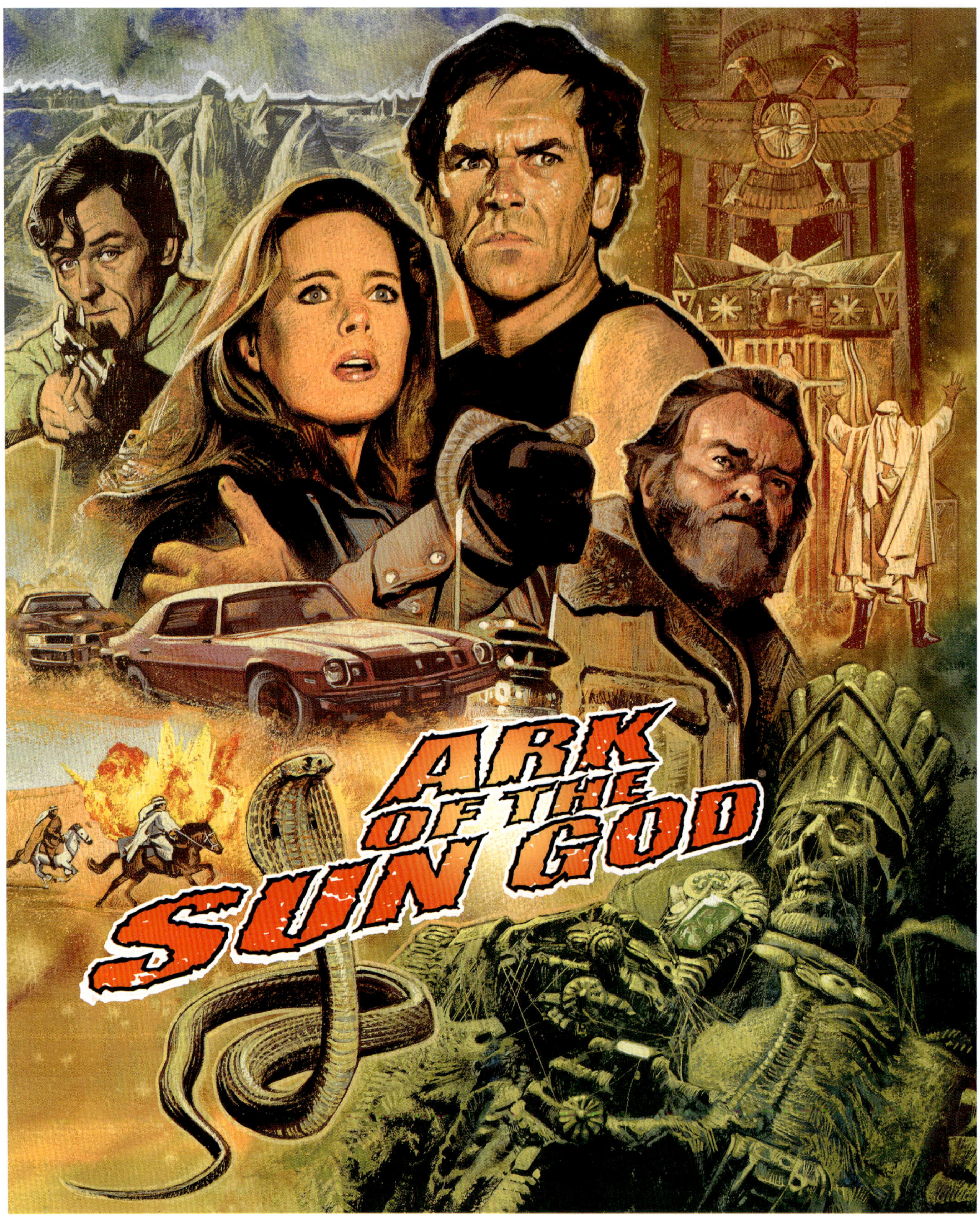

ABOVE: *Ark of the Sun God* (2022), 88 Films; Blu-ray cover.

Essentially a *Raiders of the Lost Ark* on a budget, though no less fun. It was relatively easy to identify the most visual scenes: Heroes, chases, explosions, mysterious tomb, snake, etc... and a little nod to horror.

David Warbeck has a great face for painting. It is softly rugged and has just enough gnarliness to add interest. He has been a subject in a number of commissions, mostly Italian horror films.

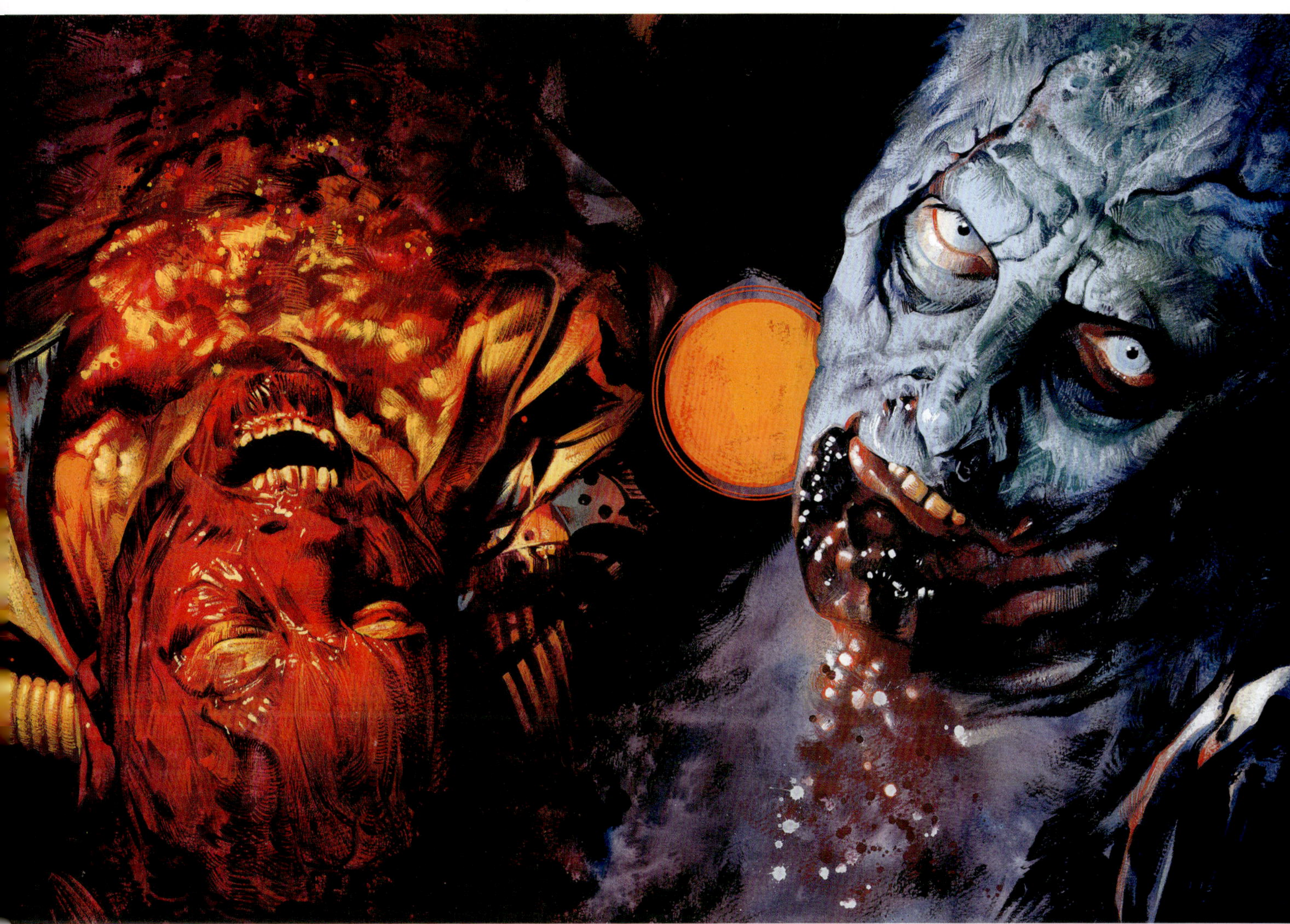

ABOVE: *House of 1000 Corpses* (2022),
Lionsgate; Blu-ray box edition cover.

A curiosity for two reasons. I'd created a UK campaign for the film in
2003, for its first release, but due to time and budget, there was no space
to paint a poster, so I opted for a photo comp, layering enough texture to
suggest a painting. Twenty years later, the opportunity to paint an image
suddenly presented itself again. I'd been working on a series of soundtrack
covers, Rob Zombie Presents (which appear in the Vinyl chapter), and had
built up some trust with the film's director, Rob Zombie. I was delighted
when he asked Lionsgate to approach me for the commission. In truth, my
sketch concepts weren't to Rob's liking, and I was sent a reworked layout
as my guide. The layout is thus not typical of mine but the colours and
textures remain my own.

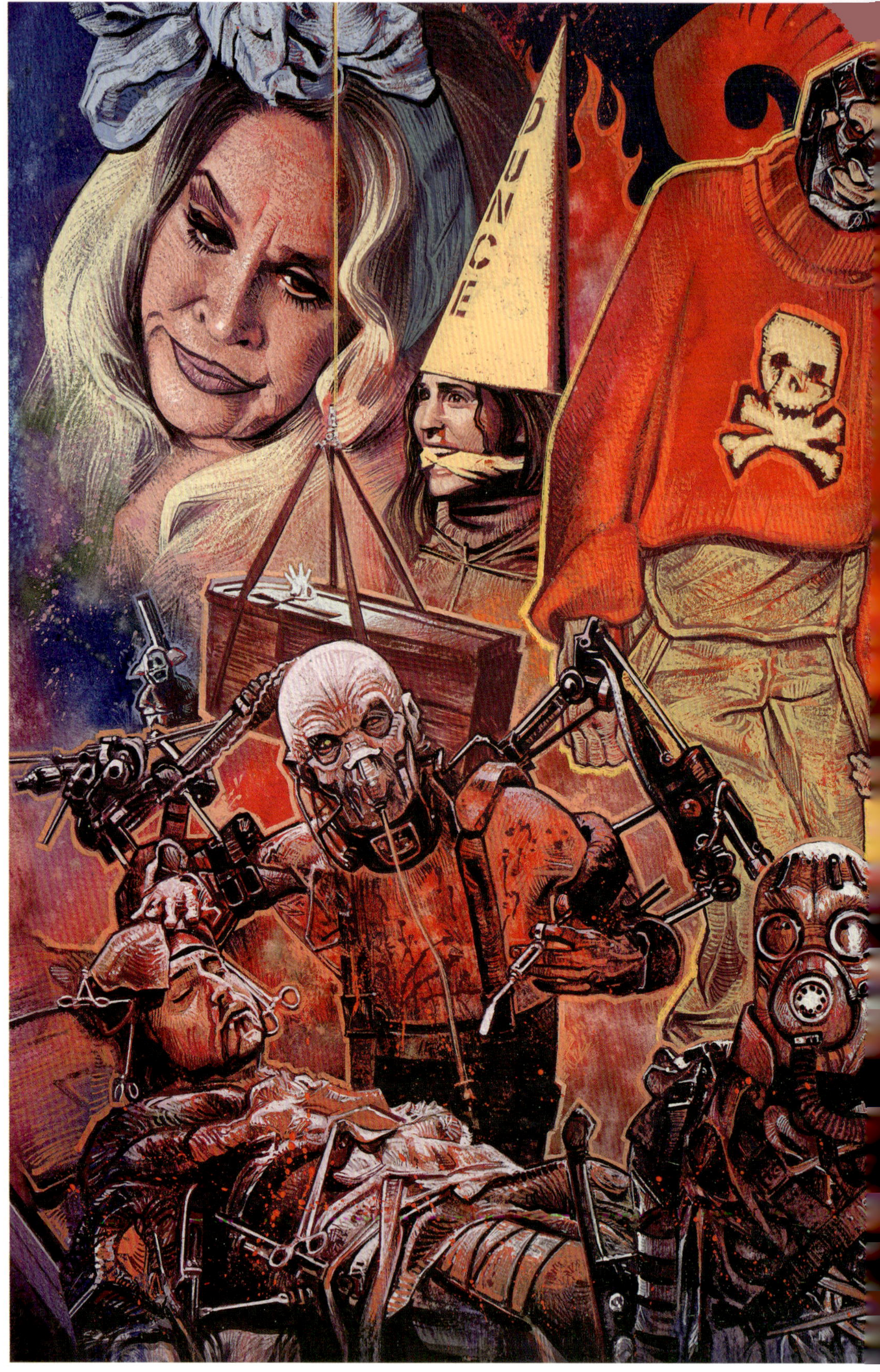

RIGHT: *House of 1000 Corpses* (2022), Lionsgate; box edition booklet cover.

Originally intended as another complex layout of alternative elements to complement the box art, I was instead sent two stills that the director wished to see on the front and back. My painting is my interpretation of the photographs, removing the gloss of the high-quality reference and piling on the aggressive textures that I felt better represented the film.

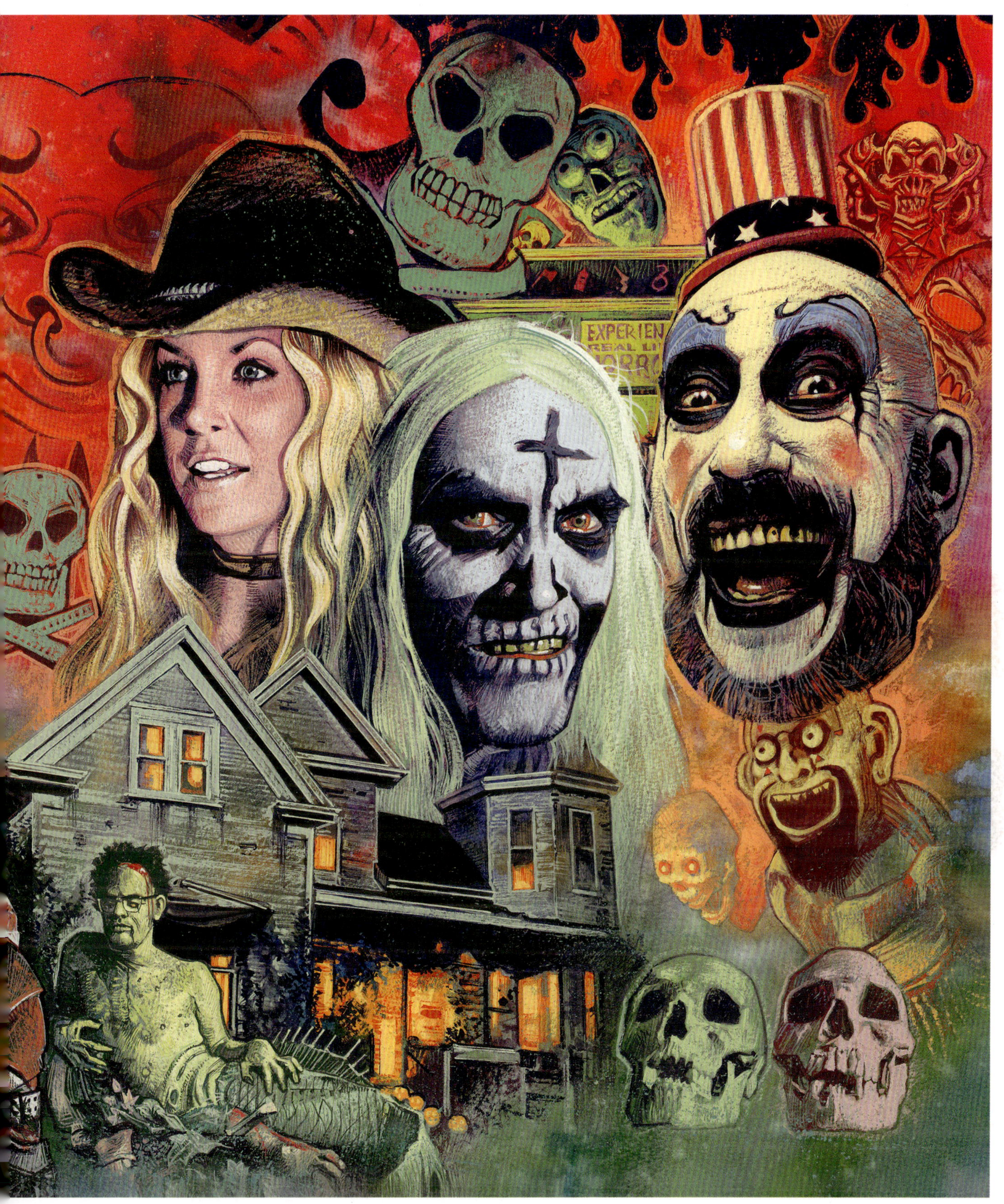

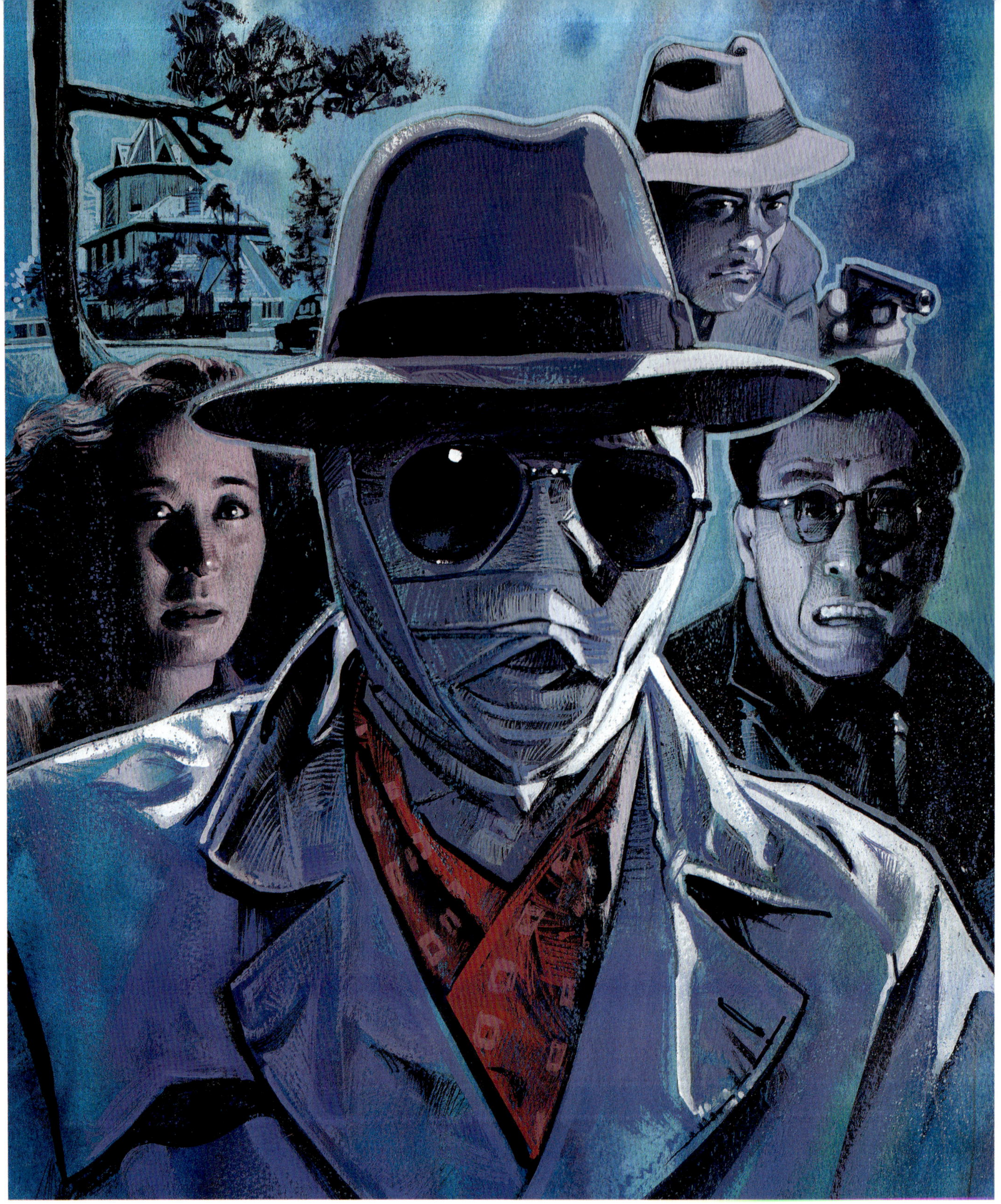

ABOVE: *The Invisible Man Appears* (2019), Arrow Films; Blu-ray cover.

Not the Universal classic but a Japanese homage from 1949. My only available reference was the unrestored film, in very bad form… It was very blurred and almost impossible to lift any images from. The key portraits are, therefore, very soft. The film is also black and white, meaning that a simple blue palette was the best compromise for a colour sleeve.

RIGHT: *It Came from Outer Space* (2020), Fabulous Films; Blu-ray cover.

A classic of the science fiction genre. I couldn't have been happier to paint this cover. I recall seeing the film at the Scala Cinema in London in the early 1980s, in 3-D, double-billed with *The Creature from the Black Lagoon*, a nostalgic re-creation of the drive-in thrills of America in the 1950s. The art references posters of the era in which the film was made. The palette represents the green colour one expects of alien life forms in a B-movie world, and the soft purples, earthly comforts.

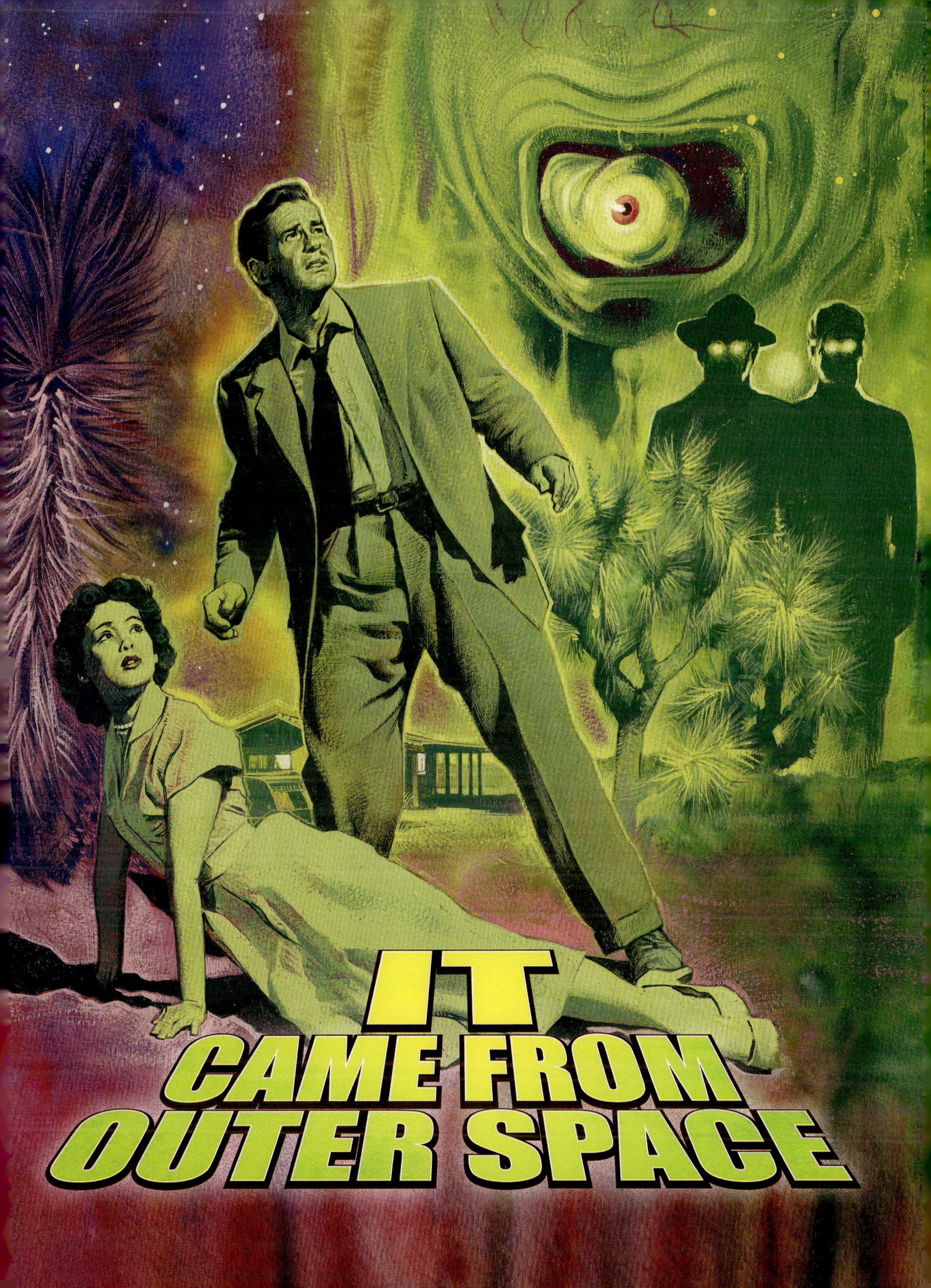

IT
CAME FROM
OUTER SPACE

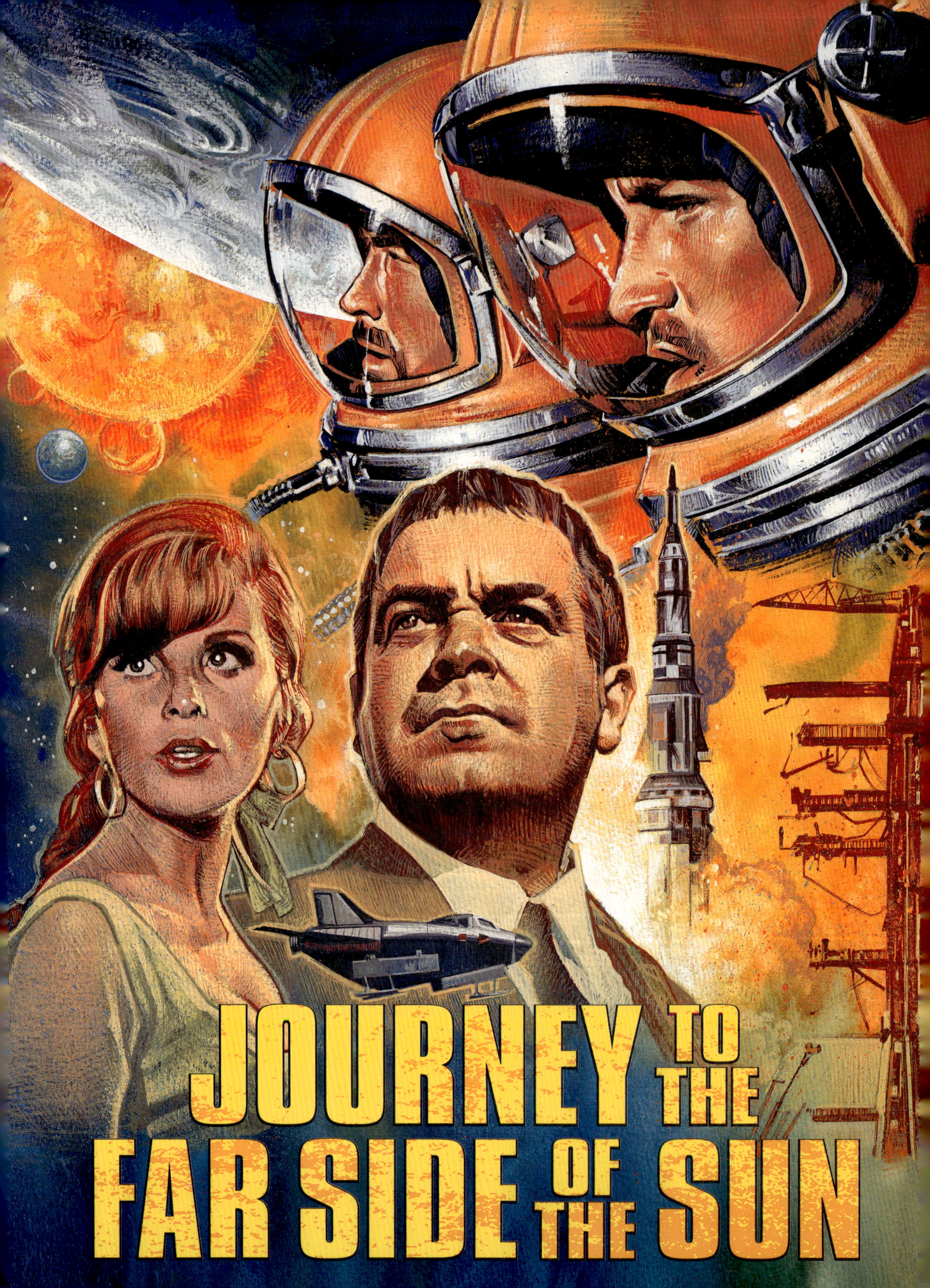

JOURNEY TO THE
FAR SIDE OF THE SUN

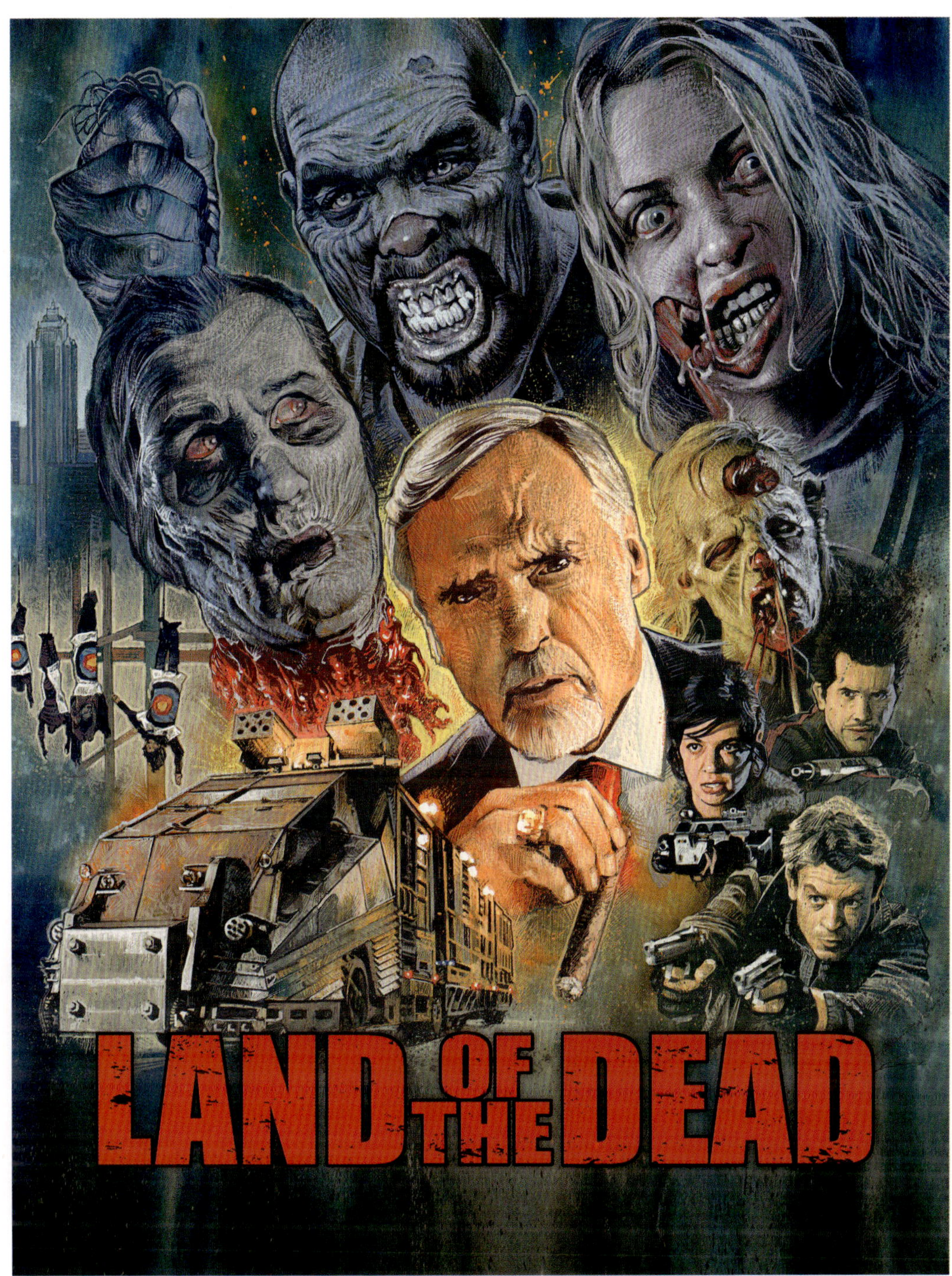

LEFT: *Land of the Dead* (2020), Fabulous Films; Blu-ray cover.

A late entry into the George A Romero zombie series, this nevertheless presents some memorable scenes and spectacular make-up effects, making it much easier to choose the elements. With so much scope, it was hard to reduce the options to make this single representation of so many parts. However, I knew that there was the key cast headed by Dennis Hopper, who clearly rules the cover, just as he rules within the narrative. The rest is zombie fun!

OPPOSITE: *Journey to the Far Side of the Sun* (2021), Fabulous Films; Blu-ray cover.

This Gerry Anderson-directed film employed many elements from his sci-fi cannon, notably his TV series *UFO* (from which elements were lifted). The presence of Herbert Lom added gravity (appropriately!) and gave my composition a commanding portrait. The primary colours were intended to reference the vintage sci-fi films and posters of the 1950s/'60s.

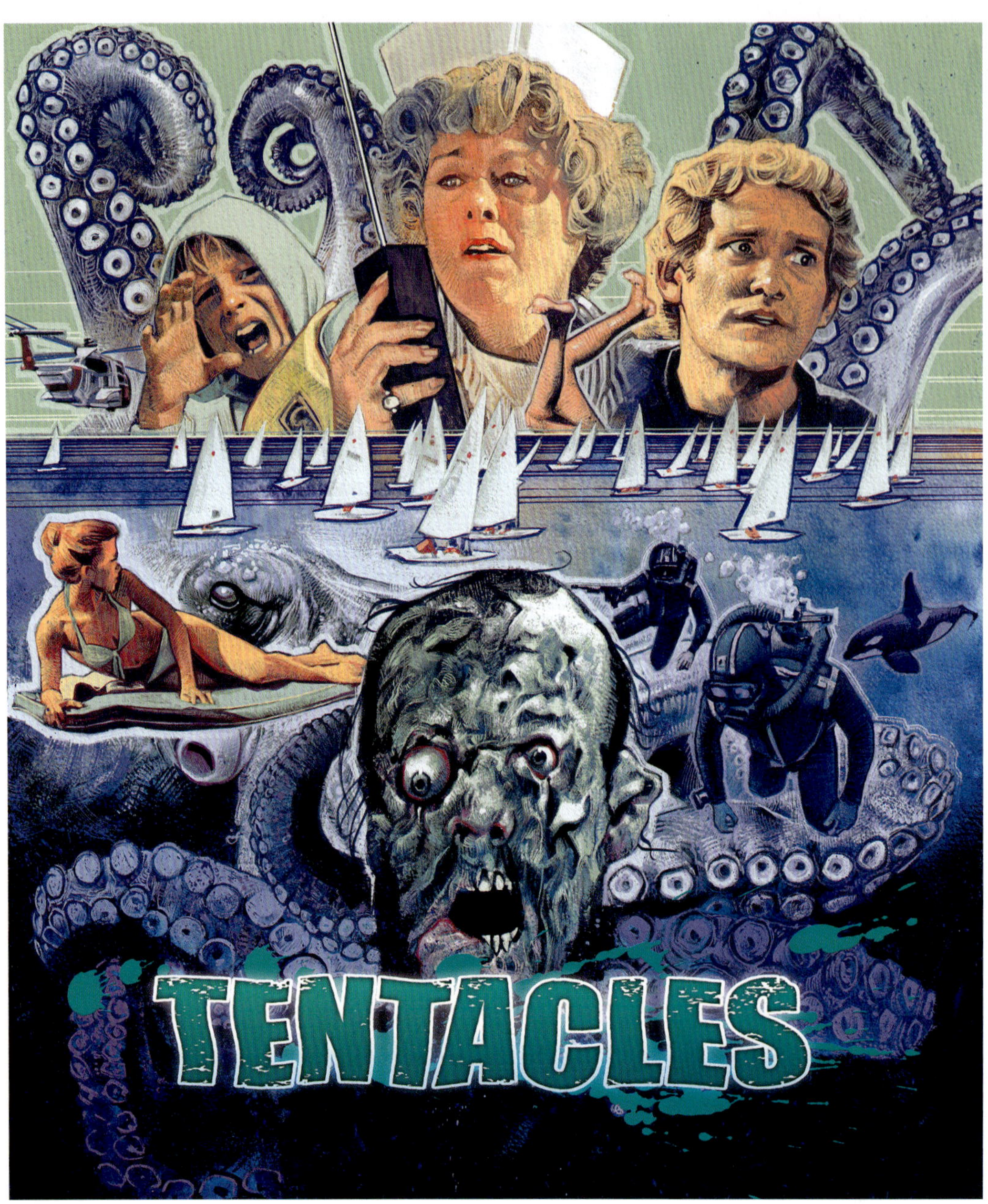

The film is one of a number
of those that were made in the
wake of the success of *Jaws*
(1975). In this instance, the sea-
themed peril is a giant octopus.
Shelley Winters had starred in
The Poseidon Adventure, which
made her a logical choice for this
late entry into the era of great
"disaster" films, a sub-genre
that featured people making
terrible choices in the face
of uncontrollable situations,
natural or man-made. It's pure
B-movie joy, and I decided to
play with the coastal theme by
making the colours look like an
advertisement for ice cream!

This BFI release comprises
two documentaries that rode
the popularity of witchcraft,
fuelled by the LSD subculture
of the early 1970s and the
"Satanic Panic" generated by
a sensationalist press. Common
to the two documentaries is the
presence of English occultist
Alex Sanders. Nudity features
heavily (doubtless part of the
reason for the popularity of the
witchcraft-related culture of
the time). My brief requested a
range of elements from the two
documentaries, and I focussed
on the Pagan, mystical elements
rather than the sensationalism.

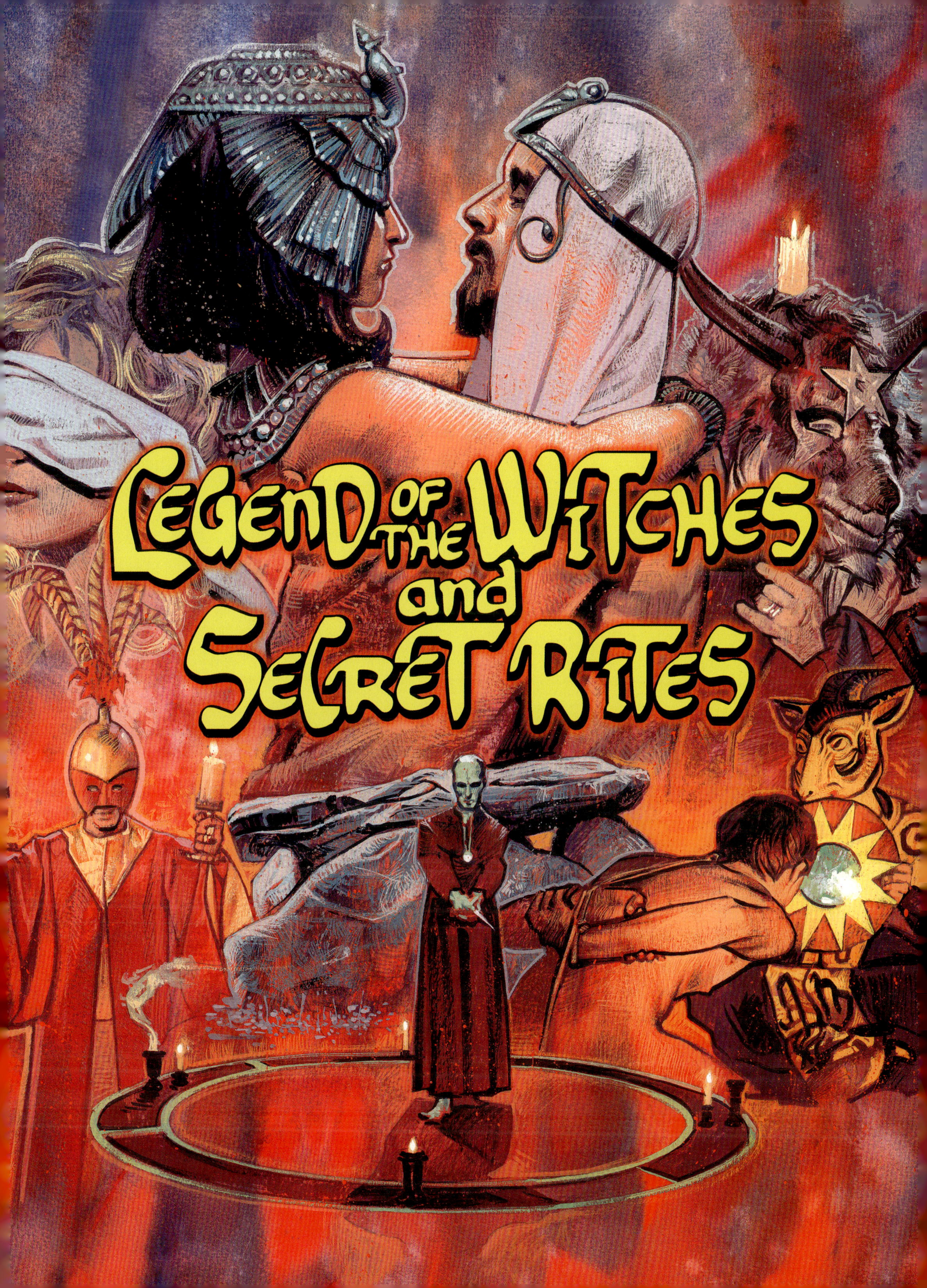

LEGEND OF THE WITCHES
and
SECRET RITES

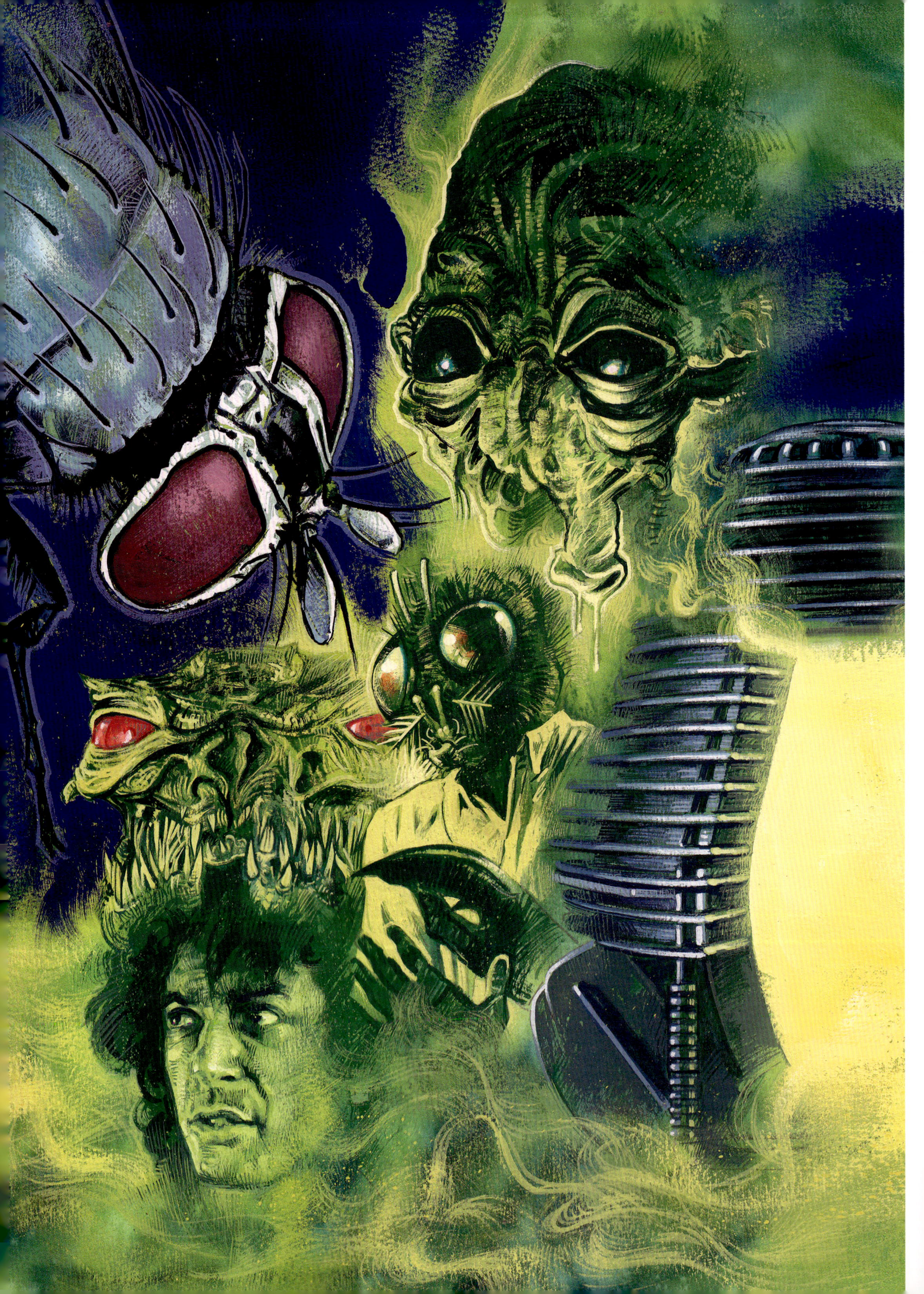

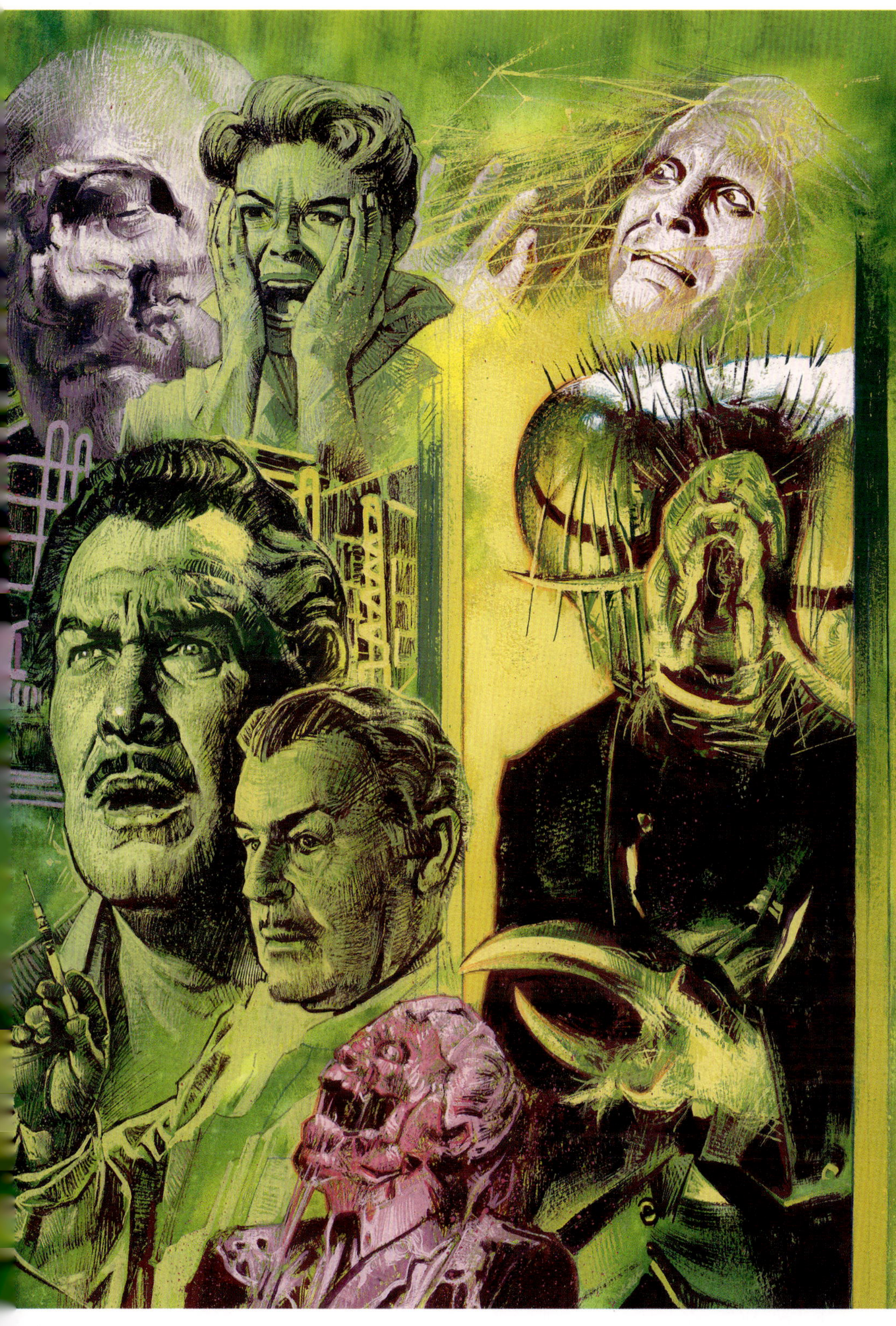

OPPOSITE: *The Fly Collection*
(2019), Shout! Factory;
Blu-ray box set cover.

This complex commission
involved a wraparound art that
would feature elements from all
The Fly films — from the original
1958 movie to the 1989 *The Fly 2*
— five in all. My original sketches
didn't feature Jeff Goldblum;
I'd hoped the pod and creature
from the 1986 film would suffice,
but the client insisted that I
add Goldblum's face, making
my composition slightly more
awkward than intended. This is
another instance where the use
of colour is vital in consolidating
so many disparate images.

LEFT: *The Fly Collection*
(2019), Shout! Factory;
Blu-ray box set cover.

The giant fly head in *Return
of the Fly* (1959) was an image
I had a particular affection
for, so I wanted it to feature
prominently on the reverse.
It was another opportunity to
paint the expressive features of
Vincent Price. As a fan of classic
horror, my layout for the reverse
is my preferred art.

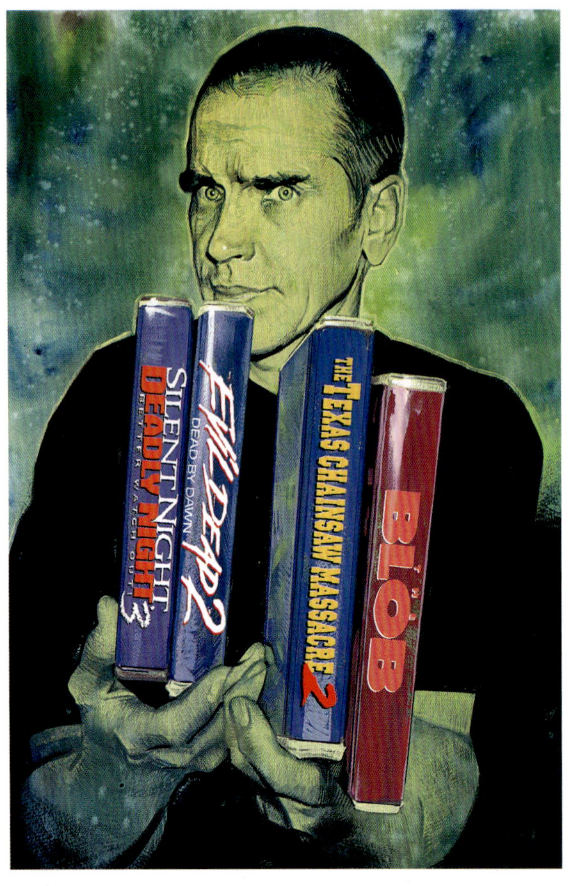

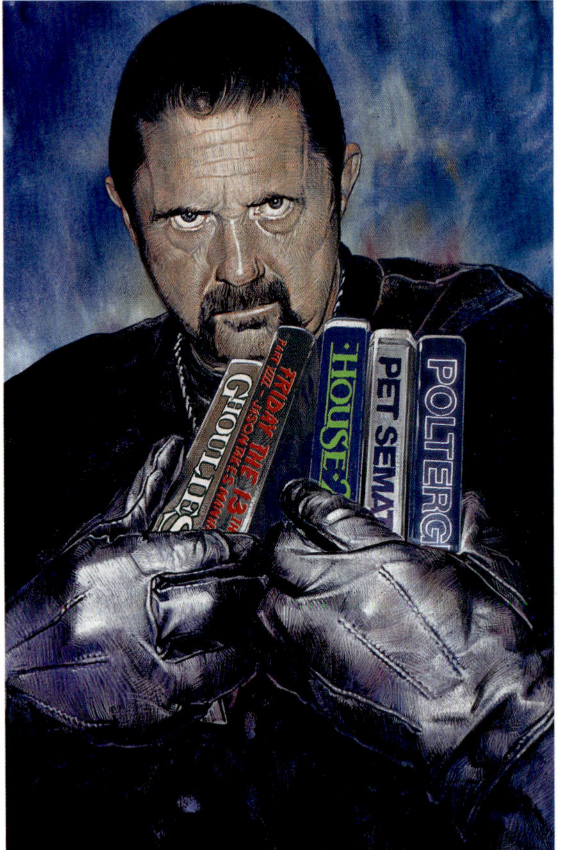

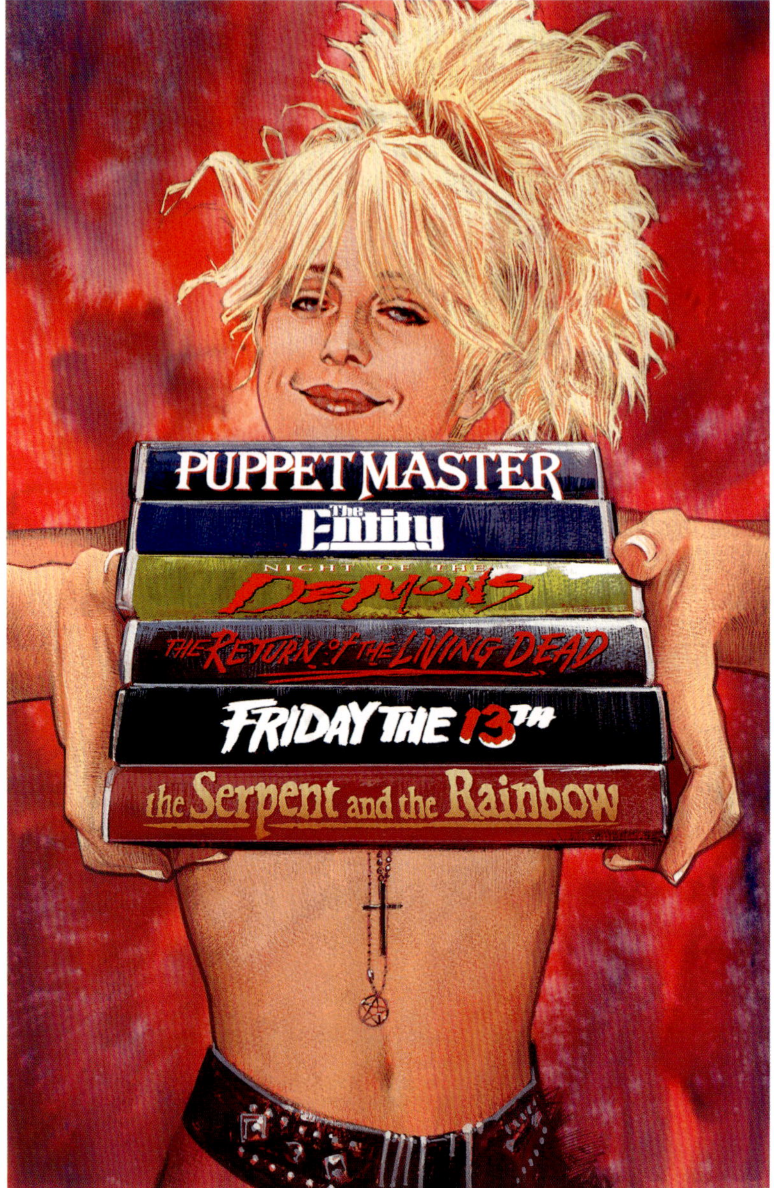

In Search of Darkness: Part II (2020), Creator VC; documentary promotion.

These portraits were intended to serve as a promotional appendage to a documentary campaign. In each instance the actors are portrayed clutching VHS boxes of films in which they'd starred.

ABOVE: Linnea Quigley

TOP LEFT: Bill Moseley

BOTTOM LEFT: Kane Hodder

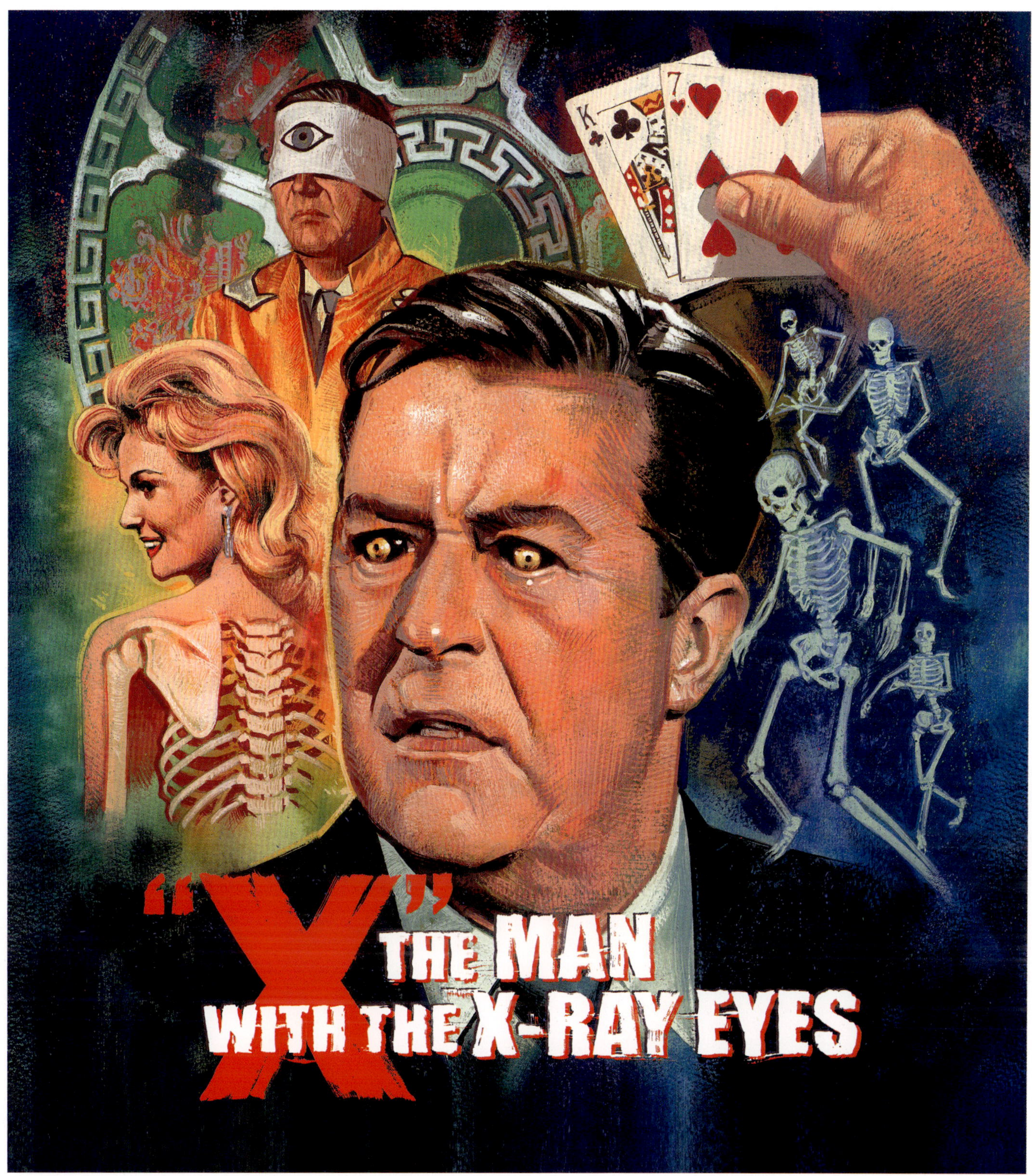

ABOVE: *The Man with the X-Ray Eyes* (2019), Second Sight; Blu-ray cover.

Ray Milland has a wonderful face to paint, and his tortured expression is all over this film. With so many possibilities, I decided to go for the full-on X-ray eyes portrait, with elements suggestive of his enhanced vision and the vices attached to it.

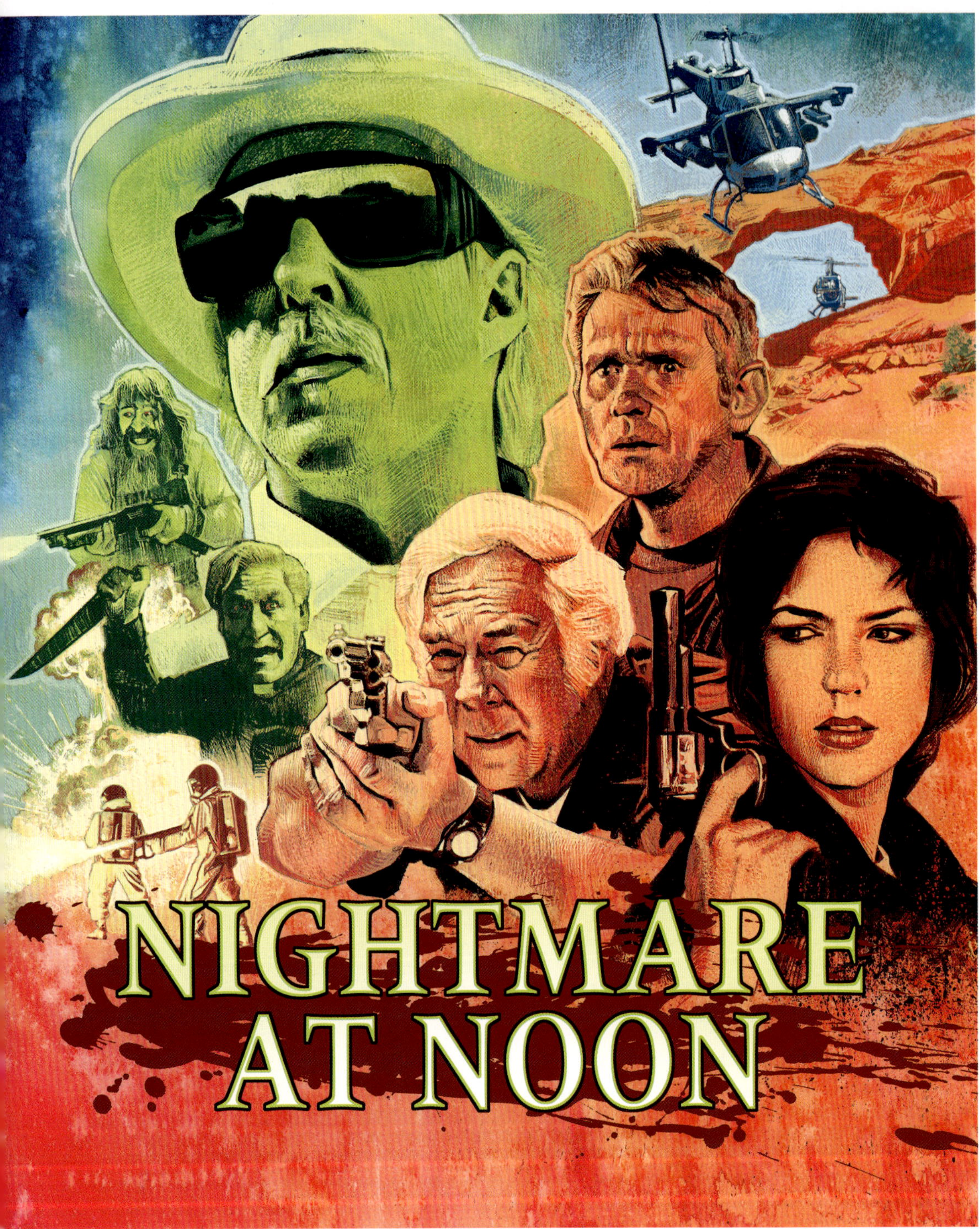

NIGHTMARE
AT NOON

LEFT: *Nightmare At Noon* (2022), Arrow Films; Blu-ray cover.

A film in the Nico Mastorakis catalogue. A hybrid of science fiction, western and action, it wasn't easy to define the film with all three genres. Some simple colour coding helped define the hero/villain balance, and green features heavily within the sci-fi scenes.

RIGHT: *Dr Terror's House of Horrors* (2022), Fabulous Films; Blu-ray cover.

There are so many good things about this film, not least an impressive cast. I'd already painted a previous cover for this release, so I needed to rethink the approach. By concentrating attention on the Death card, I could push the other elements further back whilst still giving prominence to Peter Cushing's portrayal of Dr Terror. Further consideration was given to the colour palette. The use of green and red was intended to evoke vintage train livery and signalling, as well as vintage horror posters.

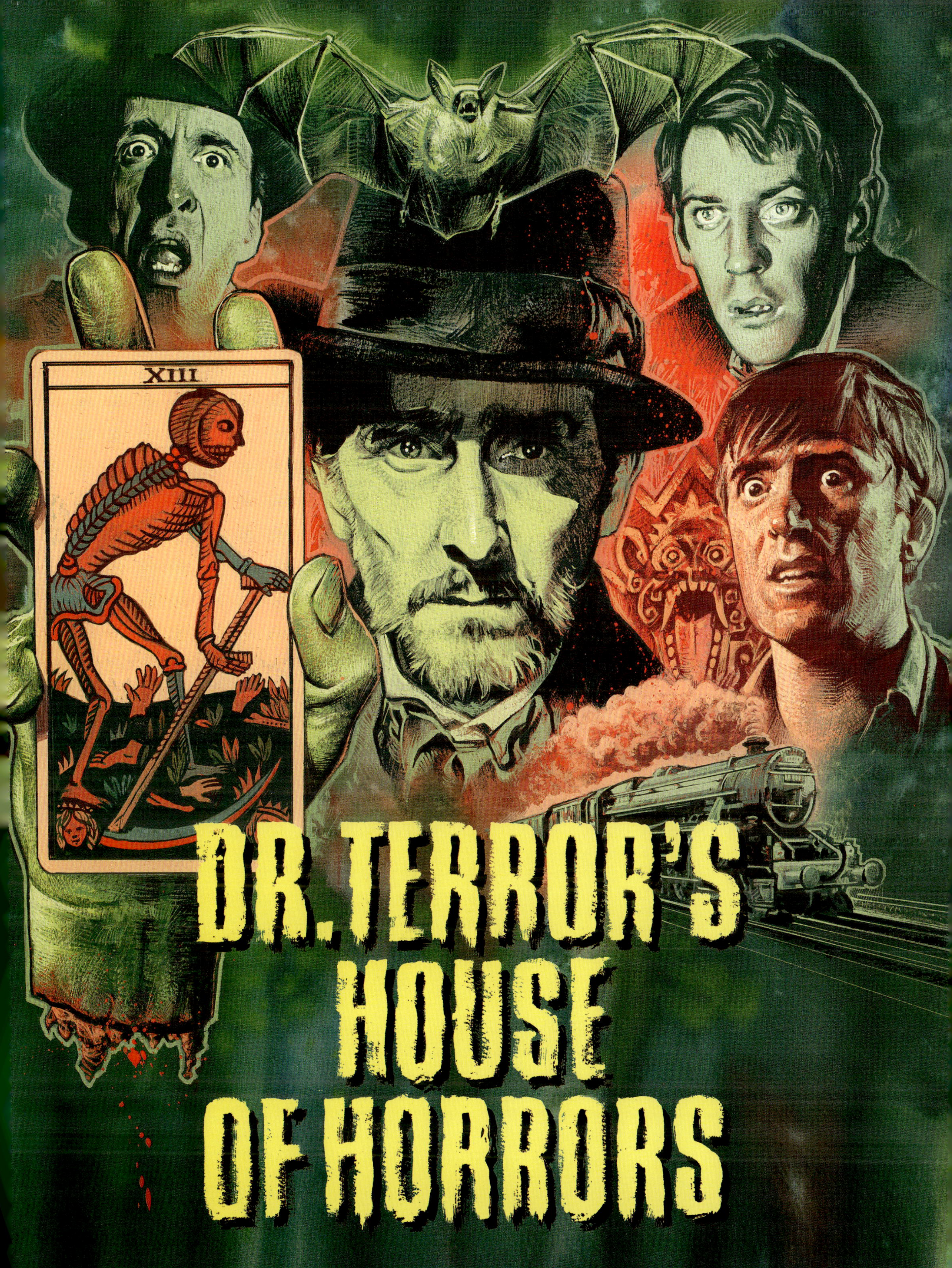
XIII
DR. TERROR'S
HOUSE
OF HORRORS

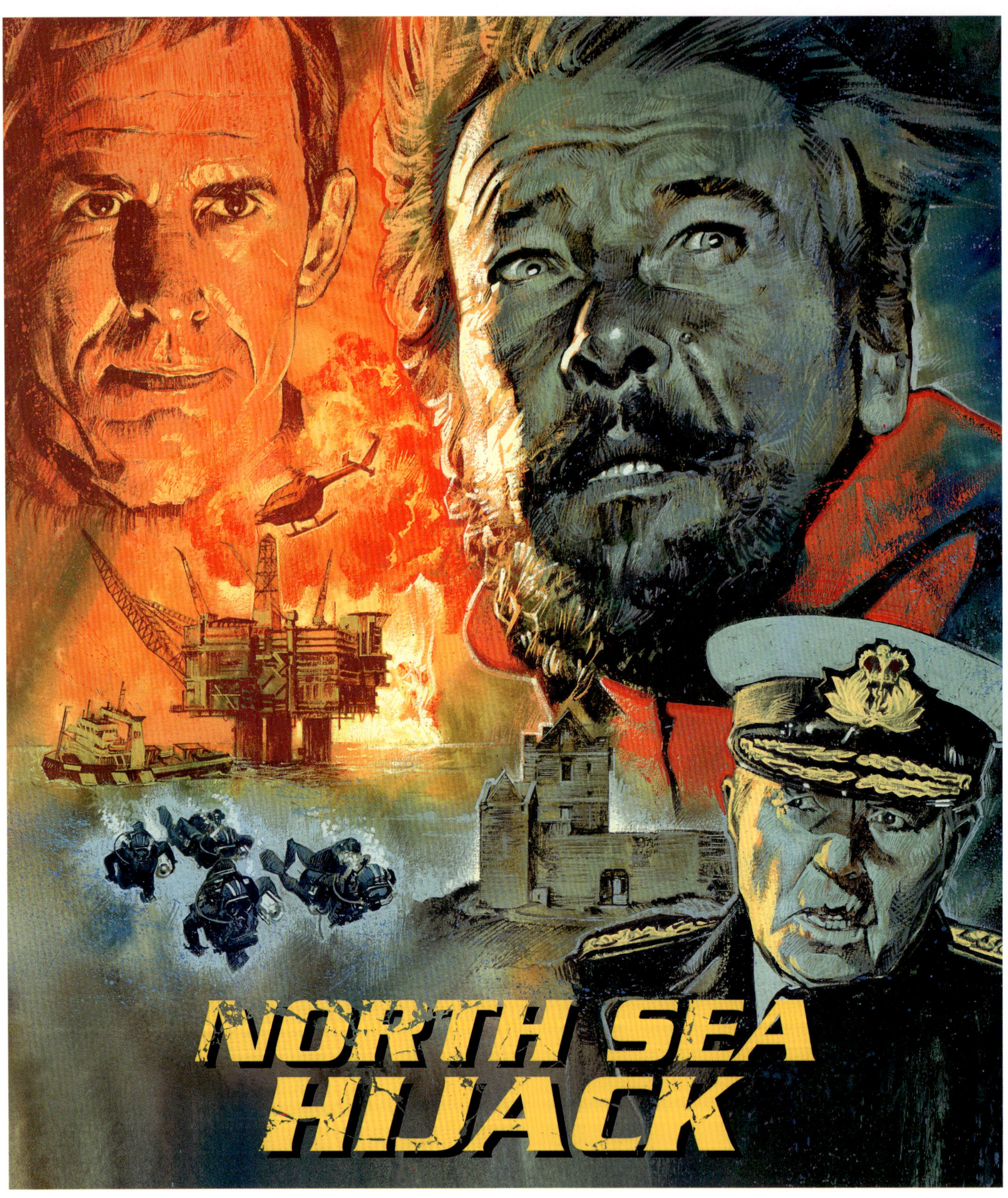

ABOVE: *North Sea Hijack* (2019), 88 Films; Blu-ray cover.

The three familiar faces would have sold the film alone, but the extra elements add context and drama. Roger Moore's character is a nod to his previous Bond role, and the film even references *Thunderball* (though not Moore's Bond) with the red diving suit and underwater scenes. Explosions always signify "action"! Some clichés are useful!

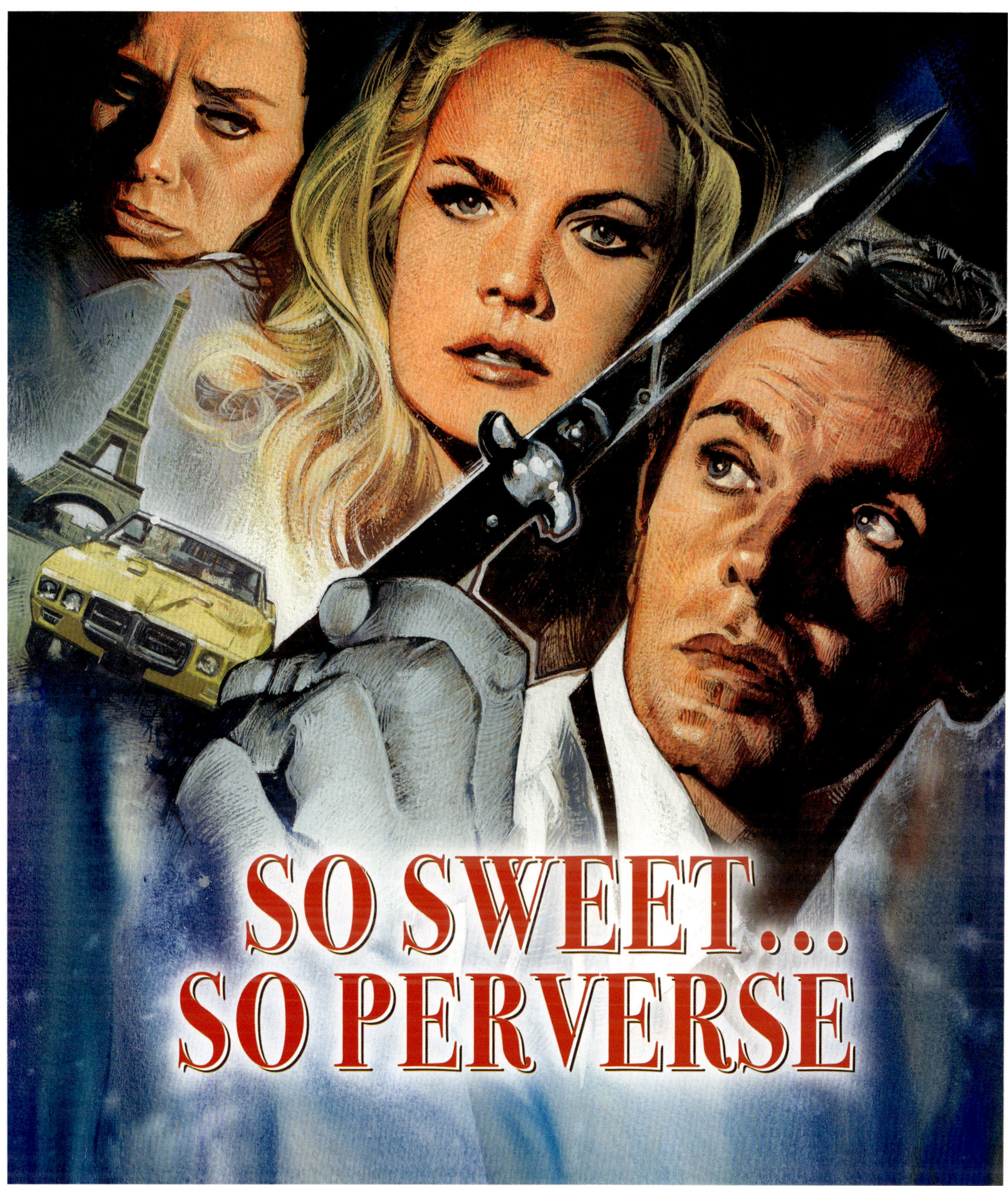

ABOVE: *So Sweet... So Perverse* (2020), 88 Films; Blu-ray cover.

Not genre, but with some giallo elements. I felt the best approach was to give the artwork a retro Euro thriller treatment, concentrating on the interaction of the emotional triangle and representative expressions that suggest a narrative. As always, this means watching the film carefully to pick precisely the right moment, which might often be so fleeting that it's easily missed — pause button and camera at the ready!

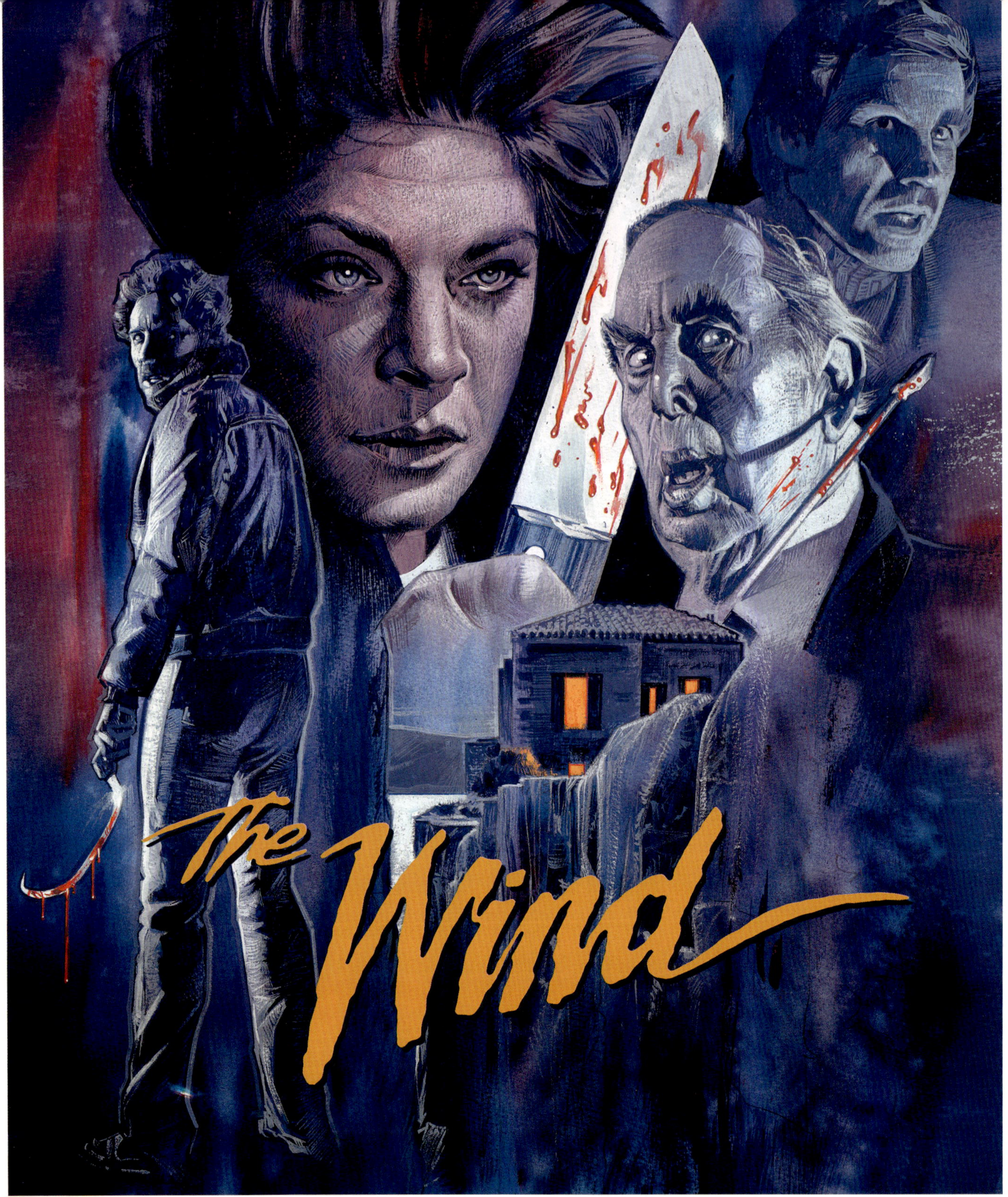

ABOVE: *The Wind* (2020), Arrow Films; Blu-ray cover.

Set on a Greek island, the film includes the colourful character actor Robert Morley and the intensely blue-eyed Meg Foster. It seemed only right that these two should occupy as much space as possible on the cover. The knife is the pivot around which the other elements revolve, but it also serves as a frame for Meg Foster's portrait.

RIGHT: *The Burning Room* (2021), BetaJester Ltd; promotional art for a VR experience.

This unusual commission resulted from a client relationship built through my artworks for the BBC TV show *Inside No. 9*. The project was written by Jeremy Dyson (the invisible member of *The League of Gentlemen*) and is still in development. The basic concept was discussed and merely required my textural and colour approach to a very simple image. The client asked for a pose that would recall the reaching Tarman in my art for *The Return of the Living Dead*. I used a timer to photograph myself as reference.

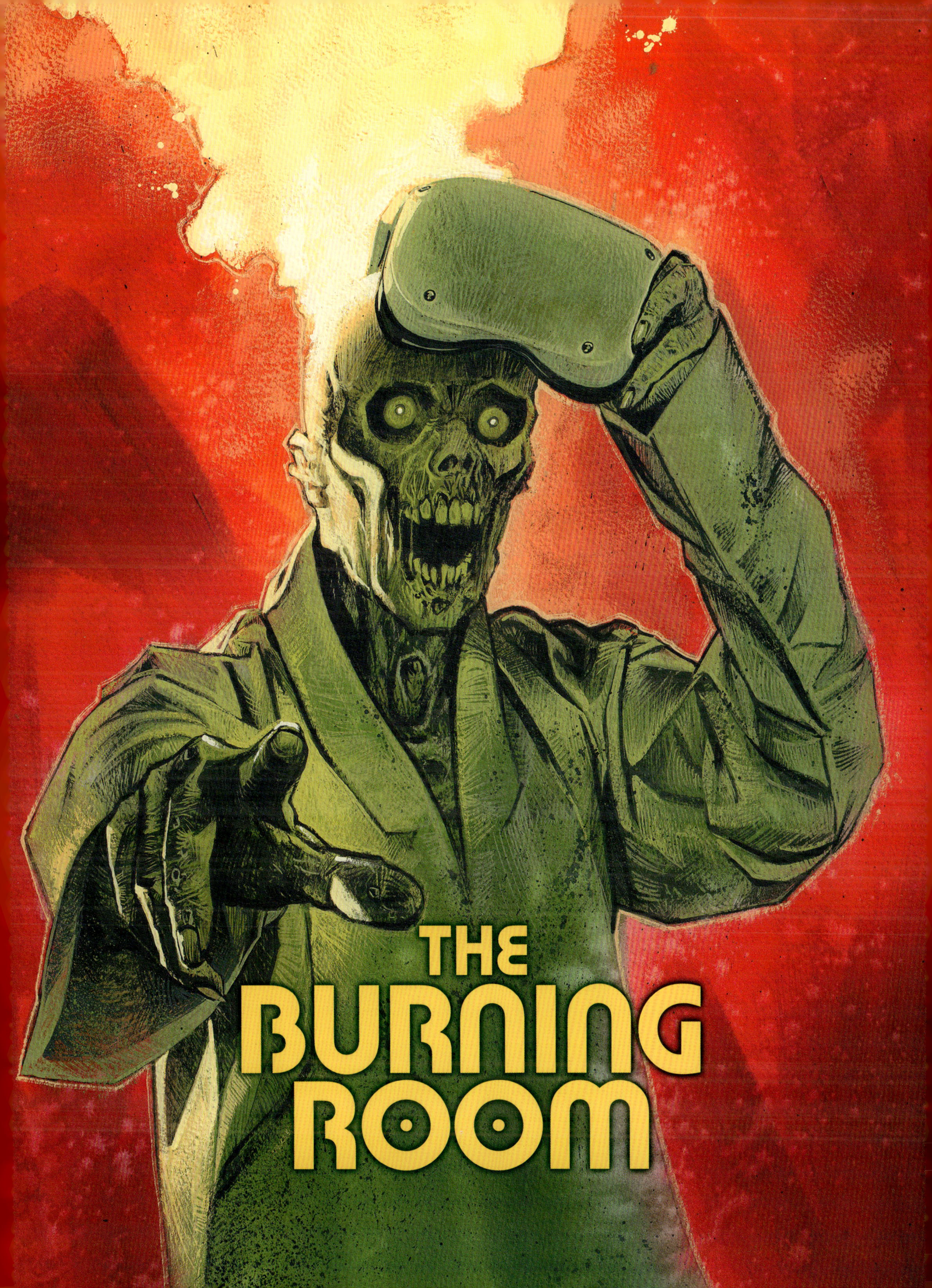

THE
BURNING
ROOM

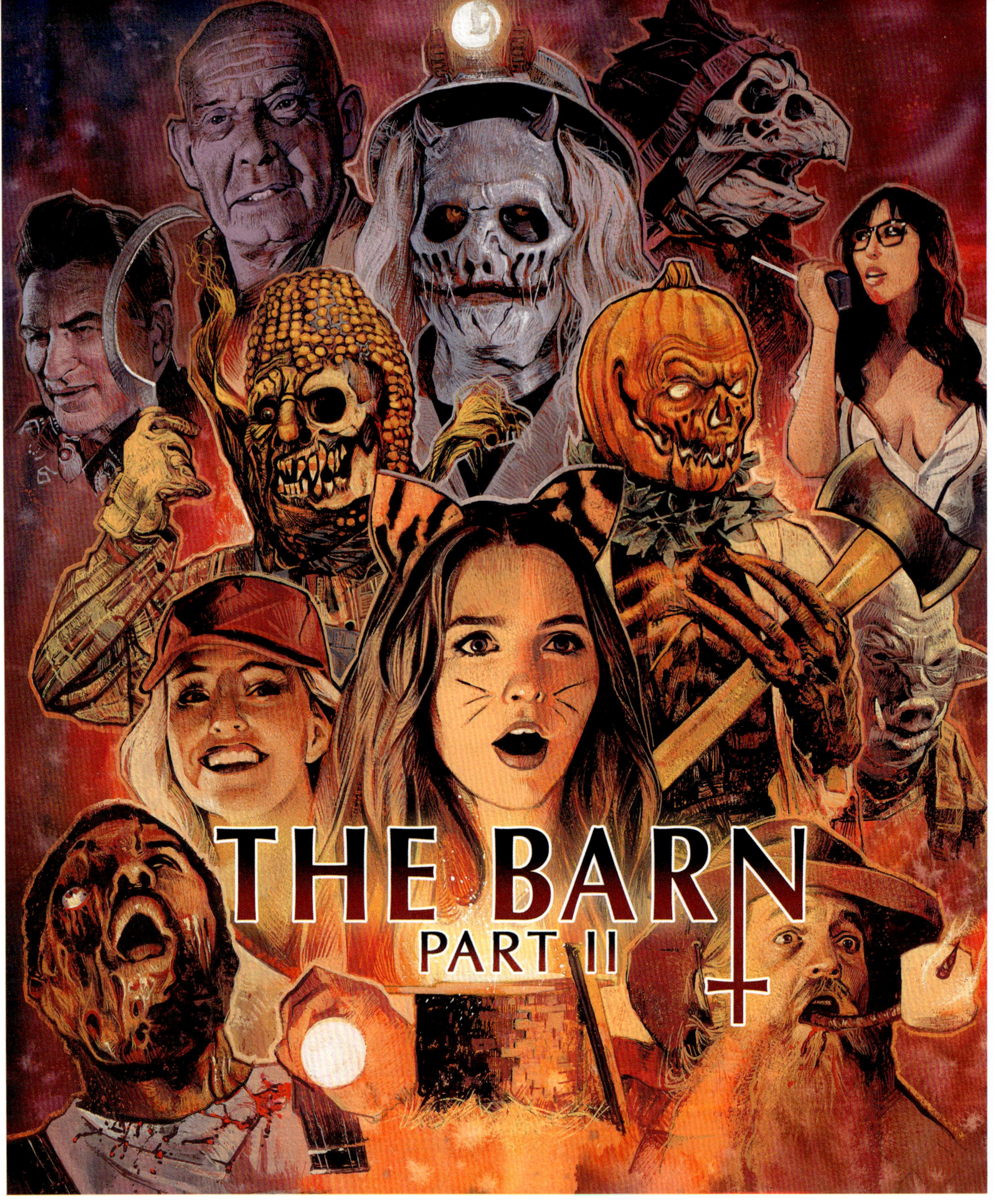

ABOVE: *The Barn II* (2022), Nevermore Production Films; Blu-ray cover.

I'd illustrated the cover for the first film, *The Barn*, and the client/director was happy enough with the result to commission an artwork for the sequel. New monsters were added to the previous line-up and thus needed to be represented, but I was trying to retain the feel and look of the first artwork to retain continuity, even using the same colour palette. As I found with the previous art, this one also required multiple elements, making it a very crowded image... which is where the colours play such an important part in creating uniformity and retaining control.

RIGHT: *Sunshine Manor* (2021), Fossil Games; retro video game cover.

This video game is designed to appeal to those who recall the crude graphics from gaming in the 1980s and film tie-ins. To emphasise the nostalgia for that era, my work was specifically chosen as a link to the period when I painted video covers. The brief determined the imagery and the required elements, which would have only existed as basic pixelated animations. It was my job to give life to the simple graphics and suggest something more filmic. A companion commission is underway at the time of writing: *Camp Sunshine*, a homage to the *Friday the 13th* films.

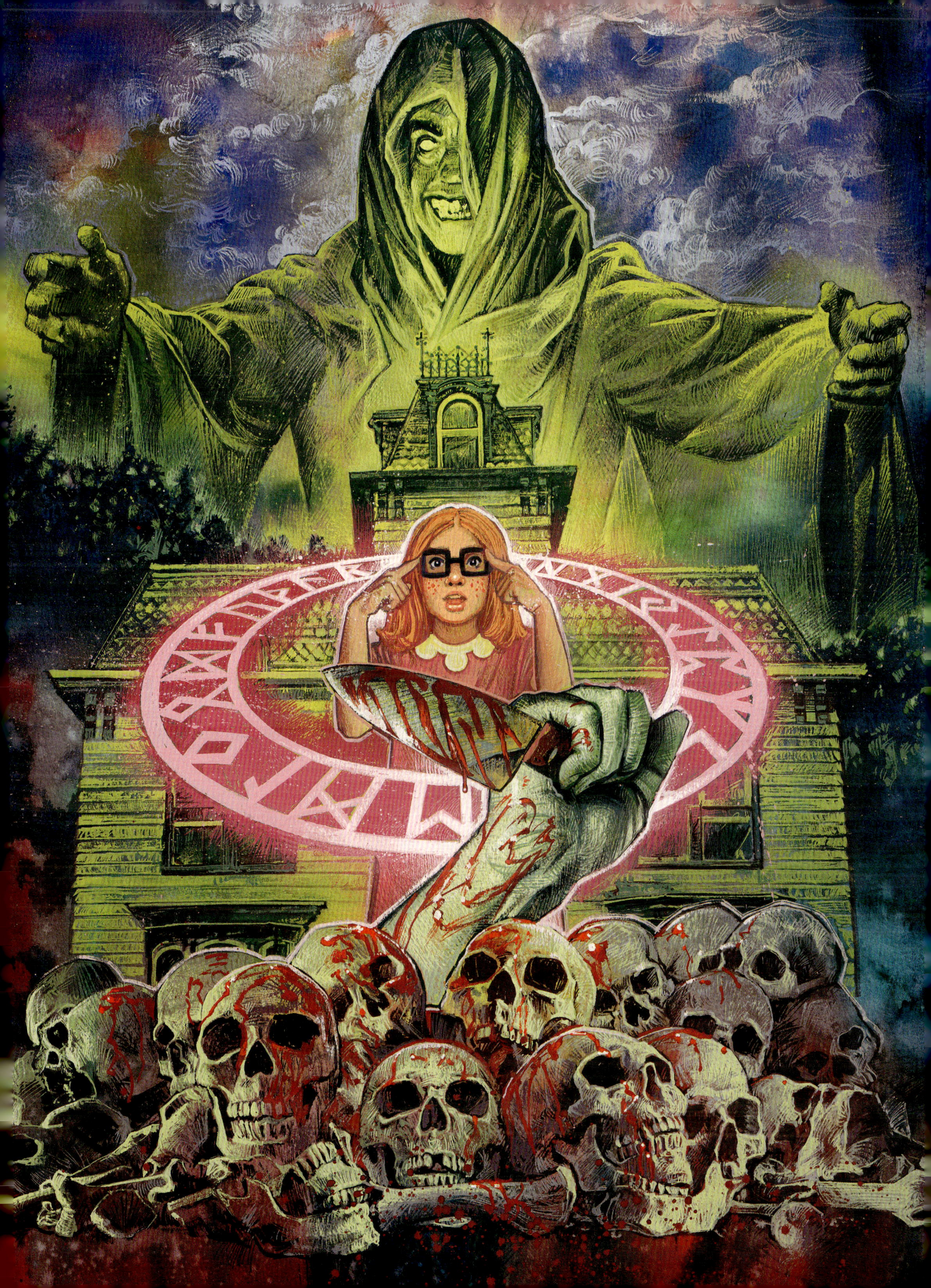

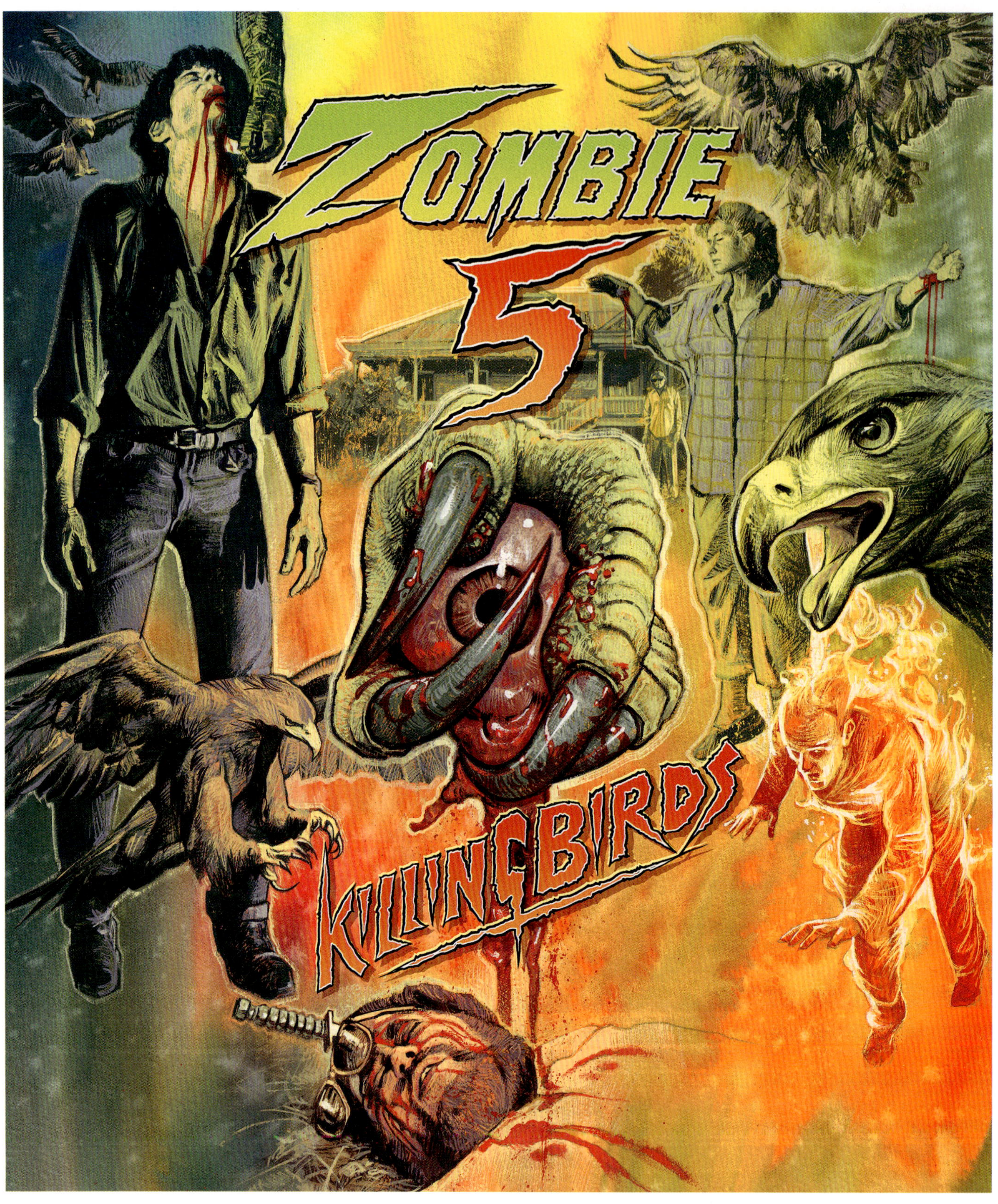

ABOVE: *Zombie 5: Killing Birds* (2021), 88 Films; Blu-ray cover.

With its scattershot plot that never quite seems to gel, it was difficult to find a focus for this film; the only notable actor was Robert Vaughn (best known for the 1960s *The Man from U.N.C.L.E.* TV series. In this film, he plays a blind man with little in narrative drive to justify a larger portrait.

In fact, Vaughn is the furthest and smallest figure within the layout. I took an early moment from the film and made it my central motif (the eyeball), scattering the other elements in a similar fashion to the plot! A bold colour theme holds the painting together.

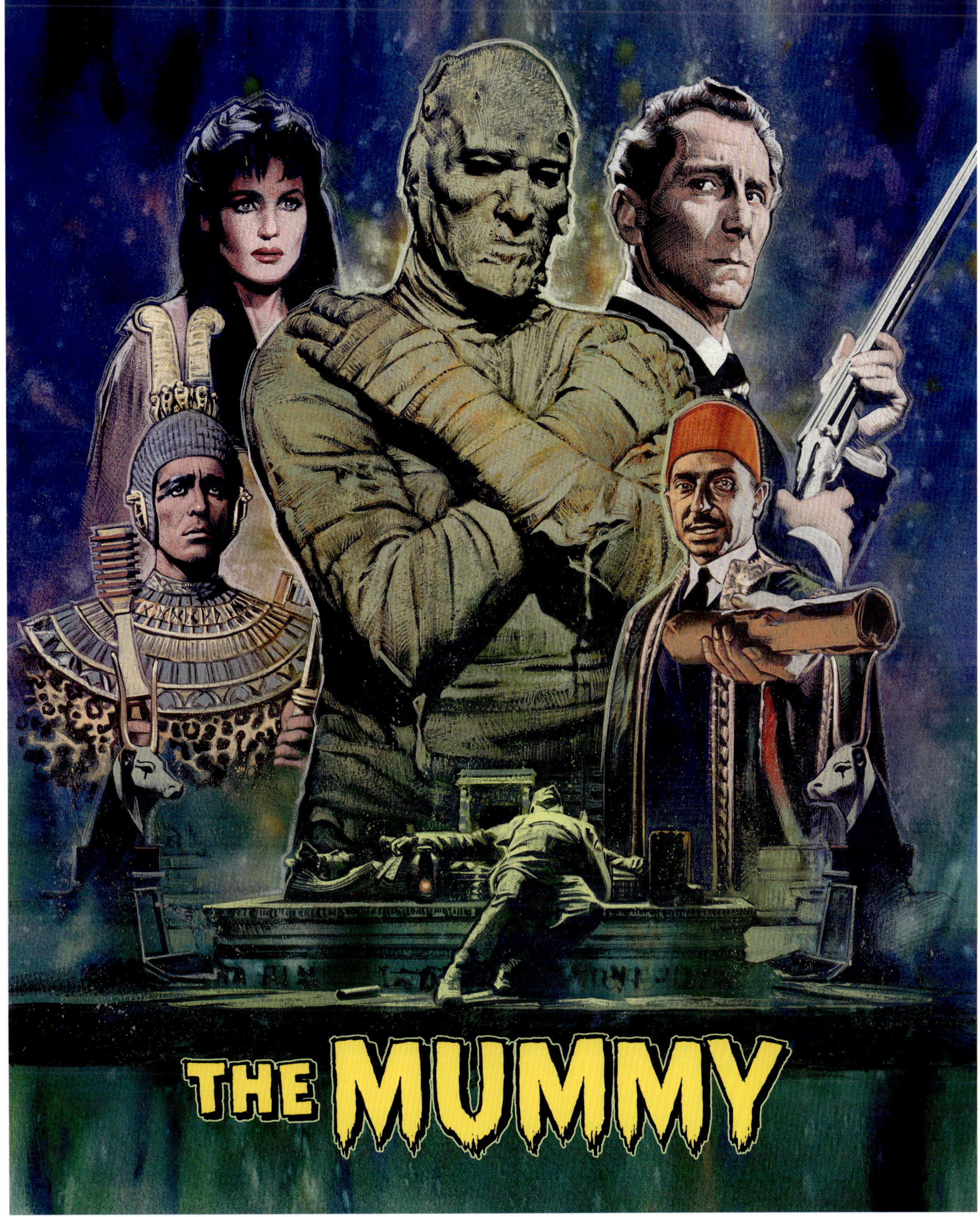

ABOVE: *The Mummy* (2020), Second Sight; Blu-ray cover.

Painted in the same period as my *Frankenstein and the Monster from Hell* art, I hoped to retain a similar feel in colour and layout. Ultimately, they remain individual rather than companion pieces. Whereas the *Frankenstein and the Monster from Hell* film proved to be the final period Gothic horror from Hammer, *The Mummy* was one of the very first films in what became Hammer Films' golden age for many horror fans. Christopher Lee's Mummy is a bandaged corpse but is seen in a pre-death sequence, so I was able to keep his familiar aristocratic features alongside those of co-star Peter Cushing in Hammer's most enduring actor pairing.

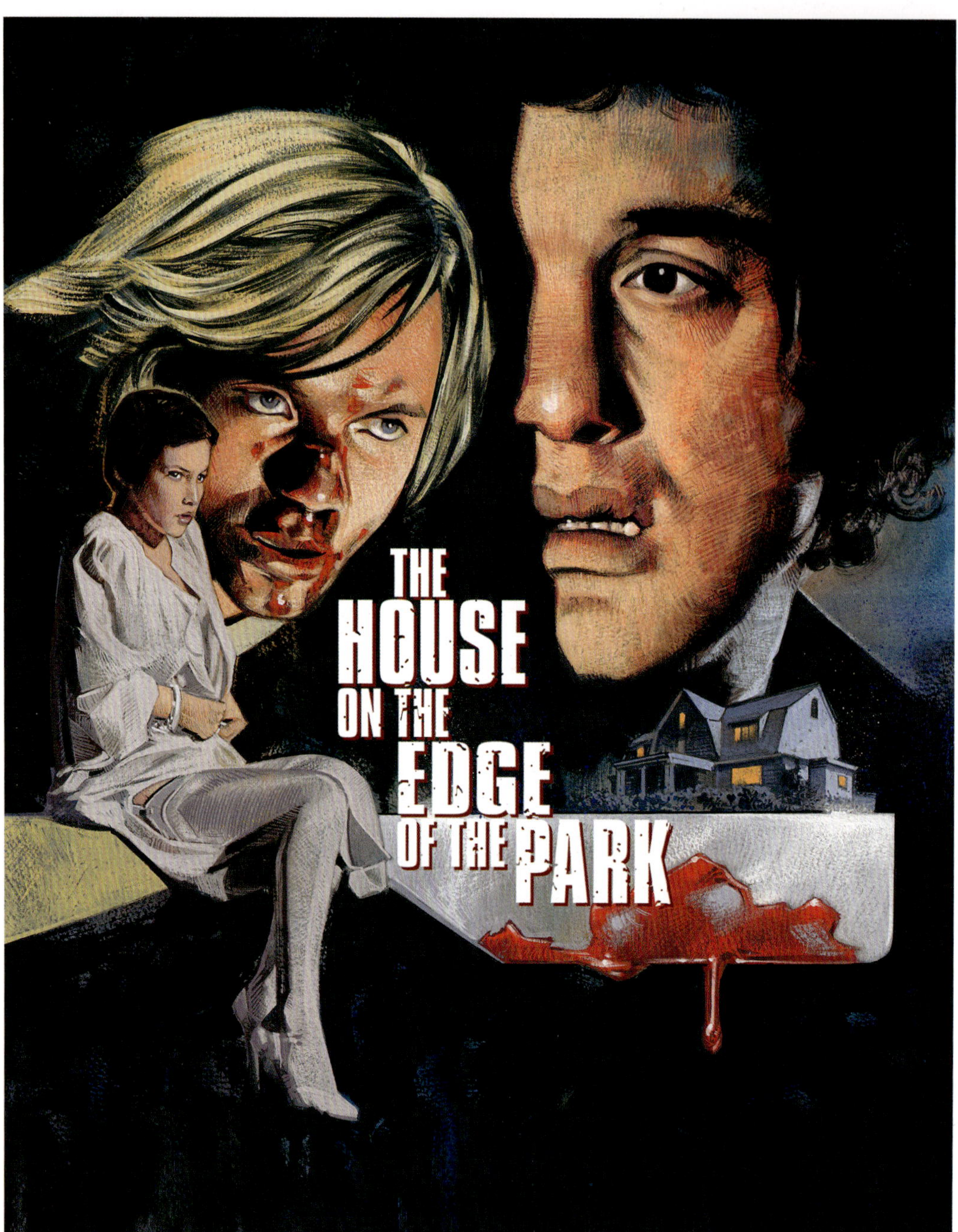

LEFT: *The House by the Edge of the Park* (2022), 88 Films; Blu-ray cover.

This is a film that carries some notoriety, and not without reason. I hadn't previously seen it, but I knew some of the content; the finale goes some way to addressing the viewers' discomfort. The challenge was to avoid exploiting the contentious, distressing content but to present the key characters in a way that created a hierarchy, eclipsing the brutish elements without giving any spoilers.

RIGHT: *Worzel Gummidge* (2022), Fabulous Films; Blu-ray cover.

Not as far a cry from horror as one might think. Gummidge is a living Wicker Man! As a youth, I found his visage deeply disturbing. Somehow, the "living dead doll" appearance of "Aunt Sally" doesn't help. This is true folk horror!

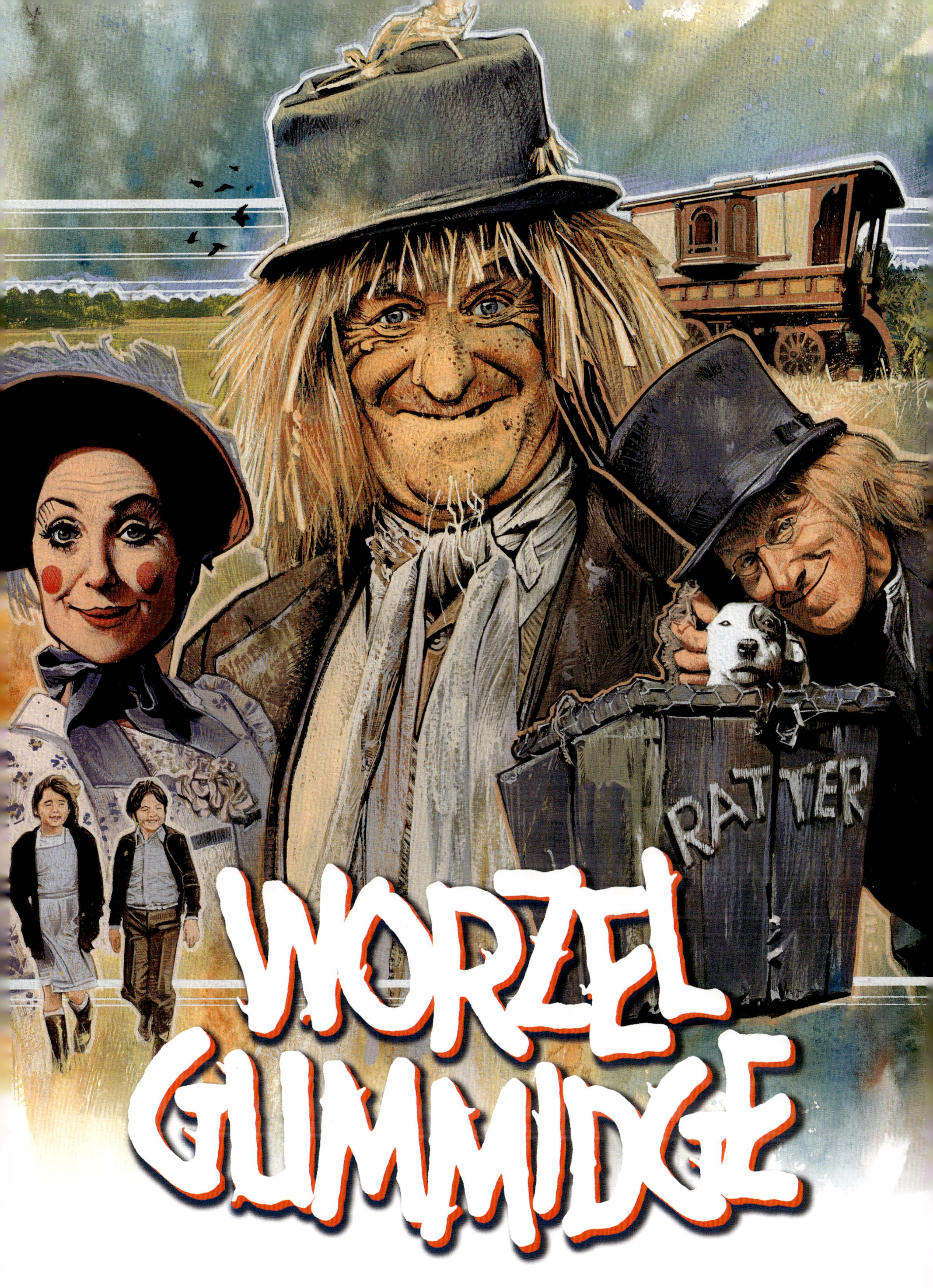

RATTER
WORZEL
GUMMIDGE

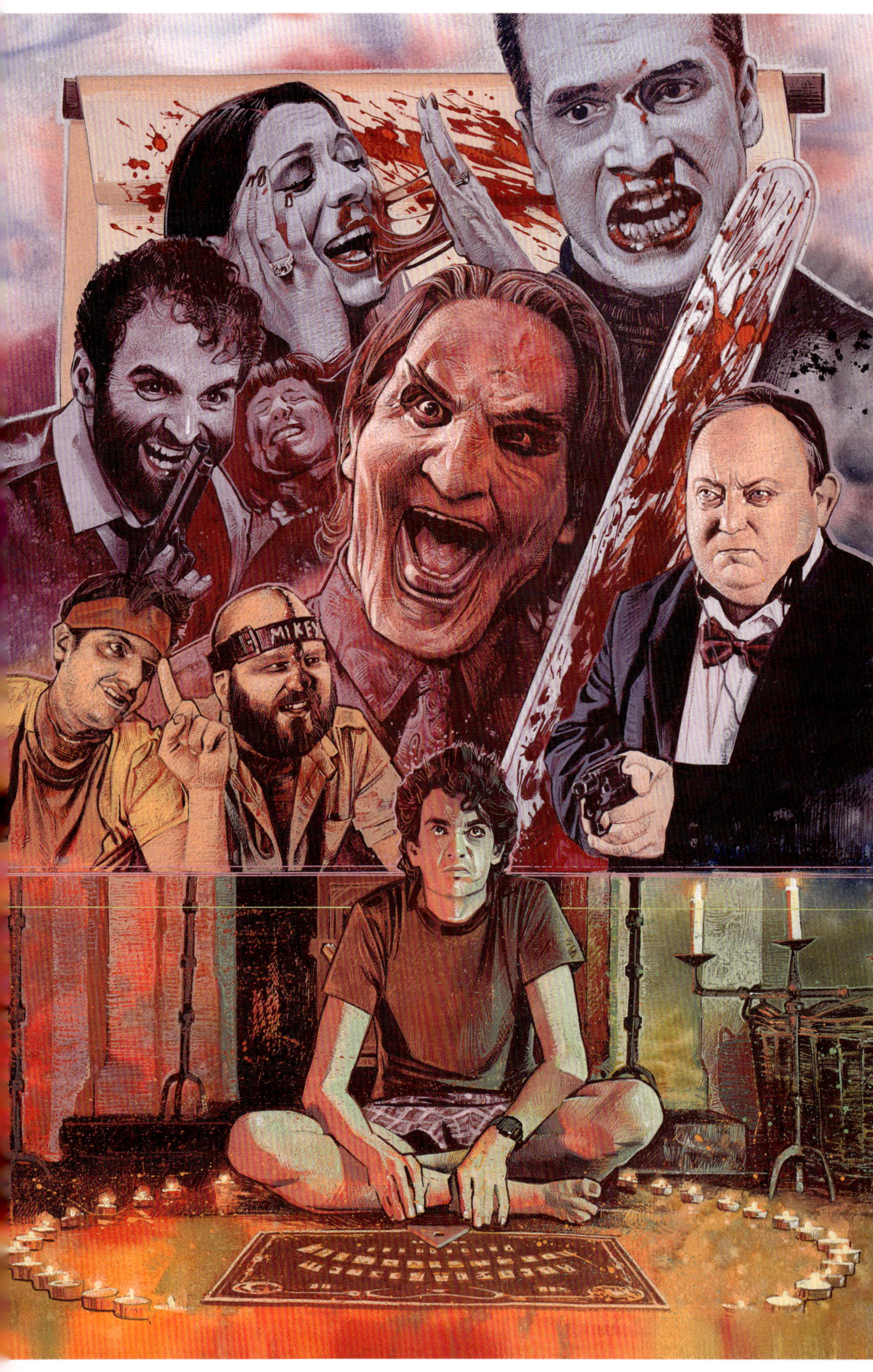

LEFT: *My Bloody Banjo* (2021); limited edition Blu-ray cover.

Liam Regan, the director of this film first released in 2015, asked me to create fresh artwork ahead of a campaign to fund his next film. The cast of main characters had to be included. I used the opportunity to elevate actor Laurence R. Harvey to 007 status (which was not, it should be said, his role in the film).

POSTERS

The poster is a form of communication that has endured through a long and varied history. Its evolution began with the invention of the printing press in the 15th century — it was a perfect format for announcing entertainment, from theatre and film to music and events. My interest in posters peaked when I began to grasp the film poster's beauty (and occasional beast) — loud declarations of wonderment and horror, the more lurid, the better, certainly for my tastes. From fly posters to massive billboards, my work has been viewed across public spaces since my earliest notable quad, *The Evil Dead*.

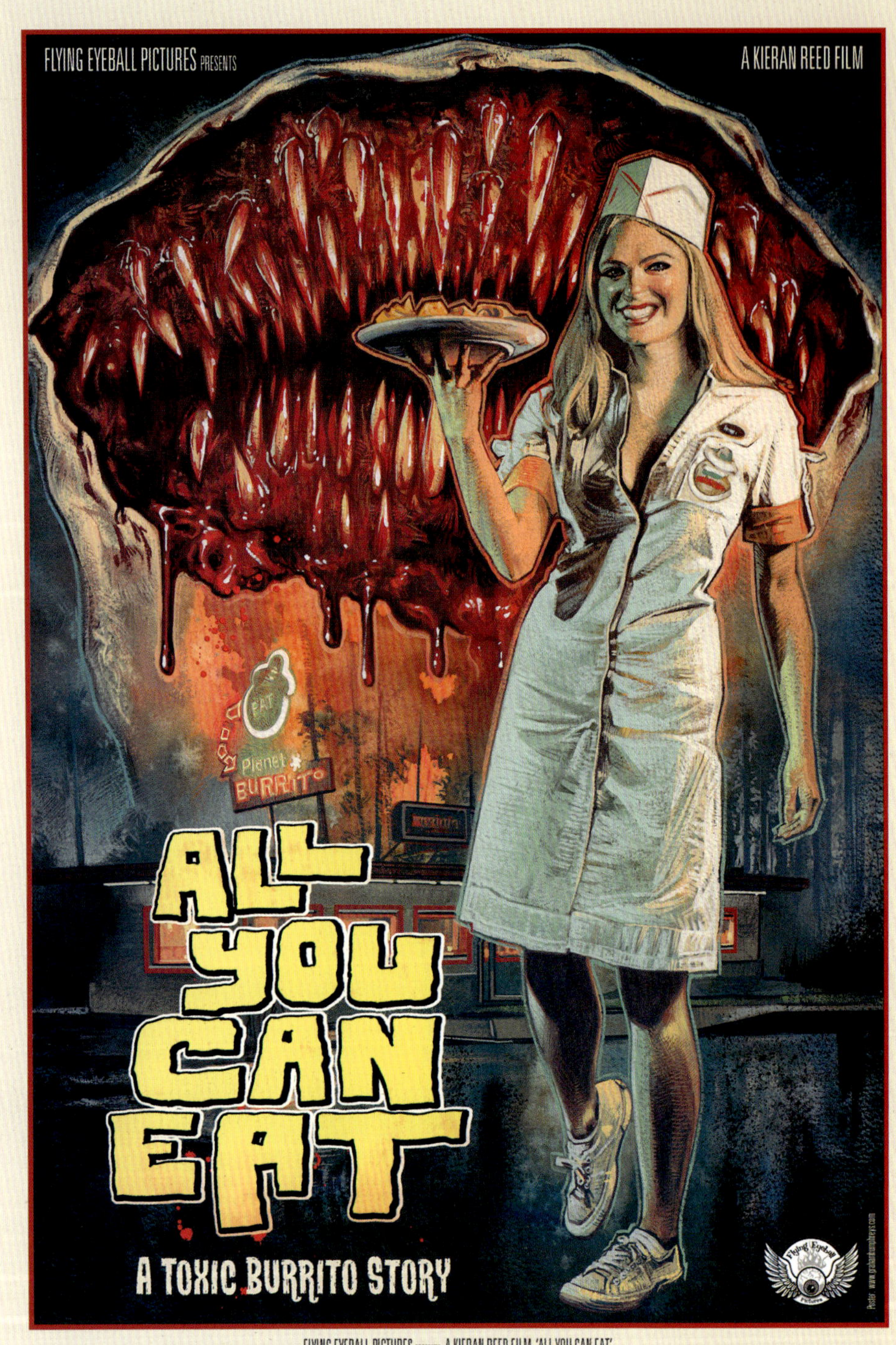

LEFT: *All You Can Eat* (2022), Flying Eyeball Pictures; film poster.

Commissioned as a tool for promoting this short film at festivals, my client requested an image that would emulate a B-movie monster poster. As the female lead was crucial to the image, I asked for a photo that would provide the best possible reference. Whilst we'd originally conceived a running shot, the photography proved too problematic for a naturalistic movement; however, the static shot worked well for a playful, kitsch approach.

RIGHT: *Creepshow* (2020), Monster Agency Productions Inc; episode promotion.

Commissioned to promote a Halloween-themed edition of the series, streamed on the subscription channel Shudder, my brief required the show's eponymous Creep to hold a carved pumpkin. The cemetery setting seemed a natural choice, and references came from my own photographs of various tombstones. I thought it would be amusing to have the lantern held high, with the robed Creep holding a copy of the Creepshow comic in the manner of the Statue of Liberty. I took timer photographs of myself in the pose for extra reference.

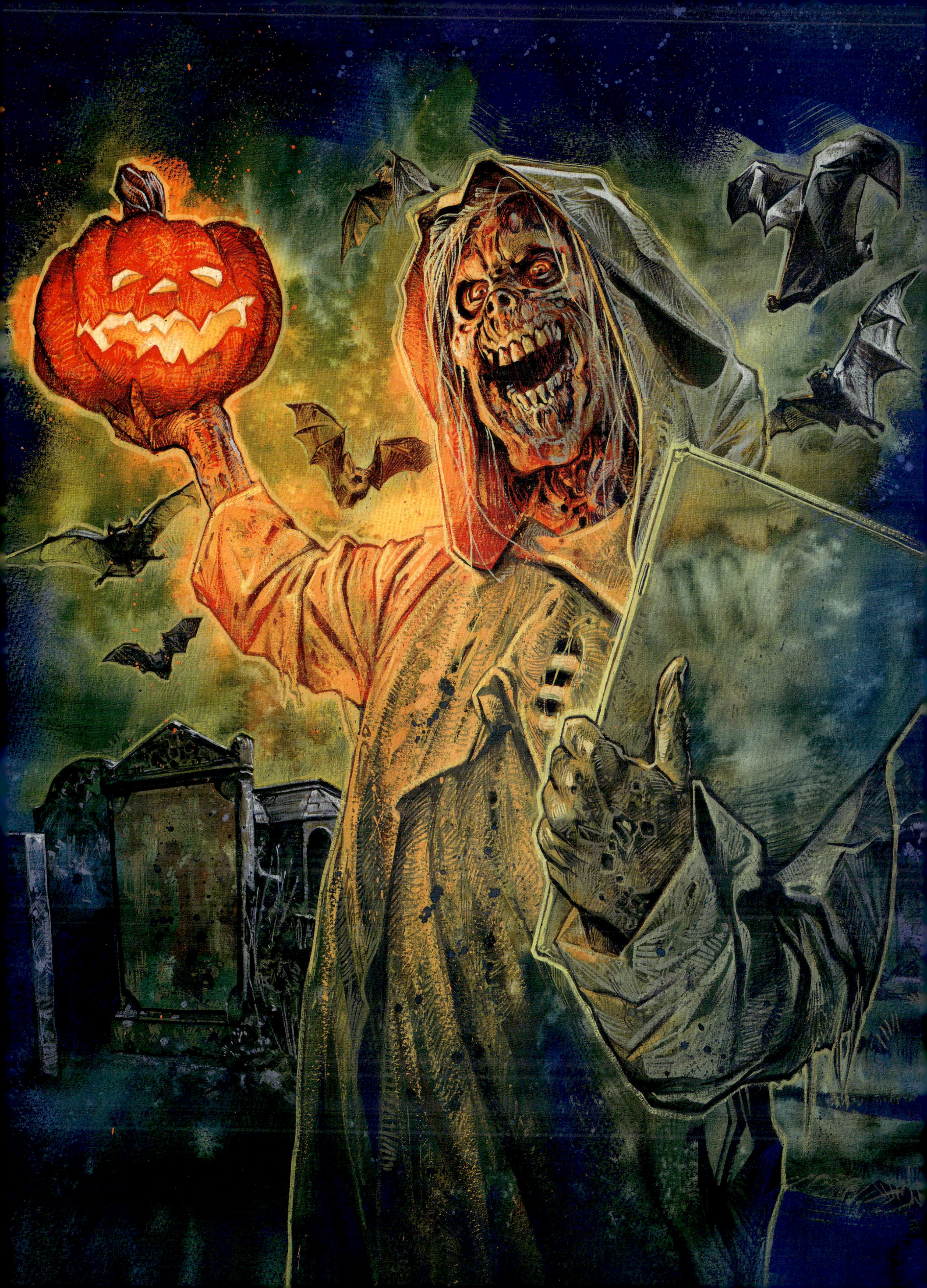

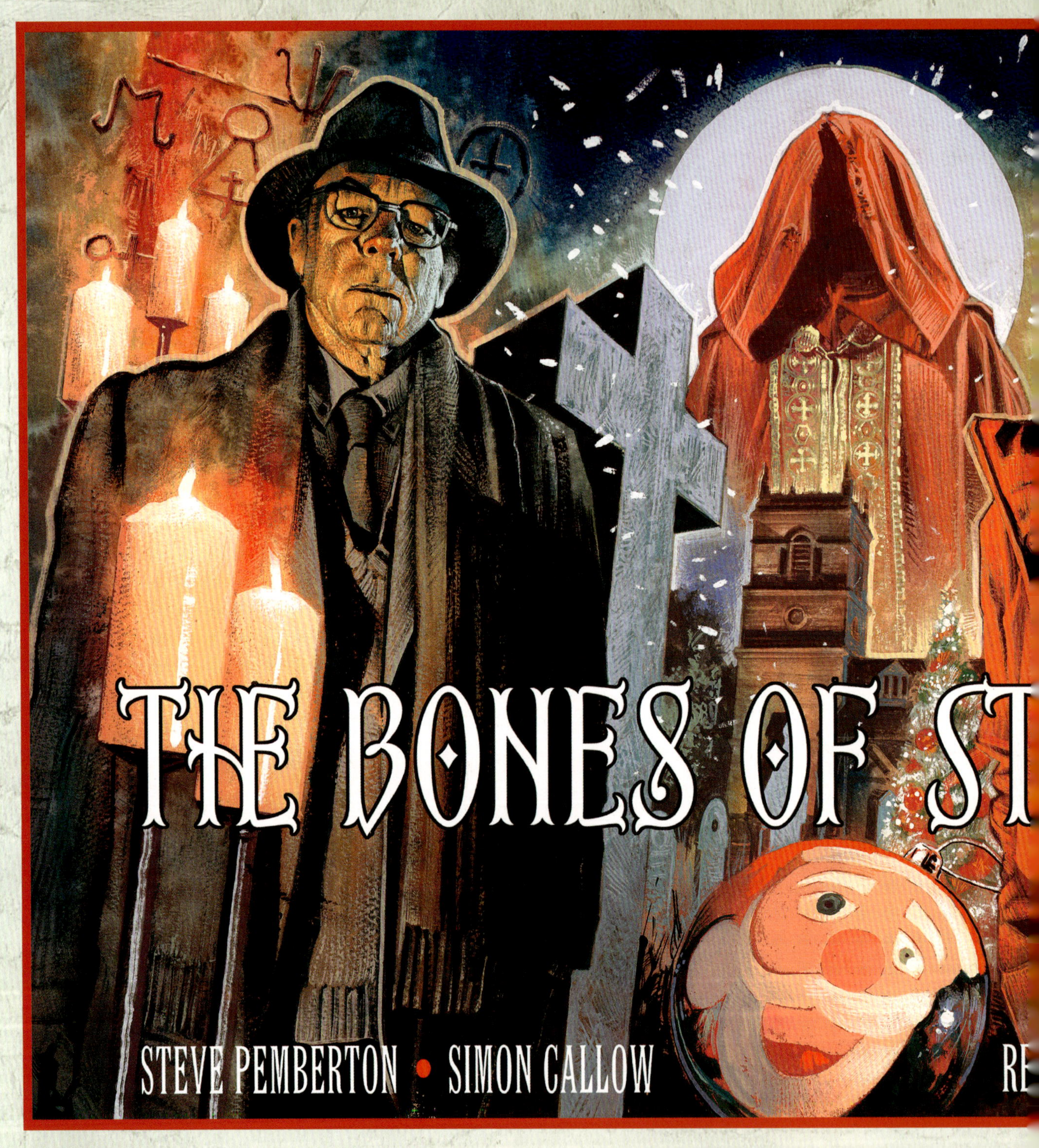
THE BONES OF ST
STEVE PEMBERTON · SIMON CALLOW · RE
BBC TWO
BBC TWO PRESENTS A BBC STUDIOS PRODUCTION AN INSIDE NO. 9 FILM "THE BONES OF ST. NICHOLAS" STEVE PEMBERTON
PRODUCTION DESIGNER PAUL ROWAN DIRECTOR OF PHOTOGRAPHY LEN GOWING COSTUME DESIGNER YVES BARRE EDITED BY PATRICK HALL MUSIC BY CHRISTIAN HEN
LINE PRODUCER URSULA HAWORTH UNA SAPLAMIDES EXECUTIVE PRODUCER ADAM TANDY JOSH COLE WRITTEN BY STEVE PEMBERTON & REEC

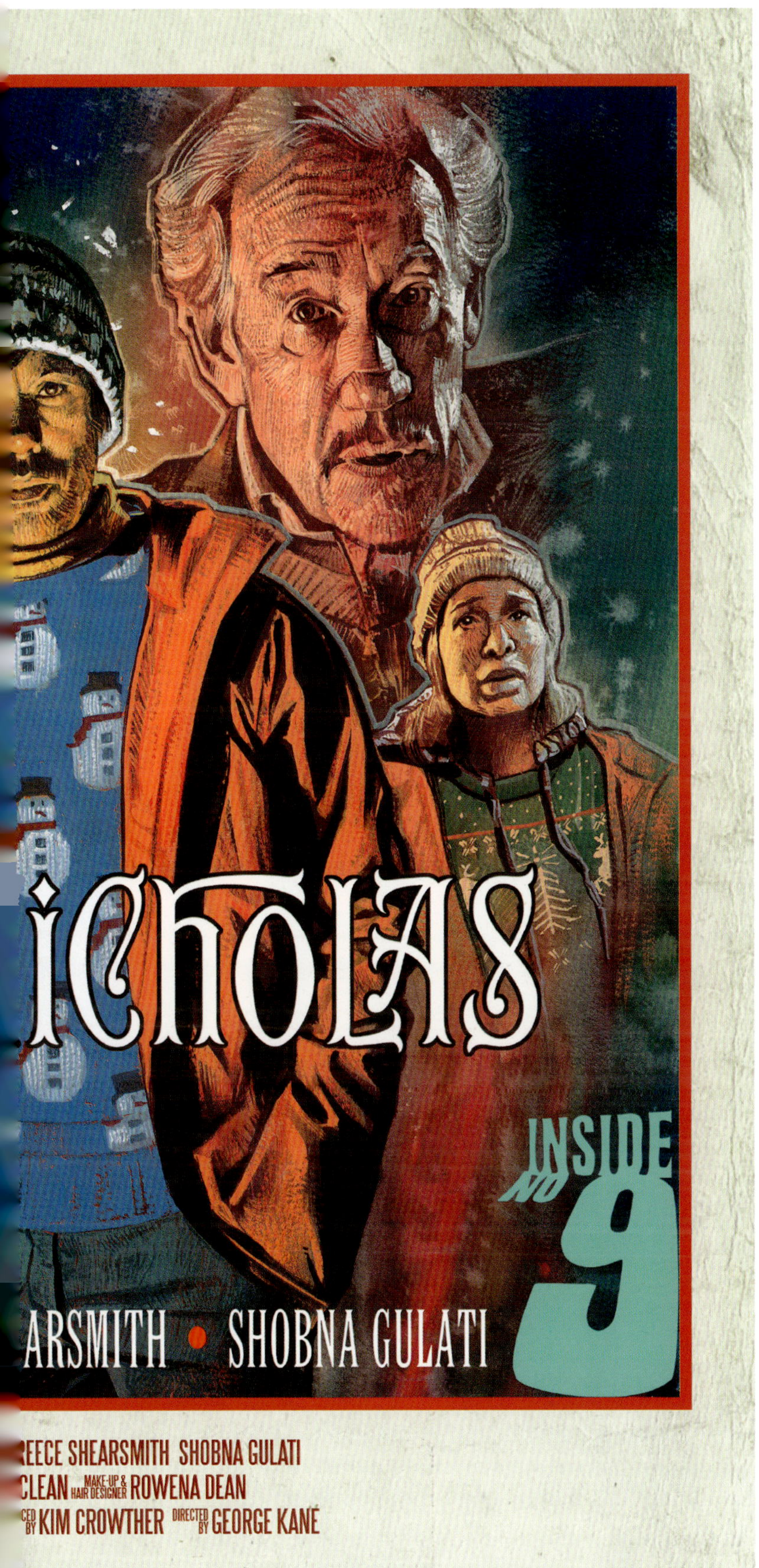

For this Christmas edition of the *Inside No. 9* TV series, I was supplied with a number of production stills and high-quality references for my work. But as often happens, subtle differences in expressions can impact the final art. Sometimes the best head isn't on the best body pose. Here, both lead heads are on different bodies from within the selection. With access to a secure link to the episode, I was able to find the extra imagery I needed to build the composition. It seemed appropriate to keep traditional Christmas colours, almost like a Christmas card. But the colouring and placement of the character on the left (actor Steve Pemberton) are suggestive of *Raiders of the Lost Ark*; indeed, a reference is made to the film within the episode's dialogue.

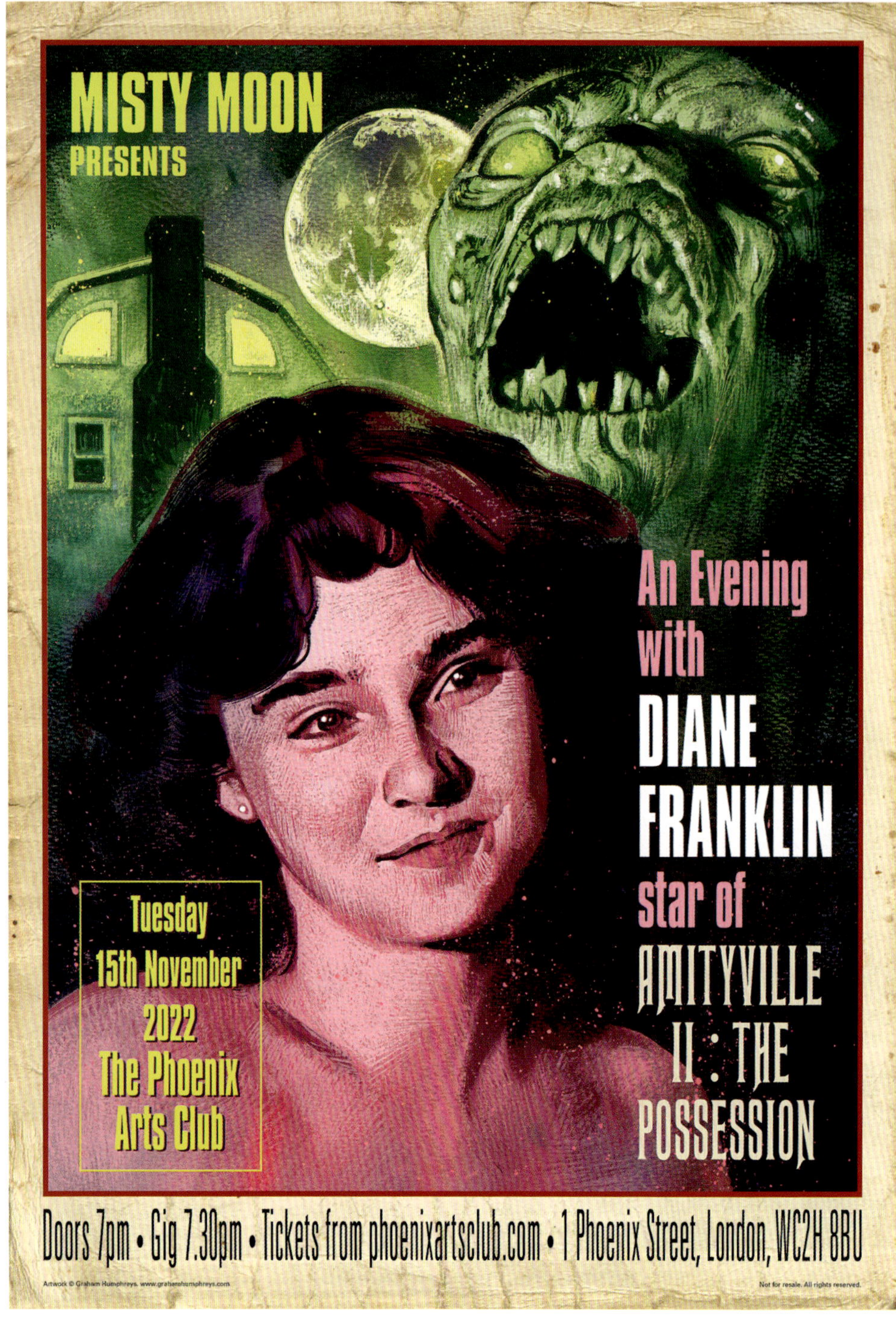

LEFT: Diane Franklin (2022), Misty Moon; event poster.

A poster for an evening in the company of American actress Diane Franklin, here represented in a role that will be familiar to horror fans. Because her performance in *Amityville II: The Possession* would be the main focus, the notorious house and finale creature are painted in contrasting colours to the portrait. As with all Misty Moon events, there's a full moon that must appear! The Misty Moon posters are usually designed and painted within a day because no fee is attached. The technique thus appears more textural and less polished. This is in the spirit of the late British poster artist Tom Chantrell, however, whose work for Hammer Films would often be delivered under similar budgetary constraints

RIGHT: *Darkadelic* (2023), Ear-Music; limited edition promotional poster.

As part of the promotion for The Damned's 2023 LP *Darkadelic*, I was asked if I could produce a fake film poster that encompassed elements from the promotional music videos for the band's new songs "The Invisible Man" and "Beware the Clown". With themes that centred around vintage horror, 1960s London, politics, and the 1960s TV series *The Avengers*, I felt a good starting point would be the poster I'd found for the 1968 film *Danger Diabolik*. With no time or budget for an actual painting, the image is composed of elements rendered with a marker pen and black paint. Each was scanned, then composed and coloured in Photoshop. The "Darkadelic" logo is a replica of the original poster's title.

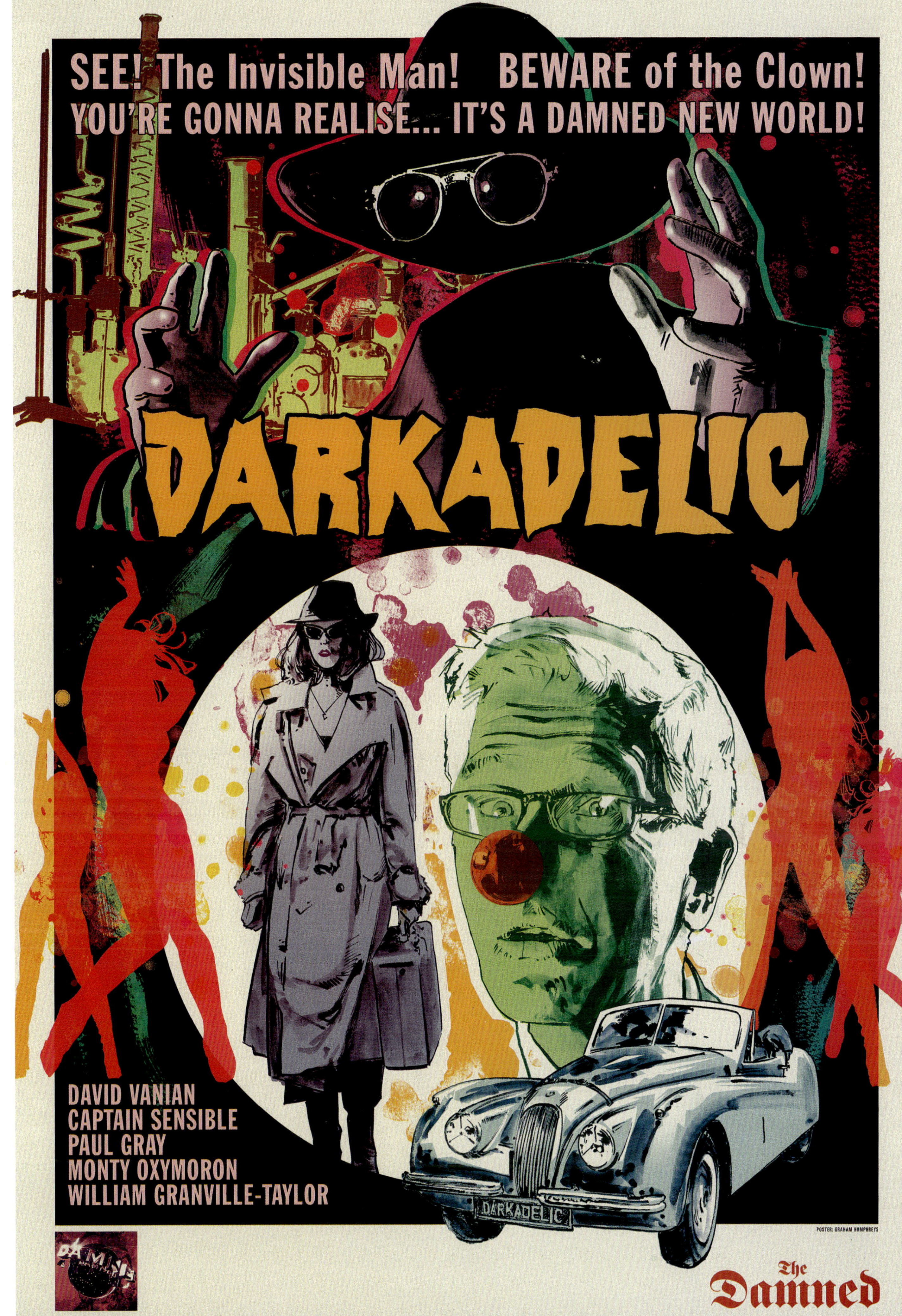

SEE! The Invisible Man!   BEWARE of the Clown!
YOU'RE GONNA REALISE... IT'S A DAMNED NEW WORLD!
DARKADELIC
DAVID VANIAN
CAPTAIN SENSIBLE
PAUL GRAY
MONTY OXYMORON
WILLIAM GRANVILLE-TAYLOR
DARKADELIC
POSTER: GRAHAM HUMPHREYS
The Damned

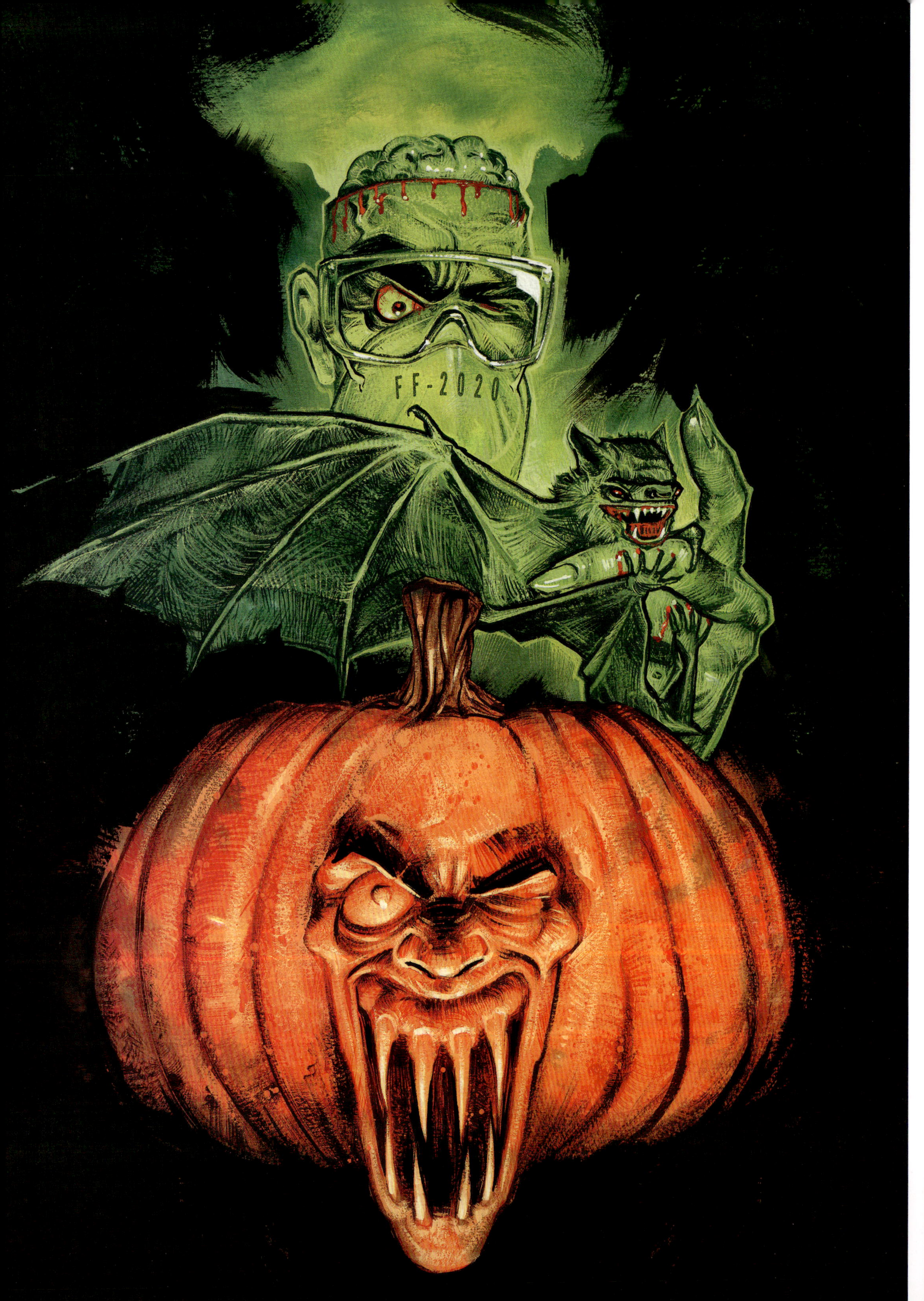
FF-2020

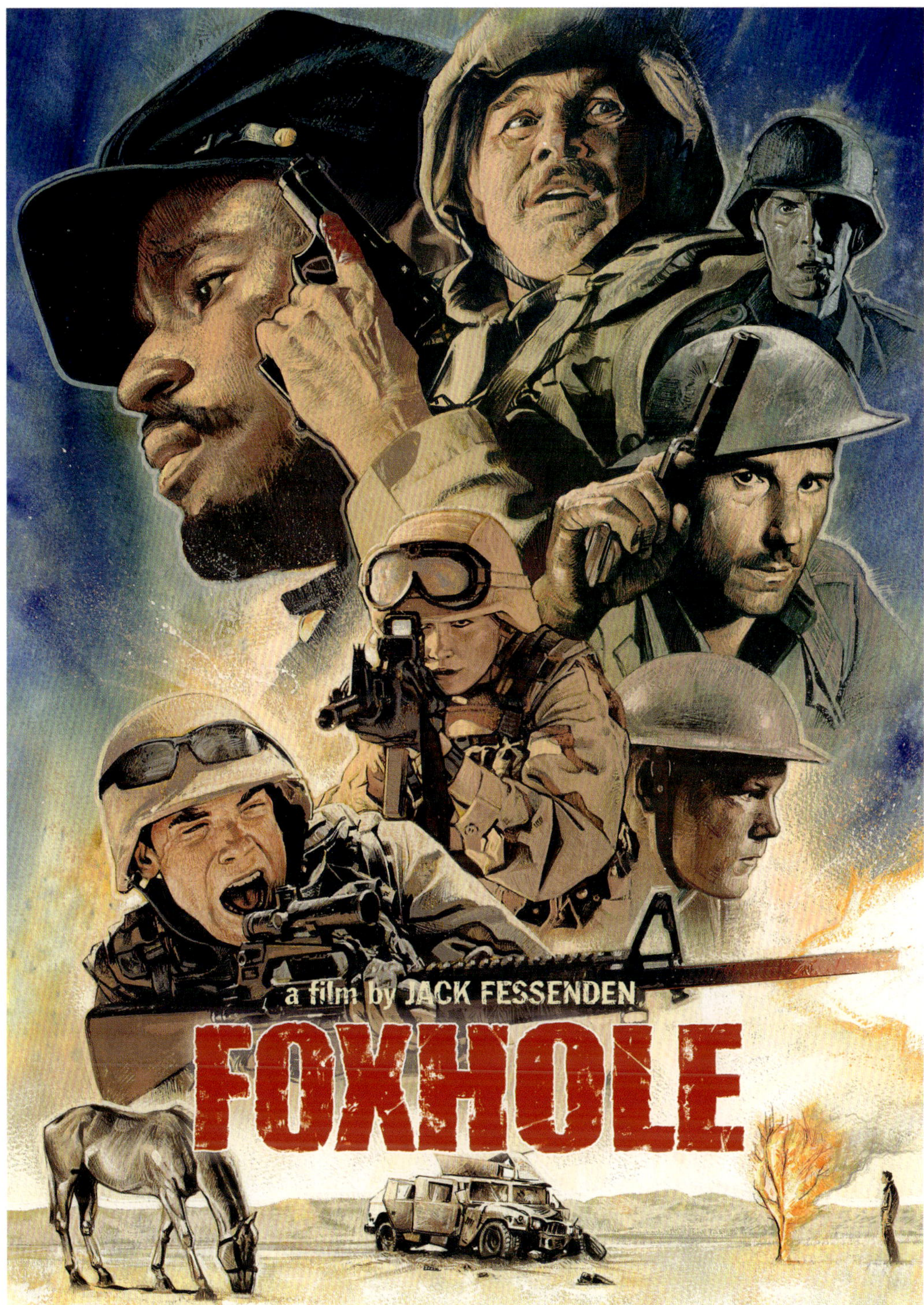

I'd worked with producer Larry Fessenden on a couple of previous projects. This film was the feature-length directorial debut of his son, Jack Fessenden. The film follows the same group of actors playing soldiers in three different war settings: The American Civil War, World War I, and the Iraq War. My poster needed to represent the cast and portray the three war periods. I'd been sent images of various classic war movie posters with the idea of emulating the general look. I had the difficult task of sifting through a large amount of supplied material and some of my own grabs from a screener link. I picked a range of expressions that would show the various faces of war. Some surreal details at the base of the artwork were removed from the final version.

OPPOSITE: *FrightFest* (2020), London FrightFest; poster.

Unable to stage an in-person event due to the pandemic, the long-running London FrightFest film festival was relegated to an online streaming service. As f ace masks were a requirement in most settings in 2020, the resident monster is complying; perched on his surgical gloved hand is a bat (at the time, there was a theory that Covid-19 had originated in bats). As the poster image would then be repurposed for an online Halloween event, the otherwise covered monster face is revealed on the pumpkin — a direct reference to the film poster for *Halloween* (obvious but reverential!).

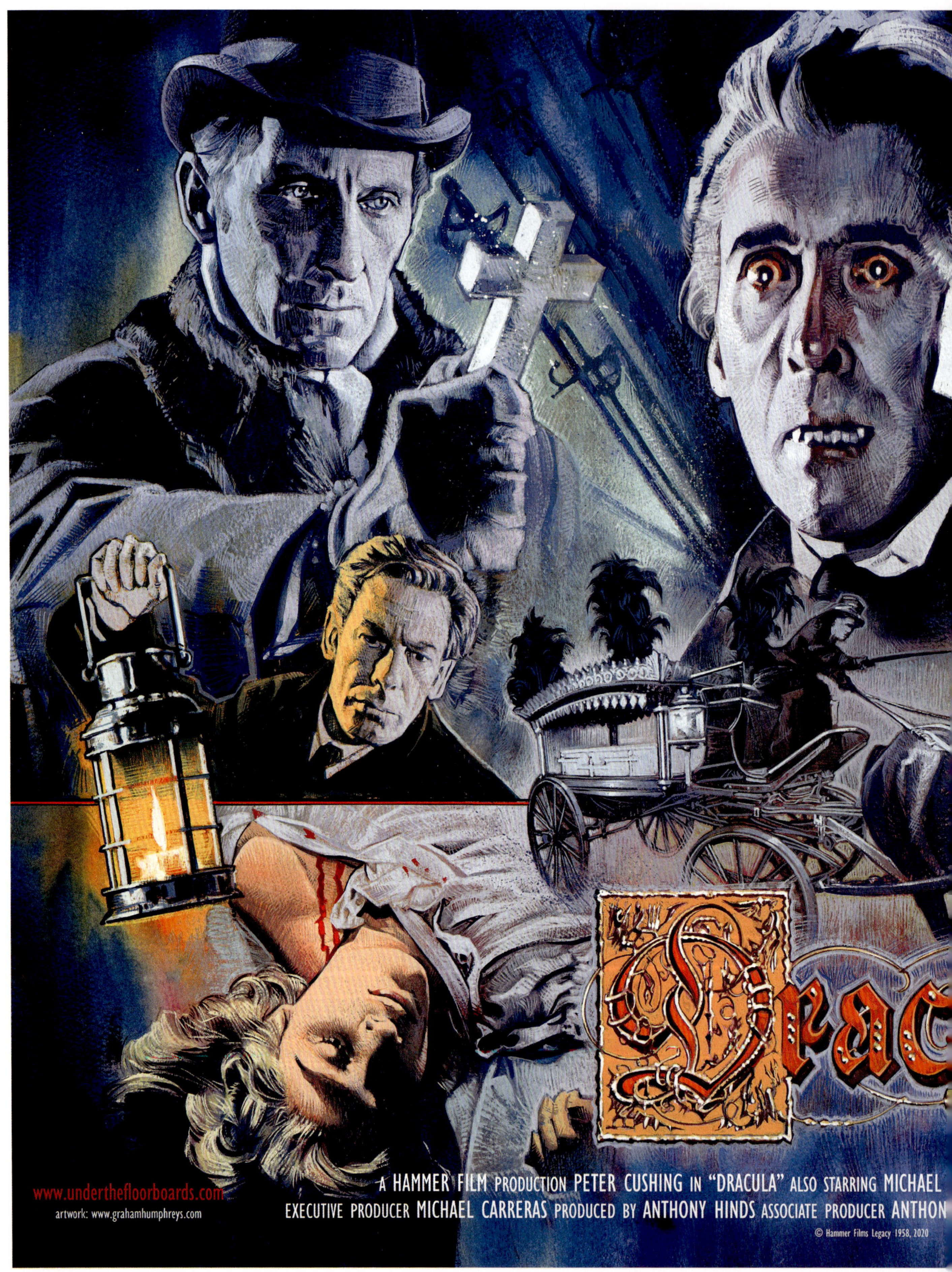

www.underthefloorboards.com
artwork: www.grahamhumphreys.com
A HAMMER FILM PRODUCTION PETER CUSHING IN "DRACULA" ALSO STARRING MICHAEL
EXECUTIVE PRODUCER MICHAEL CARRERAS PRODUCED BY ANTHONY HINDS ASSOCIATE PRODUCER ANTHON
© Hammer Films Legacy 1958, 2020

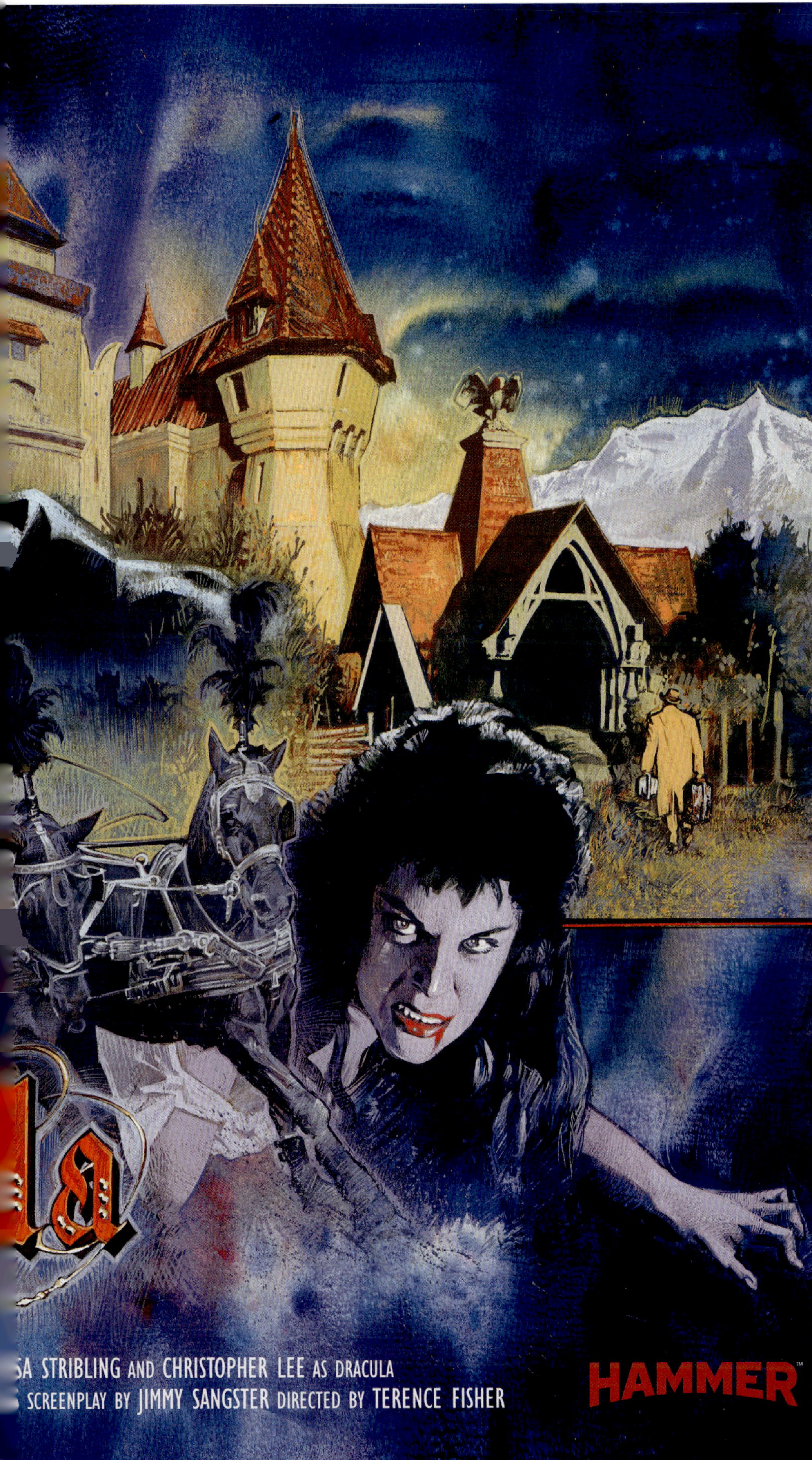

LEFT: *Dracula* (2020),
Under The Floorboards;
licensed poster art.

My love of Hammer horror is recognised by those who know me. This opportunity to create a new poster, a limited edition print, allowed me to explore the images in the 1958 *Dracula* film and try to capture elements of the production design and vibrant colours to which I'd responded the first time I saw the film. I particularly wanted to feature the carriage that conveys Dracula's coffin from the castle, even adding a hint of the tower at Oakley Court (the famed Hammer location next to Bray Studios, where *Dracula* was filmed) among the trees! Christopher Lee and Peter Cushing became internationally associated with many of Hammer's best-known films and are rightly the focus of the poster's composition.

I was thrilled when Graham pointed out that he's probably drawn me more than anybody else (with the possible exception of Vincent Price). For many "Monster Kids" like myself, Graham and his beautiful poster artwork are a direct link back to how we all became obsessed with horror and fantasy as a genre in the first place. Far too young to actually watch these treasures in the cinema, and before they started popping up late at night on BBC2, many of our first tastes of these films were via the artwork of their posters.

Often lurid and shocking, they would evoke such expectations regarding the films they advertised. Who could resist the looming skeleton holding a noose over the *House on Haunted Hill* or the *Halloween* poster — a monstrous pumpkin made of orange knife stabs; *Cannibal Holocaust* depicted a cannibal chewing on a rope of bloody intestines! These images brought so much to the experience of discovering these classics. They are as valuable and influential as the movies themselves.

That feeling remains today, and I always cherish it. Graham has created many of the truly great posters for *Inside No. 9*, and it's always such a special moment to see what he will come up with. The thrill of seeing a new, beautifully drawn genre poster elevates the craft and has you fall in love with it all over again. Graham is a true master, and long may he keep alive the art of the painted poster in an increasingly digital world.

REECE SHEARSMITH,
London, England

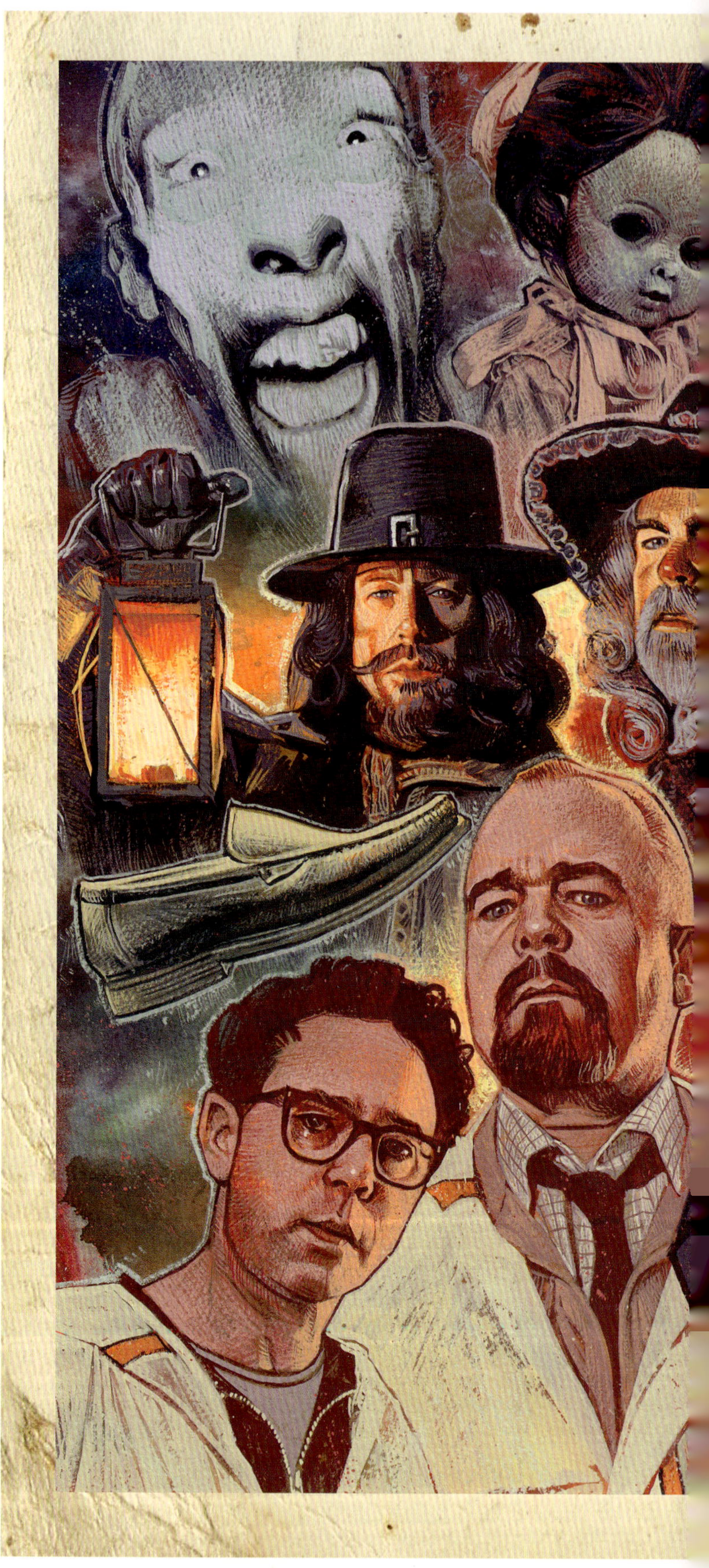

RIGHT: *Insider's Guide to Inside No. 9* (2021). Hodder & Stoughton; poster print.

Because of the number of posters I'd made for the TV series *Inside No. 9*, it was decided that I should create a composite of various key characters from the series. The resulting print would be signed by the two key actors, the author, and myself. The initial list of inclusions was far too extensive, so I requested a definitive shortlist from which to find my reference. The idea was to celebrate the breadth of the series. They kindly skewed the selection towards the horror-themed episodes!

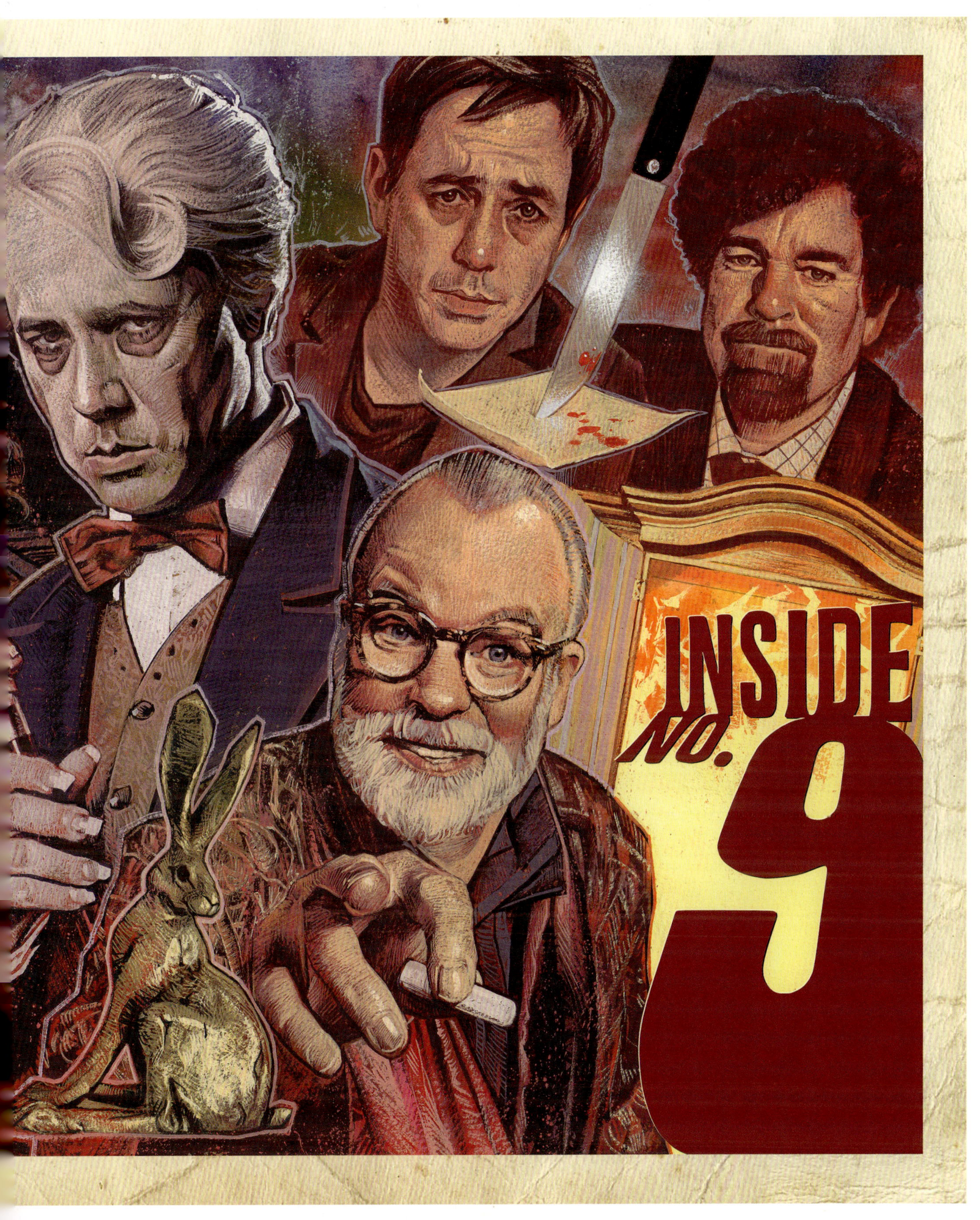
INSIDE
NO.
9

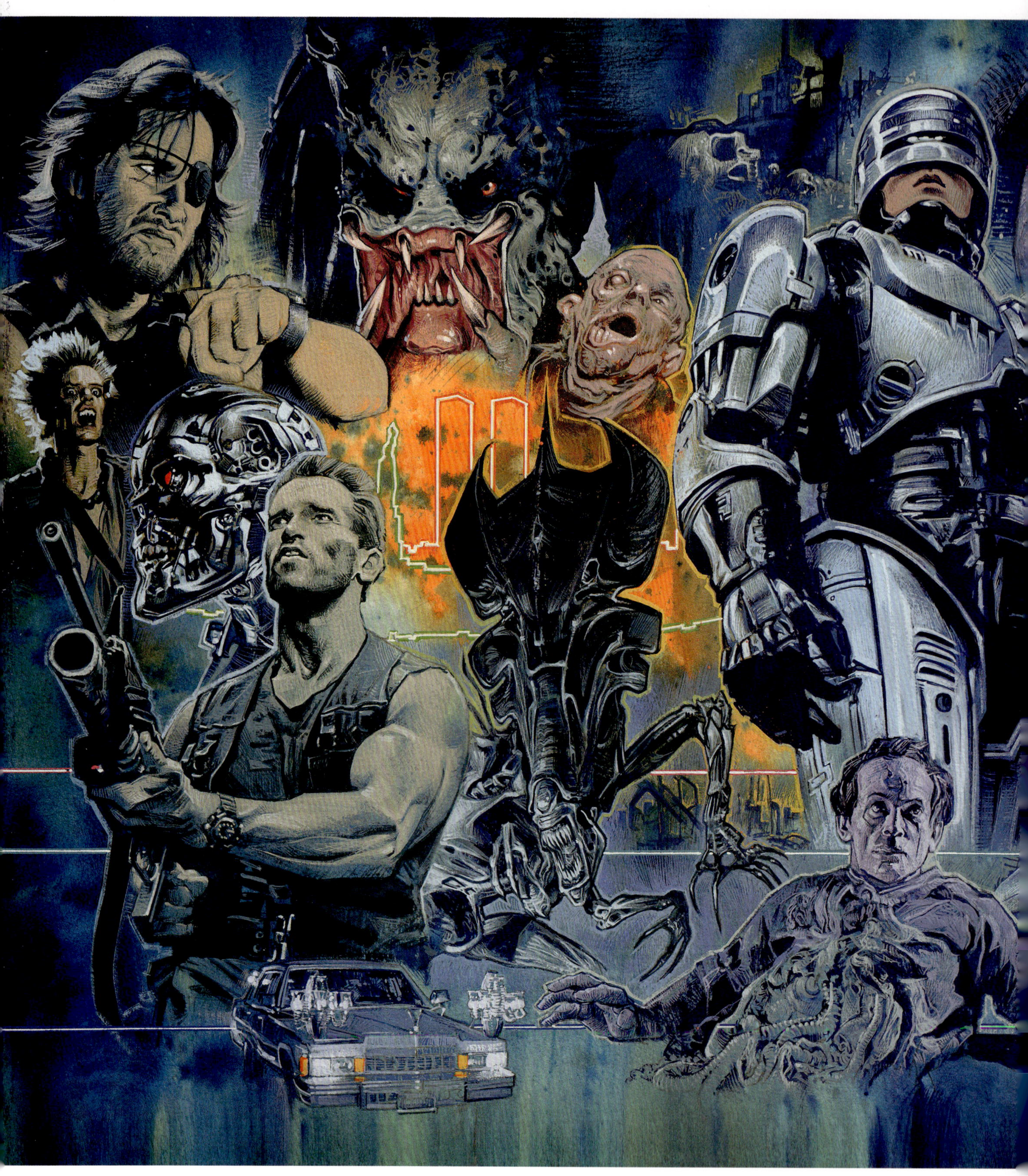

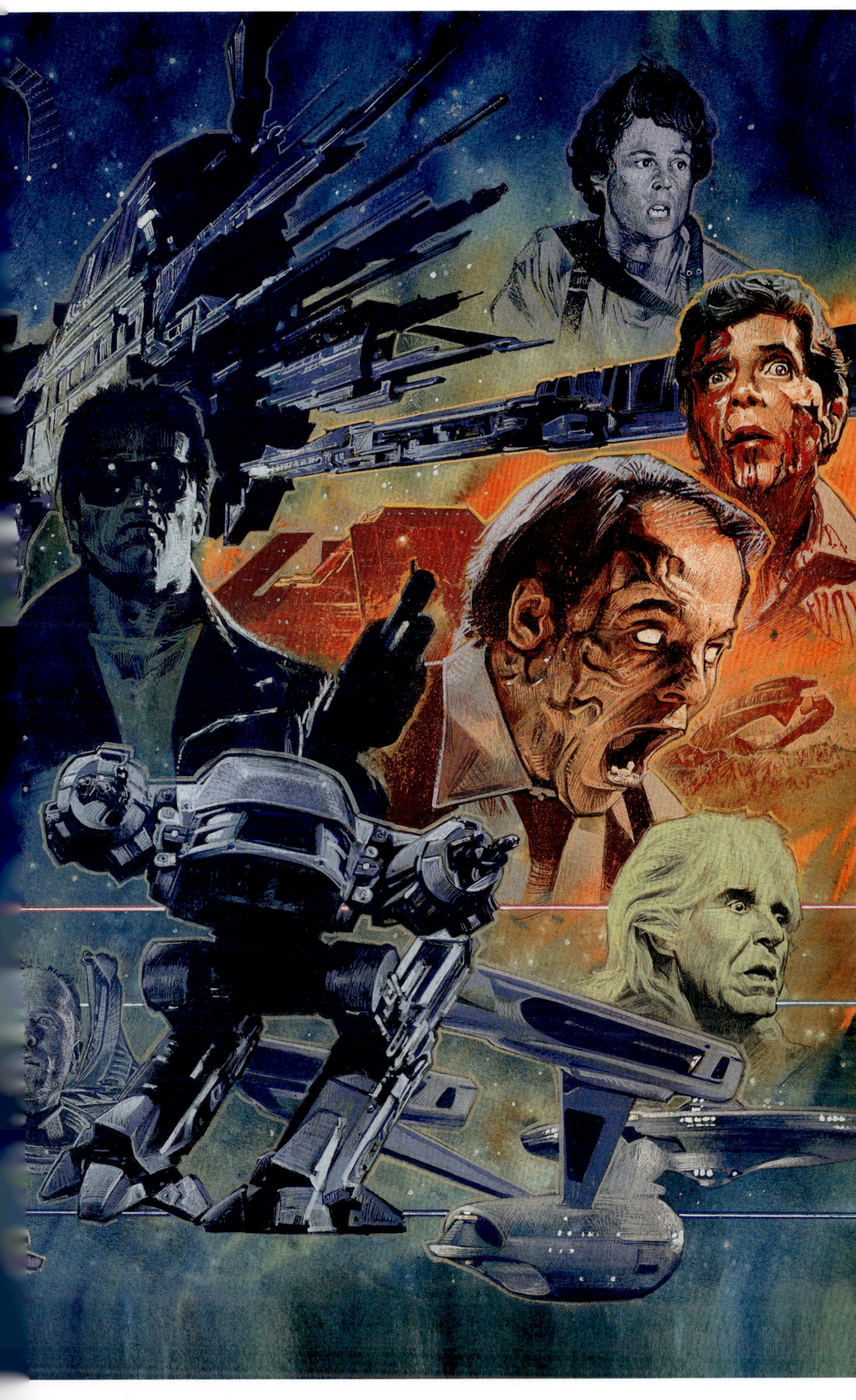

LEFT: *In Search of Tomorrow*
(2020), CreatorVC;
promotional poster.

On one of the most complex
commissions I've received, my
task involved portraying the
cream of 1980s science fiction
from a (very long!) shortlist.
My preference is a mix of online
searches and screen grabs.
I needed to spend a weekend
watching many of these films!
This is very much a reflection of
my favoured moments, naturally
concentrating on the horror
aspects! The colour palette was
particularly important in keeping
control of so many parts.

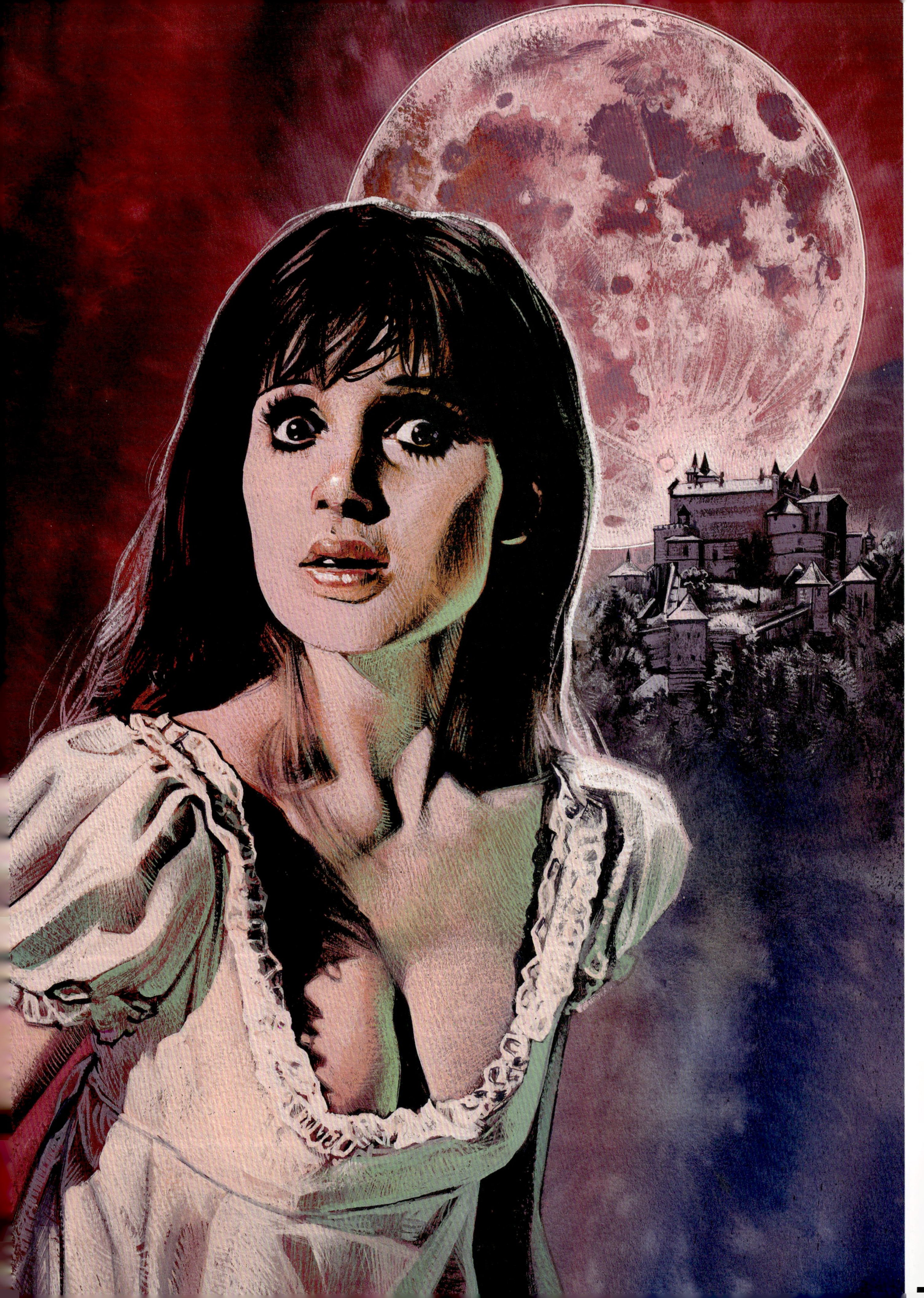

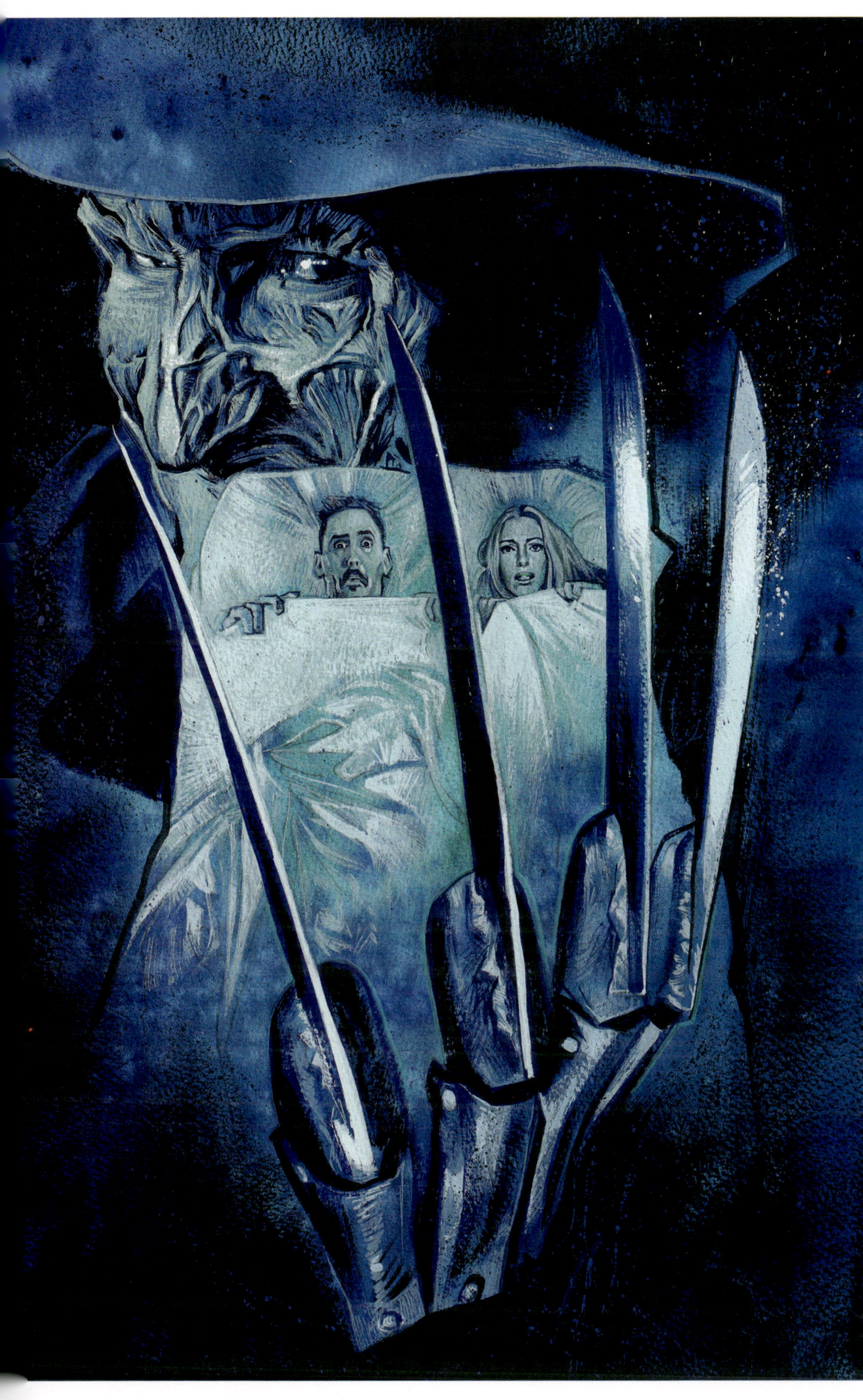

LEFT: *Up All Night* (2019),
Shaw Thing Productions;
project promotion.

I'd met Matt Shaw at an industry convention, where he was promoting his books and I was promoting my work. He'd already discussed his desire to move into film before this project arrived. Described as *A Nightmare on Elm Street* fan film, I was asked to paint Matt and his choice of female lead being menaced by Freddy. No other elements were required, which is just as well as the budget wouldn't have covered a day's work!

OPPOSITE: *Madeline Smith* (2022), Misty Moon; event poster.

One of a series of posters that were painted gratis for an event organiser. Madeline is someone I've had the pleasure of meeting on numerous occasions, and her astonishing career includes work with Hammer Films and the 007 franchise. Here, she's in character for her performance in *Lust for a Vampire* (1971). As a point of interest, the castle in the background is Hohenwerfen Castle in Austria — it appears in Hammer's *The Horror of Frankenstein* (1970), though only as a frozen still.

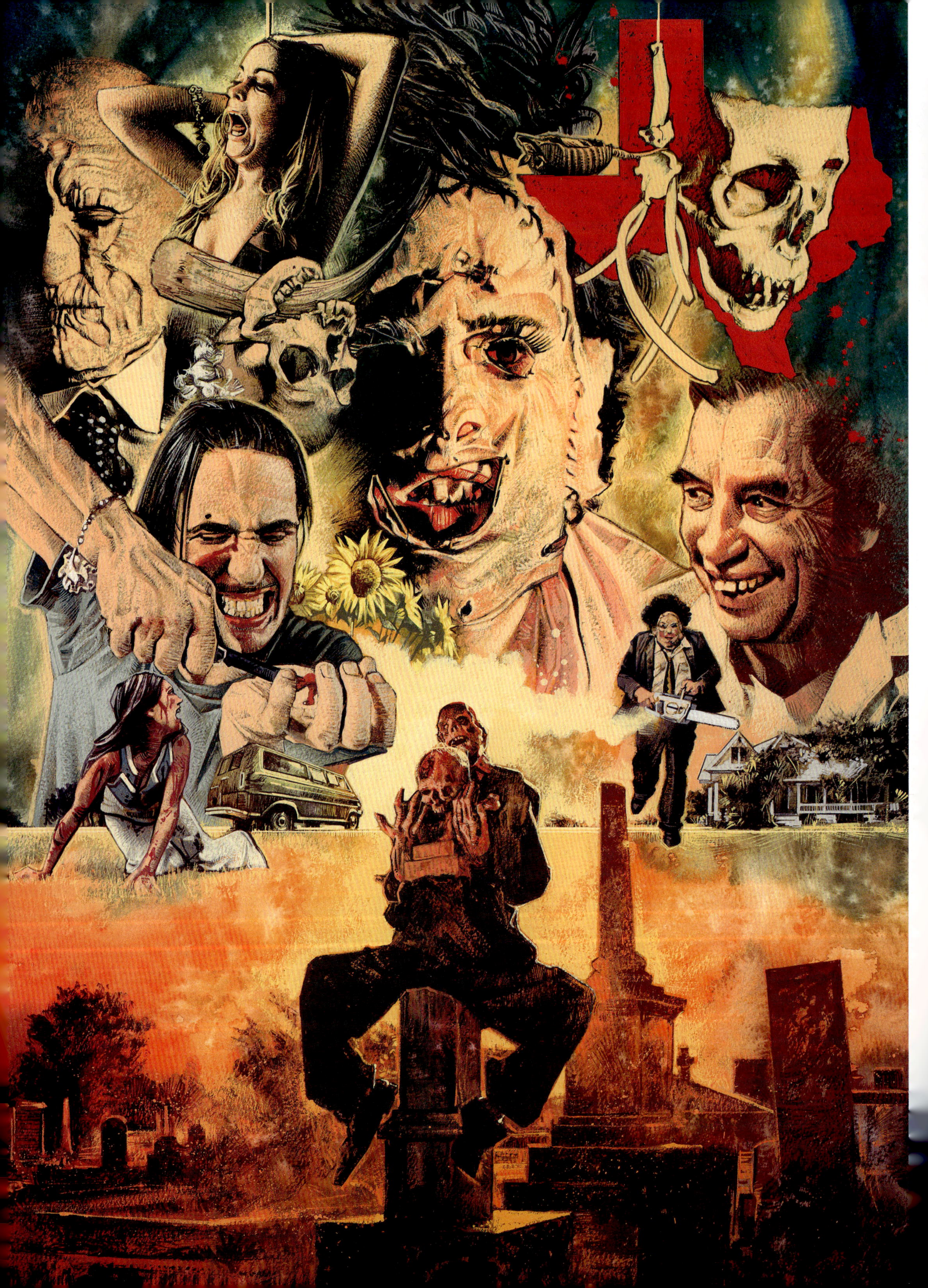

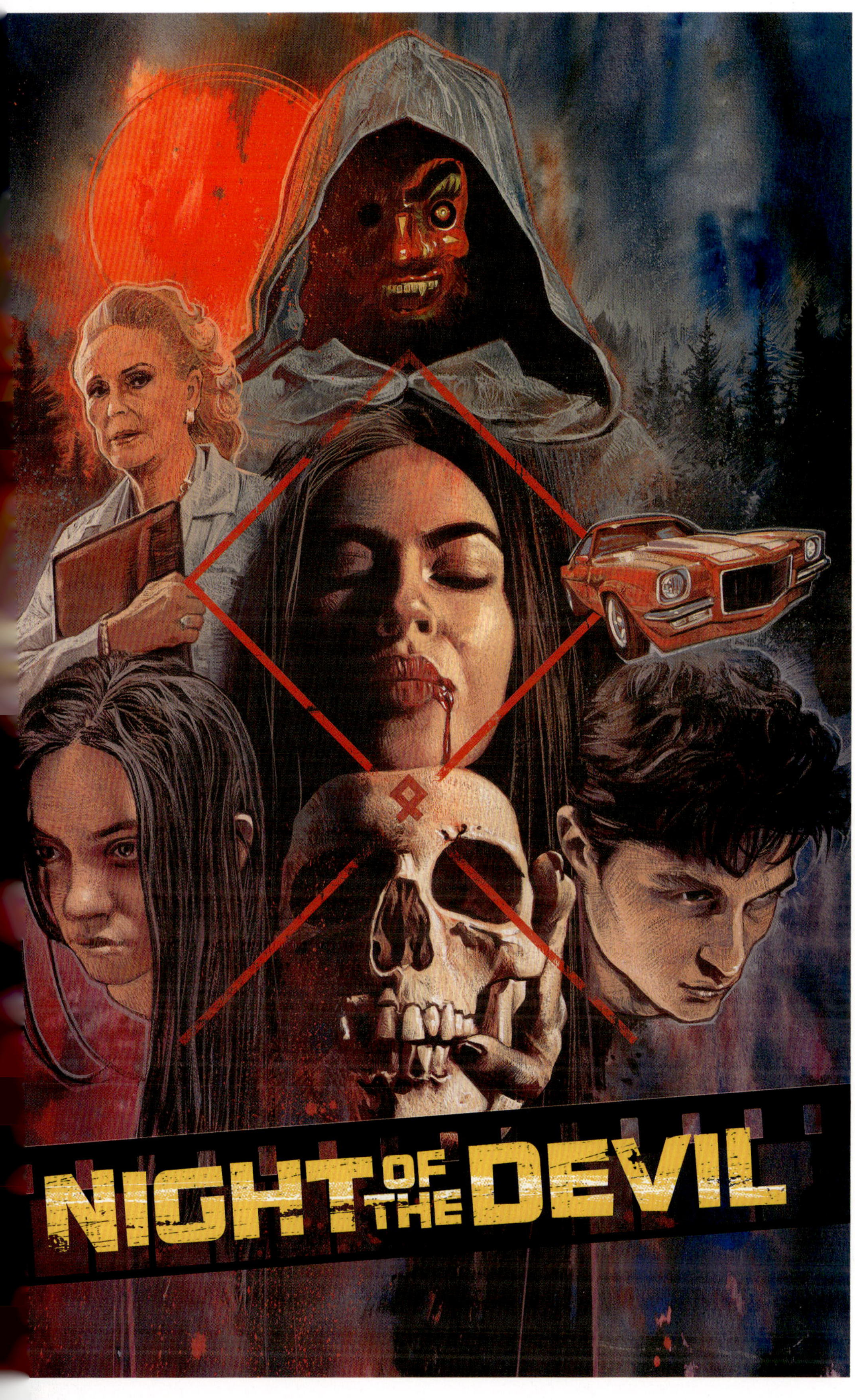

A low-budget feature which boasts a performance from Hammer horror actor Veronica Carlson (*Dracula has Risen from the Grave, Frankenstein Must be Destroyed*). The director provided guidance on the elements required, and the reference images were pulled as screen grabs, apart from the skull (from one of my own photographs) and the car (an image search that matched the vehicle used in the film). The "devil" image is a direct reference from the film, and it's a mask rather than a make-up effect.

It's a special day when you're commissioned to design a poster for a film that's risen to the status of legendary! Knowing how treasured the film is by its many fans, it's daunting to tread the subject without fear of disappointing customers, yet retain the integrity to employ your personal response to the film. I rewatched the film three times to identify the specific elements and expressions that would unfold the narrative. It was important for me to look at other posters and not simply repeat what had come before, so adding my own extras was vital. The client had suggested I steer clear of some of the obvious and iconic imagery (the dead armadillo and the desecrated corpse, for example), but I argued that these are the totems that are the core of the film and inseparable from the legend. Fortunately, everyone agreed.

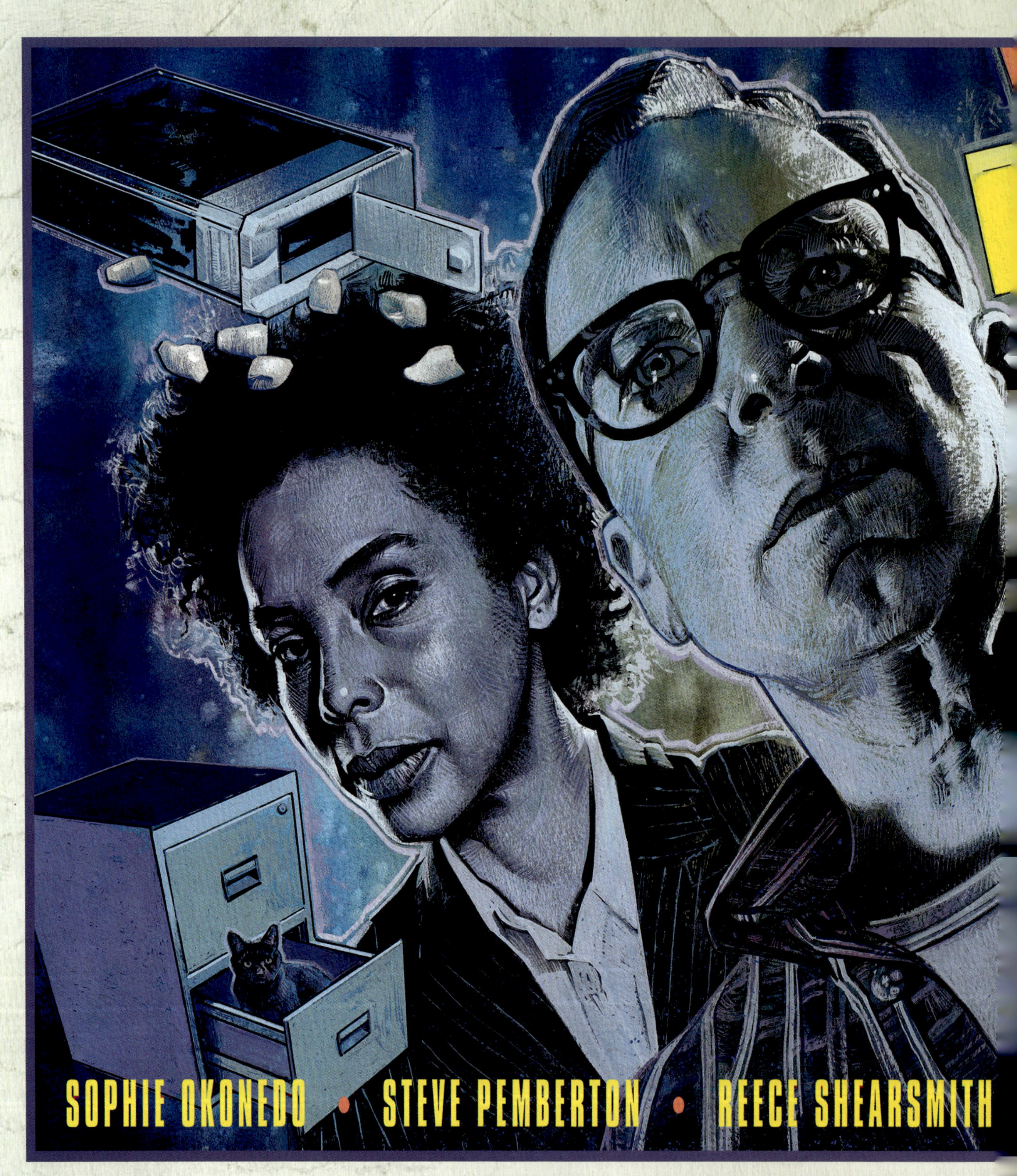

SOPHIE OKONEDO · STEVE PEMBERTON · REECE SHEARSMITH
BBC TWO PRESENTS A BBC STUDIOS PRODUCTION AN INSIDE NO. 9 FILM "NINE LIVES KAT" SOPHIE OKO
SIOBHAN REDMOND COCO-LILI HODER DIRECTOR OF PHOTOGRAPHY JAMES MOSS CASTING BY TRACEY GILLHAM
LINE PRODUCER UNA SAPLAMIDES WRITTEN BY STEVE PEMBERTON & REECE SHEARSMITH EXECUTIVE PRODUCER A

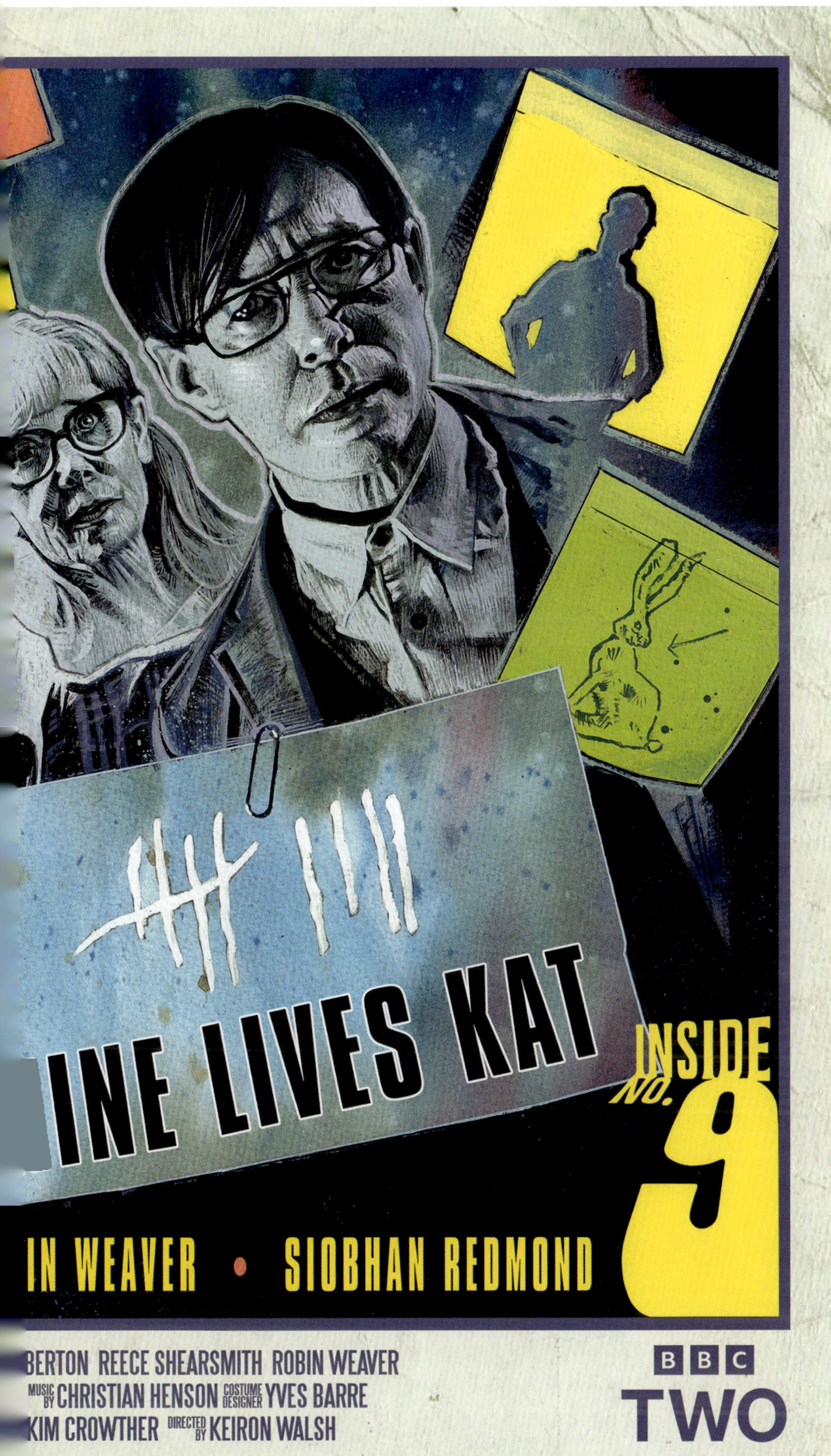

LEFT: *Nine Lives Kat* (2022), BBC Comedy; poster.

An episode in series seven of *Inside No. 9*, the title is a clue to the complex series of characters and interactions in the show, with additional narrative elements added to create intrigue in my composition. As ever, the two constants, actors Steve Pemberton and Reece Shearsmith, feature prominently in the poster — always providing the expressive faces that make a project like this seem so cinematic, particularly in a widescreen format.

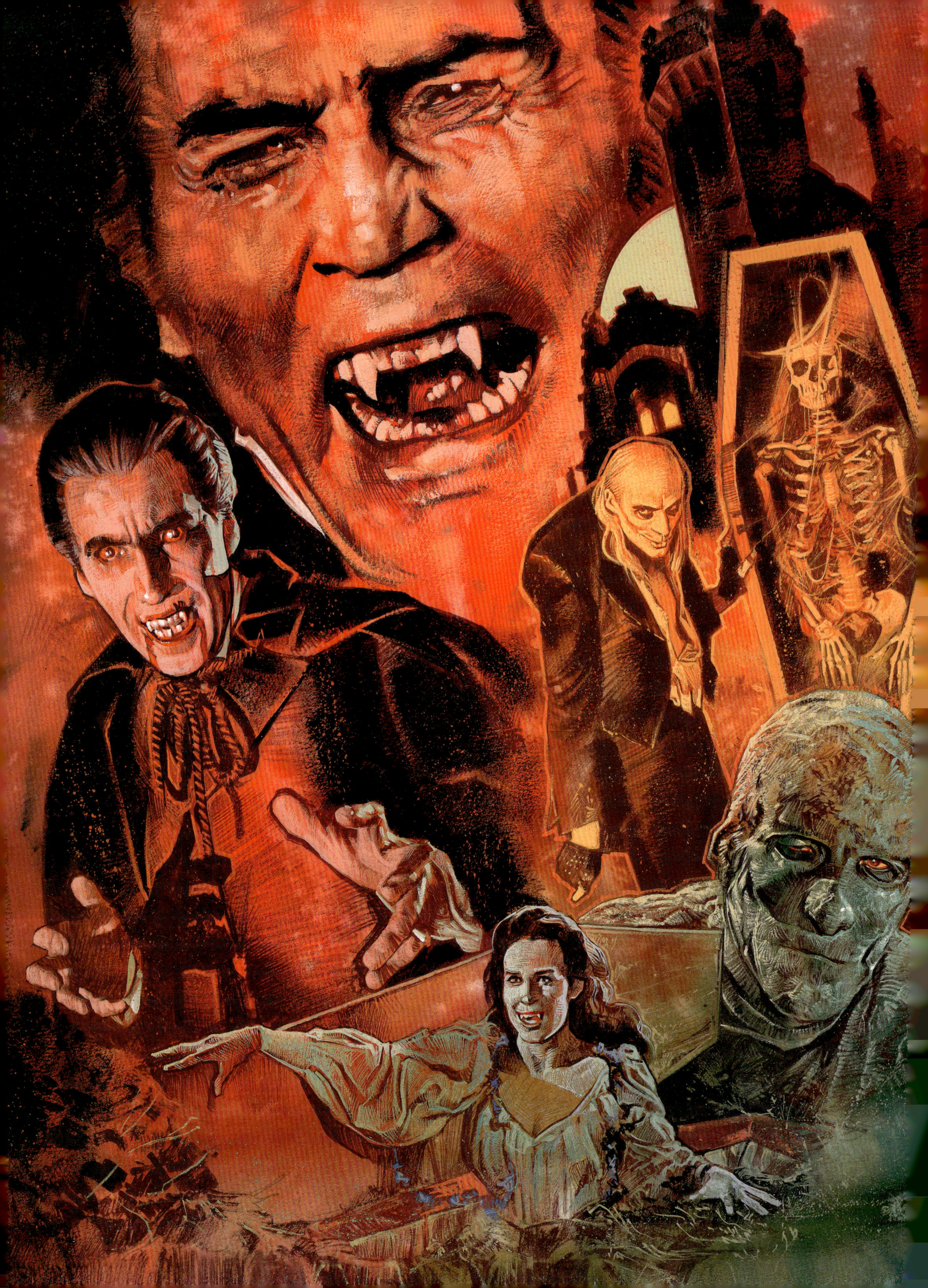

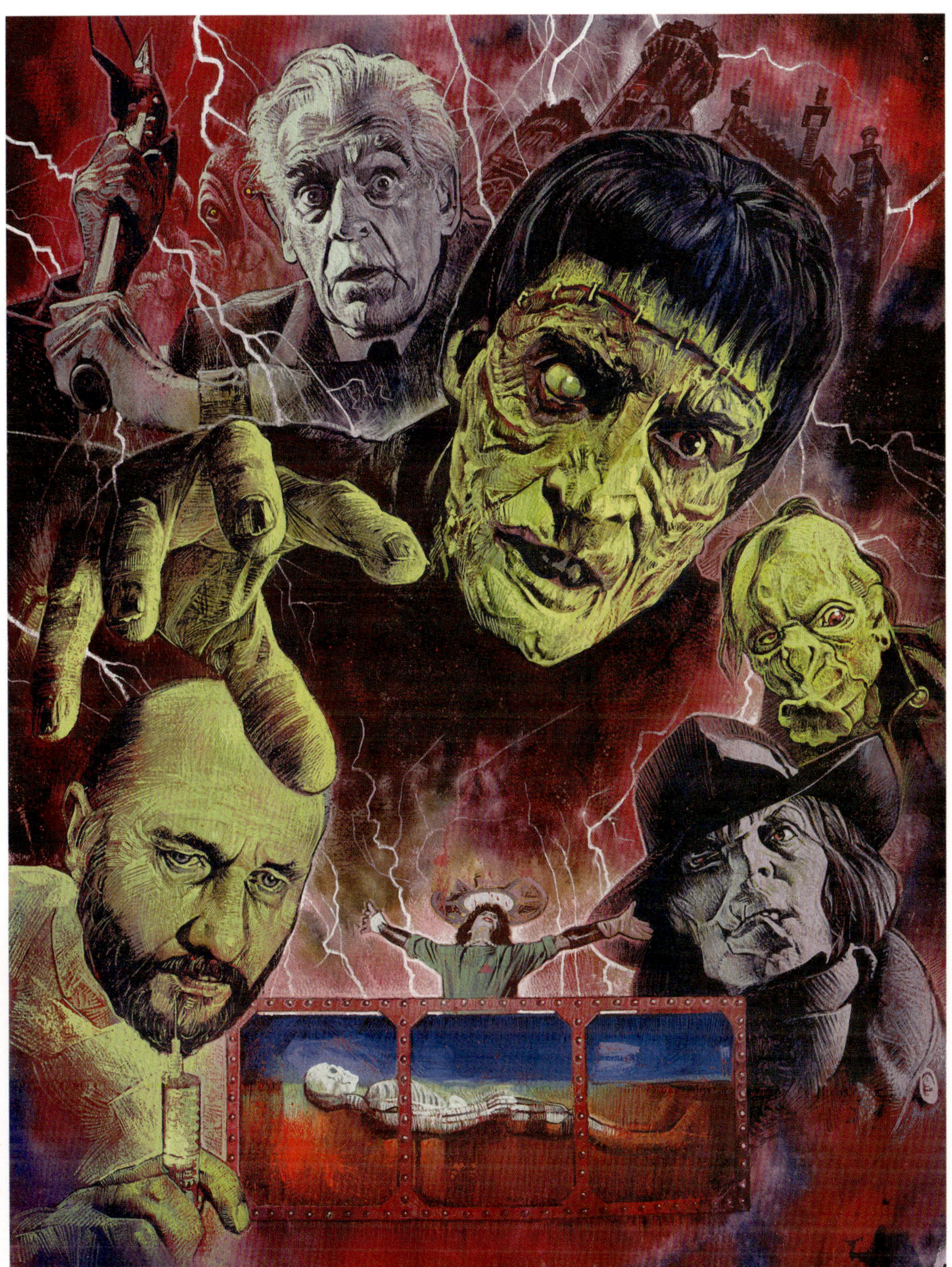

OPPOSITE: The Oakley Court Film and Memorabilia Fair (2019); event poster.

The second poster designed to celebrate the films that used Oakley Court (situated next to Bray Studios, Windsor) as a location. Bray Studios is known for the early Hammer horror films, and parts of its building and grounds are seen in numerous films. Oakley Court also provided the setting for *The Rocky Horror Picture Show*, as did the surrounding grounds. A special guest at the event was Dacre Stoker, great-grandnephew of Bram Stoker, hence the Dracula-themed composition. The Dan Curtis film *Dracula* (1974) makes particularly good use of Oakley Court's interior (then derelict); it is a little-seen film that features a ferocious performance from Jack Palance as the Count.

LEFT: The Oakley Court Film and Memorabilia Fair (2021); event poster.

My third poster for the event, again using images from films that had been shot at Oakley Court. The main theme — "Dracula" from the previous event — was (inevitably) "Frankenstein". A break of two years between the previous event and this one was due to the pandemic. Related to that, unfortunately, an elite hotel chain has stepped in and declared Oakley a "luxury spa destination" and it no longer welcomes visitors who wish to celebrate the films' legacy — unless they're prepared to pay the eye-watering room rates.

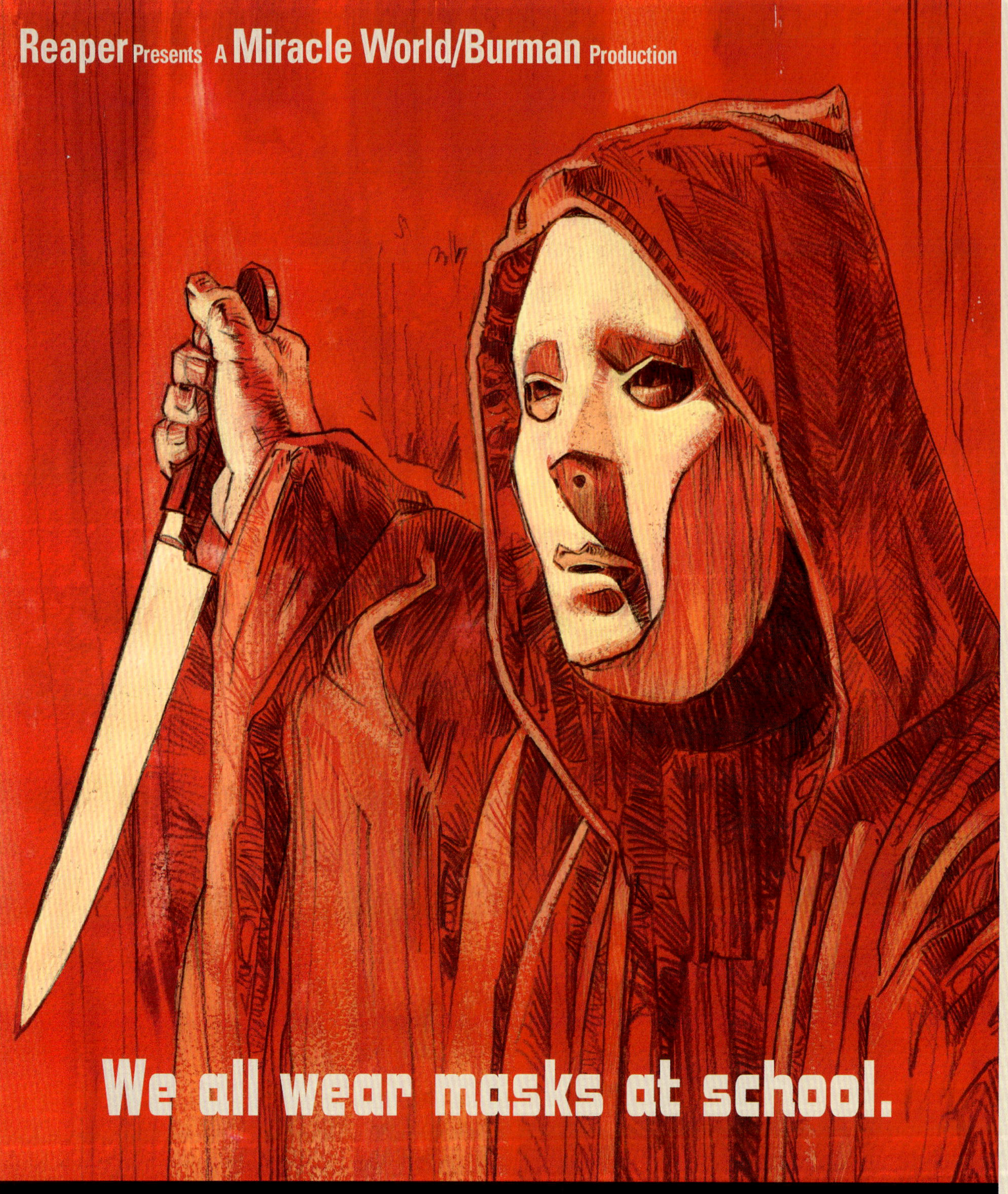

Reaper Presents A Miracle World/Burman Production
We all wear masks at school.
A MARIO COVONE film
OVERTIME
REAPER Presents A MIRACLE WORLD/BURMAN Production A MARIO COVONE Film OVERTIME
BETHANY RUMBELLOW • CHRIS SPYRIDES • JACK CLARK • HEATHER-MAE CUTTS • ANNA BEER with GARY BAXTER and introducing PIPPA HADDOW
Casting Director TARA BORZONI Music TOM RUMBELLOW 'WINE OF GODS' written by JACKAL Performed by THE CRIMSON GHOSTS Wardrobe SIOBHAN PENN Make up Effects SOPHIE GOODMAN Production Design BETHANY CLARKE
Editor REBECCA HUDSON Director of Photography OLIVER MACKINLEY Executive Producers RICHARD STEWART & CAMERON LUSTY Producer JACK BURMAN Written by MARIO COVONE & CAMERON LUSTY Director MARIO COVONE
© 2020 All Rights Reserved.

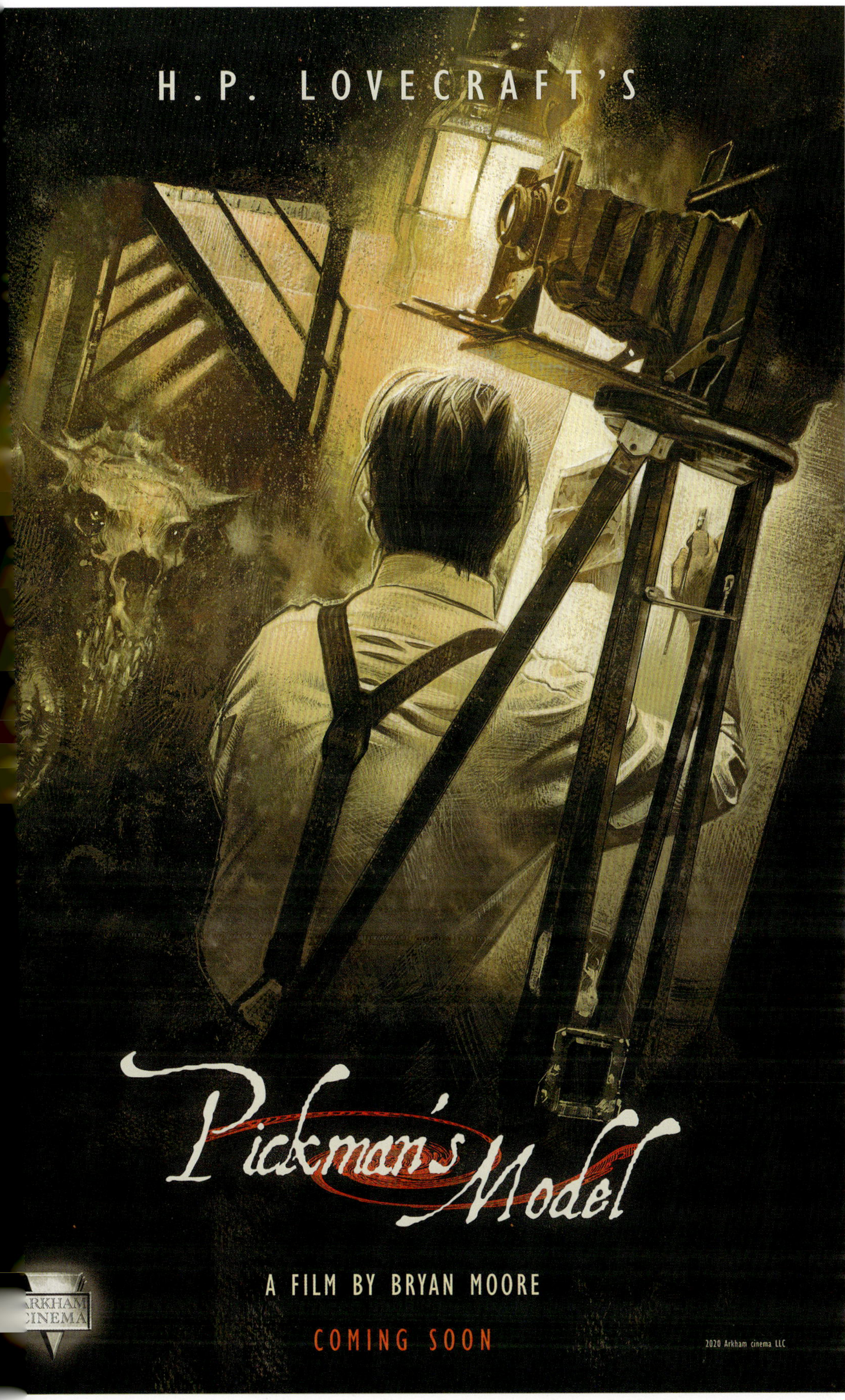

LEFT: *Pickman's Model* (2020), Arkham Cinema LLC; poster.

A pre-production artwork for a film by the multi-talented Bryan Moore (sculptor, writer, director, and actor). Designed to a precise brief, my reference uses sourced images and a photograph of Bryan himself, posed as Pickman. The palette is intended to convey a sickly sepia, a reference to a plot point.

OPPOSITE: *Overtime* (2020), Reaper — Miracle World/Burman; poster.

With a limited budget, my initial design featured a collage of simple elements created in black and white, then overlaid as colour in Photoshop. The client felt it didn't represent their vision of their film, so I changed my approach and painted an image that was inspired by the poster style of some of Sergio Leone's spaghetti westerns. The client was happy.

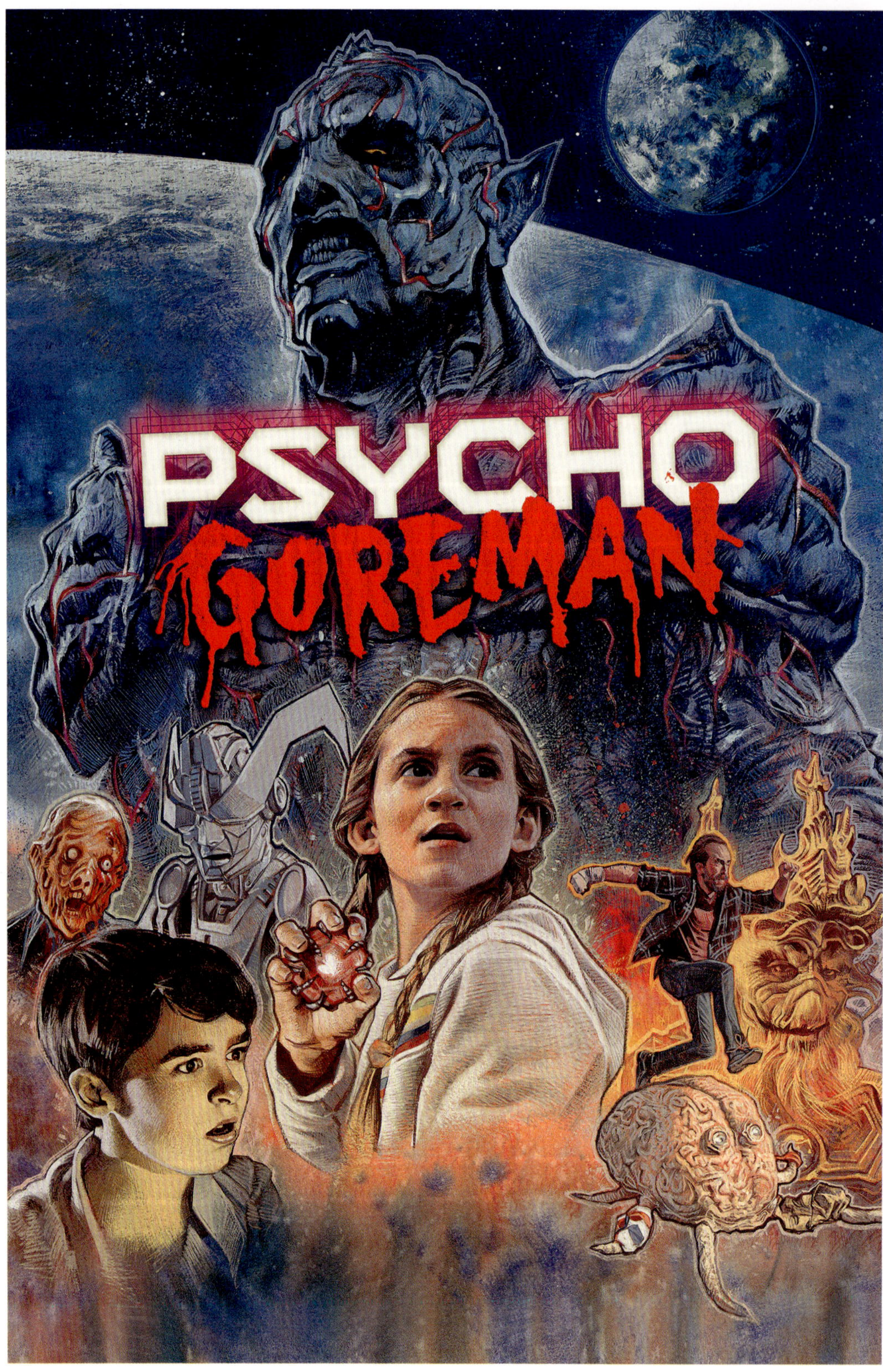

LEFT: *Psycho Goreman* (2020), RLJE Films; poster.

A Canadian science fantasy, action, horror-comedy film written and directed by Steven Kostanski, *Psycho Goreman* defies expectations with a delirious plot that crosses genres with playful abandon. I was left to my own devices to compose an image that would cover as much material as possible — I supplied several sketch options using many of the bizarre and colourful visual elements that appear in the film. But ultimately, it was down to the client to decide what would appear on the poster.

RIGHT: *The Rocky Horror Picnic Show* (2022), TimeWarp Fan Club; poster.

Commissioned to be printed as a giveaway at an event, the poster was going to have limited use. I'd always wanted to show the turreted castle (Oakley Court) as a spaceship — although the title covers the blast. The client requested the entire array of characters, leaving little room for any narrative elements. As it was designed for a summer picnic, I kept the palette bright and floral. (I may amend the art at some point to create a darker feel.)

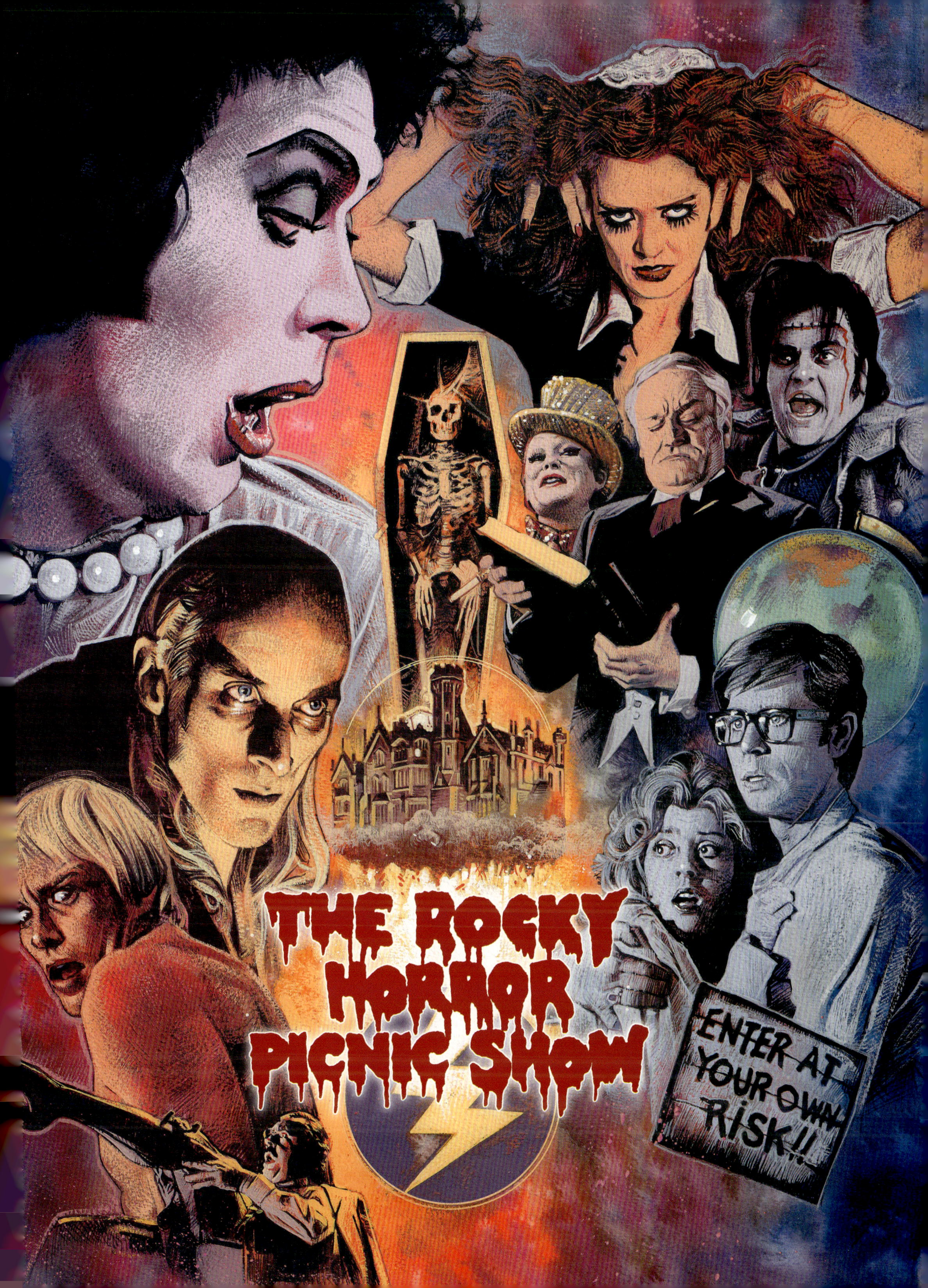
THE ROCKY
HORROR
PICNIC SHOW
ENTER AT
YOUR OWN
RISK!!

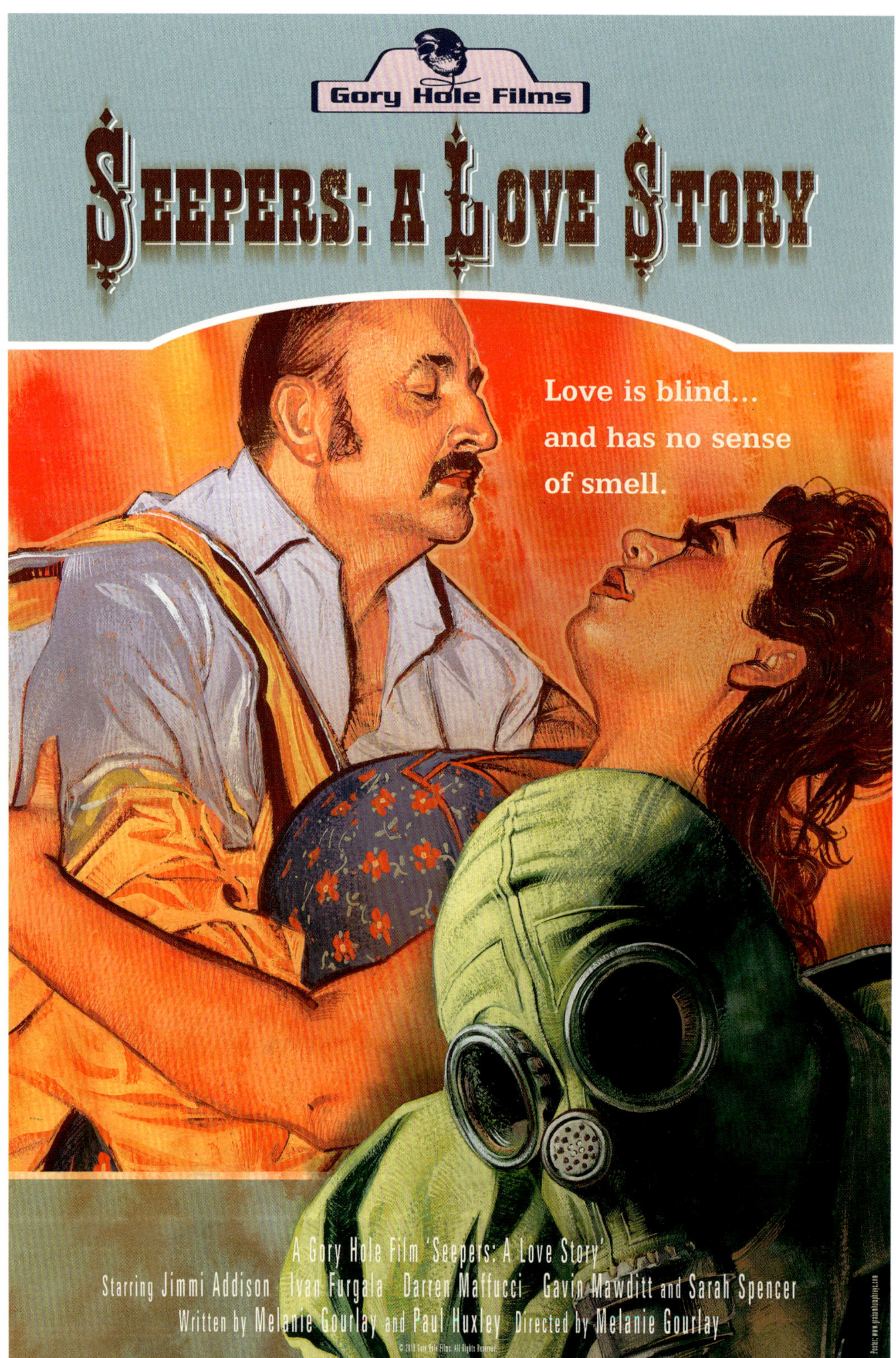

LEFT: *Seepers: A Love Story* (2019), Melanie Gourlay; poster.

The poster was designed as a pastiche of the popular Mills & Boon romance paperback covers. Posed photography was provided as a reference for the two leads and masked character. The finished layout was composed of two scanned paintings, with the framing graphics generated digitally.

RIGHT: *Trieste Science+Fiction Festival* (2022), La Cappella Underground; poster.

Alan Jones, a long-time friend and founder of the annual London FrightFest, invited me to produce a poster for the Italian festival that he was curating.

Celebrating 100 years of science fiction, my poster was expected to reference the entire spectrum of classics, from the silent era to the present day. It clearly required some pruning, so I requested a practical shortlist for inclusion and built my image around a central character who could represent a number of key films. The surrounding imagery makes additional film references (*Metropolis*, for example, is clearly seen), whilst others are more abstract.

The challenge was more acute because the image needed to be pulled apart to facilitate many formats and uses. My paintings are always produced as single entities, so they're not created in digital layers. My only option was to make a collage of elements that could be moved around and reconfigured as required. Rather than use paint, the elements are marker drawings, scanned and coloured in Photoshop, with the addition of overlaid paint textures I'd made especially for the work.

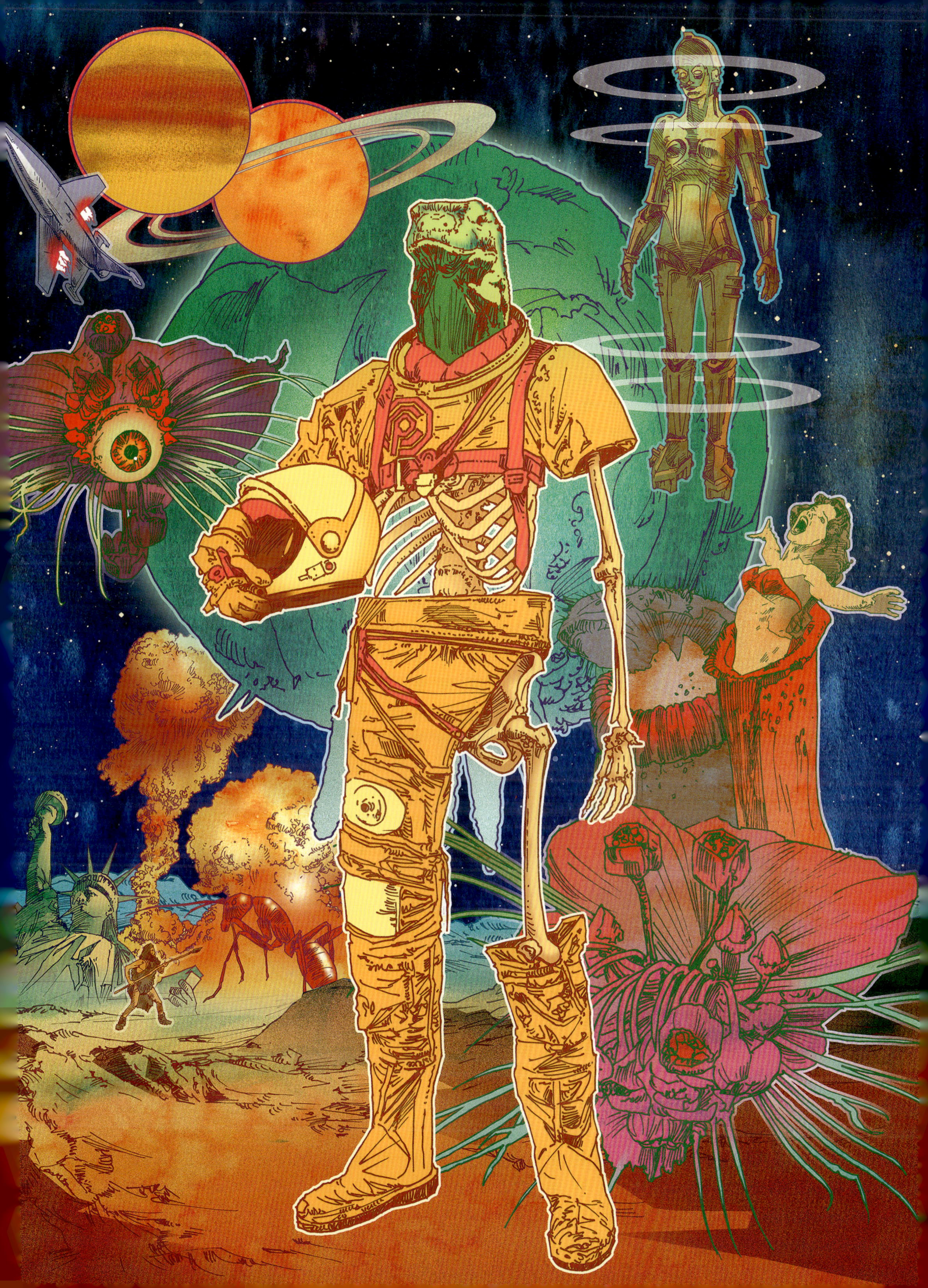

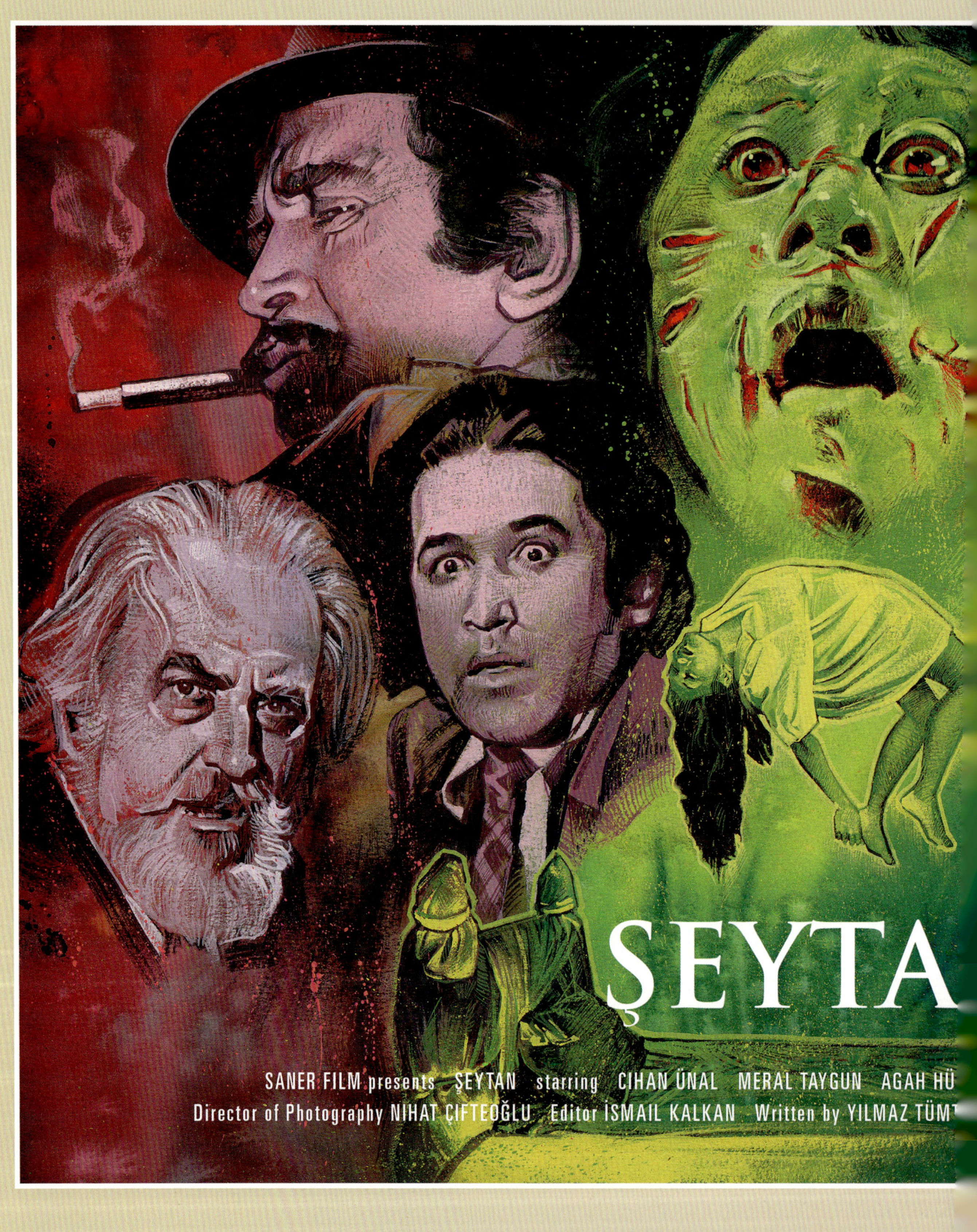
ŞEYTA
SANER FILM presents ŞEYTAN starring CIHAN ÜNAL MERAL TAYGUN AGAH HÜ
Director of Photography NIHAT ÇIFTEOĞLU Editor İSMAIL KALKAN Written by YILMAZ TÜM

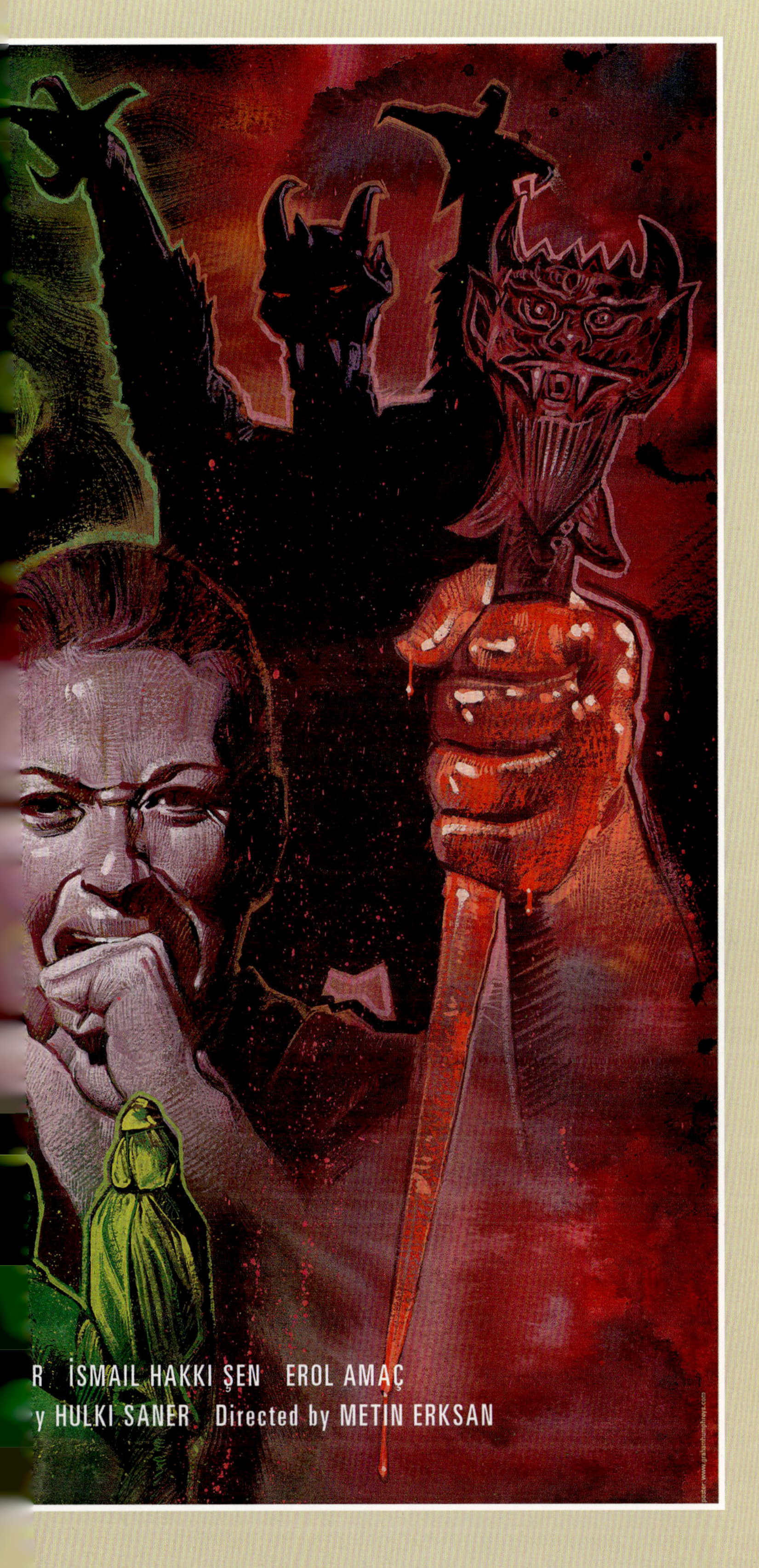

Seytan (1974) is also known as "the Turkish Exorcist". The film was being restored for posterity as part of an ongoing mission to celebrate the Turkish remakes of popular films. With a Vimeo link as my only reference, I had to use some low-quality screen grabs to design the poster. My reference for the levitating character was constructed from three separate sourced images; the bed was referenced from a still from the original film *The Exorcist* (1973). The additional elements are as they appear in the film — the less-than-scary statue and the ritual dagger.

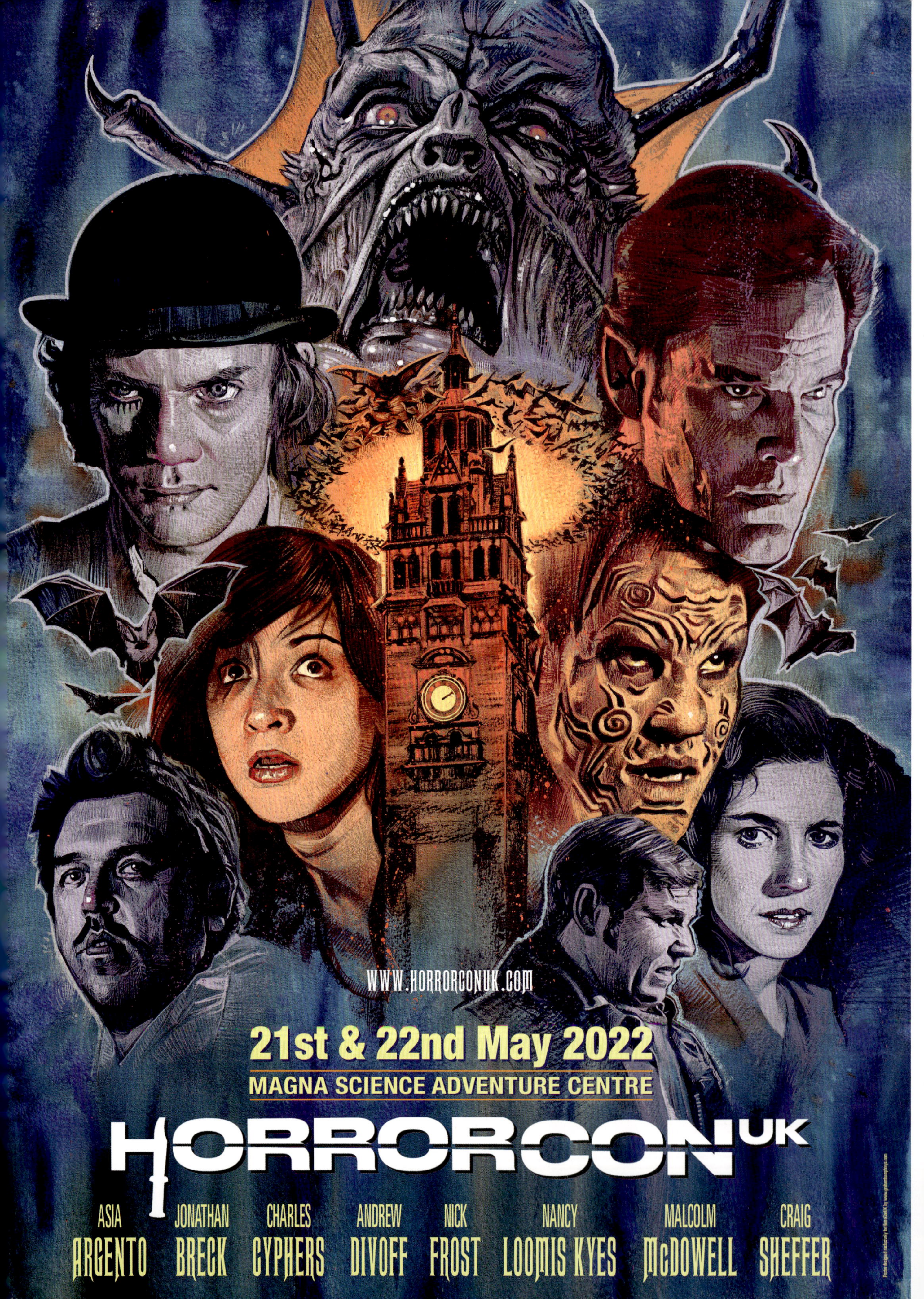
WWW.HORRORCONUK.COM
21st & 22nd May 2022
MAGNA SCIENCE ADVENTURE CENTRE
HORRORCON UK
ASIA ARGENTO
JONATHAN BRECK
CHARLES CYPHERS
ANDREW DIVOFF
NICK FROST
NANCY LOOMIS KYES
MALCOLM McDOWELL
CRAIG SHEFFER

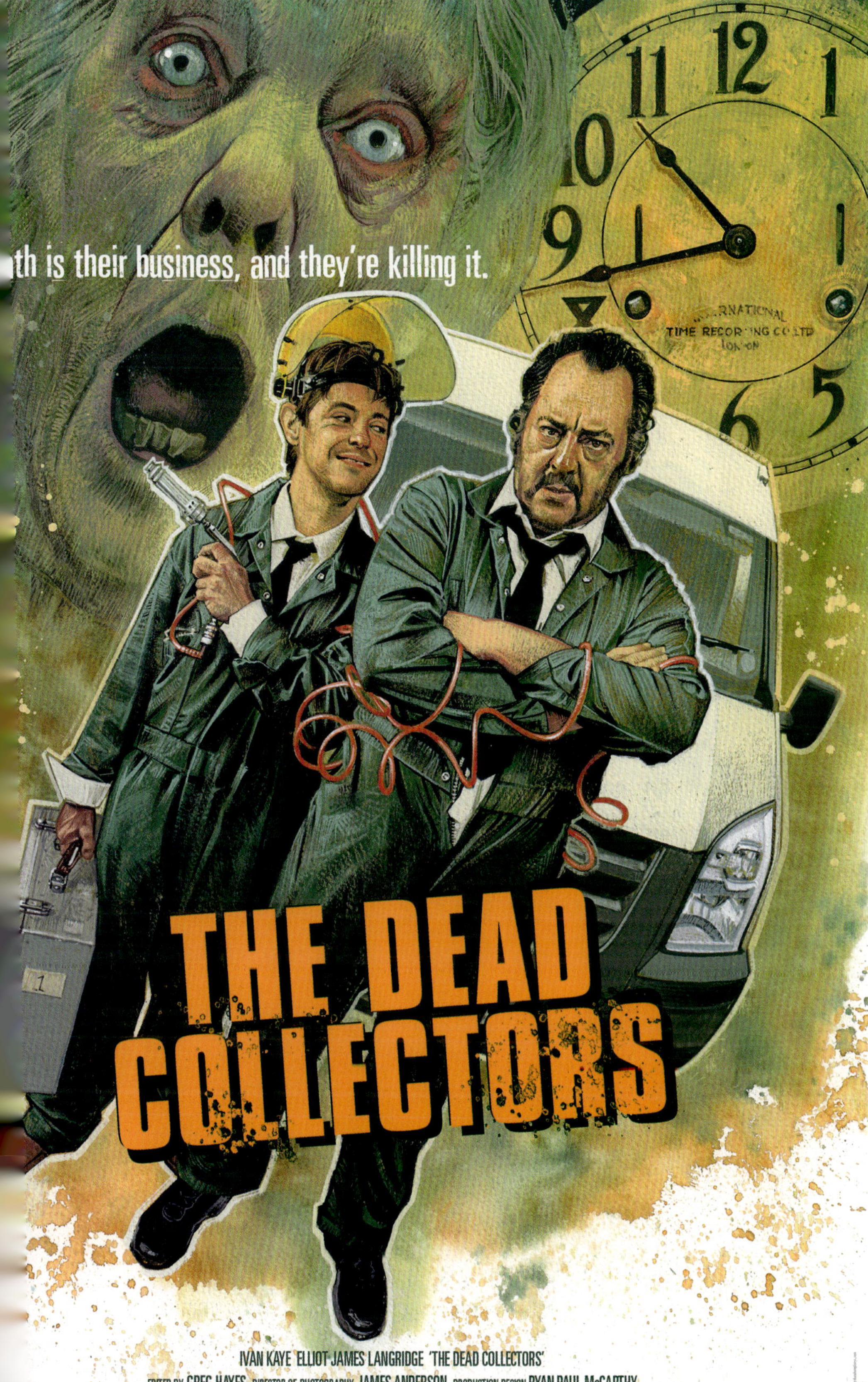

LEFT: *The Dead Collectors* (2021), Fear Army Ltd; poster.

A short film that introduces two key characters whose professional relationship (old hand and novice) drive the plot. With such prominence required in the composition, I requested a photo shoot that would give me the best possible reference to make it work. The additional images serve to add layers of narrative.

OPPOSITE: *Sheffield HorrorCon* (2022); event poster.

One of a series of posters painted for this annual convention. My poster is expected to represent all of the invited special guests, generally in the roles that make them valued at the event. I've always added an element of the city of Sheffield itself to create a focal pivot and point of interest.

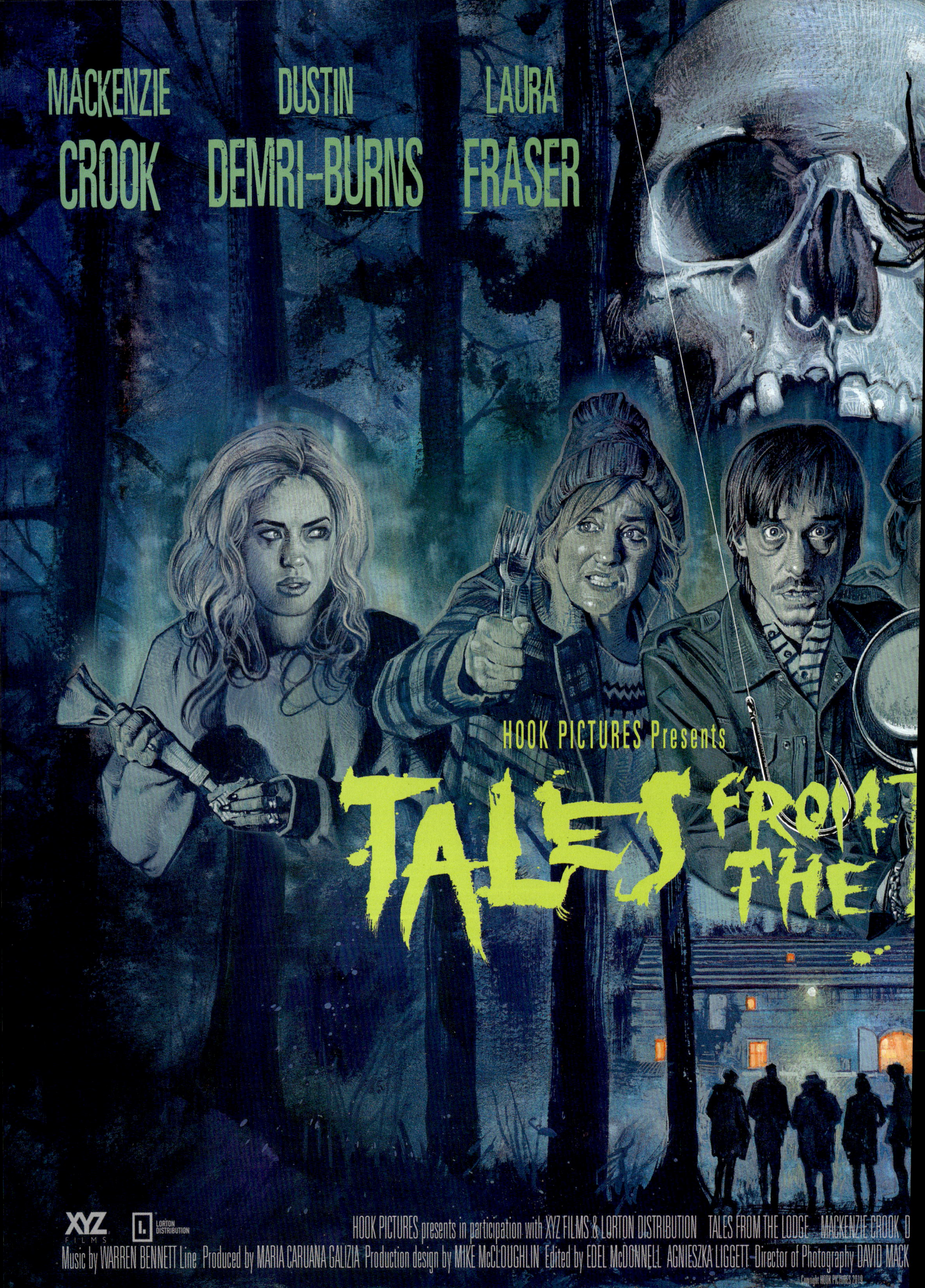

MACKENZIE CROOK
DUSTIN DEMRI-BURNS
LAURA FRASER
HOOK PICTURES Presents
TALES FROM THE
XYZ FILMS
LORTON DISTRIBUTION
HOOK PICTURES presents in participation with XYZ FILMS & LORTON DISTRIBUTION   TALES FROM THE LODGE   MACKENZIE CROOK   D
Music by WARREN BENNETT Line Produced by MARIA CARUANA GALIZIA Production design by MIKE McCLOUGHLIN Edited by EDEL McDONNELL AGNIESZKA LIGGETT Director of Photography DAVID MACK

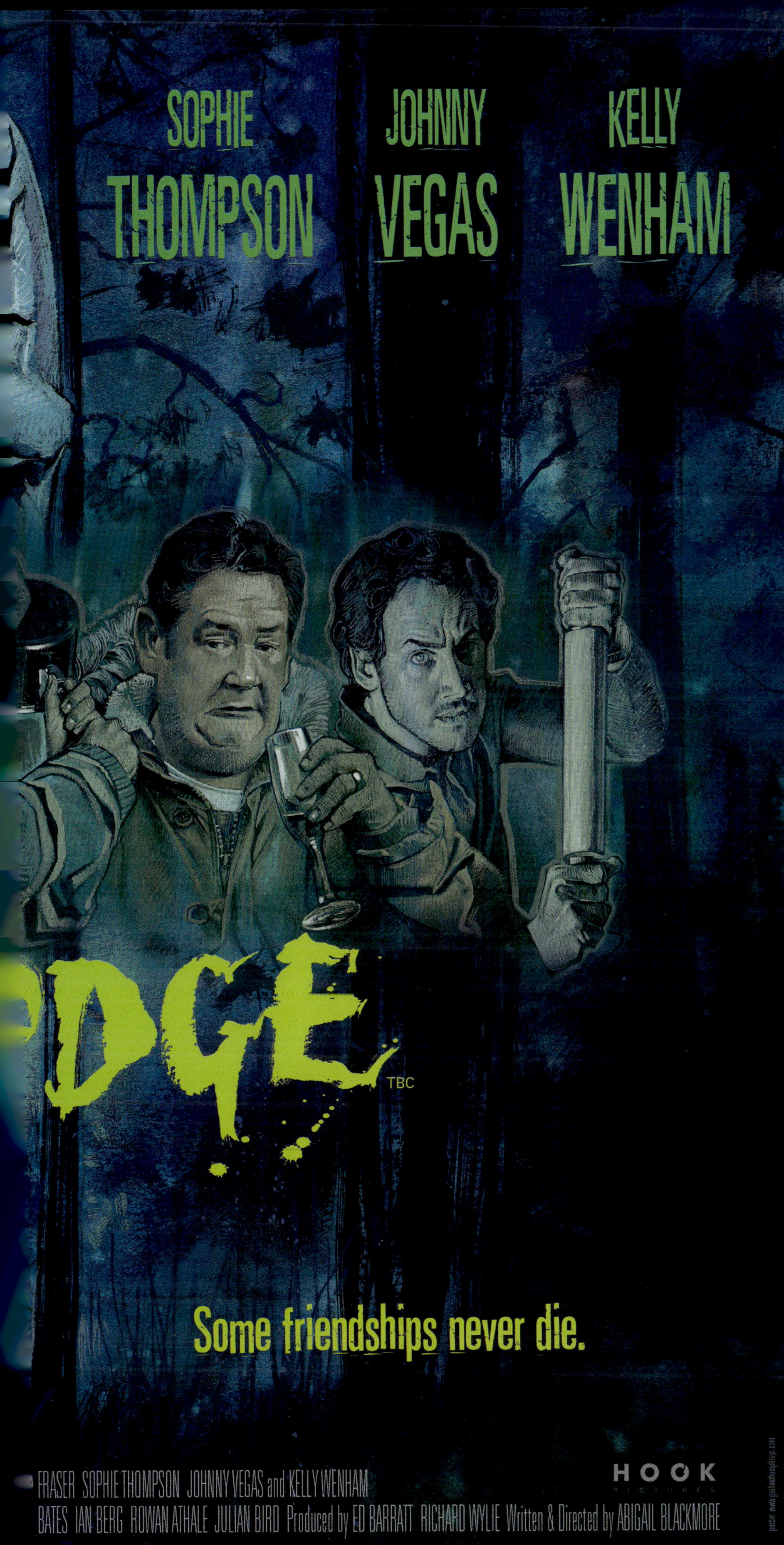

The tradition of anthology films is a joy that's best encapsulated in the Amicus films of the 1960s and '70s. The format involves seemingly unconnected stories with a wraparound link — they never end well! This contemporary take on the genre is a comedic homage which required the one element that can always link the legacy of horror across the decades: a skull!

I love painting skulls (have you noticed?). The first thing I could draw in my infancy (aside from Daleks) was a skull. I had in mind posters for *Tales from the Crypt* (1972), *The House that Dripped Blood* (1971), and *Dr Terror's House of Horrors* (1965).

These anthologies, also known as portmanteau films, had one common feature: a cast of great British character actors; in *Tales from the Lodge* (2019), the line-up includes some equally familiar faces, notably Mackenzie Crook and Johnny Vegas.

One problem I encountered, not an uncommon one, was the need to repurpose the art for both portrait and landscape formats. I resolved this by painting the forest and skull as one artwork and the cast line-up as another, giving me the freedom to resize digitally to accommodate the two formats.

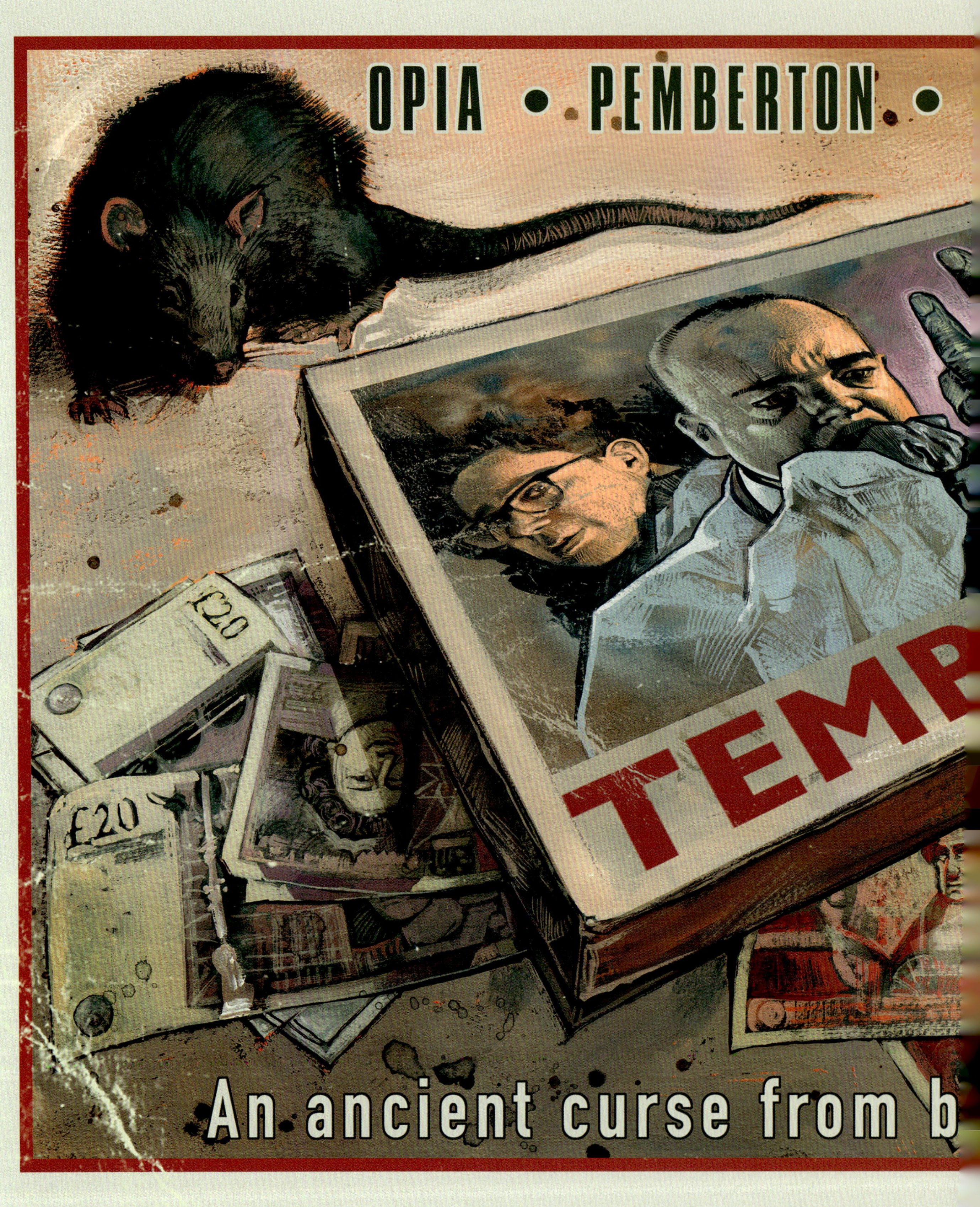

OPIA • PEMBERTON •
£20
£20
TEMB
An ancient curse from b

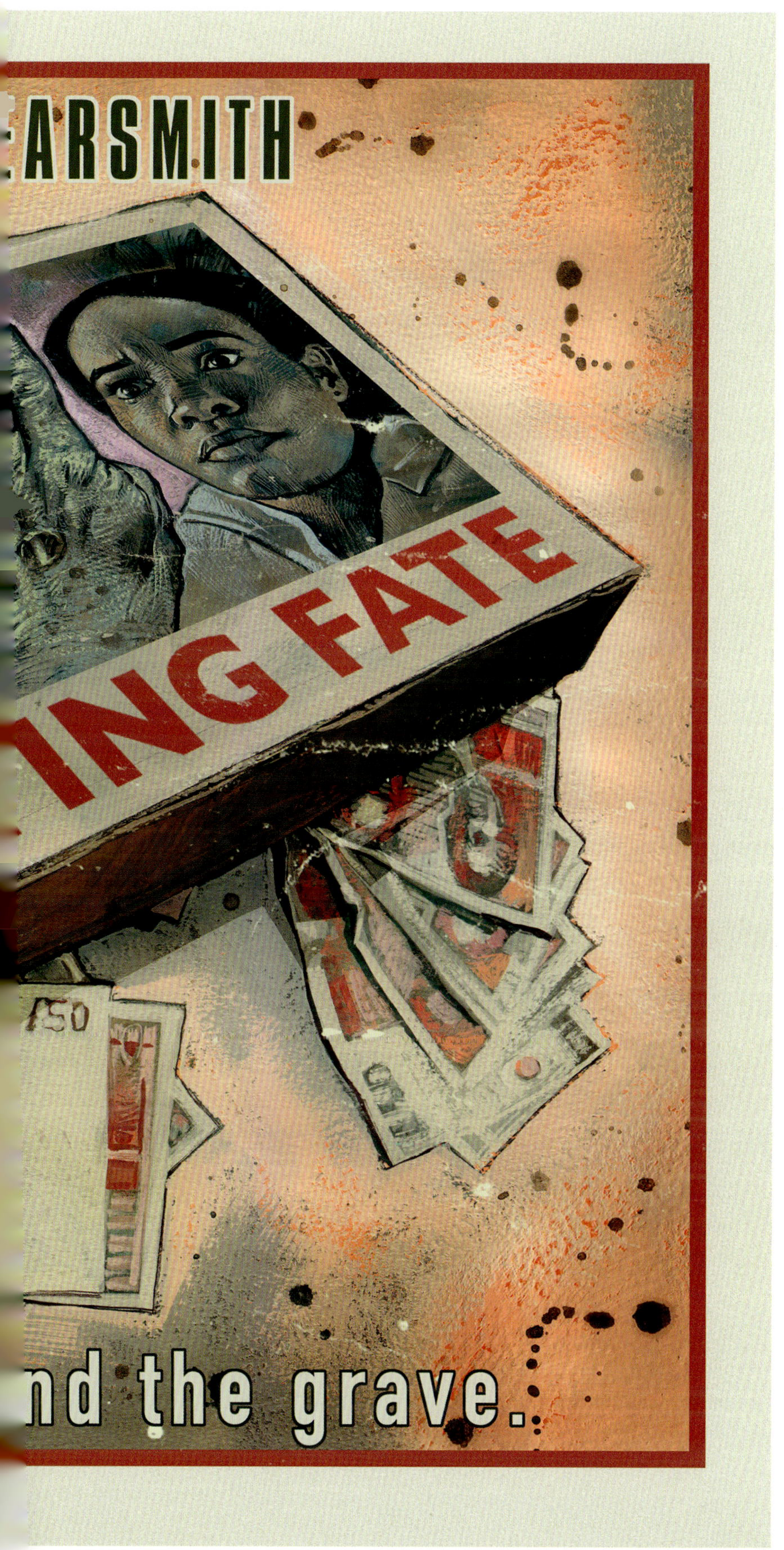

LEFT: *Tempting Fate* (2020), BBC Comedy; poster.

Created for an episode of the TV series *Inside No. 9*, this is one of a number of "poster" commissions for the show. In this instance, it was important not to reveal any surprise elements but to allude to the situation-led drama that unfolds.

LEFT: *Vampirella* (2019), De Montfort University; event poster.

Commissioned by the university that protects the Hammer archives, this poster promoted a live script reading of the original screenplay for one of Hammer Films' eagerly anticipated yet unmade projects — "planned to be a big-budget Hammer horror in the 1970s with Peter Cushing signed on to star, along with former Beatle Ringo Starr and Hollywood legend Orson Welles, with Barbara Leigh as the superhero vampire", according to information from the university. Another name touted to play Vampirella was Hammer actor Caroline Munro (she was later to star in the 1978 film *Starcrash*, in a similar outfit). I was asked to imagine a poster that would incorporate narrative elements from the script, with the casting of Caroline Munro (who was one of the evening's readers, alongside her daughter performing the role of Vampirella) and Peter Cushing (I sourced my reference from his Hammer films of the period).

RIGHT: *The Reckoning* (2020), Neil Marshall; poster.

Commissioned by the director as one of three variants, this is a classic composite of content revolving around a focal character. There was enough interesting imagery in the production to give me plenty to work with. I had issues with the lead actor's face. She wasn't happy with the first version, despite its accuracy to the approved material. It took two further attempts with different references before approval was given. Once the art was complete, I decided to darken the image considerably, adding to the gloom (achieved in Photoshop). I tend to trust my judgement in how dark or light an image should appear, but in this rare instance I had second thoughts, only after considerable time investment that didn't allow me to adjust the image in paint.

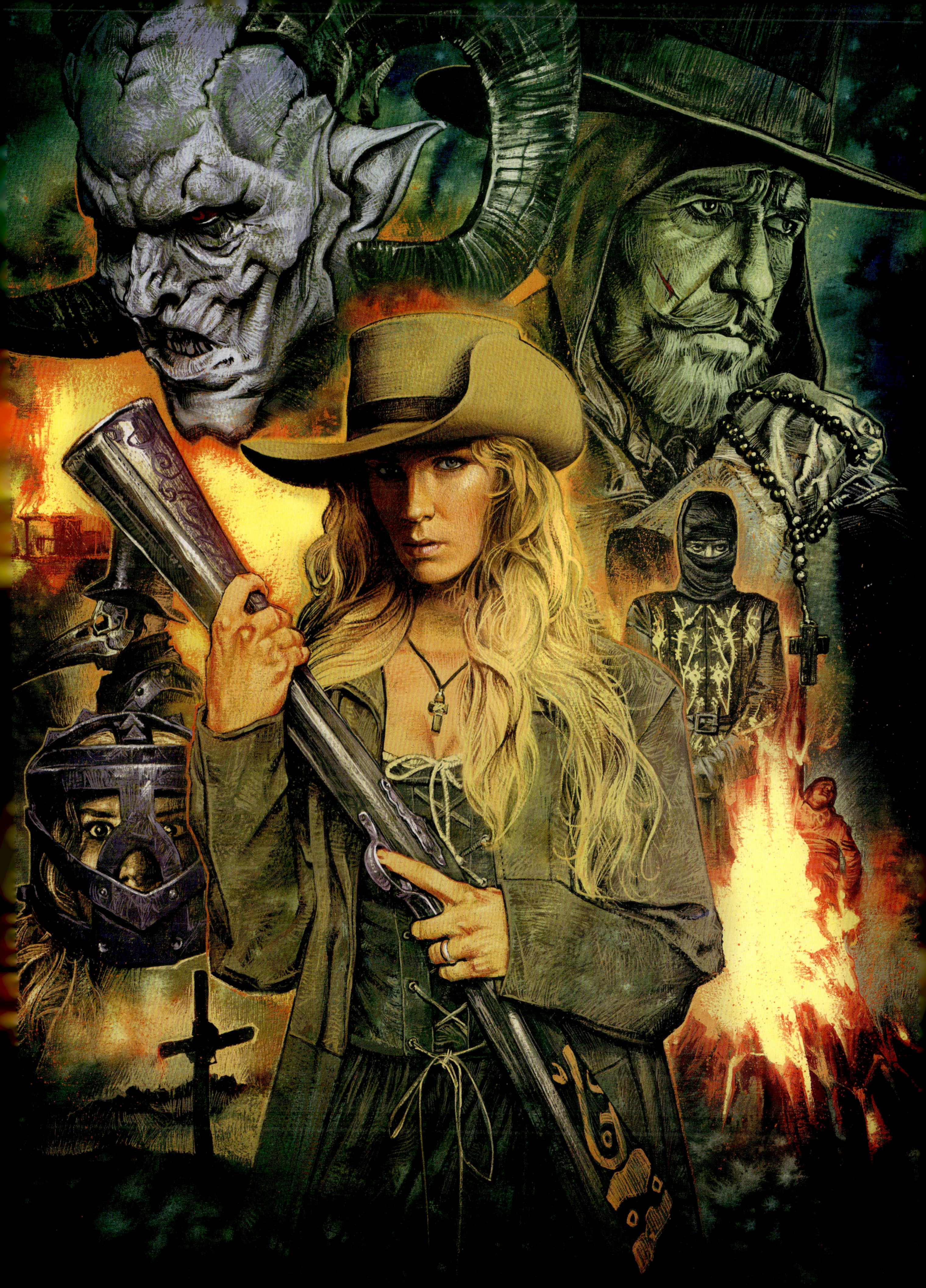

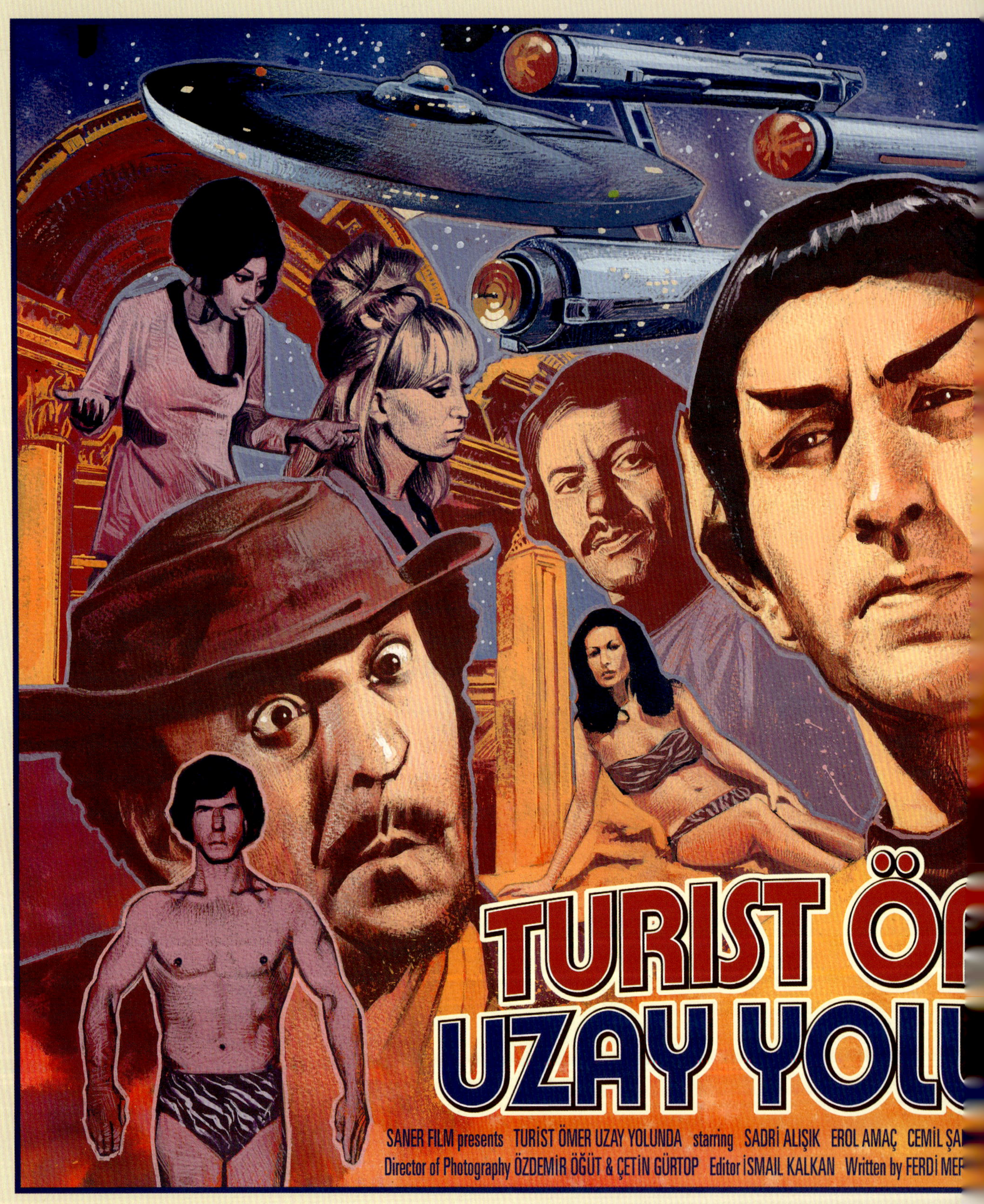
TURIST ÖMER
UZAY YOLU
SANER FILM presents TURİST ÖMER UZAY YOLUNDA starring SADRİ ALIŞIK EROL AMAÇ CEMİL ŞA
Director of Photography ÖZDEMİR ÖĞÜT & ÇETİN GÜRTOP Editor İSMAİL KALKAN Written by FERDİ ME

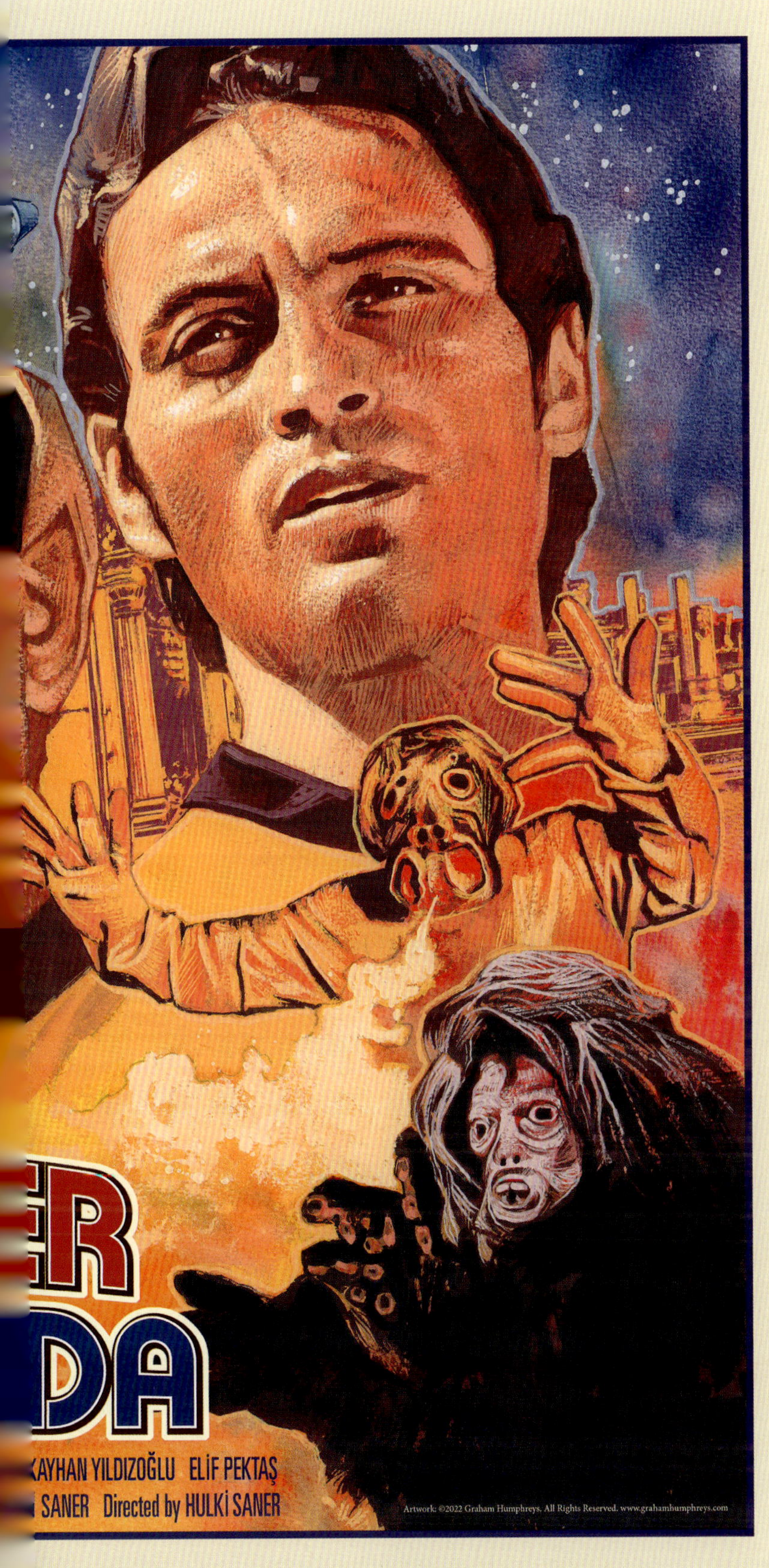

LEFT: *Turist Ömer Uzy Yolunda* (2022), university commission; poster.

The "Turkish Star Trek", as it's also known, is a shameless steal from the 1960s US TV series, even pinching footage from the show. It's loosely based on one particular episode, "The Man Trap". Oddly, it almost manages to trump the original material by use of actual outside locations (the ruins of Ephesus in Turkey).

My references came from a supplied link to the film (for key portraiture and peripheral characters) and some image searches (for instance, the ruins are sourced from a tourist site, and the spacecraft from a photo of a model kit rather than the original licensed show).

I decided to limit my use of colour to primaries and pastels, giving it a retro toy-like quality.

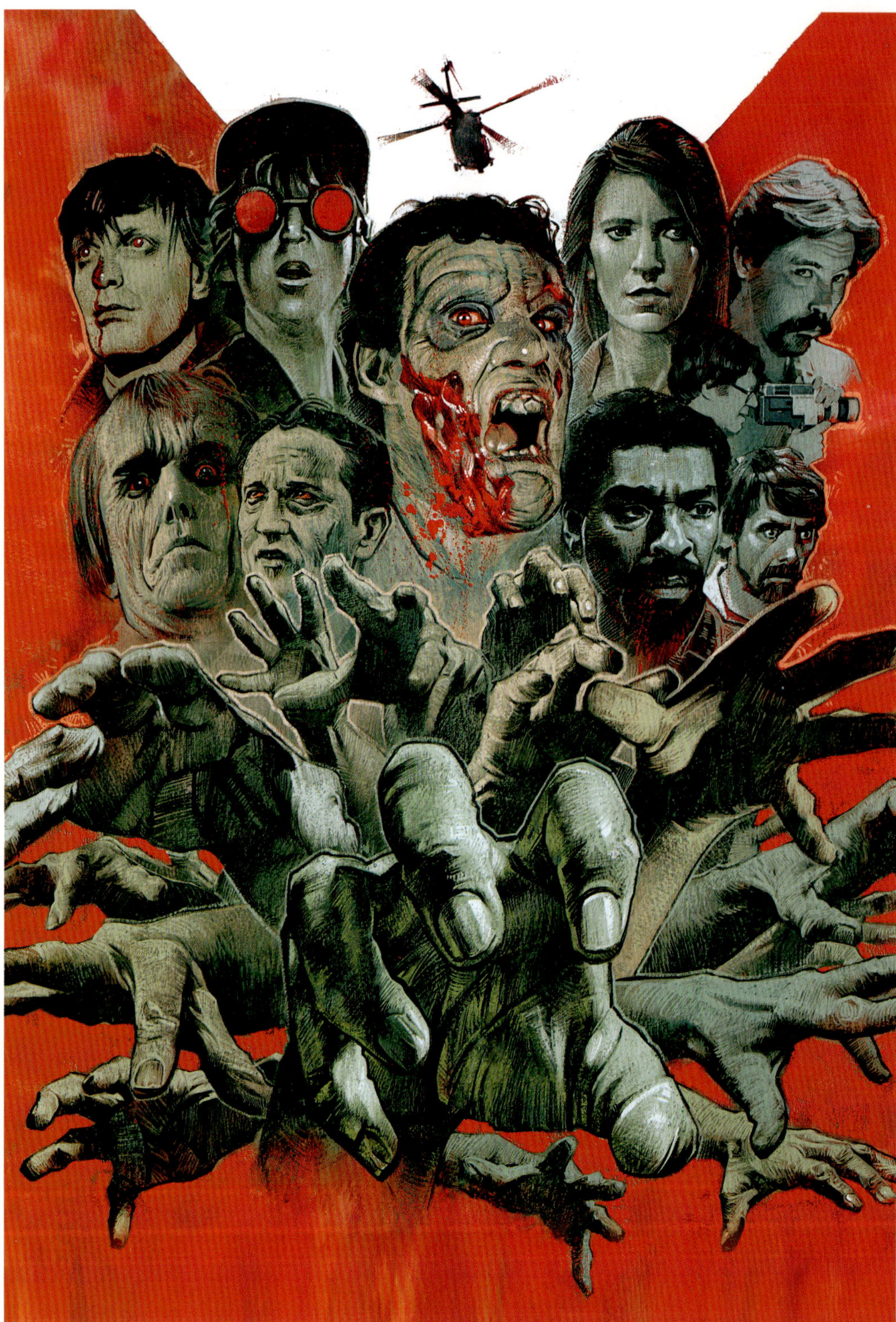

PAGE 108: *Vincent Price* (2021), Tomorrow's Ghosts Festival; poster.

A special guest appearance of Victoria Price (the daughter of Vincent Price) was planned as part of a Goth weekend in Whitby, Yorkshire, England. The poster celebrates Vincent at his menacing best. Originally a smaller portrait of Victoria was going to be added at the bottom to promote her appearance as part of a series of screenings and talks; however, circumstances prevented Victoria from travelling, and the event was cancelled. Fortunately, the art exists and is a personal favourite of the many times I've painted Vincent Price.

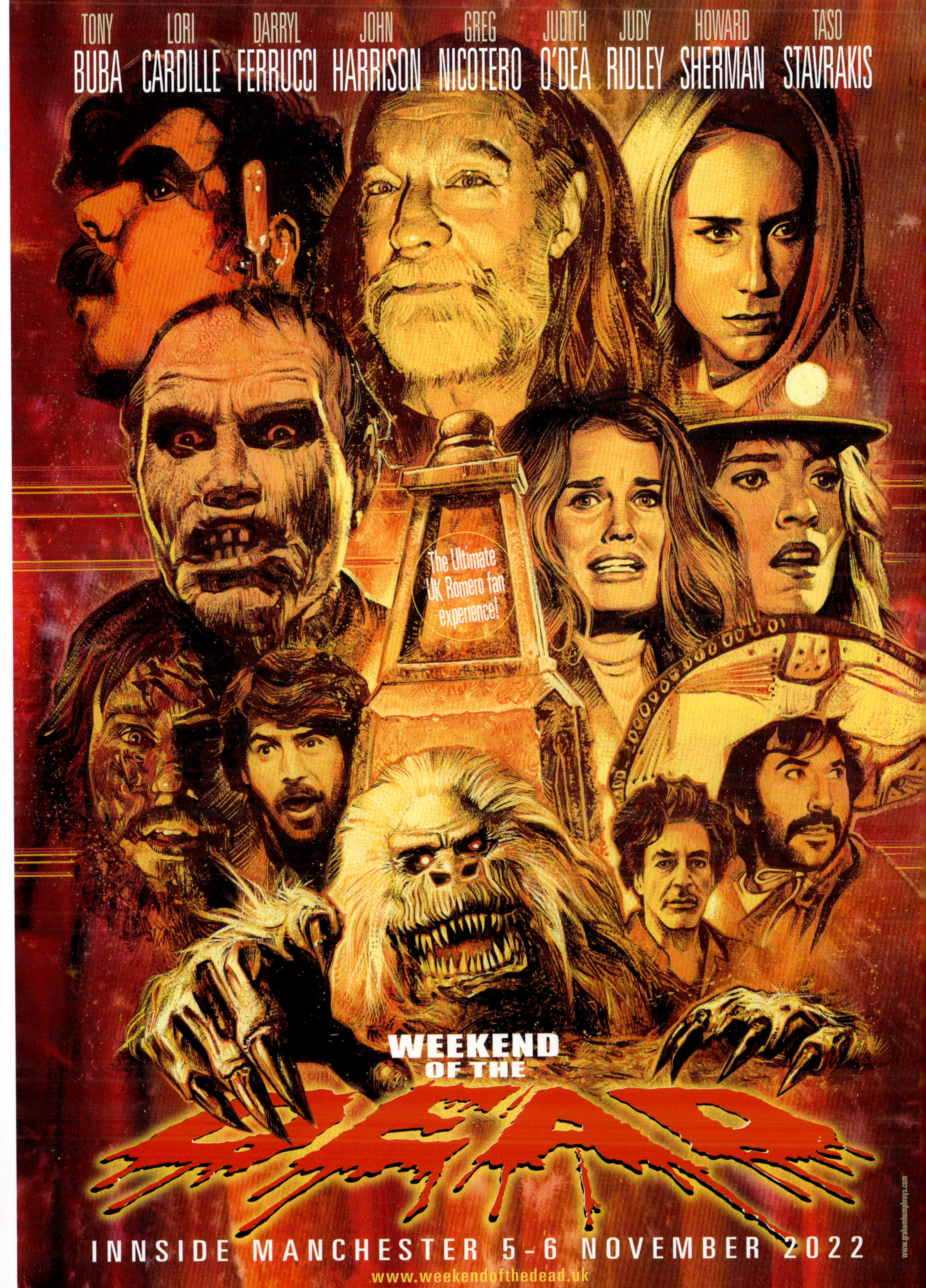

TONY BUBA
LORI CARDILLE
DARRYL FERRUCCI
JOHN HARRISON
GREG NICOTERO
JUDITH O'DEA
JUDY RIDLEY
HOWARD SHERMAN
TASO STAVRAKIS
The Ultimate UK Romero fan experience!
WEEKEND OF THE DEAD
INNSIDE MANCHESTER 5-6 NOVEMBER 2022
www.weekendofthedead.uk
www.grahamhumphreys.com

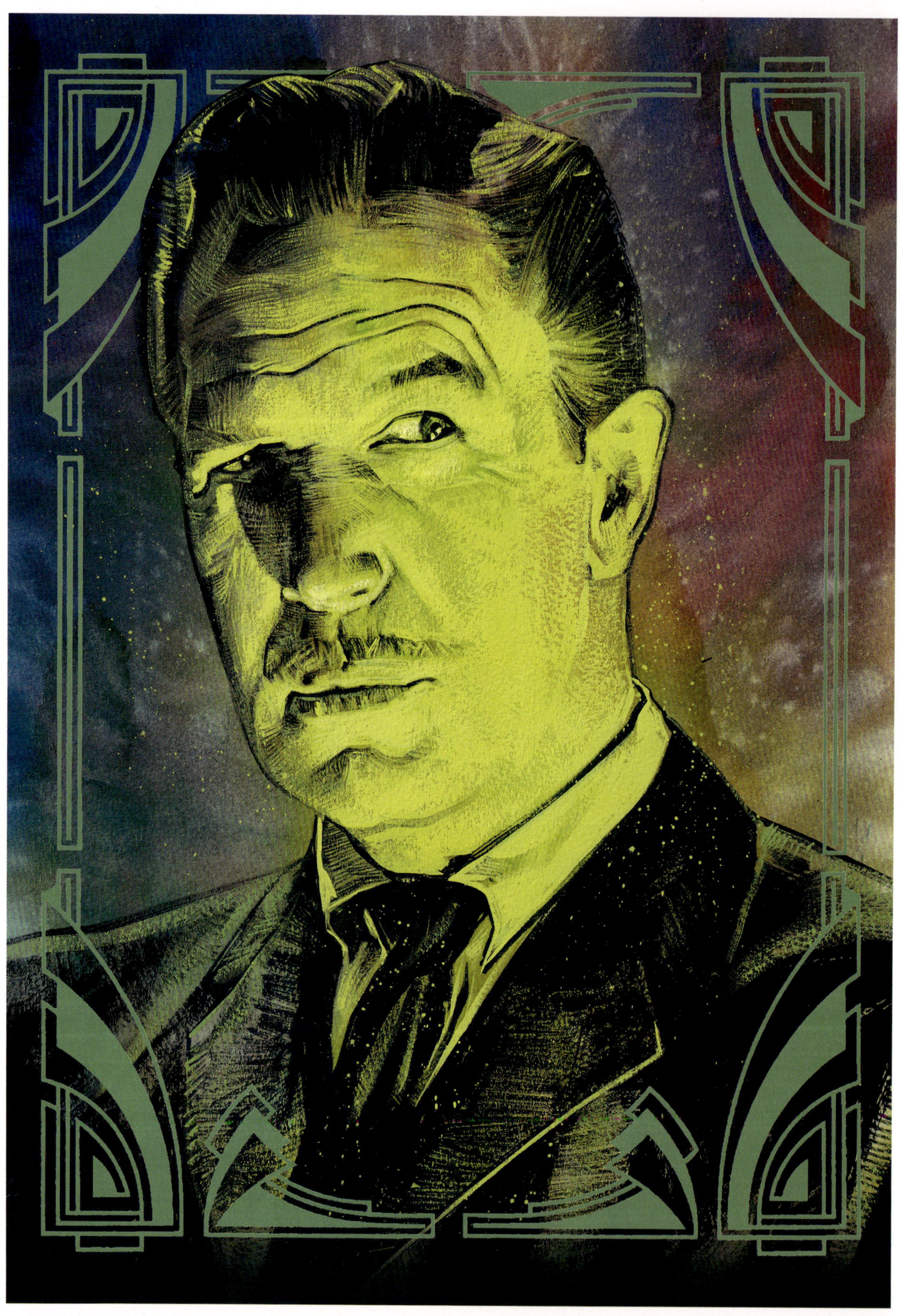

PRIVATE COMMISSIONS

The appeal of a private commission — one that doesn't function in the public domain and doesn't generate profit at the expense of a license holder (which would be piracy) — is the freedom to imagine the advertising without the constraints of legal requirements and billing, or the demands of agents and actors. Commissioned by individuals or closed groups, these items exist for film fans in limited editions. It is, if you must call it so, "fan art", but it's a case for experimentation within an art form that's often been the subject of scorn, written off as low-brow and vulgar (two descriptions that I delight in!).

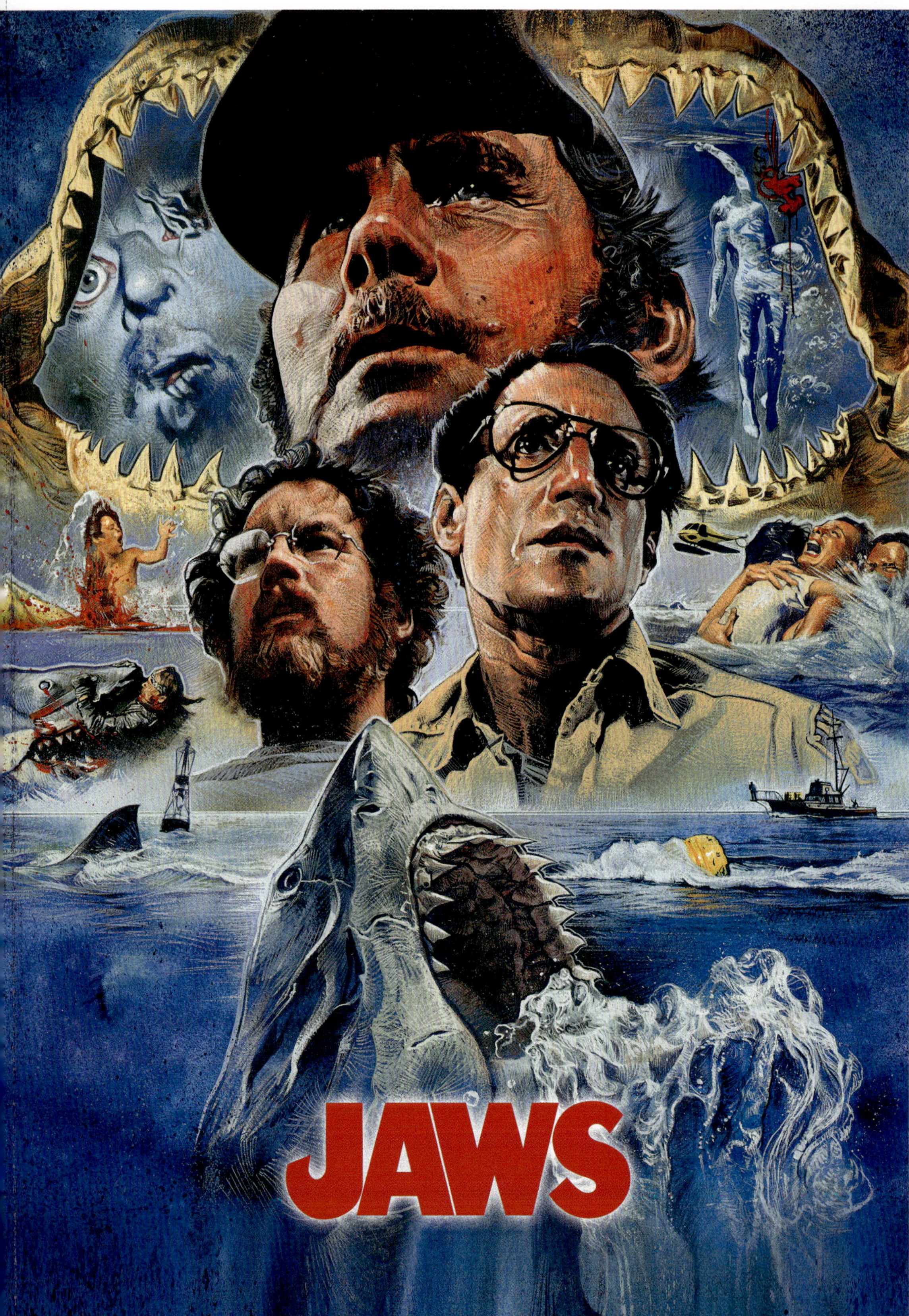

LEFT: *Jaws* (2020).

One of the drawbacks of any commission is the non-negotiable client requirements! The original poster for *Jaws* is a magnificent example of stark imagery; it's one of my favourite posters. My client sent me a list of scenes and characters he wished to include. The resulting composition is an exercise in assigning a hierarchy. A latter-day Moby Dick and Captain Ahab, Robert Shaw and "Bruce" are the central pillar. The floating head was the memorable jump scare for me as a 15-year-old, which is why I added the extra element. The shark is an amalgamation of the animatronic versions in the film and sourced wildlife photography. I wanted it to look as monstrous as possible. There are two horizon lines, as one wasn't enough to hold all the images.

RIGHT: *Mandy* (2021).

I was unfamiliar with the film until I received this group commission, but I was instantly a fan. There were many options for imagery, so I chose those which could best represent my response to the film. I tried to steer away from existing posters for the film and represent a feature that was less explored. The original selected sketch didn't include the Bill Duke character, but he was added at the group's request.

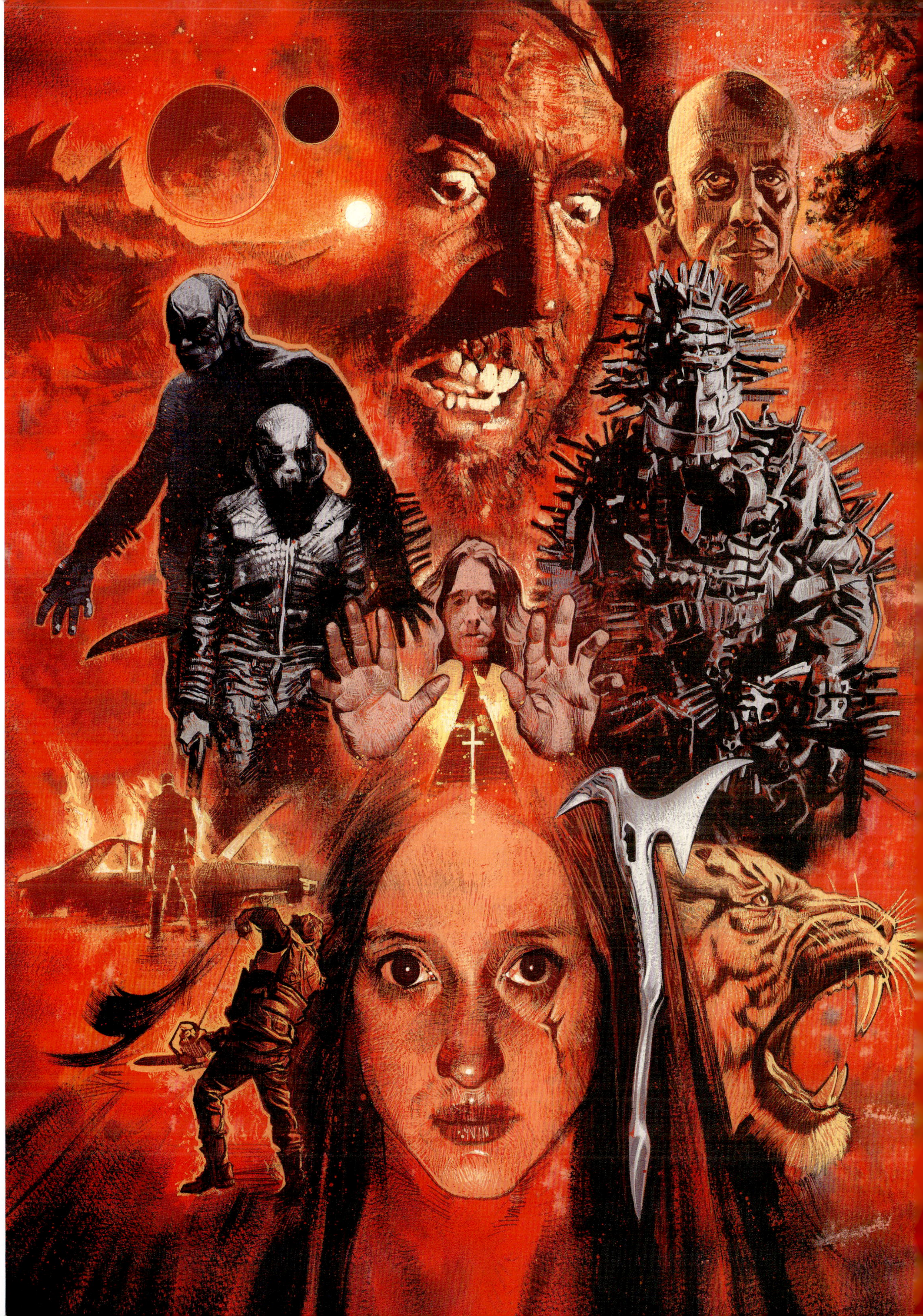

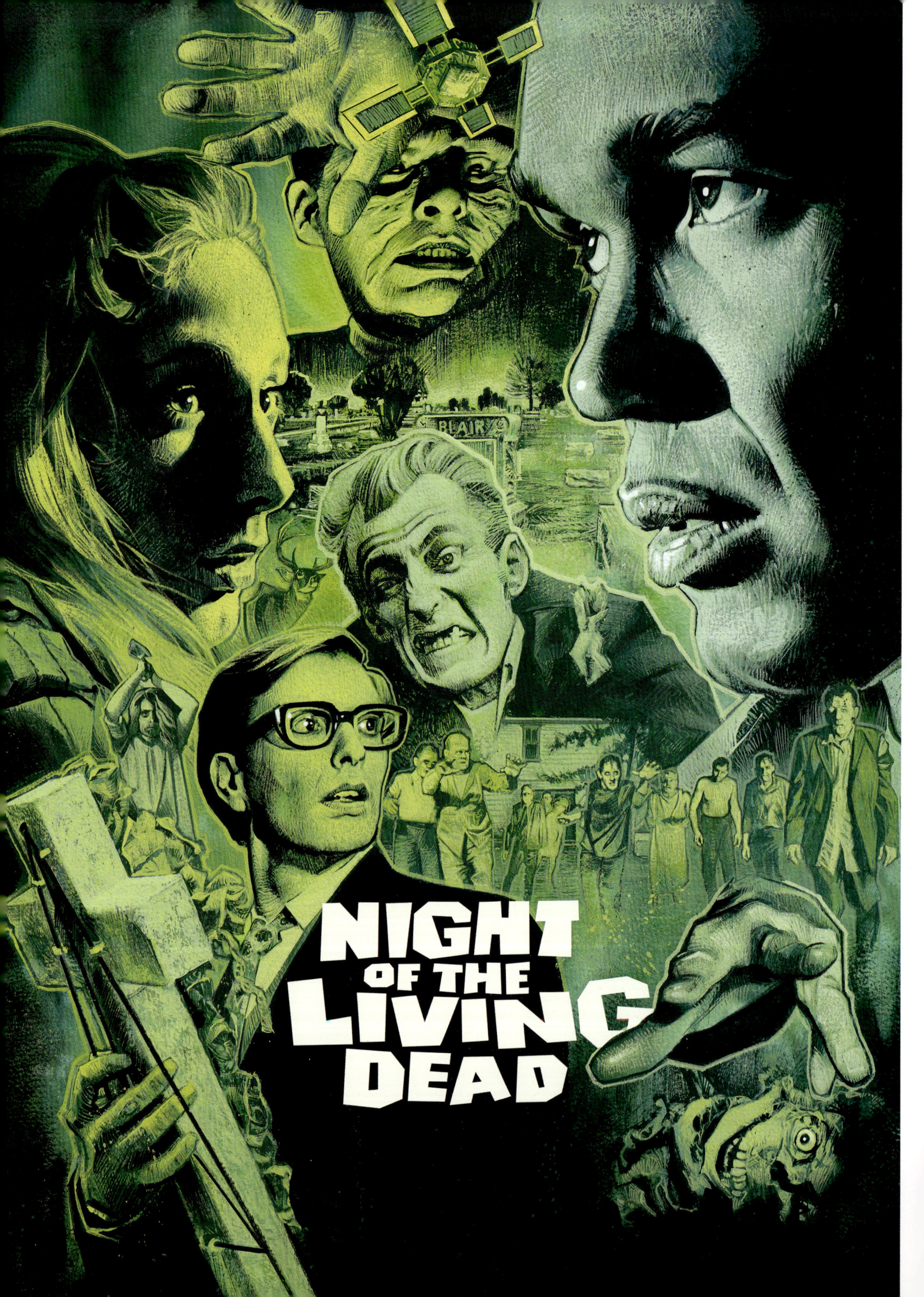

BLAIR
NIGHT OF THE LIVING DEAD

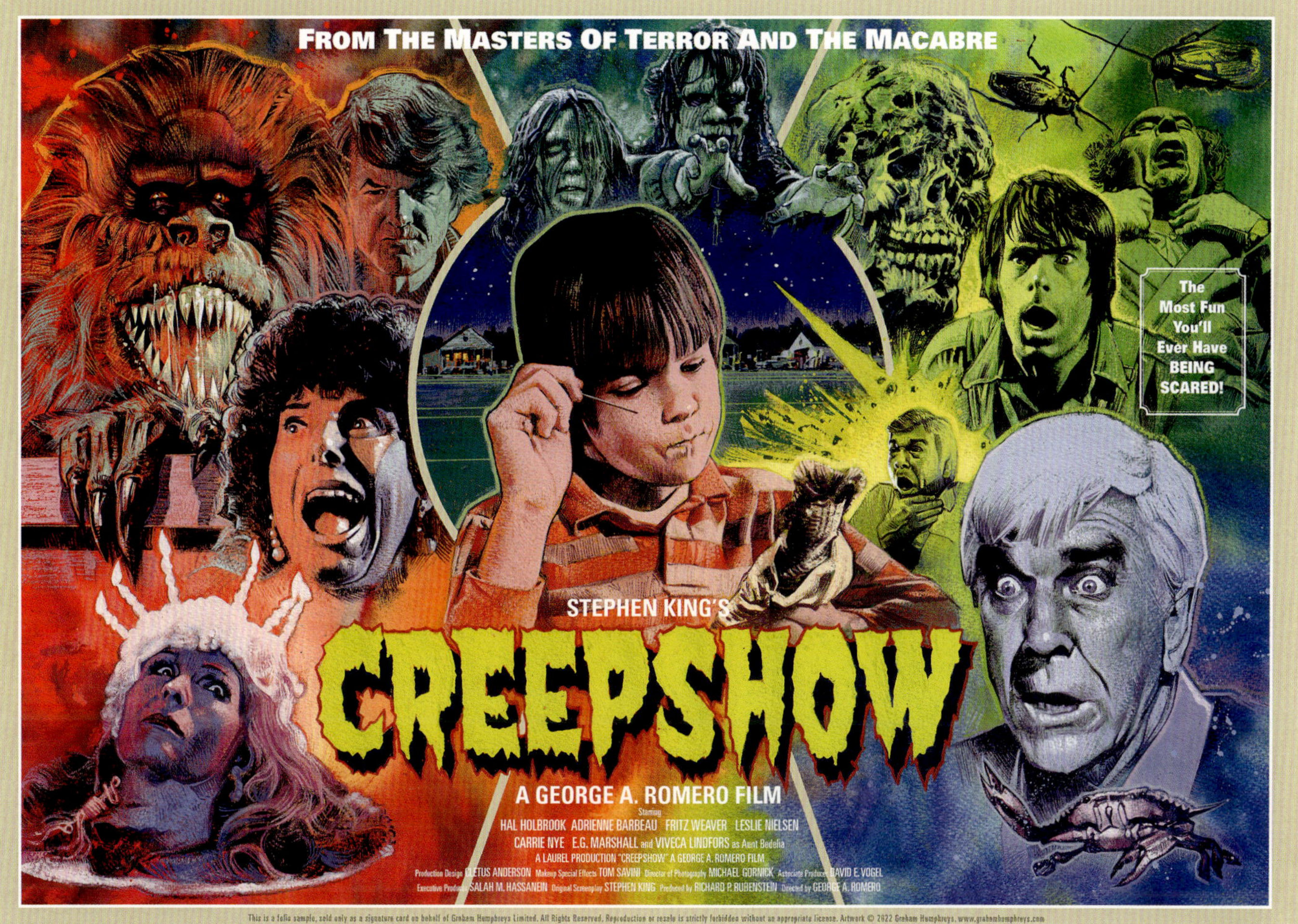

ABOVE: *Creepshow* (2022).

Initially commissioned as a fundraising vehicle for GARF (George A Romero Foundation) by a friend, the foundation chose to reject the commission, for reasons unknown. However, the artwork was already completed and exists in this poster form. My layout takes inspiration from a comic-book framing device. The colours are also intended to convey a comic-book feel. Each narrative segment is represented by my choice of the best expressions I could grab from the film.

LEFT: *Night of the Living Dead* (2022).

The client specified a black and white poster to best reflect the film. Although I've painted mono images from the outset of my career (when full-colour printing was still prohibitively expensive for some publications), I always prefer to use colour. I stated that I could deliver the mono image but would use a colour as my starting point. This allowed me to offer two versions. Always hoping to add underrepresented elements, I chose to include the satellite, which is referred to in the film as the "Venus Probe" but is never actually seen. Being the identified cause of the zombification, it seemed critical for the visual narrative (however, the term "zombie" is not used in the film — they're referred to as "ghouls").

I will never forget climbing the dark staircase, moving through a dim hallway and arriving quietly at an ominous door. With a few resounding knocks, the door swung open to reveal a young and engaging Graham Humphreys. The year was 1989. I'd travelled to London for a fan-funded film festival. It was an adventure, to say the least. Scott Spiegel and I were promoting his first (and KNB'S first) film, *Intruder*, and ended up sleeping on the floor of someone's flat in London, drifting through the city somewhat aimlessly. The last night before we flew back to the States, I found myself in the company of someone whose work had influenced and inspired me. Graham had done the UK poster art for Scott and Sam Raimi's opus *Evil Dead 2*, so our host thought it would be fun for us to meet.

I'd grown up with a fascination for movie poster art. I was instantly drawn to the style and composition that, in those days, was one of the premier ways to fill movie theatre seats. Of course, you had trailers and radio spots (yes, radio), but it was the newspaper ads/movie posters that seduced and lured unsuspecting patrons into a dark theatre with promises of monsters, madmen, and mayhem.

A true art form that is sadly underappreciated. I didn't attach names to the artists back then. Still, I quickly learned about Reynold Brown (*Creature From the Black Lagoon*, *Tarantula*), Robert McGinnis (*Thunderball*, *Breakfast at Tiffany's*), Tom Jung (*The Empire Strikes Back*, *Raging Bull*), John Berkey (*The Towering Inferno*, *King Kong*), Frank McCarty (*The Valley of Gwangi*, *Where Eagles Dare*) and Bob Peak (*Apocalypse Now*, *Rollerball*), to name but a few. Graham's body of work stands alongside these men who single-handedly touch upon evocative imagery, use of contrast, and, most notably, colour to draw you in and make you want more. Graham's style is distinct and ferociously original in its execution. His collage-style layout and near-perfect likenesses celebrate the material in its entirety. Adding in his penchant for and love of horror and monsters leaves us with his unique celebration of everything from Christopher Lee in *Dracula* to reimagined poster art for *Jaws* and Romero's *Dawn of the Dead* (the original of which I had to purchase immediately).

It's exceedingly difficult to describe the allure, but it's immediate and lasting. Graham's dedication and affection show through in every pencil sketch and coloured wash; he creates life like a modern-day Dr Frankenstein in each of his creations, which are distinctly his yet somehow familiar, as if they belonged to the film all along. I'm proud to have several of his original pieces adorning the walls of my house in Los Angeles. If he keeps going like this, I'll need more walls.

GREG NICOTERO,
Paris, France

RIGHT: *Dawn of the Dead* (2020).

Armed with a shopping list (appropriately!) of moments and characters requested by the client, my alternative film poster plays with the idea of heaven and hell, with blue as the predominant colour over the fiery oranges below. With so much to represent, I required three horizons, a device I used in a follow-up commission, *Jaws*. My original sketches featured more bikers. However, the client didn't like that particular plot feature, so they became more background.

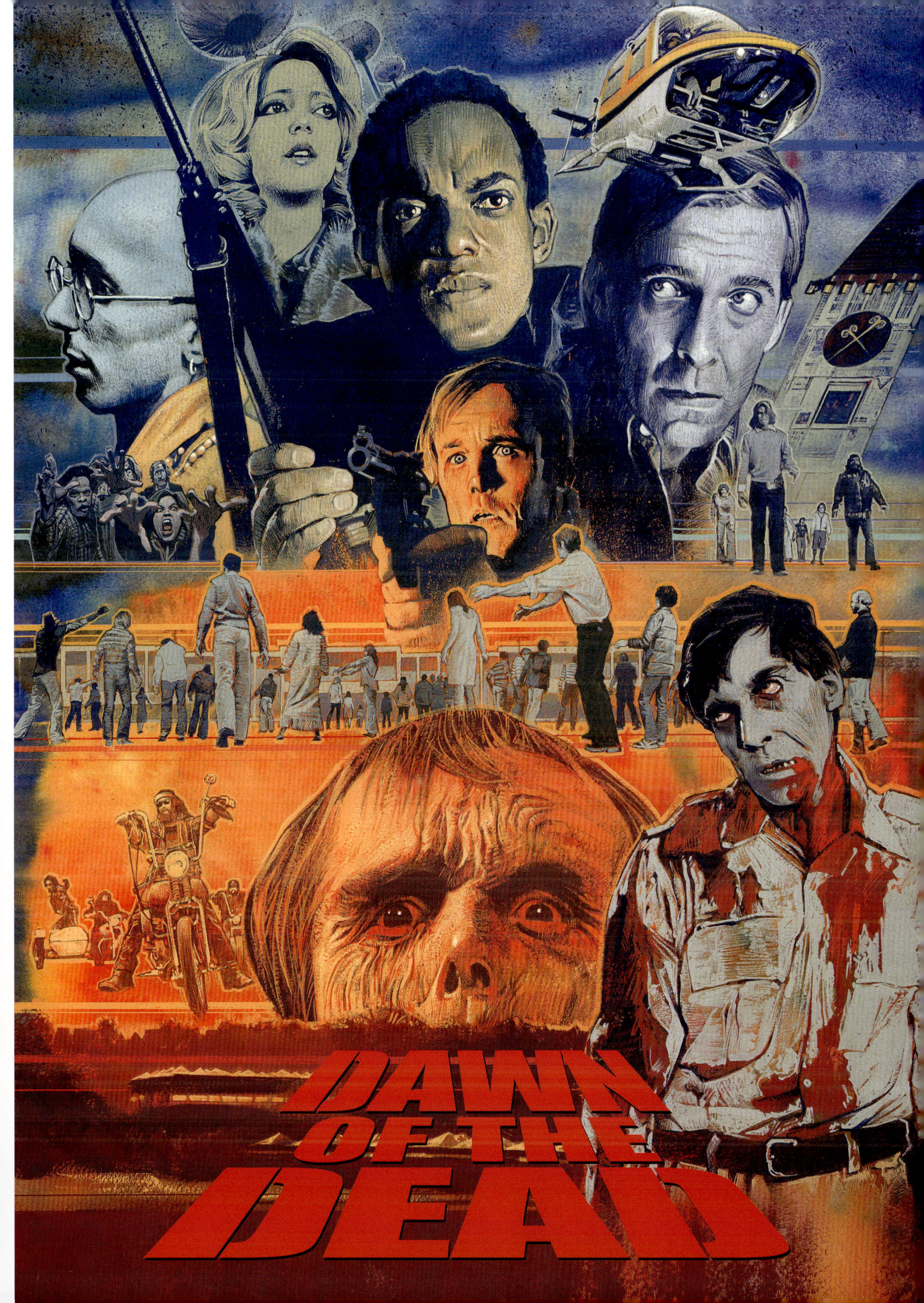

DAWN OF THE DEAD

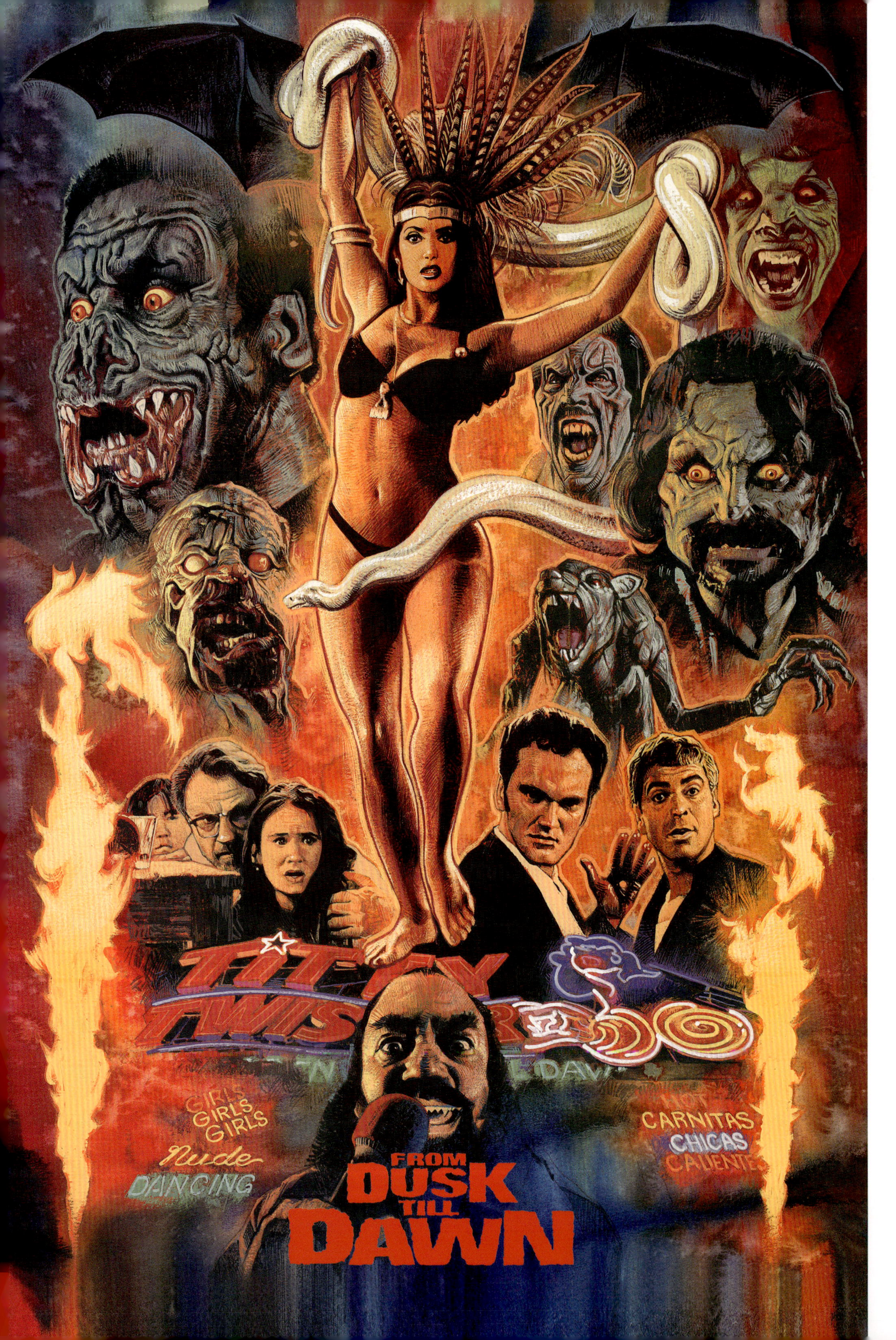

TITTY TWISTER
GIRLS GIRLS GIRLS
Nude
DANCING
HOT
CARNITAS
CHICAS
CALIENTE
FROM
DUSK
TILL
DAWN

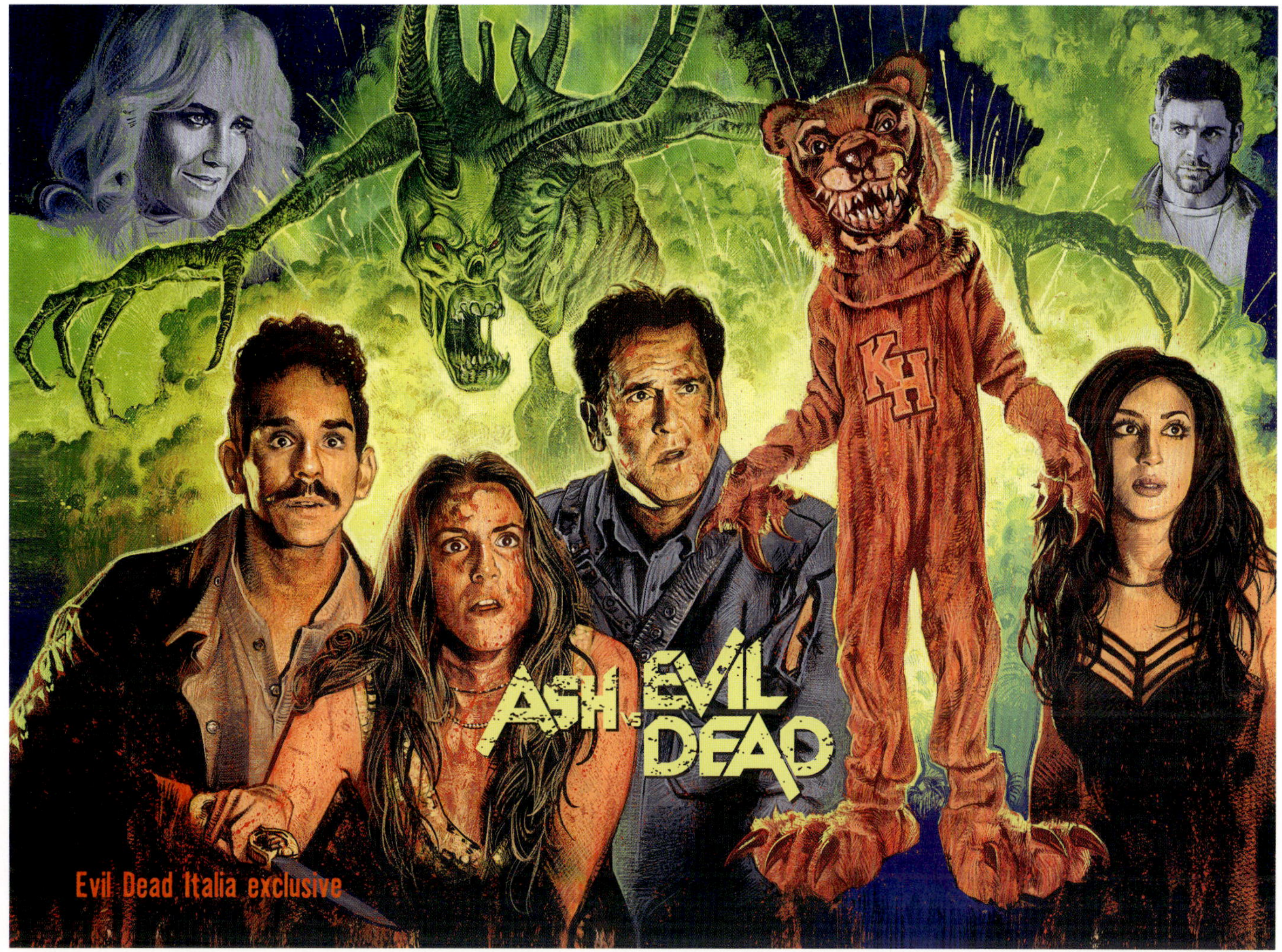

ABOVE: *Ash vs Evil Dead* (2021).

My client was specific about the choice of imagery and supplied
good reference material, so my composition was already locked down.
My input was putting paint to paper and making the colour choices.

LEFT: *From Dusk Till Dawn* (2021).

One of the first Photoshop posters I created for a UK quad campaign
was for this film (illustration having fallen out of favour in 1996). Here
was my opportunity to throw some paint at the subject, free of commercial
constraint. With no requirement to withhold the horror twists that arrive
midway through the plot, I was able to make the poster a full-blooded
vampire study.

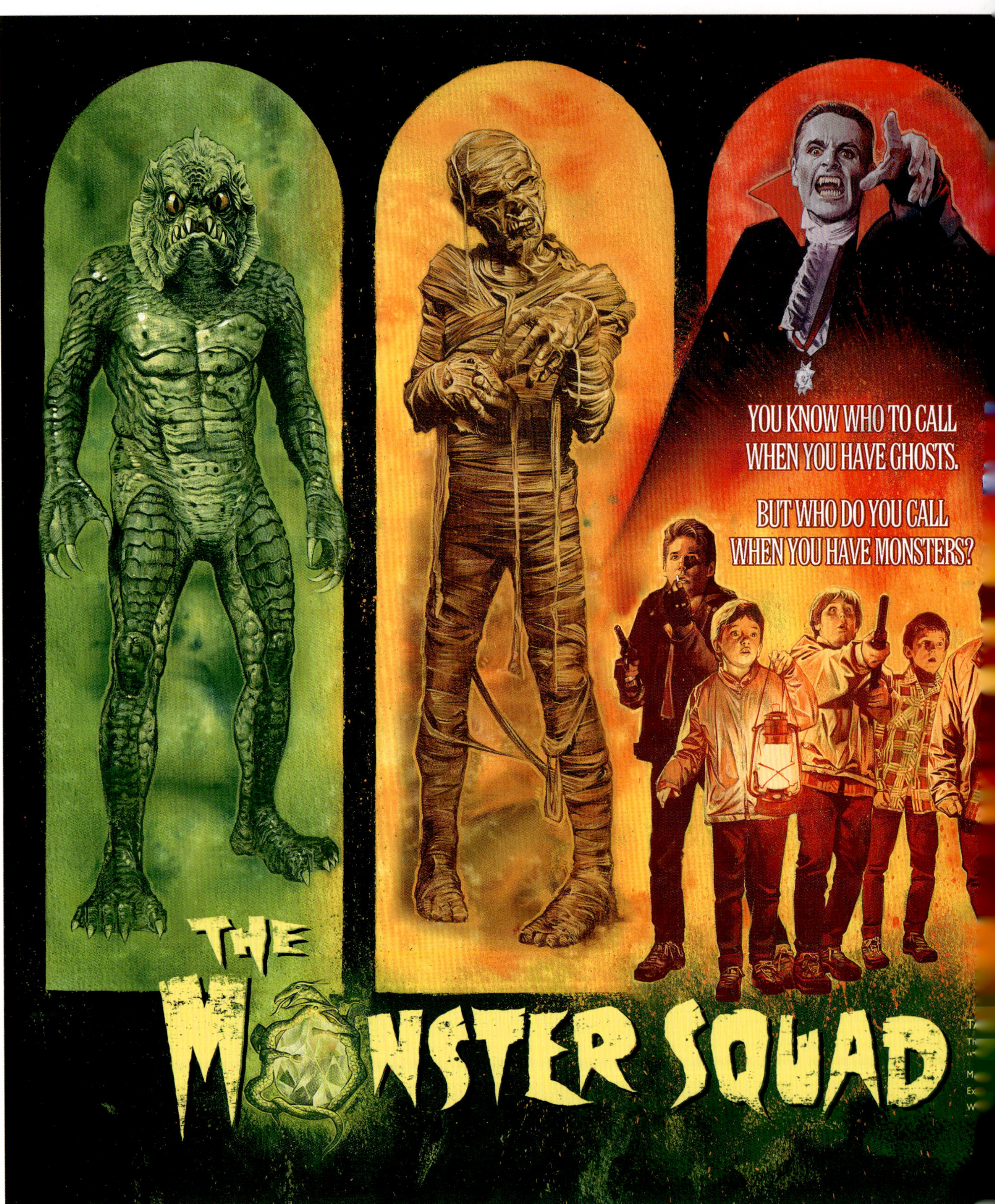
YOU KNOW WHO TO CALL
WHEN YOU HAVE GHOSTS.

BUT WHO DO YOU CALL
WHEN YOU HAVE MONSTERS?

THE MONSTER SQUAD

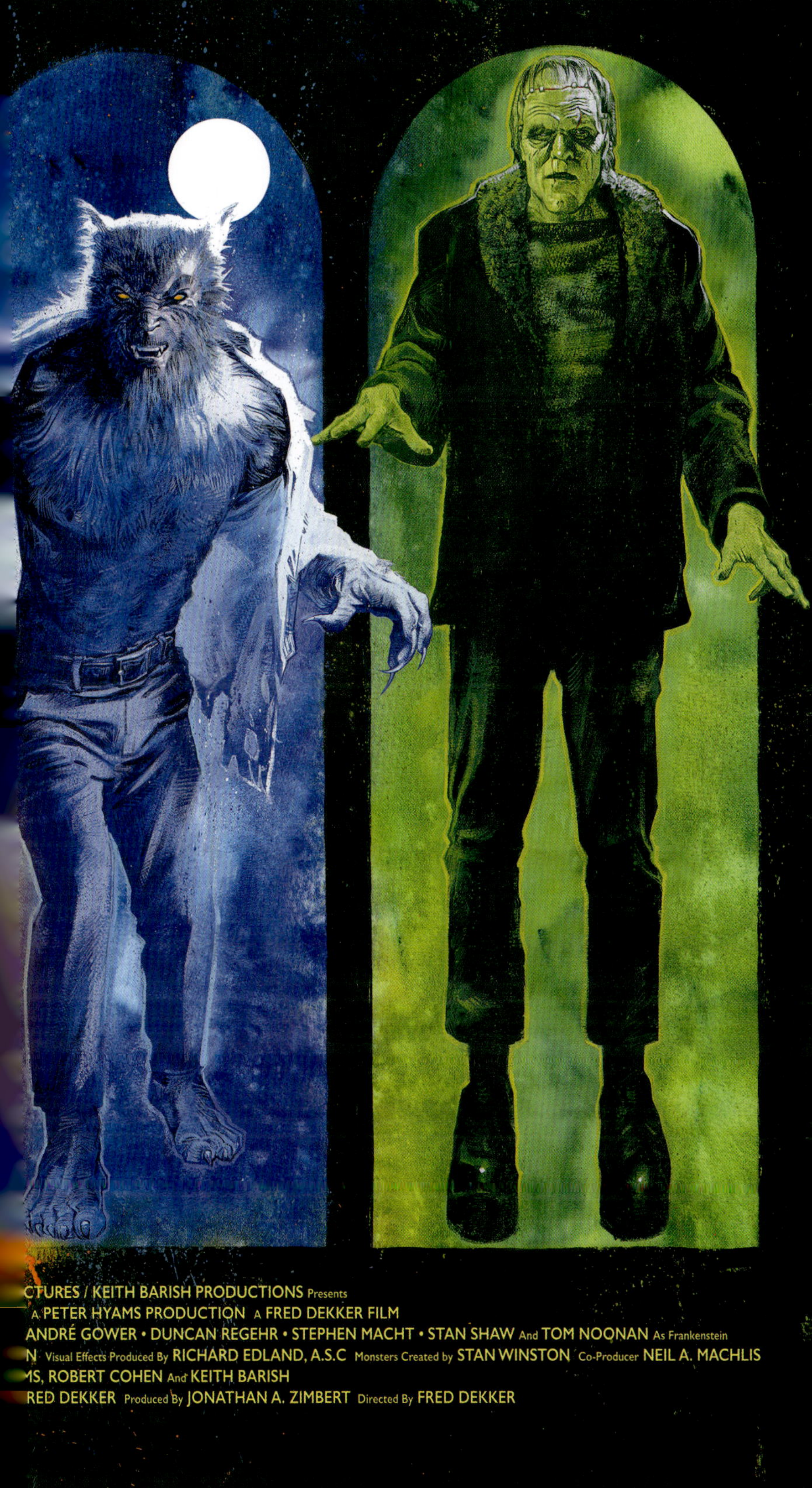

LEFT: *Monster Squad* (2020).

The film is a fan favourite, partly because of its loving homage to the Universal monsters of the 1930s and '40s, which, despite the film's sub-Spielberg family appeal, managed to deliver some convincing micro-horror.

The brief required all the main cast — monsters and boys — as full-length figures, making it impossible to fulfil within the painting dimensions I normally work with (detail is too difficult to retain at a small scale). The only solution required painting individual elements that would need Photoshop to bring them together. Composing the 10 characters without compromising the brief was a challenge. I recalled an advert for the Aurora Monster hobby kits from the 1960s, each character within an arched frame, arranged in a row. My design is a homage to those hobby kits as much as to the film.

As is common to many of the films from which I'm sourcing my material, there were few full-body shots of the boys that had any reasonable quality (they were mostly blurred and soft focus, and in still form). I had no option but to photograph myself in the various poses, distorting as necessary before adding the sourced close-up headshots. It's why they're all wearing the same clothes!

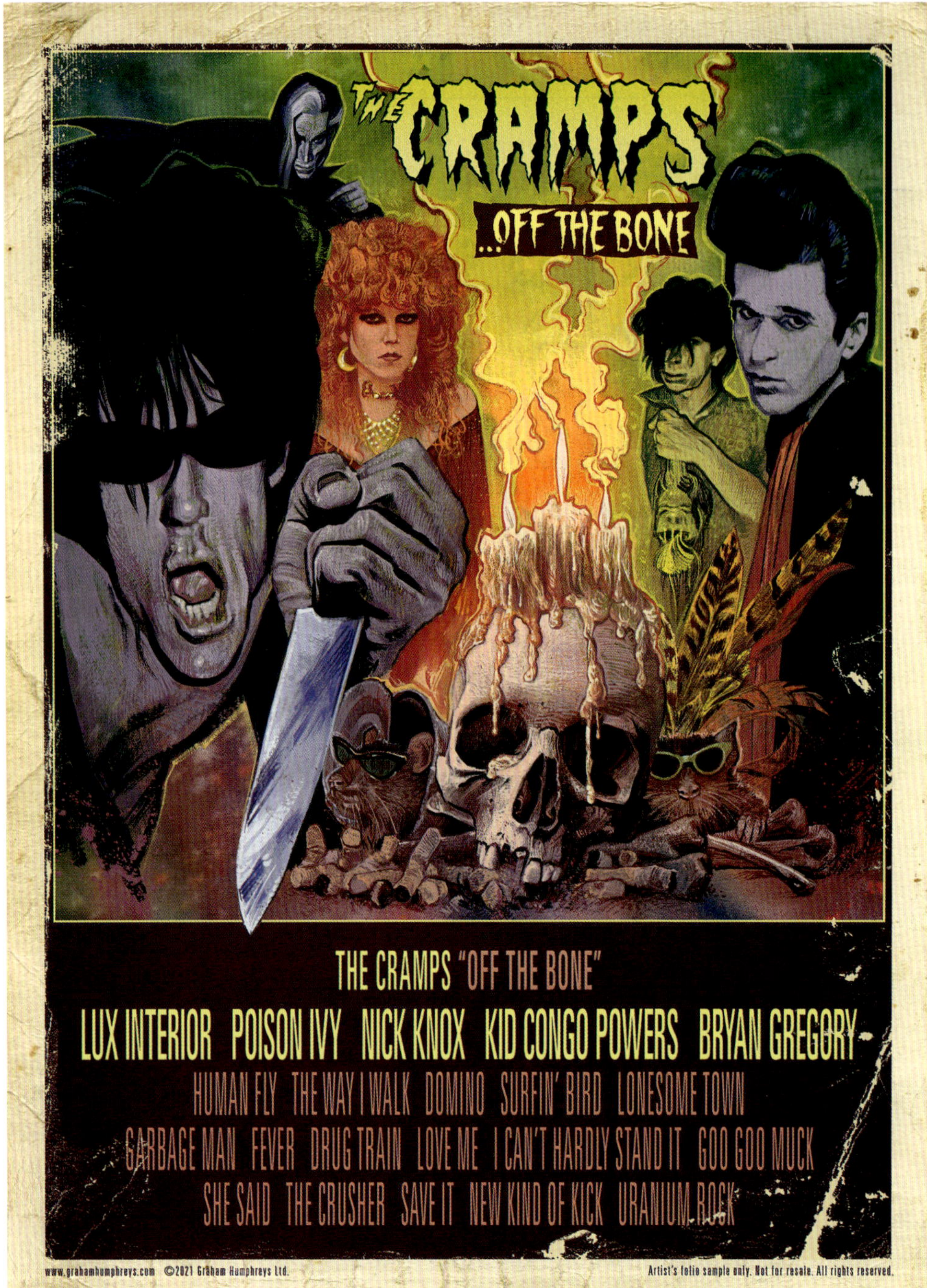

LEFT: *Off The Bone* (2021).

In 1983, I designed an LP cover for a compilation of songs by the US band The Cramps. In capturing some of the B-movie aesthetic represented in many of their tracks, I thought a 3-D cover (requiring red and green filter glasses) would match perfectly. It was constructed using black and white painted elements, photocopied and pasted onto sheets of acetate. This allowed me to shift the layers for a second capture of the artwork to create the second-eye view.

The album proved popular among the group's fans. Some years after I'd designed the cover, I felt that the level of work was crude and resolved to re-create it in colour. A window of opportunity allowed me to revisit the project and achieve my aim. I used the image to create an imagined film poster.

RIGHT: *Hellraiser* (2020).

This film has a wide fan base, so I knew I had to create something reverential to the subject. I watched the film twice to decide on my focus. Most of the existing posters for the film centre on the Cenobite characters, in particular, "Pinhead". However, the film centres on the characters Julia and Frank, with the Cenobites providing background interest. This is reflected in my composition. The windows in the background interior are mirrored in the exterior of the house below. I also chose imagery that tends to get overlooked (such as the carnation and vagrant character). As this was painted during a lockdown, I used the opportunity to have some overdue work done on my flat — pieces of exposed plasterwork provided reference material.

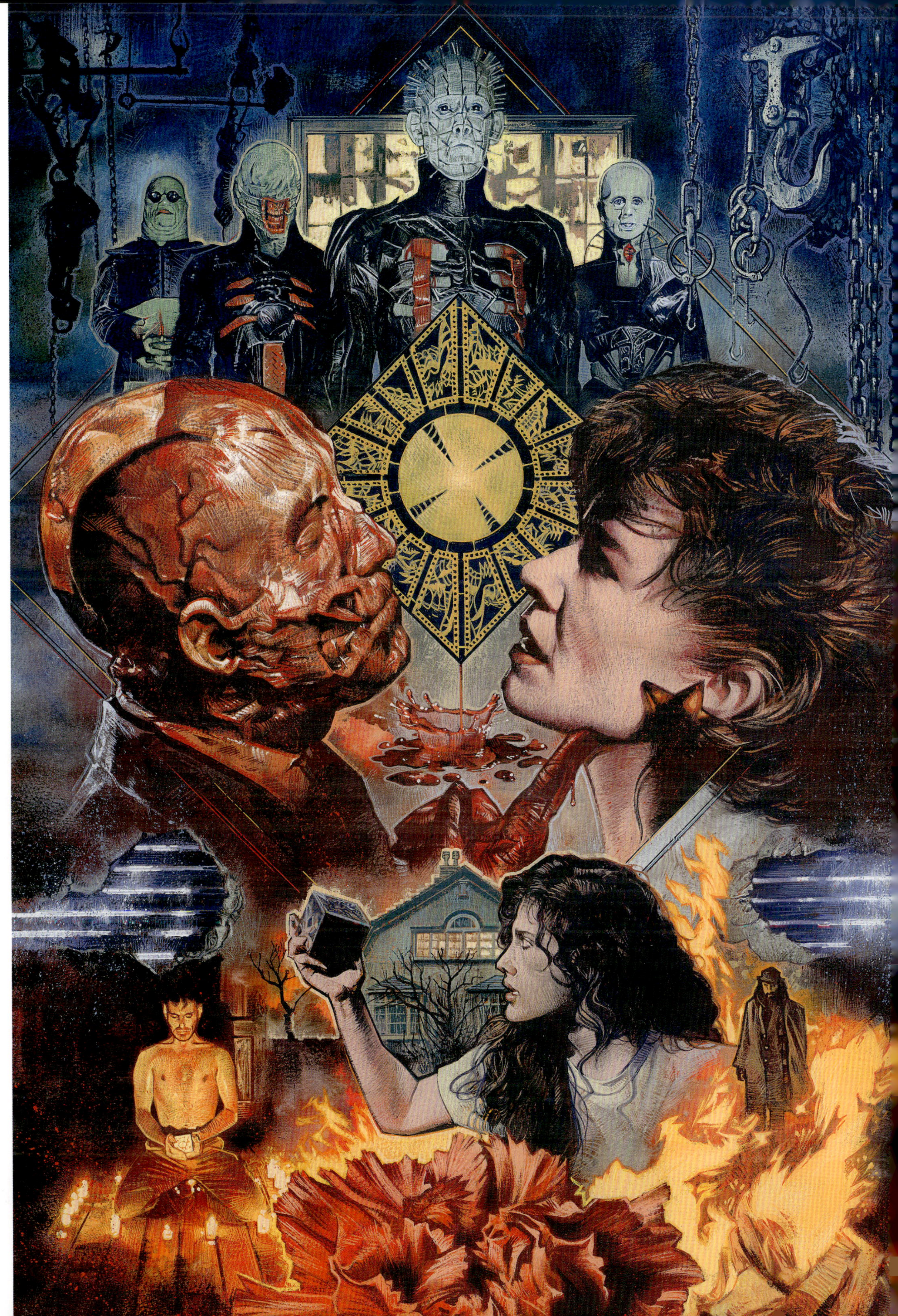

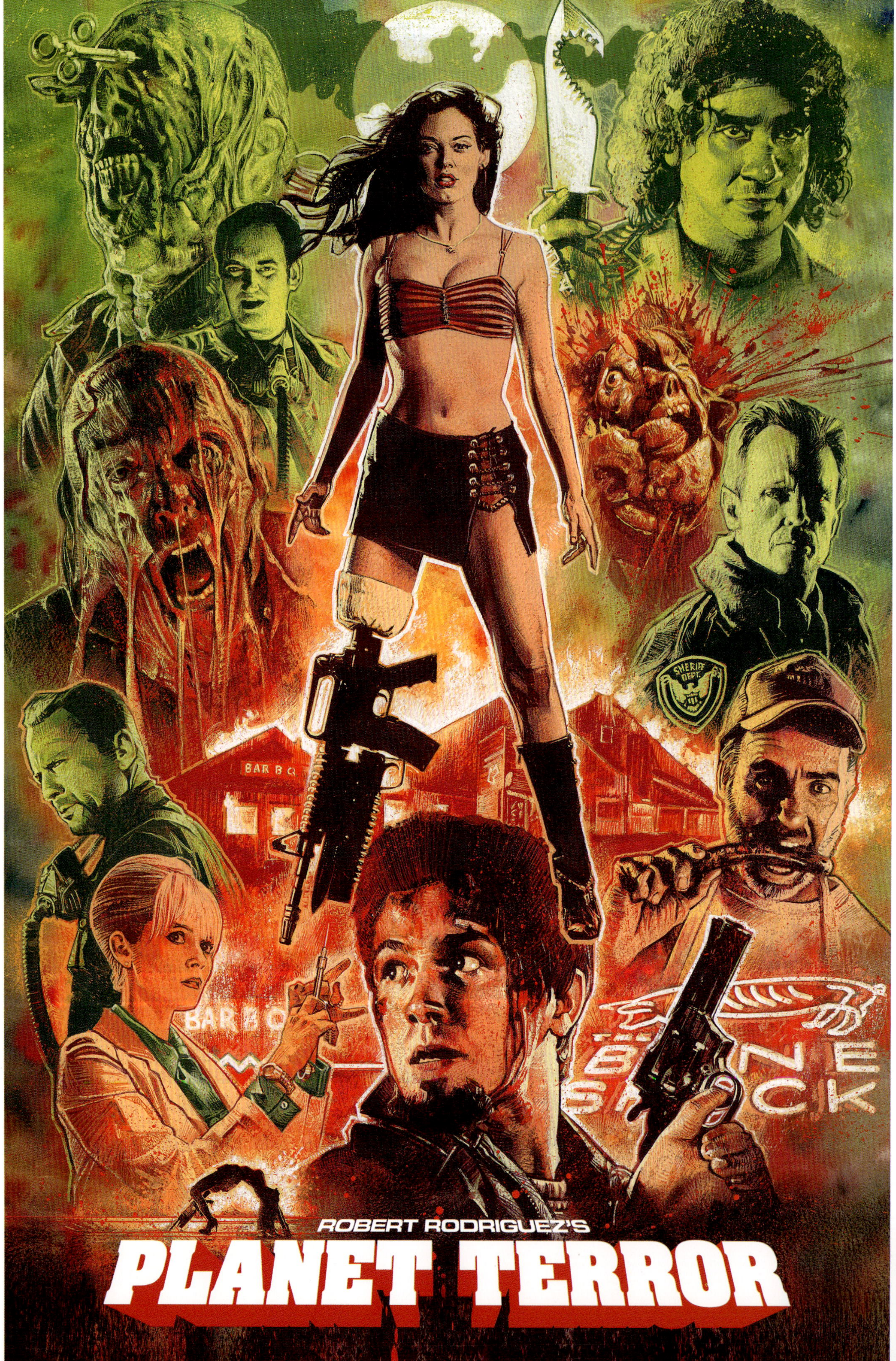
BAR B Q
SHERIFF DEPT
ROBERT RODRIGUEZ'S
PLANET TERROR

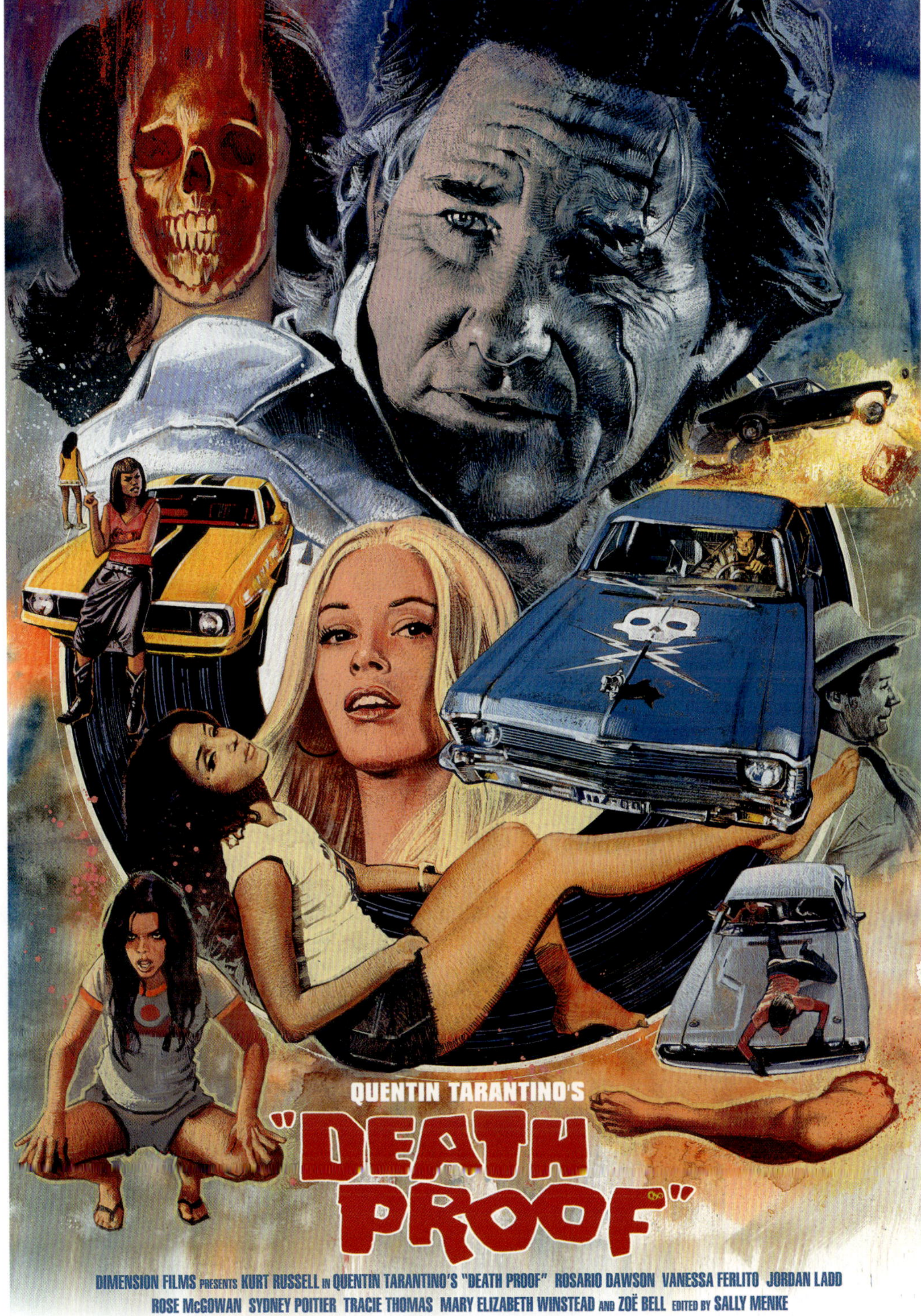

LEFT: *Death Proof* (2023).

Completing the Tarantino/ Rodriguez trilogy (*From Dusk Till Dawn, Planet Terror, Death Proof*), this was not a commission I would have accepted otherwise (I'm not a fan of the film). But I kept a professional approach and completed it to the best of my ability, considering the source material was very difficult (due to the artificial film distressing). The client insisted on including all the characters, making it a complex layout to control. There was some resistance to the skull at the top (this was a group commission with feedback on four sketch options), but although this isn't seen in detail, the scene exists in the film, so I argued it should remain.

OPPOSITE: *Planet Terror* (2021).

A companion piece to *From Dusk Till Dawn*, the layout is built in a similar way but using a different colour theme. With so many elements competing, colour is the only way to control the composition.

PAGE 124: *Halloween III* (2019).

A private commission allows me to explore the parts of a film otherwise ignored or underrepresented. Pivotal to the plot in *Halloween III* is the stolen pillar from Stonehenge. I wanted to ensure it was given a special place in the poster.

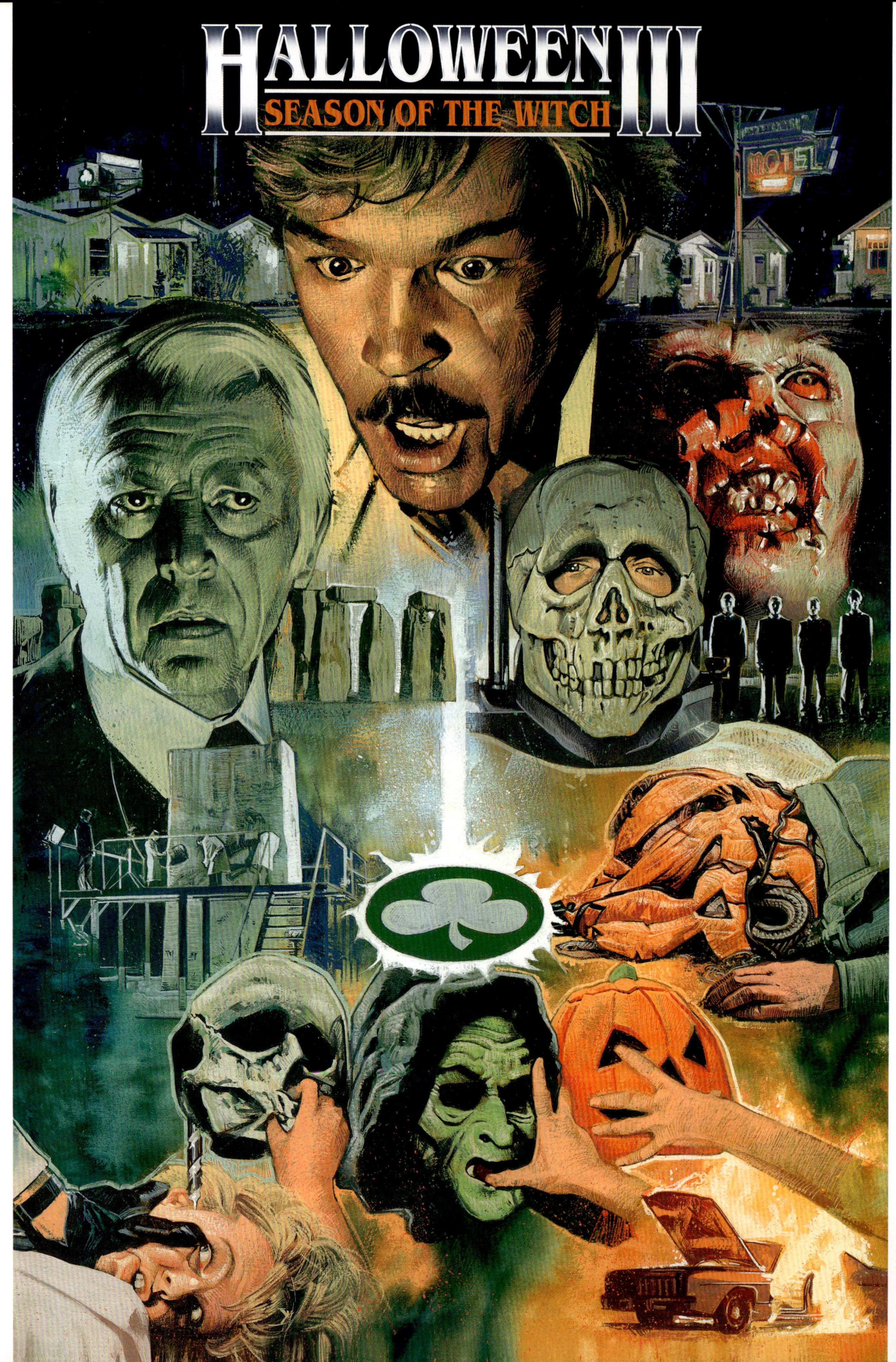

HALLOWEEN III
SEASON OF THE WITCH
MOTEL

EDITORIAL

My first post-college, real-world commissions came from publishers of magazines and educational books. I worked for the music press at the same time as providing illustrations for various journals. In the 1980s, prohibitive print costs meant that a significant percentage of my editorial work was black and white. I had to learn techniques that would ensure my work still carried an impact. These lessons in texture and contrast would later influence all my colour work. Book covers were always exciting because they afforded a fantastic opportunity for exposure and an entry-level form of respectability.

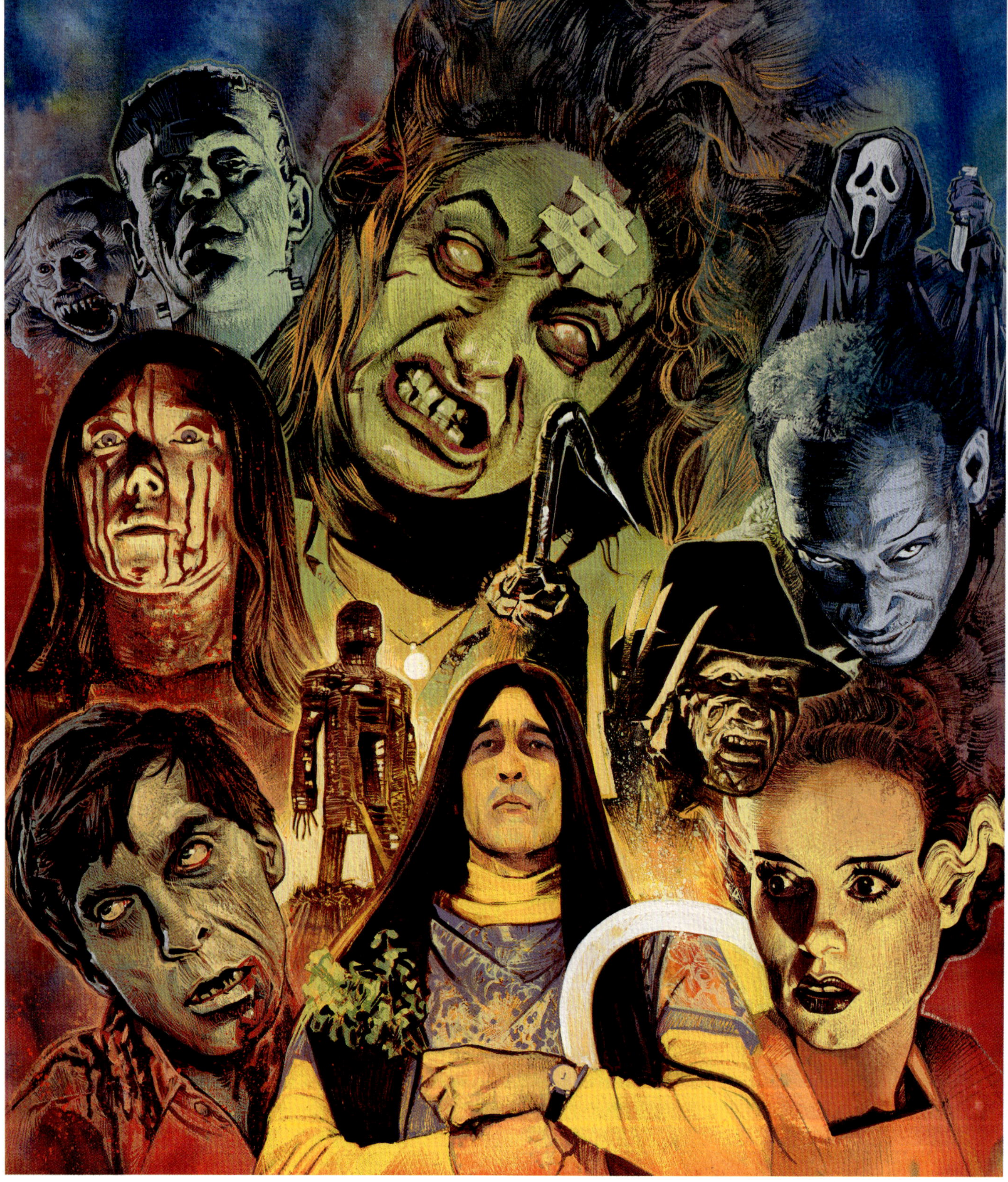

ABOVE: *Starburst* (2021), Starburst Magazine Ltd; magazine cover.

My cover for a special Christmas edition illustrates several films that are featured in the Top 100 Greatest Horror Films listed within. I was asked to pick some of the best-known characters, arranged as I wished.

RIGHT: *The Long-Lost Autobiography of George Melies* (2020), self-published (Jon Spira); book bonus print.

This required little more than a central portrait of the pioneering filmmaker surrounded by images from his fantasy creations. As all the reference material is monochrome, I just needed to add the colours I imagined the images might have been.

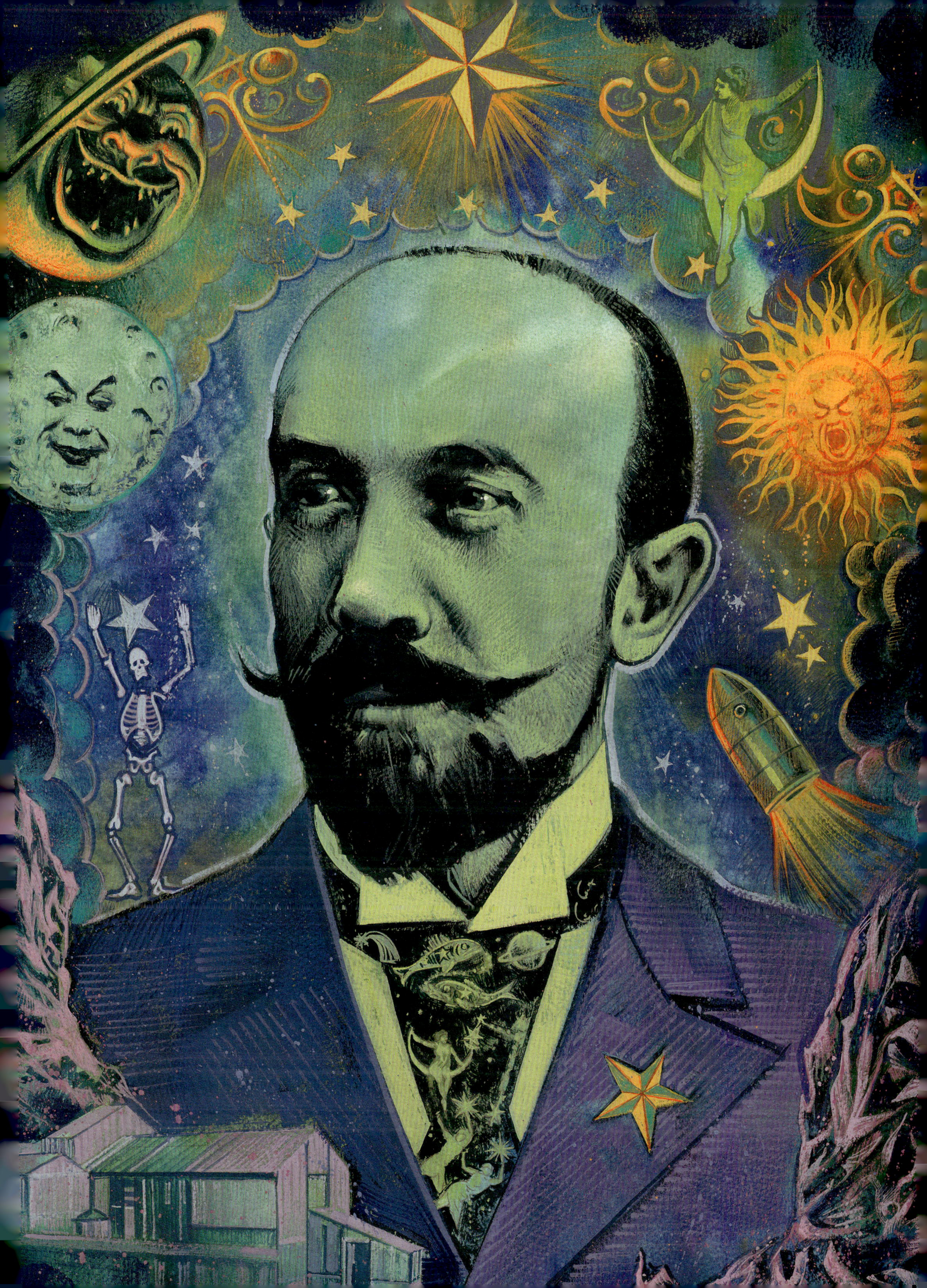

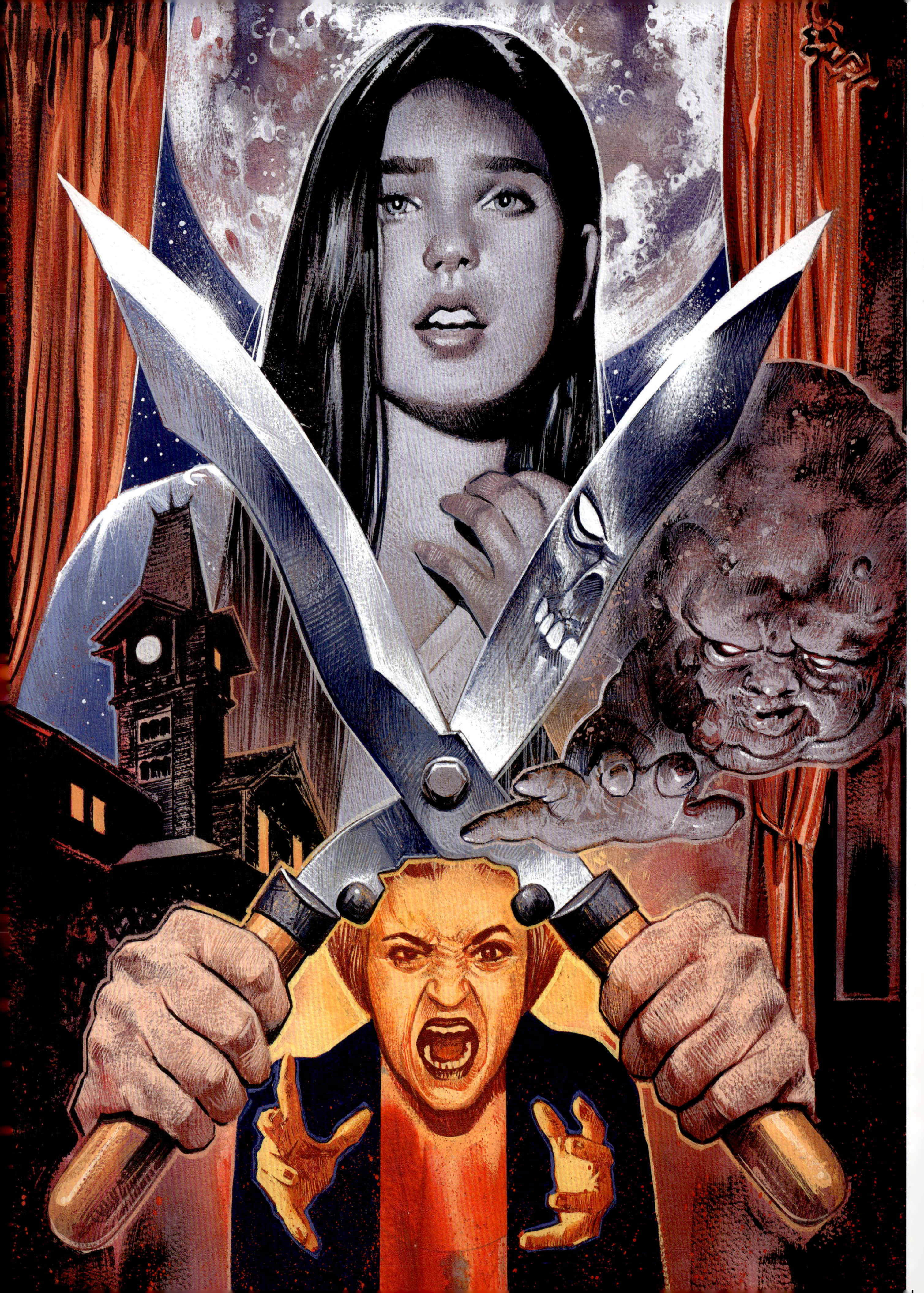

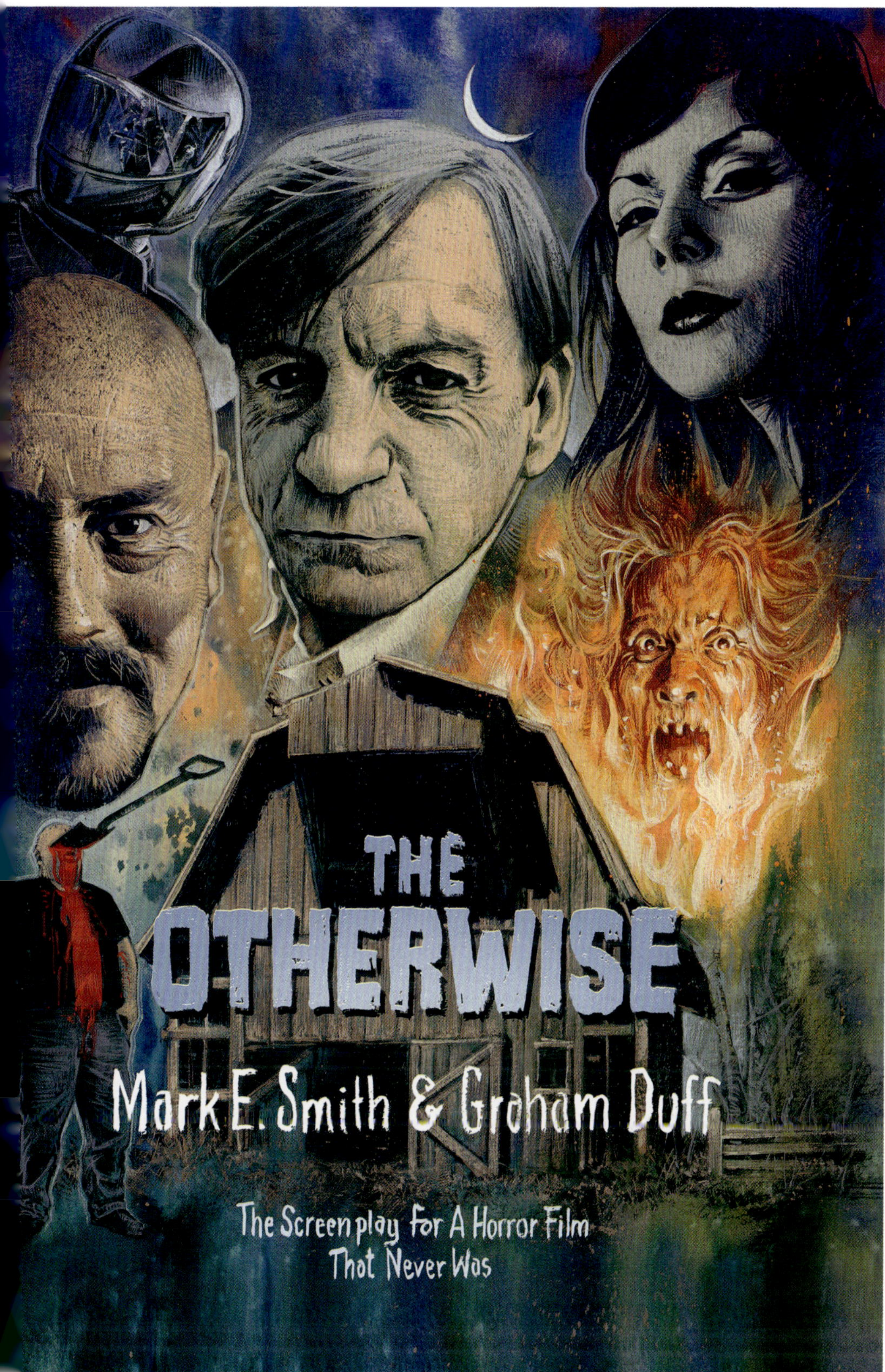

The book is the film treatment of
an unrealised horror film project
conceived by Mark E. Smith (of
the pioneering British band The
Fall) and writer Graham Duff.
The two authors are the focus
of the cover, plus elements that
relate to the screenplay.

OPPOSITE: *Clock Tower* (2022),
Lost In Cult; specialist magazine
cover.

Described as "a survival horror
point-and-click adventure
video game" (a series created
by Hifumi Kono), the plot is
described thus: "the story follows
Jennifer Simpson, a young girl
searching for a way out of a
mansion in Norway while evading
Scissorman." I was asked to
create a homage to the game,
which is itself a homage to
Dario Argento, specifically the
film *Phenomena*. The character
Jennifer Simpson is based on
Jennifer Connelly, from Argento's
film. My artwork for the original
UK release of *Phenomena* (re-
titled *Creepers* for the heavily
cut UK release) was one of the
reasons I was approached with
the commission.

When I was 12, my uncle returned from a holiday in the UK and visited our house with an armful of gifts for all of us. He handed me a cardboard tube, and I opened the end to pull out what was inside. To my amazement, it was a watercolour-painted movie poster in the good old Hammer horror films style, but with my name replacing those of the actual people who worked on the film!!! *Vampire Circus*, directed by Howard Berger! Written by Howard Berger! Produced by Howard Berger! It quickly became my prized possession as although my name littered the poster, it was the painted artwork that made my head spin and my heart pound! It immediately took pride of place on my bedroom wall, between my original *Jaws* poster and the Hildebrandt Brothers' *Star Wars* poster. By the way, those two posters are my all-time favourites.

There was always something extraordinary about the Hammer movie posters. They were so well illustrated — so much so that I felt I could see the figures on the posters breathing. I also loved all the blood and boobs on these posters, as everything was heightened to thrill us young adolescent boys dying to see these films. I'm a huge fan of illustrated horror, sci-fi, and fantasy book covers, so much so that when I was writing my book, I went to the publishers and pleaded my case to have the great Graham Humphreys do a hand-painted cover for it. They couldn't see the importance it had to the book and me! I knew all Monster Kids would love it! I even did a poll online, and the illustrated option won! In the end, I lost the battle with the publisher and found another place in the book to feature Graham's beautiful work. Even Guillermo del Toro said the art should have been the cover, and who knows better than GDT?!

Seeing a well-illustrated film poster takes me back to the days when movies were magical. They promised an event and not a product. You knew from Drew Struzan's *Raiders of the Lost Ark* poster that seeing Harrison Ford for the first time as Indiana Jones would be something special. It was a promise the artist made to the audience that this would be a great film, and I was never disappointed.

HOWARD BERGER,
Los Angeles, California

RIGHT: *Masters of Make-Up Effects* (2022), Welbeck; book illustration.

Originally conceived as the book cover by my client (Howard Berger, one of the authors), it was relegated to the chapter heading section by the publisher, who decided on a photographic option. The painting has been widely used to promote the book, so it has a life of its own. My brief required a composite of multiple make-up effect portraits, risking an unfocussed mess.

We whittled the list down, and a hierarchy was established. Lon Chaney's originally sourced image (with his legendary make-up box) didn't seem monstrous enough, so I substituted the headshot from another source. The primary red of Tim Curry's "Darkness" character suggested the contrasting blue background. This is a particularly colourful painting as a result.

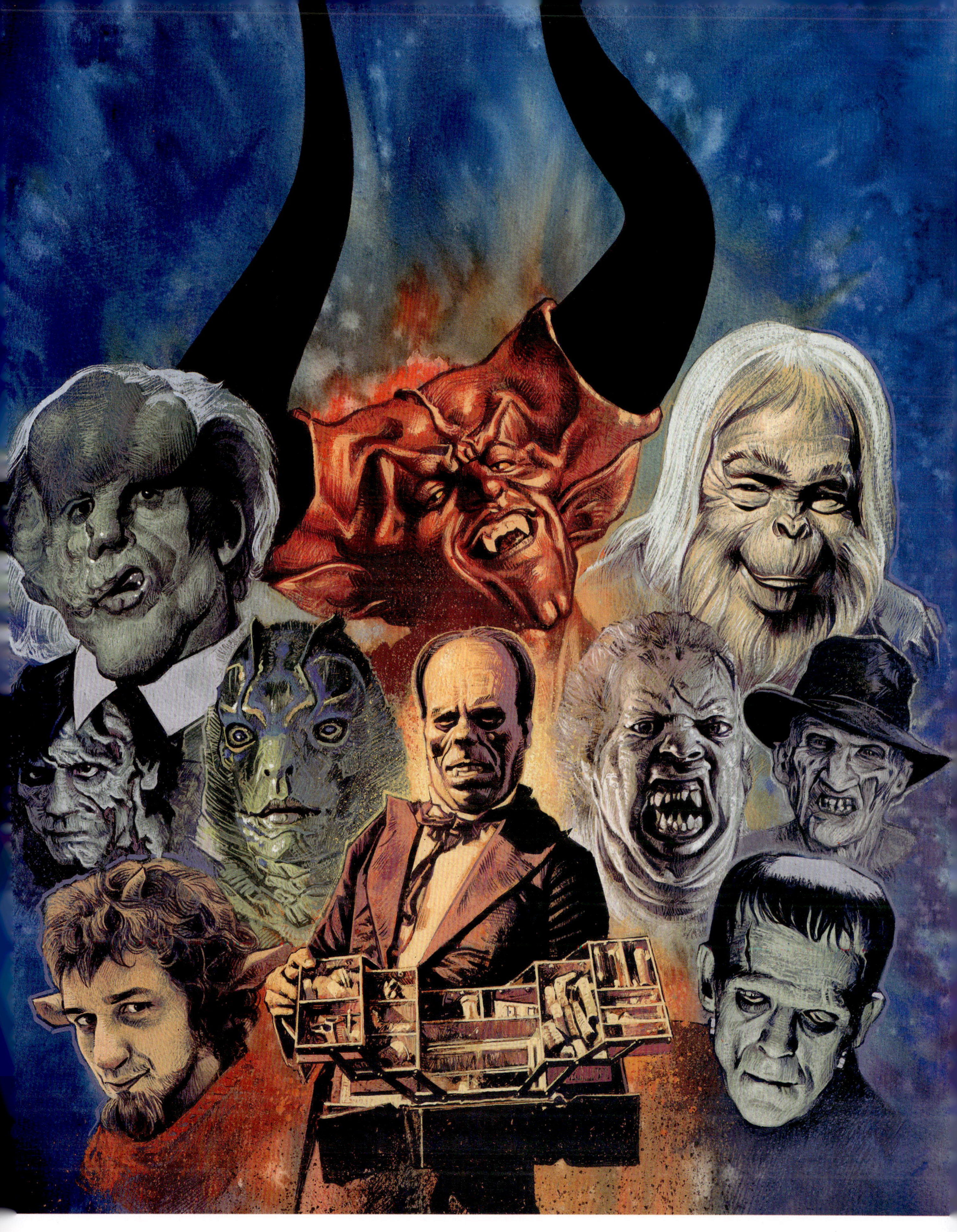

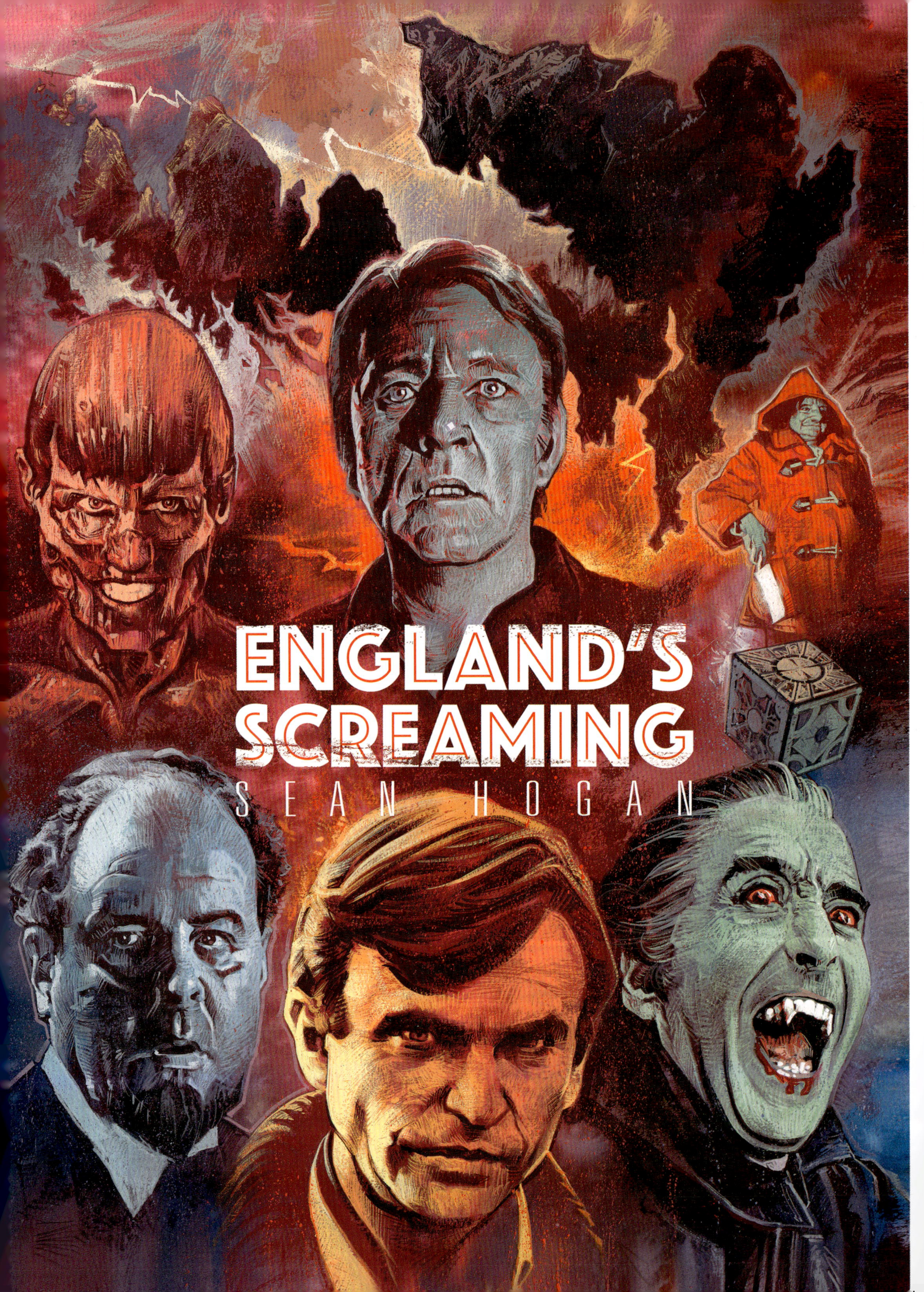

ENGLAND'S SCREAMING
SEAN HOGAN

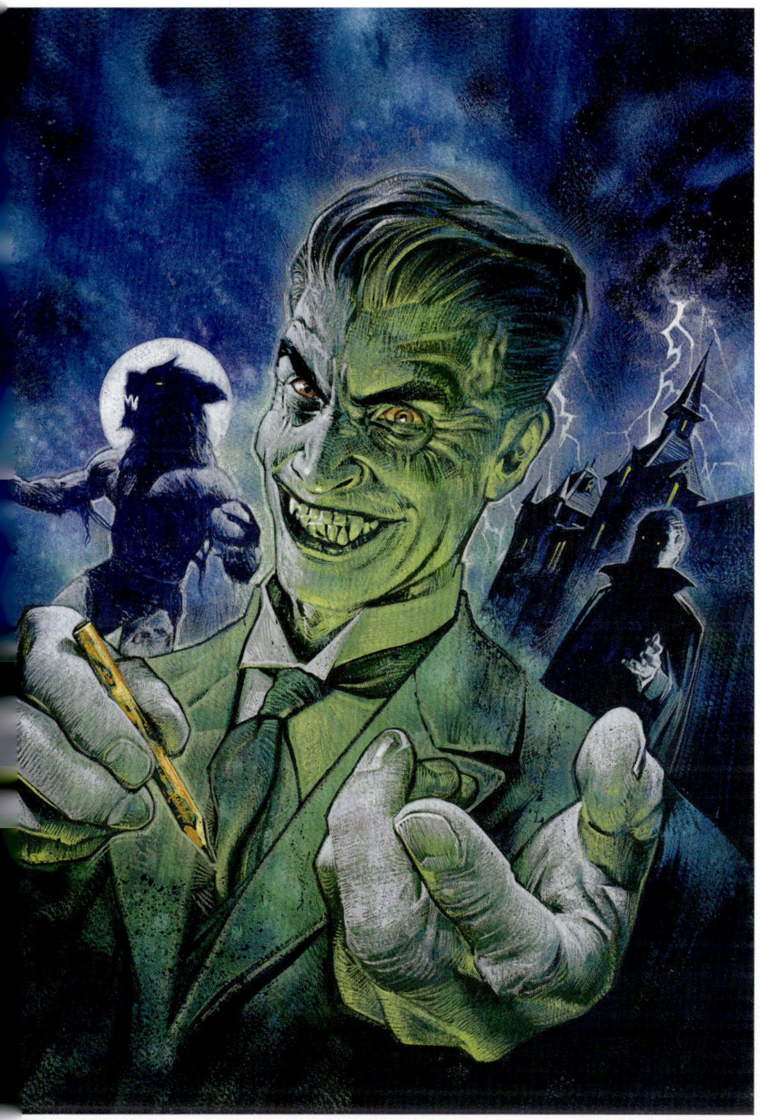

My good friend David Read asked me to paint the cover for his horror-themed
crossword book, with a simple brief requiring a sinister character beckoning
the viewer to take a pencil. It was suggested that adding some well-known
horror characters might add to the interest, although we were concerned
about potential license issues. For that reason, the Werewolf and Dracula
characters are in silhouette. The focal entity is made up of several references,
including a photo of my hand. The background building was referenced from
one of my photographs of a nearby neo-Gothic building, formerly The Royal
Victoria Patriotic Asylum.

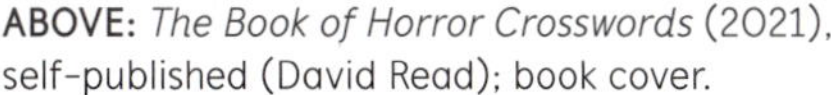

Sean Hogan's book weaves the characters and narratives of British cult films,
most from the horror genre. Damien from *The Omen* (1976), Morlar from *The
Medusa Touch* (1978), and *Dracula* (Christopher Lee's performance) battle to
take control of the planet, with a myriad of known characters from the British
horror genre. My brief requested a shortlist of definite inclusions. The book
seems to reference Brexit and the break-up of British unity, which made me
think of the epic artwork of painter John Martin (1789–1854) and his *The
Great Day of His Wrath*, which I reference at the top of the cover art.

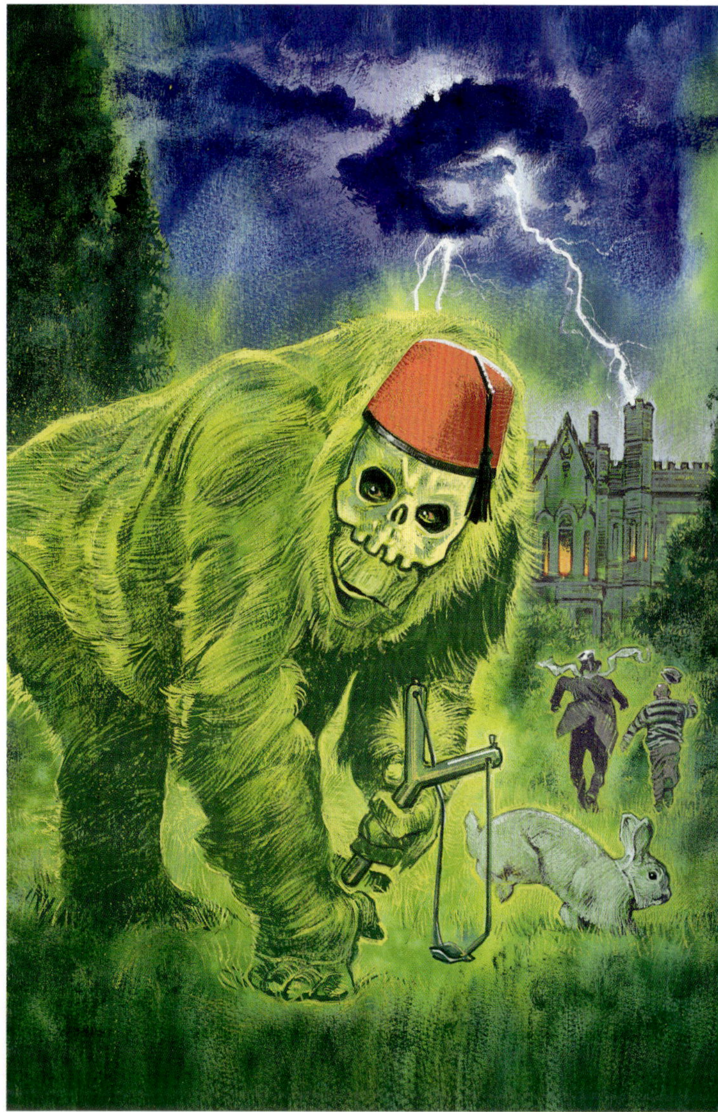

Commissioned by author Kim Newman to illustrate a short story,
"The Green Gorilla". A comical whodunnit with Gothic elements...
including the green gorilla. I'd love to see this filmed!

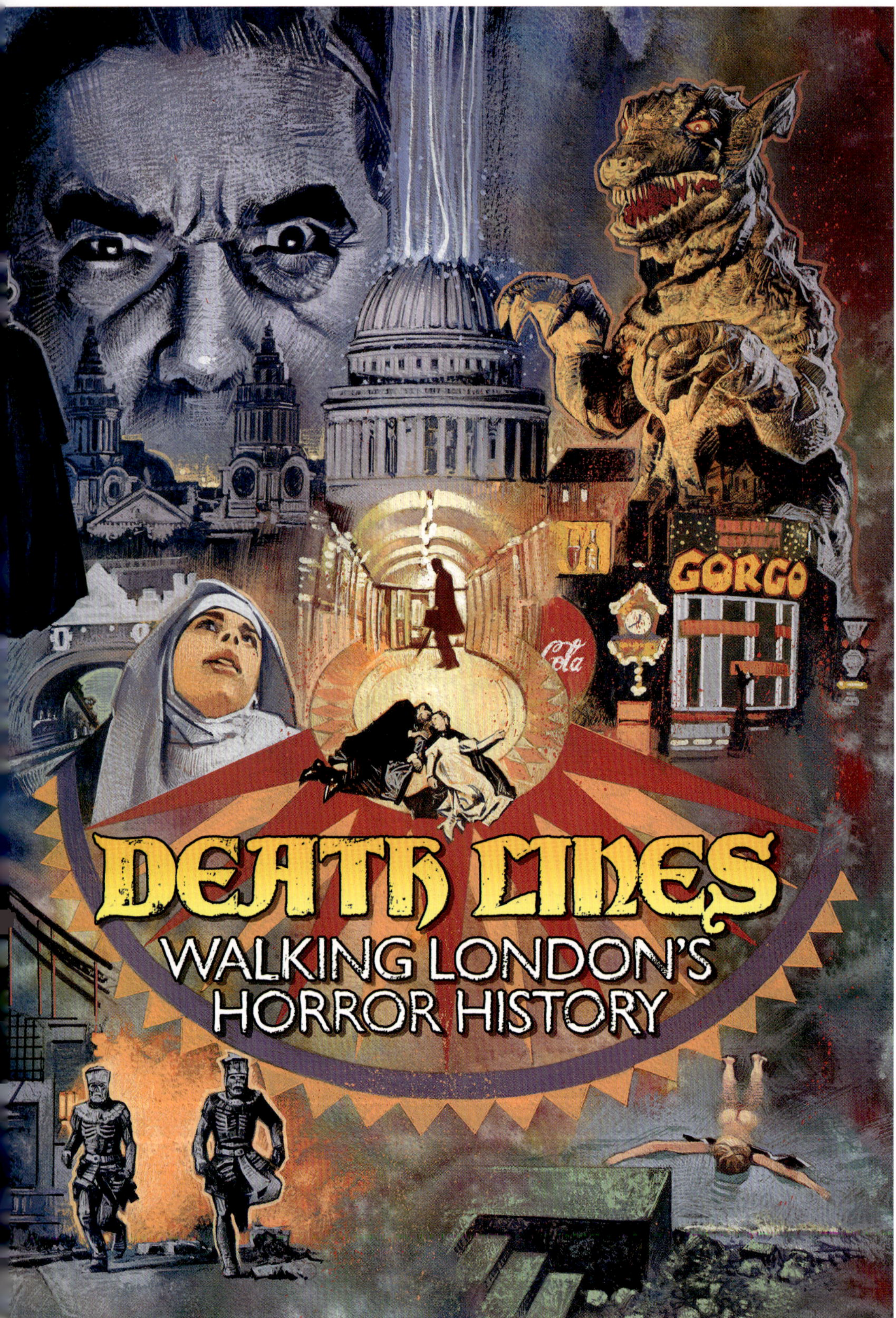

LEFT: *Death Lines* (2022), Strange Attractor Press; book cover.

This book cover highlights some of London's film locations accessed through a walking guide. The client gave me a shortlist of well-known films that are referenced in the guide, including *An American in London* (1981), *Gorgo* (1961), *The Dark Eyes of London* (1939), and *Lifeforce* (1985). Some of the reference material was very poor, and it was difficult to control the quality of the composition. I tried to make use of the marble flooring (St. Paul's Cathedral) from *Hands of the Ripper* (1971) to create a geometric device around which to place the disparate elements. The cover extended to the back with a simple further element.

RIGHT: *Scala Cinema* (2018), FAB Press; limited edition book cover and print.

Authored by my friend Jane Giles, the book is a history of the notorious Scala Cinema in King's Cross, North London, which was known for its eclectic programming; there were always firm favourites among the frequent visitors. I was asked to illustrate some of the key films that were screened there regularly, such as *Thundercrack!* (1975), *The Evil Dead* (1982), *Pink Flamingos* (1972), as well as a host of stars — including King Kong (the 1931 film played on the opening and closing nights at the King's Cross building, which had once been a Primatarium, with images of apes and jungle foliage painted up its staircase and foyer walls!).

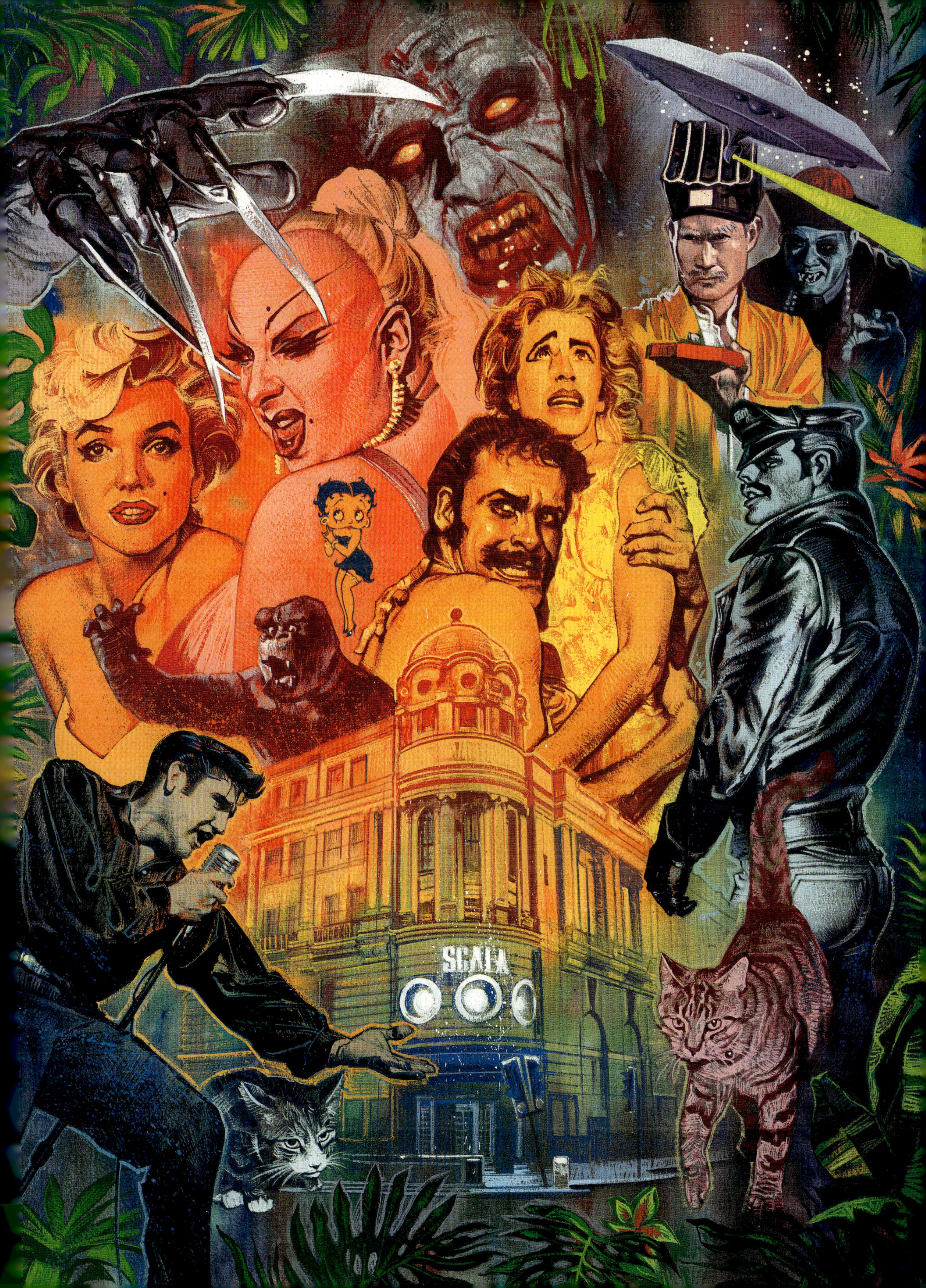

SCALA

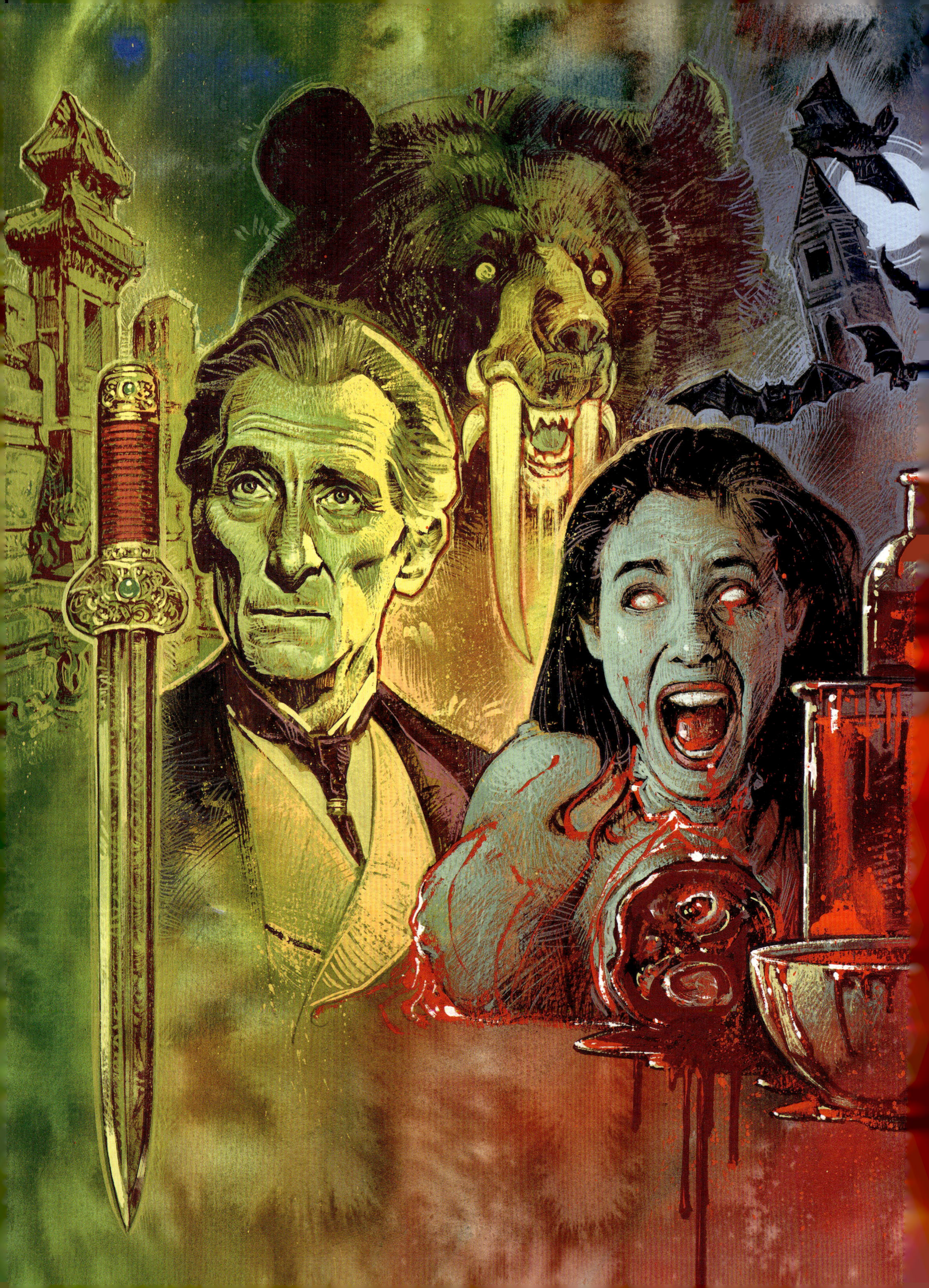

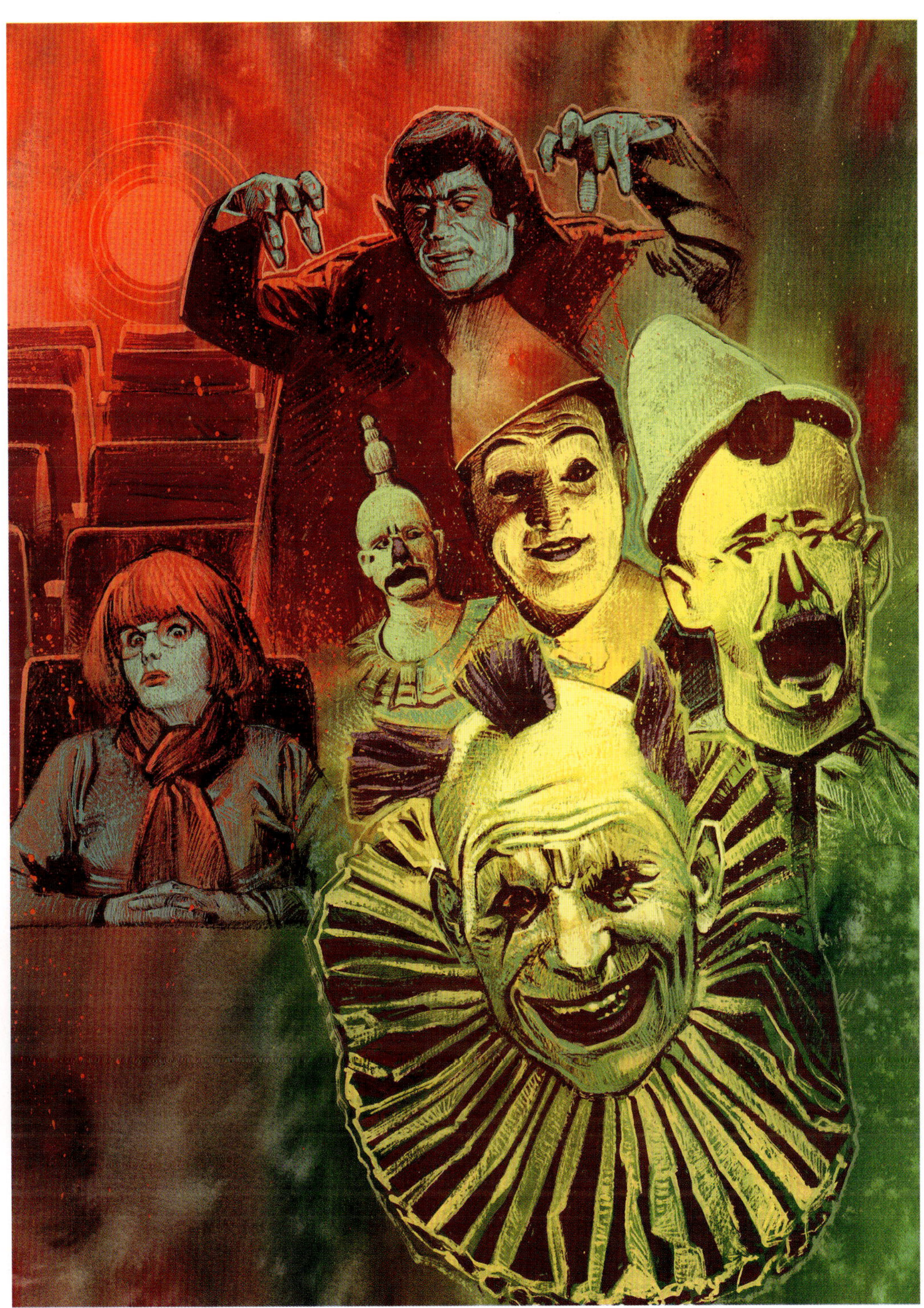

LEFT: *Studio of Screams*
(back panel) (2020),
PS Publishing; book cover.

This panel features the
likeness of actor Oliver Reed,
as suggested by the author
of one of the short stories.

OPPOSITE: *Studio of Screams*
(front panel) (2020),
PS Publishing; book cover.

The cover is a mix of images
that illustrate elements from the
collection of stories within, each
from a different author. Like the
Amicus portmanteau films of
the 1960s and '70s, there's a
wraparound story that involves
a fictional production company.
The book clearly references
Hammer Films and Amicus.
Some of the characters in the
stories were assigned real actor
likenesses, which is why Peter
Cushing is represented on this
front panel.

PAGE 138: *Twilight's Last
Screaming* (2022), Black Shuck
Books; book cover.

Following the success of Sean
Hogan's book *England's
Screaming*, the sequel features
characters from American cult
film and TV. If the first book was
a response to Brexit, the second
is a response to the presidency
of Donald Trump. Martin Sheen's
bid for the presidency in the
David Cronenberg film *The Dead
Zone* (1983), based on the 1979
novel by Stephen King, is pivotal.
In the manner of the previous
book, key characters are
represented in my artwork.

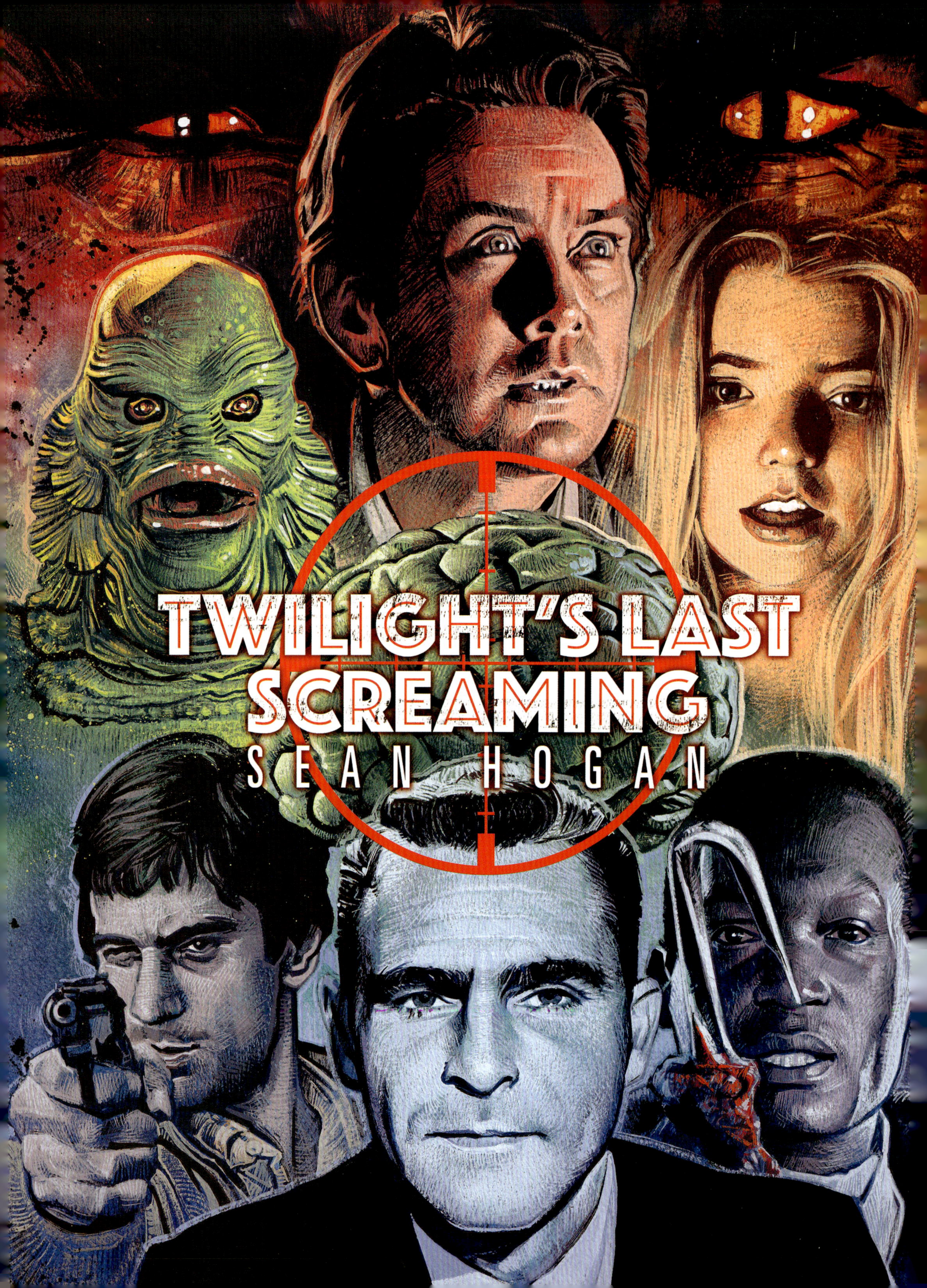

TWILIGHT'S LAST SCREAMING
SEAN HOGAN

THE ARTIST'S MUSE

Always being open to new stimuli was the key takeaway from my training at art college. Aside from the life advantages of keeping a broad set of interests, focusing on a single topic would have limited the opportunity to earn a living. I visit public galleries and major exhibitions across all subjects and disciplines, to add a new dimension to my work and keep it ever evolving. Inspiration is found not only in the subject on which the artist might focus but from the kaleidoscope of life experiences and encounters. Like pigments in paint, influences can be mixed to add colour. The following is a demonstration of how this can work.

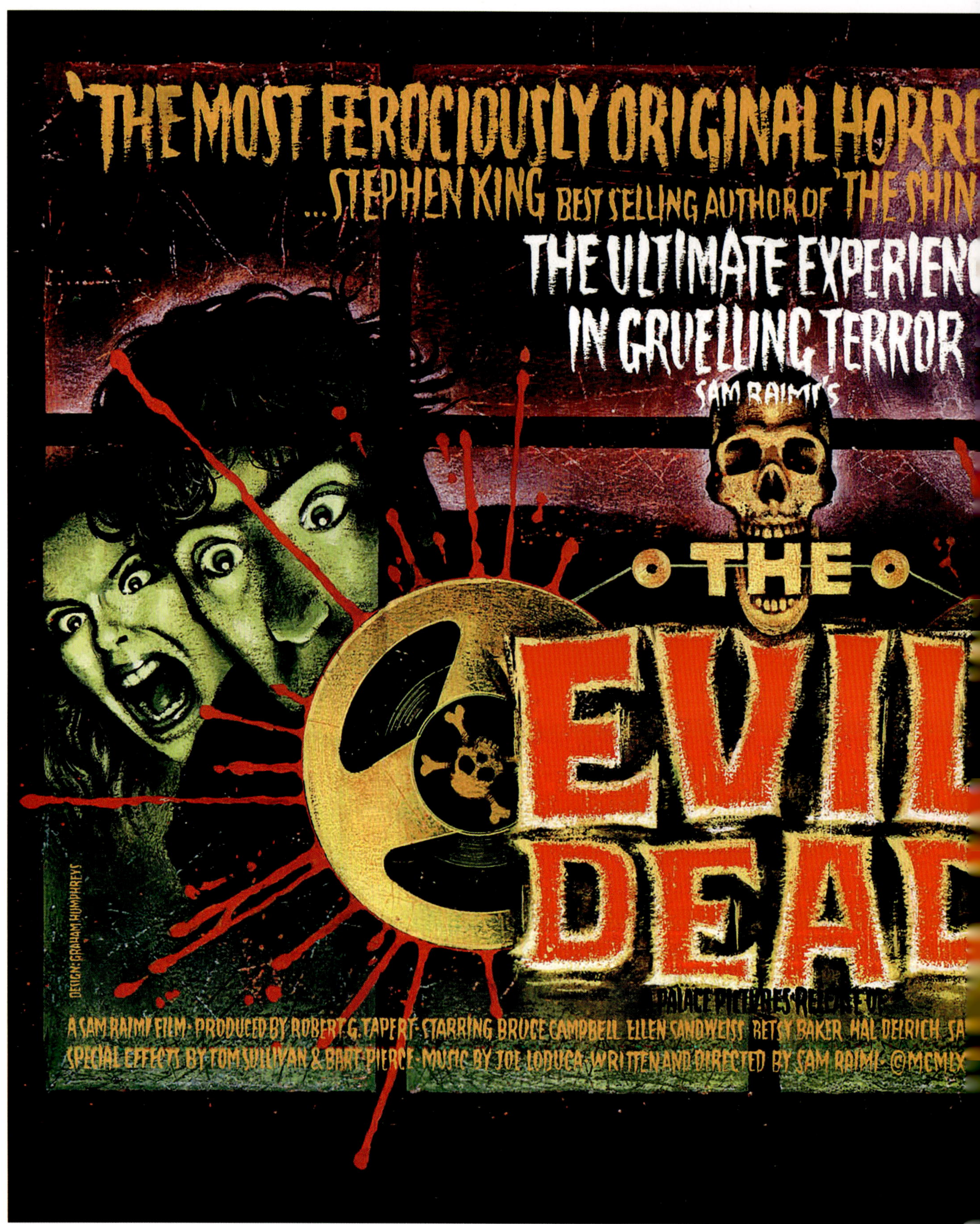

'THE MOST FEROCIOUSLY ORIGINAL HORRO
...STEPHEN KING BEST SELLING AUTHOR OF 'THE SHIN
THE ULTIMATE EXPERIENC
IN GRUELLING TERROR
SAM RAIMI'S
THE
EVIL
DEAD
DESIGN: GRAHAM HUMPHREYS
A PALACE PICTURES RELEASE OF
A SAM RAIMI FILM · PRODUCED BY ROBERT G. TAPERT · STARRING BRUCE CAMPBELL · ELLEN SANDWEISS · BETSY BAKER · HAL DELRICH · SA
SPECIAL EFFECTS BY TOM SULLIVAN & BART PIERCE · MUSIC BY JOE LODUCA · WRITTEN AND DIRECTED BY SAM RAIMI · ©MCMLX

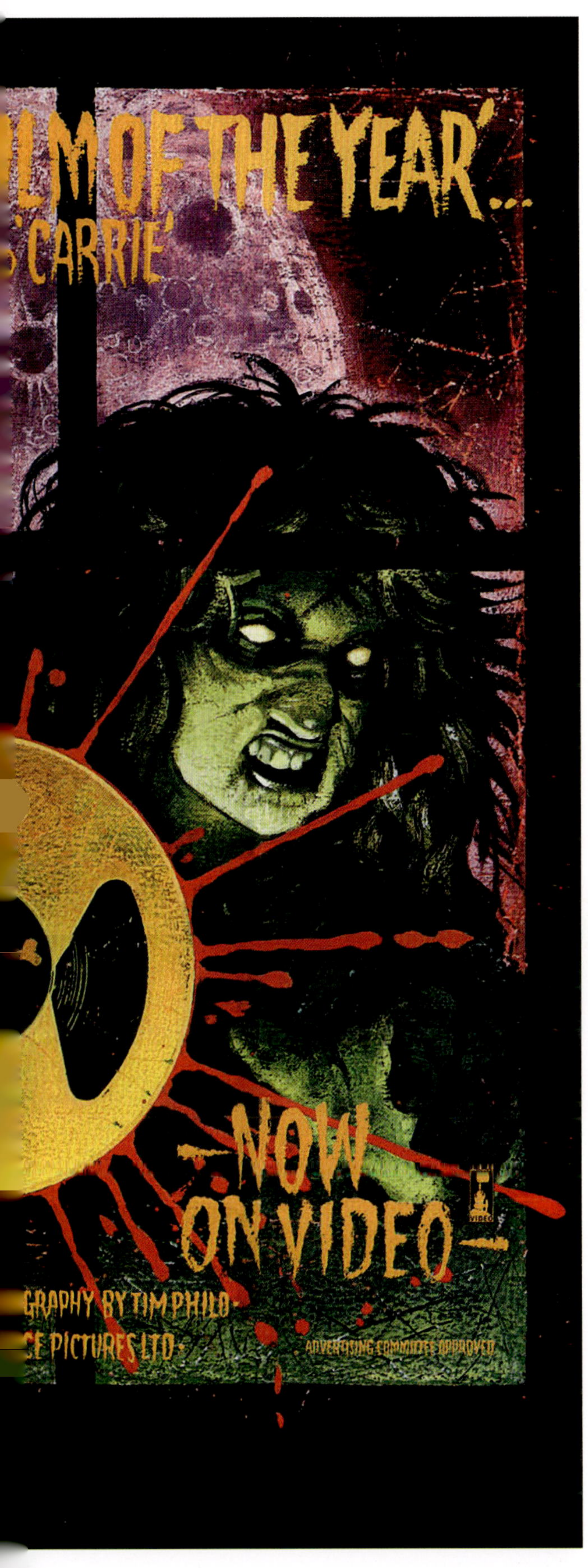

THE EVIL DEAD (1981)

Towards the end of 1981, I was thrilled to accept the commission to design a poster for the Palace Pictures, UK distribution of a low-budget horror movie called *The Evil Dead*. The title alone was the hook. It's since become one of my best-known posters, and something I'm immensely proud of, given that I expected it to have a shelf life of no more than a month, during which the movie made its run through the provinces, art houses, and flea pits.

Some 40 years later, I can now be candid about the origins of my design and how the commission might just be entirely down to the intervention of Hollywood actress Joan Crawford! At the age of 21, my knowledge of film was scant, and I focused on the popular films of the time. The 1970s disaster movies coloured my mid-teen years: *The Poseidon Adventure, The Towering Inferno, Earthquake,* and *The Hindenberg,* whilst late night TV (on my cheap little portable mono set) was filled with Universal Monsters, Hammer horror, Amicus anthologies, and the Roger Corman/Poe films. I watched a lot of old Hollywood films on Sunday afternoons because there was little else on offer. After leaving college at 20 and moving to London, I could access the independent theatres that showed golden-era re-runs alongside transgressive cult cinema, and my venue of choice was the notorious Scala Cinema in King's Cross.

In my teens, I'd seen *Straight-Jacket, Berserk, What Ever Happened To Baby Jane,* and *Trog,* which each starred Joan Crawford. In my naivety, I believed she was a seasoned horror star, and was fascinated by her angular features and heavy brows, in the same way I'd been fascinated by Christopher Lee's aristocratic presence, Peter Cushing's emaciated features, and Vincent Price's Gothic turns.

In my first professional year, with few commissions to occupy my time, I'd hawk my folio around town and use any other spare time to paint images that I thought would best represent the sort of work I wanted, scouring the local library for inspiration, listening to new music, and tapping into popular culture.

Among these early pieces of work, two were to provide me with one small step for Graham and a giant leap for my career. One I'd called *Vamp* (nothing to do with the Grace Jones movie, as yet unmade), an image of "horror actress" Joan Crawford in an imaginary vampire-themed film; in the other I'd imagined a sci-fi film called *Planet Claire* (after the B-52's song). As these were folio samples without any specific art direction, I took the opportunity to experiment with techniques and colour. It was these two artworks that caught the eye of the team at Palace Pictures when I presented my folio at their office (above the Scala Cinema).

Looking at the *Vamp* image today, it's possible to see a clear lineage to *The Evil Dead* poster, from the exaggerated colour palette to the depiction of a window frame. Joan Crawford was my horror star and a conduit to a career in the genre I love!

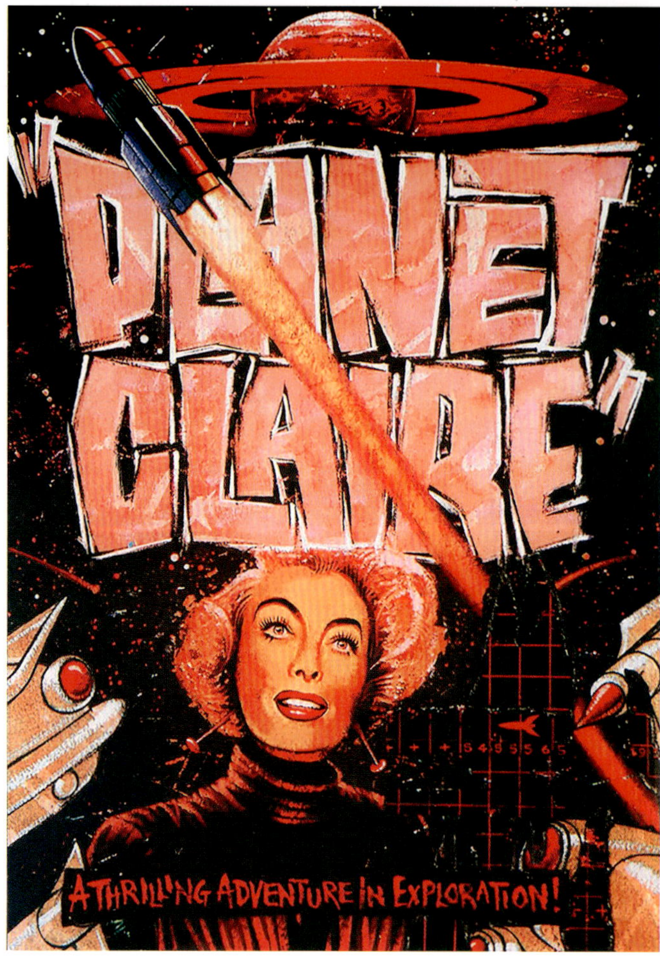

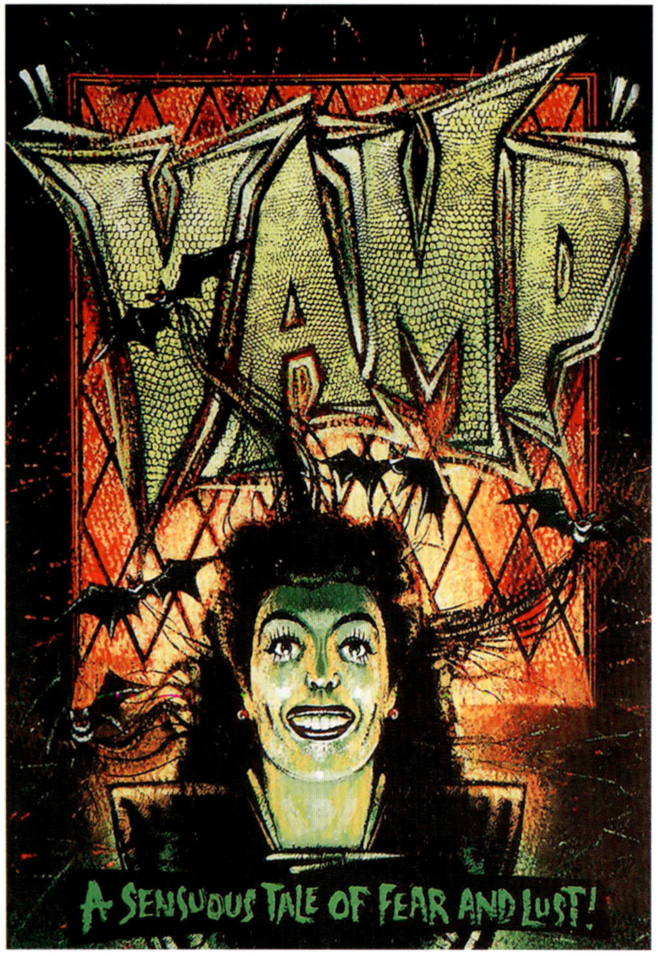

A further point of exploration is evident in my design. The window frame is the poster — a virtual window through which to view the promised horrors. Where had I seen this before? What was going through my mind when I composed this image? Only years later did I understand my inspiration as the stained-glass windows of churches!

I've always argued that the Bible is the world's first anthology of horror and science fiction. For an impressionable young mind, it's full of terrifying images: murder, genocide, torture, rape, monsters, the living dead, magic, the abyss, the apocalypse, rivers of blood, pestilence, smashed cities, extinction events — it's all there. Little that I've seen on screen matches the fearful happenings I've read in the Scriptures. If horror is your thing, you can never be short of inspiration with a Bible in hand!

Centuries ago, for those who couldn't read but were in need of visual reckonings, stained-glass windows were the movie posters, and churches the movie theatres. Every Sunday, a horror double bill! The sainted heroes, the sinners, the demons, the torture, the murder… My *Evil Dead* poster is a stained-glass window, a residual memory of church-induced fear! For an itch that had to be scratched, I took a weekend course in "leading", and the humble homage to stained-glass horrors below was among the items I produced.

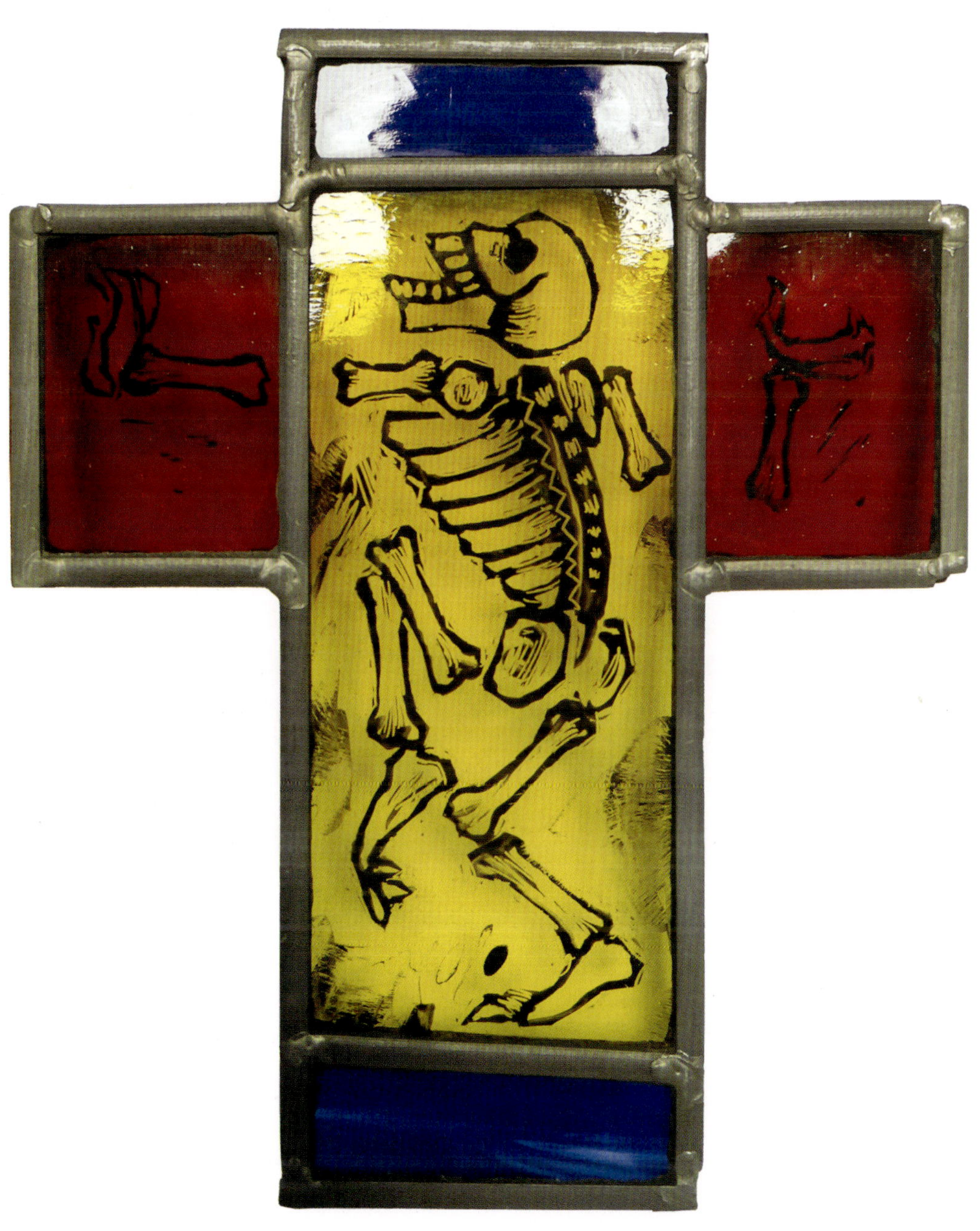

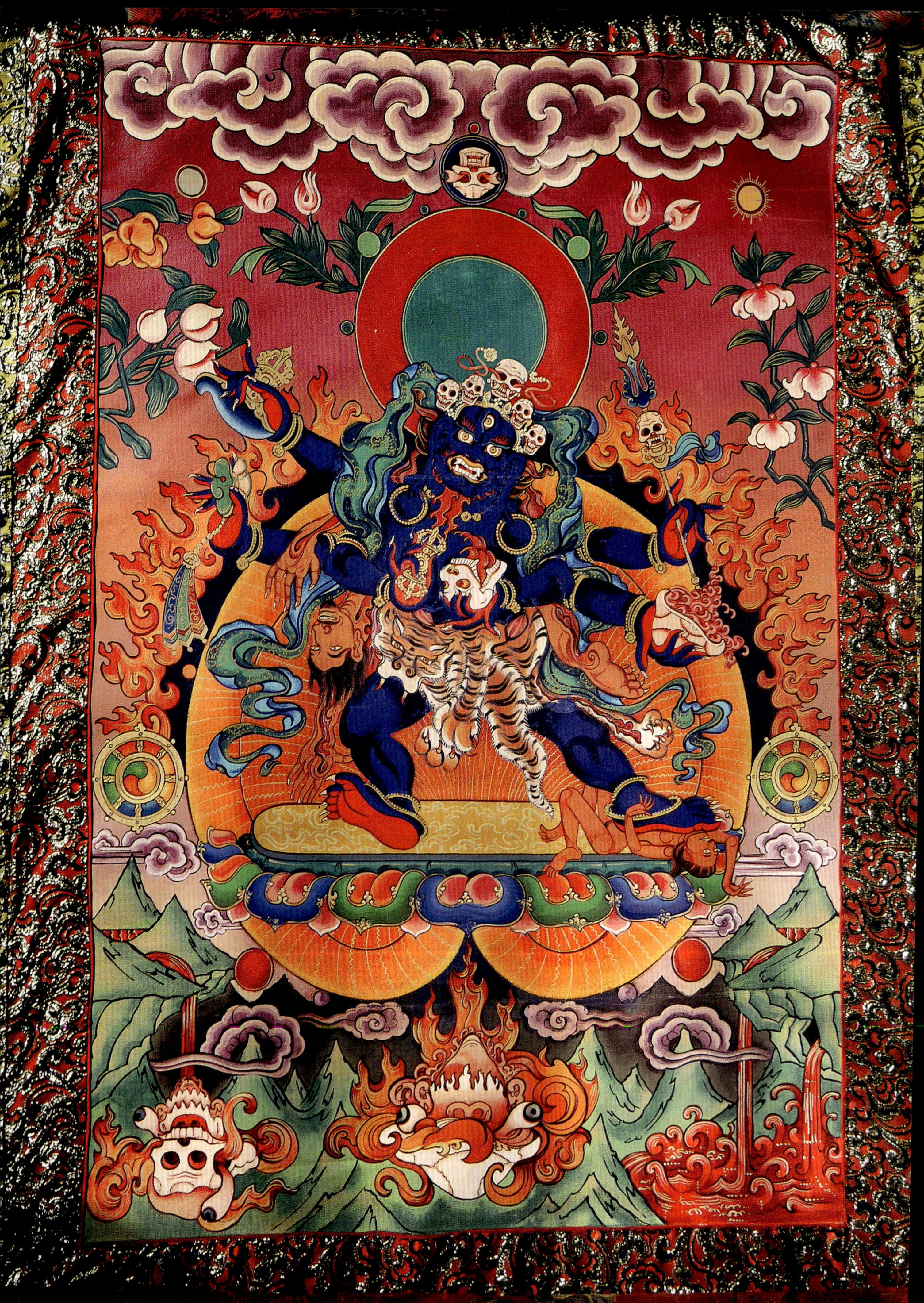

HARDWARE (1990)

Working with director Richard Stanley — then recently returned from Afghanistan, where he'd been filming *Voice of the Moon* (described as "an experimental documentary on the Russian invasion of Afghanistan") — and at the invitation of Stephen Woolley of Palace Pictures, I dived into the deep end of movie storyboarding for the British science fiction horror film *Hardware*.

My storyboards were crude, little more than simple line sketches, but they helped focus the production on many levels: action, effects, and directing among them. During this period, I took a small window of opportunity to fulfil a dream and travelled to Tibet. This kindled an interest in Tibetan sacred art, a highly disciplined and distinctive form with some extreme imagery. Easily misinterpreted, the images of skeletons, flayed flesh, severed heads, and fanged monsters supping on human blood may not appear to be usefully

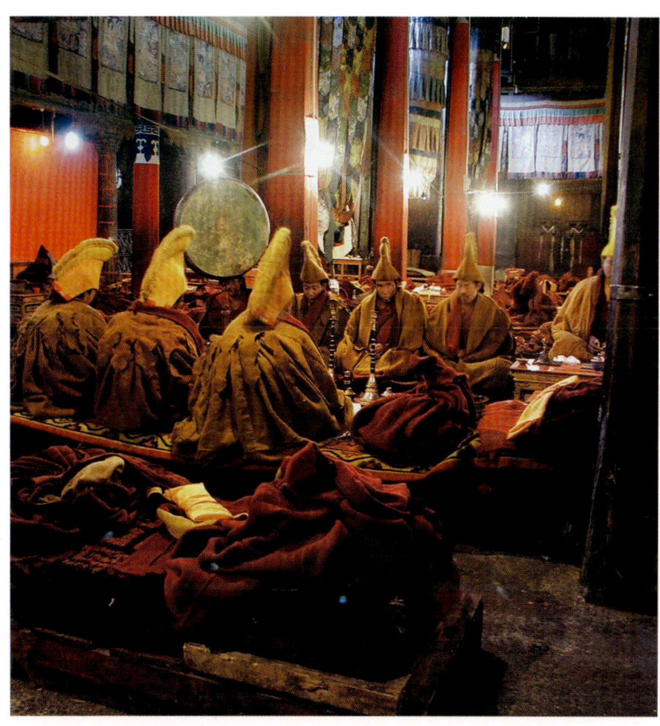
Photograph taken in Tibet by the artist.

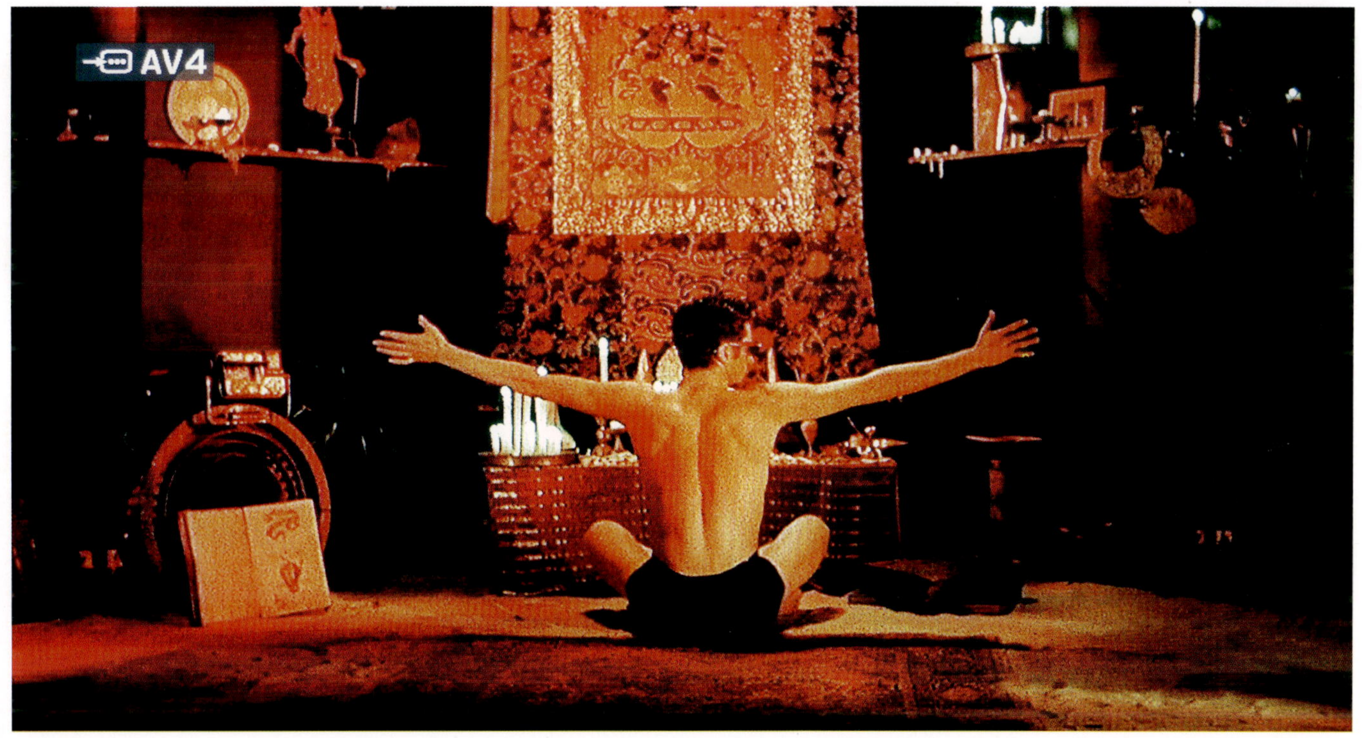

Screen shot: *Hardware* (1990), Palace Pictures.

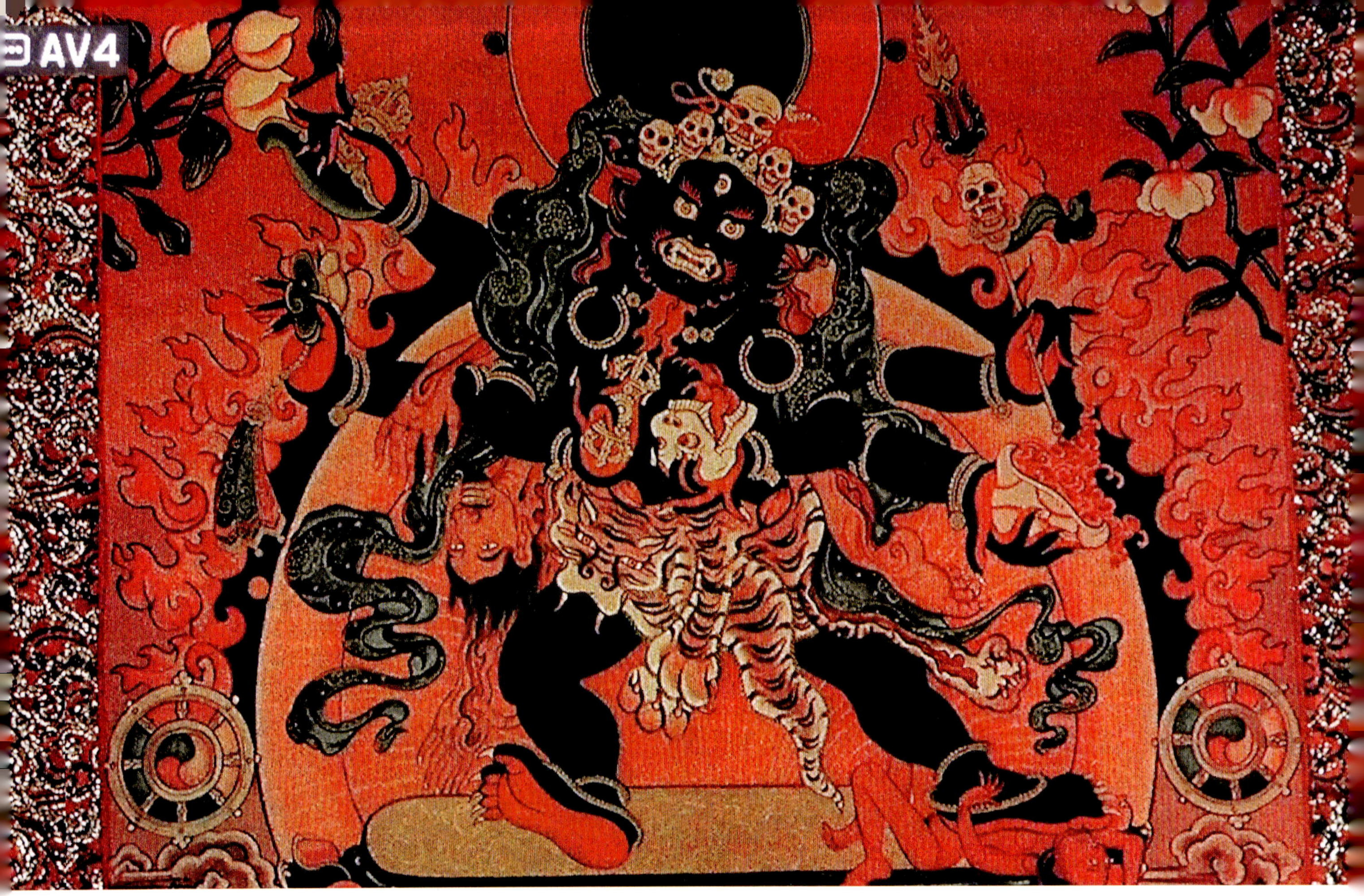
AV4

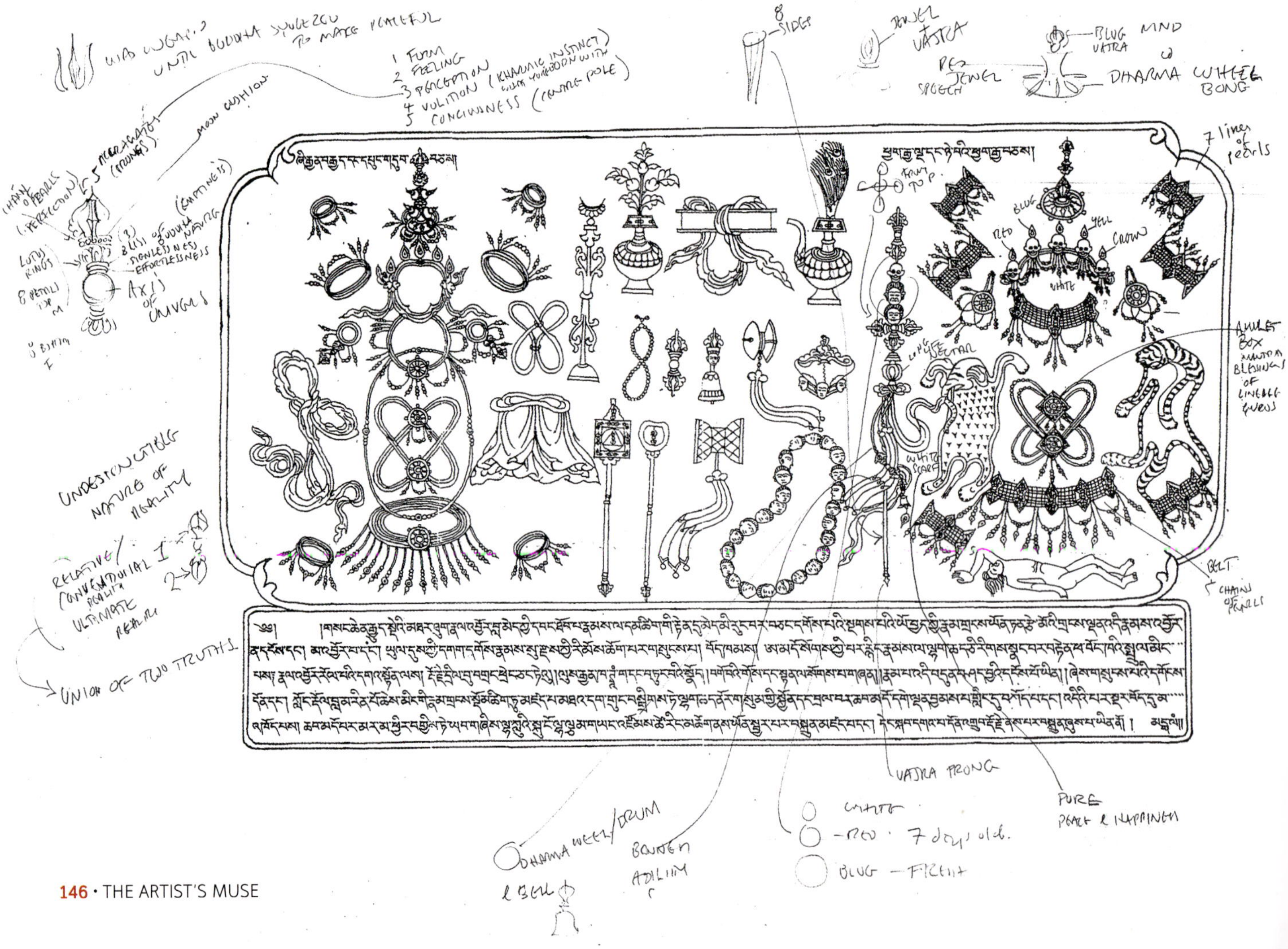
1 FORM
2 FEELING
3 PERCEPTION
4 VOLITION
5 CONCIOUSNESS
MOON CUSHION
8 SIDES
BLUE MIND VAJRA
DHARMA WHEEL
7 lines of pearls
CROWN
WHITE
AMULET BOX
BELT
UNDESTRUCTIBLE NATURE OF REALITY
ULTIMATE REALITY
UNION OF TWO TRUTHS
VAJRA PRONG
PURE PEACE & HAPPINESS
WHITE
BLUE
DHARMA WEEL/DRUM

representative of a peaceful Buddhist philosophy, but within the images are layers of meaning and models for existence that might not be apparent in the familiar Abrahamic traditions that dominate European and American culture, even though Christianity has and does employ visceral and violent imagery for its own purposes. Among those on the guided tour in Tibet was an American missionary who took offence at the images, describing them as "the black arts" — it didn't seem appropriate to point out the discrepancy.

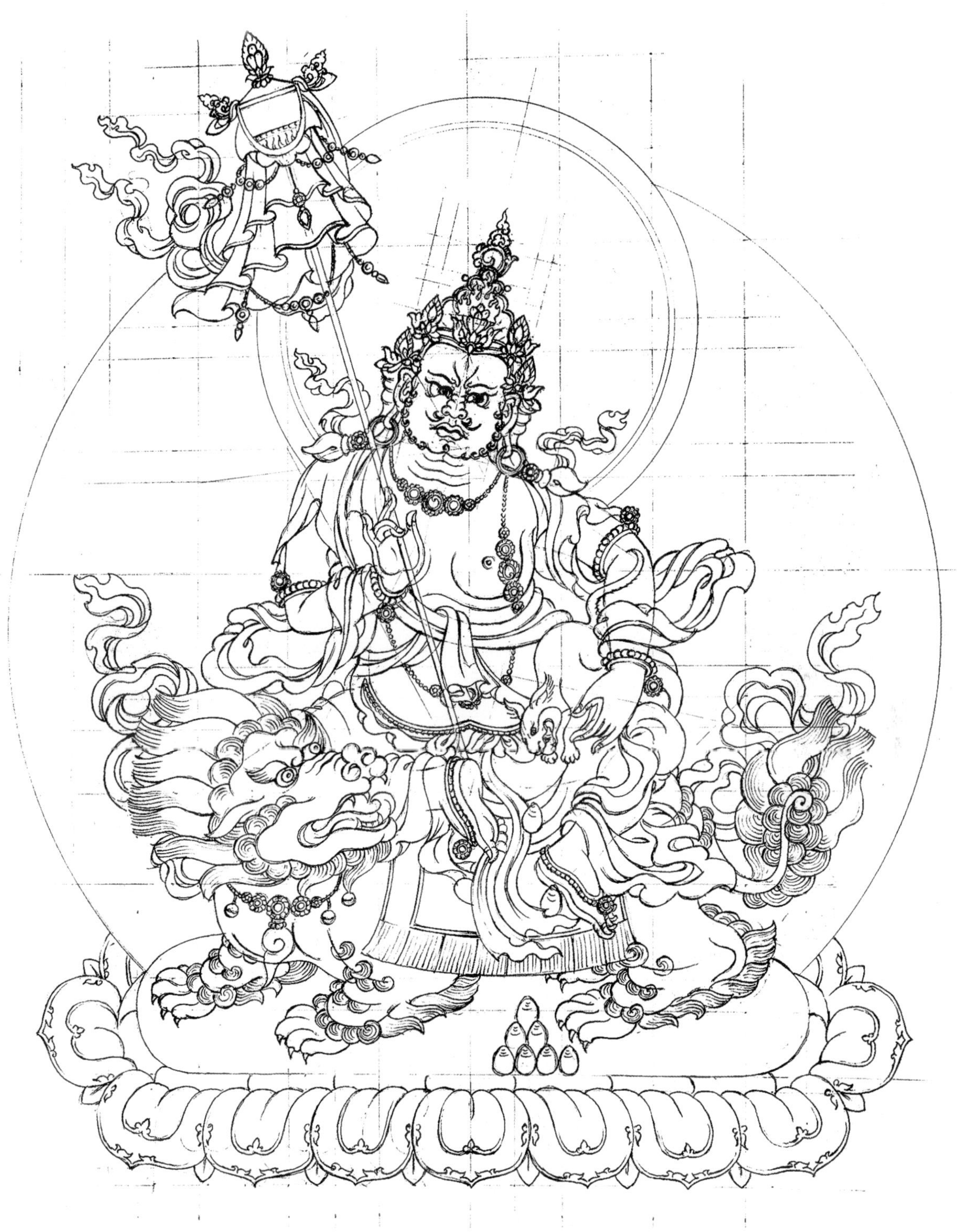

Inspired by the art I'd seen on my trip, I proposed a thangka* painting for a key scene in Richard's film, which took place in the apartment of the character Shades, who clearly had spiritual aspirations through meditation and "herbal assistance".

I intended the representation of a wrathful demon to bear a resemblance to M.A.R.K. 13, the murderous robot in the film. The painting becomes a source of focus in a couple of additional hallucinatory scenes.

The actual painting is acrylic on canvas, stitched into a fabric frame. I made it a labour of love by hand-sewing the fabric myself. Now a little dusty, with just a few parts of the paintwork chipped, the prop has survived well.

Many years later, I decided to learn more about the art form and attended some courses about the construction of the thangka paintings. The images are built on complex grids that ensure a painting from centuries before will be replicated in exactly the same form today. Likewise, the colours are also decreed. I still have a couple of drawings (see below) which show the careful measuring. Notes were made to assist in understanding the complex symbolism. Although I didn't pursue the art form any further, it profoundly impacted my work.

If there's any point to this small chapter, it's to demonstrate that influences can come from anywhere. Whilst I can name punk rock and Hammer horror as key to my work, an open mind and an inquisitive eye are needed to progress and evolve.

* A thangka is a Tibetan Buddhist painting on cotton surrounded by silk appliqué, usually depicting a Buddhist deity, scene, or mandala, that's intended for personal meditation or the instruction of monastic students.

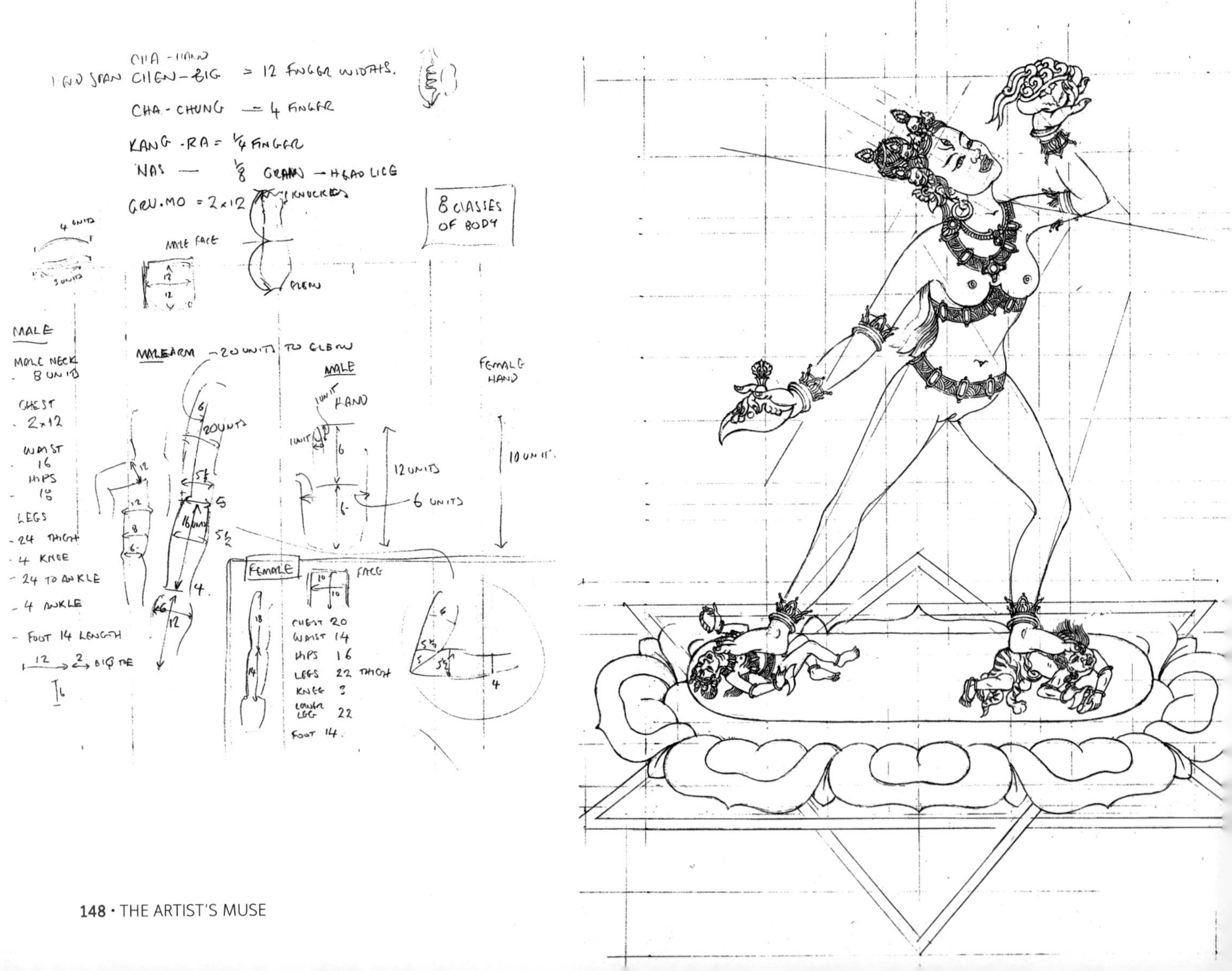

VINYL

Early in my career, I designed several LP sleeves with limited ability and experience. The format was always exciting. Without the need to worry about issues of reformatting (quad into VHS, for example), I found the humble square a perfect canvas for the imagination. With the resurgence of vinyl, once declared dead, now clawing its way through the cultural sod, the collector's market has embraced the return of the movie soundtrack. Newly licensed soundtracks (some never before released) are feeding the eager appetite for collectable artefacts. The gatefold sleeve is a playground for any artist.

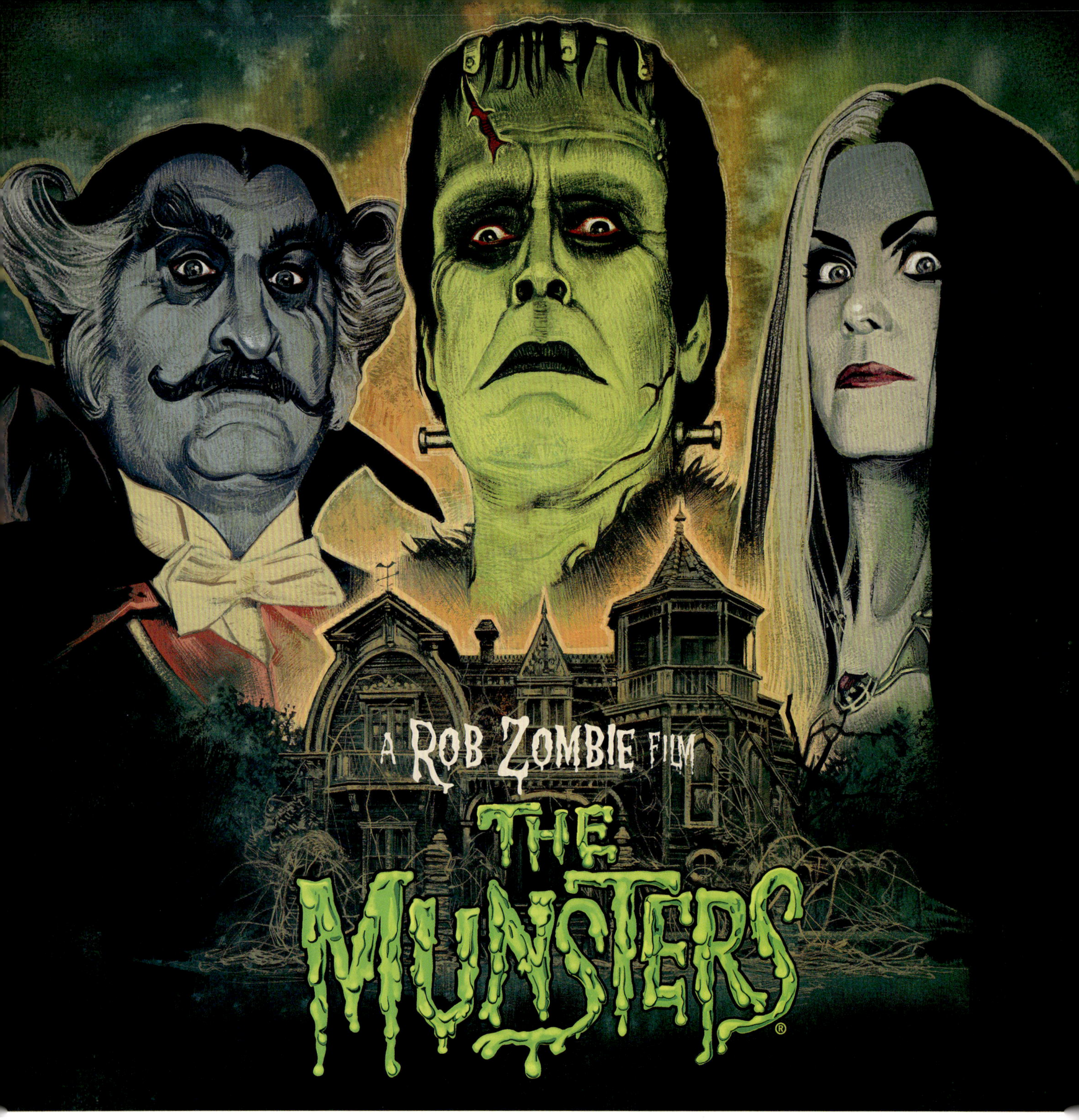

ABOVE: *The Munsters* (2021), Waxwork Records; LP cover.

Whilst working on the first two titles for the *Rob Zombie Presents* soundtrack series, I was commissioned to paint the art for the soundtrack for the as yet unfinished Rob Zombie *The Munsters* project. My brief was to retain the look of a Universal monster film, without the campiness of *The Munsters* TV series but using the available reference material (then, very limited due to confidentiality issues). In fact, the whole soundtrack project was completed before the film, and some key casting announcements. I had no access to a script or synopsis to understand how the narrative would stitch together. I did, however, have a good reference for the famed Mockingbird Lane residence, re-created for the film.

OPPOSITE TOP: *The Munsters* (2021) Waxwork Records, LP gatefold.

"An origin story" was the one plot point I was offered that helped with my work. It was logical that the creation of Herman Munster should feature in the gatefold, suggestive of Universal's 1931 *Frankenstein* movie. Lily and Grandpa add the future family unit. My colours were representative of the images available. Having seen the final film, I can see where my artwork might have otherwise taken a different direction in colour choices and in the inclusion of key characters; for example, Sylvester McCoy's casting as "Igor" had not then been announced, and therefore he doesn't appear.

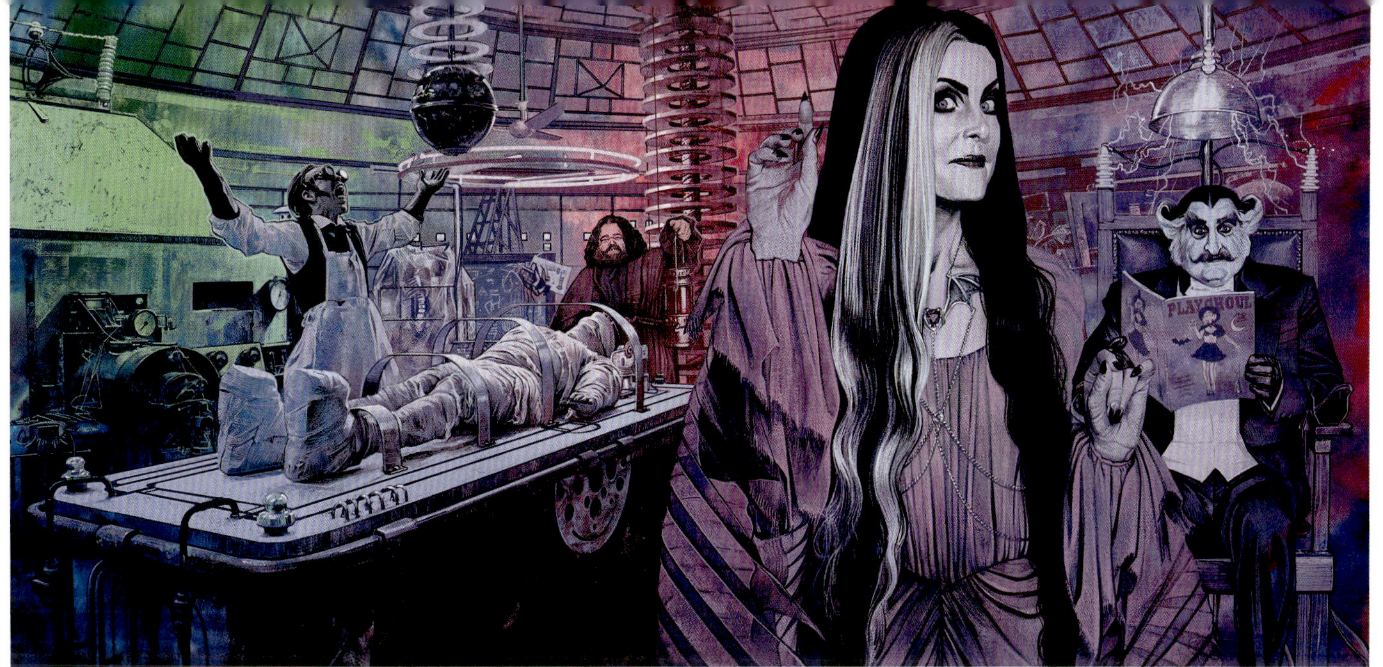

RIGHT: Vinyl labels.

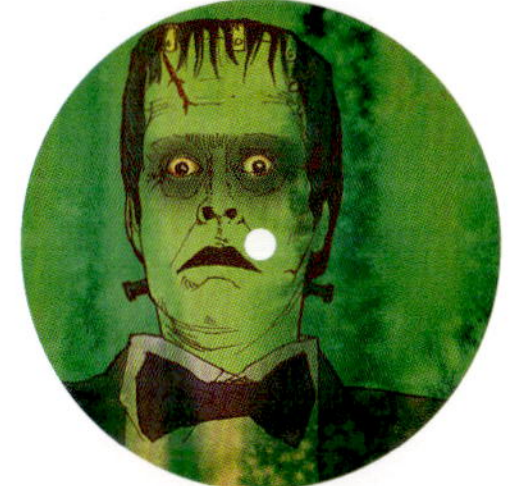
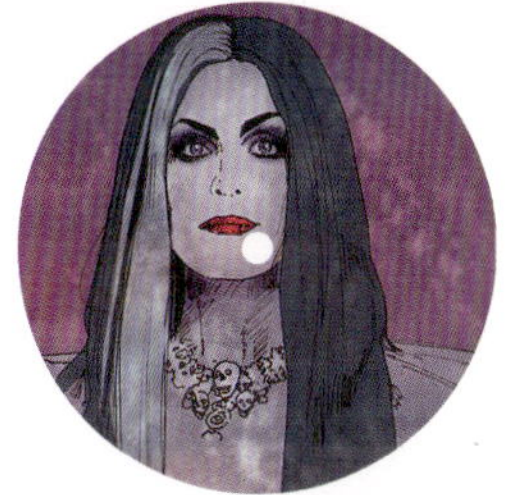
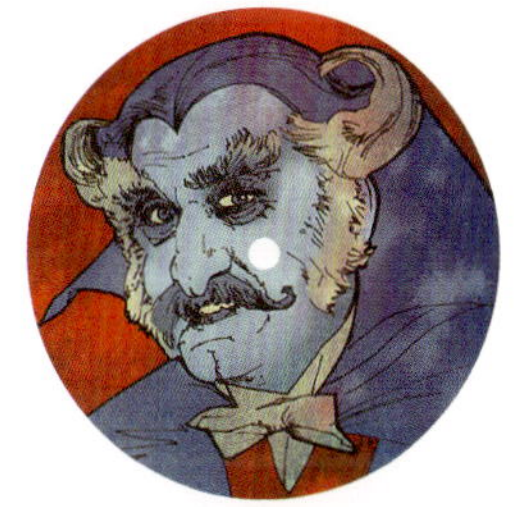
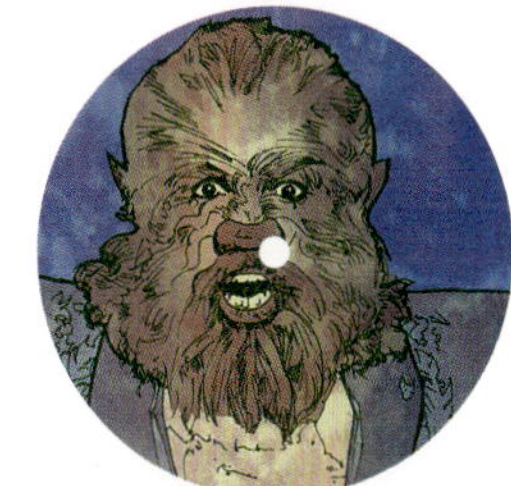

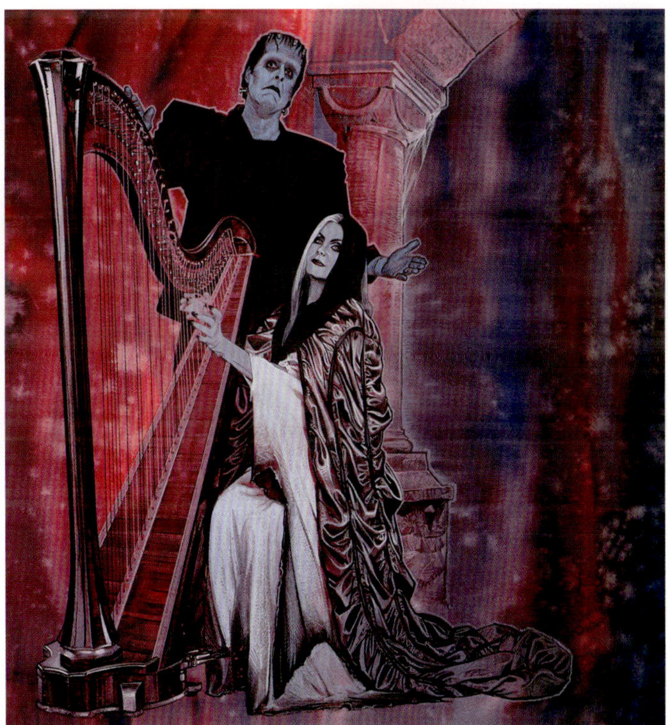
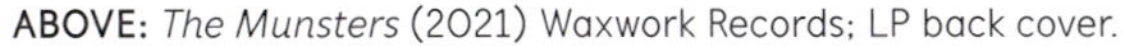

ABOVE: *The Munsters* (2021) Waxwork Records; LP back cover.

With minimal reference options available, I was drawn to this publicity shot, a re-creation of a similar publicity shot for the 1960s TV series. Knowing that a substantial track listing needs space, this seemed to be the perfect image without requiring the unknown narrative!

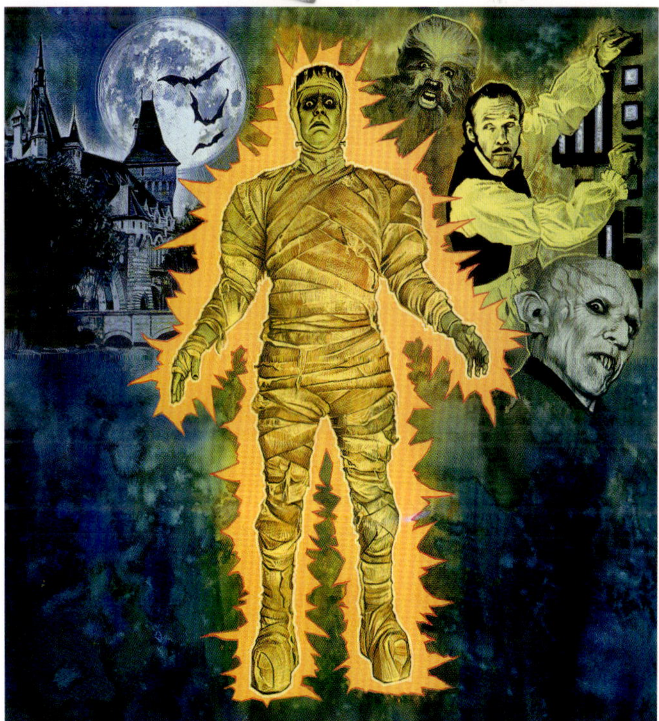

ABOVE: *The Munsters* (2021). Waxwork Records; LP bonus insert.

One image that I had been allowed to view presented itself as the perfect reference for this insert. I took inspiration from a poster for the 1941 film *Man-Made Monster*, which portrays Lon Chany Jr's character framed in a very cartoonish electrical field. The remaining elements available to me at the time add the background interest.

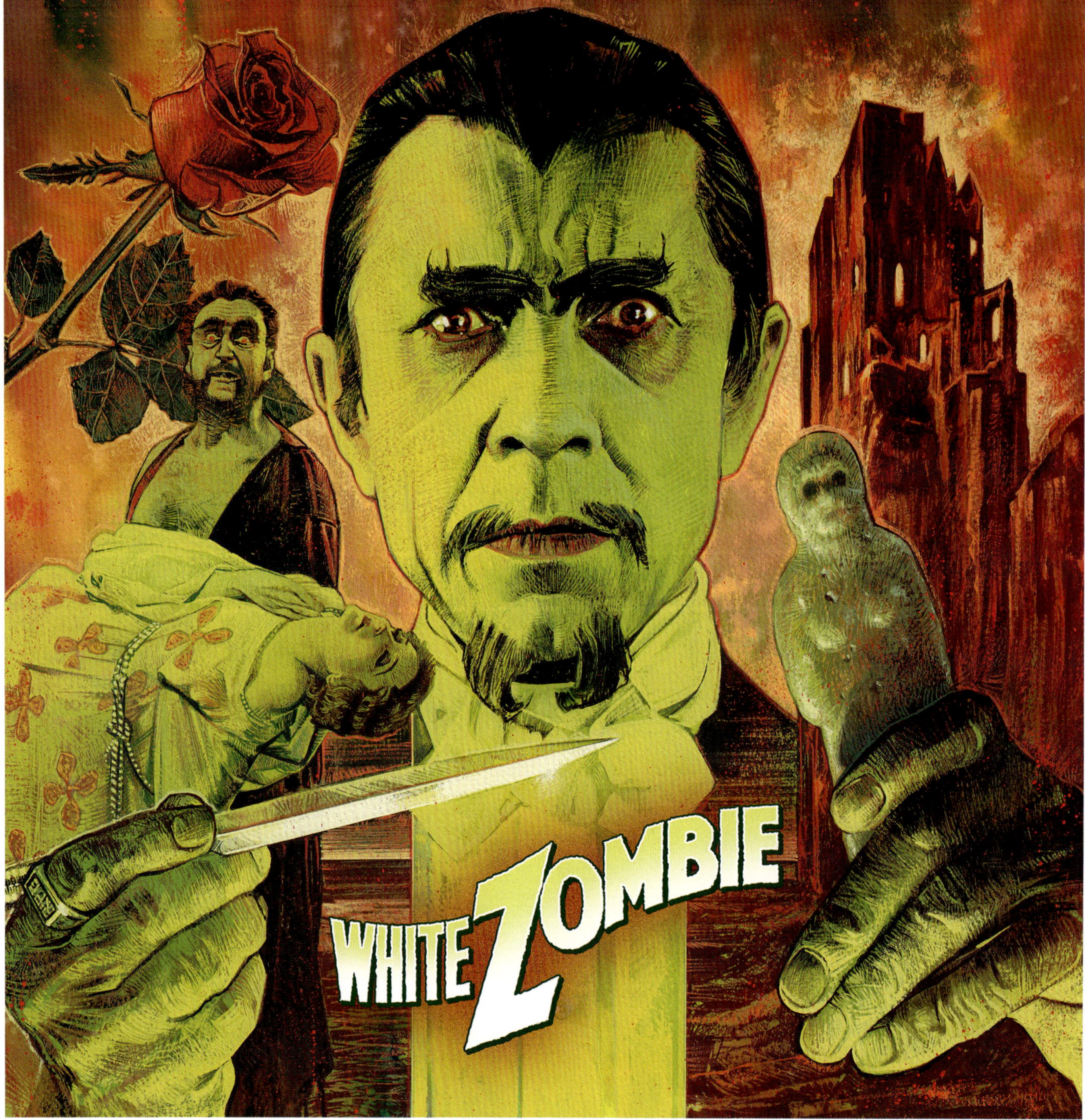

ABOVE: *White Zombie* (2021), Waxwork Records; LP cover.

At the time of writing, this is scheduled to be the first release in the *Rob Zombie Presents* soundtrack series (though not the first commissioned).

Although some were still available to source, there didn't seem to be a restored version (that I was aware of) to view for locating good reference material. The film that I could access was very poor quality, with no crisp images. I wanted to re-create a scene where Lugosi's character, "Murder Legendre" (very much in the mould of his "Dracula" released the year before), is carving a wax effigy. The quality of the footage was too poor to lift any usable reference, so I resorted to a staple solution, photographing my own hands. The backdrop signifies the Gothic elements, and the additional characters are spellbound by Murder Legendre's Voodoo. The rose is significant — it's the means by which his toxic agent is transmitted.

OPPOSITE TOP: *White Zombie* (2021) Waxwork Records, LP gatefold.

I made the decision to paint the gatefold as a single panel (a mistake I repeated with the gatefold for Carnival of Souls - when it was necessary to paint extensions to either end, to accommodate the substantial bleed required for printing). Subsequently, all gatefolds are painted as two panels stitched together in Photoshop. I'm limited by the paper stock I use. My maximum width means reducing the artwork size, where the required bleed allowance is substantial.

However, paint restrictions aside, I used the gatefold to present the array of "zombies", each perceived enemies of Murder Legendre and thus zombified. (Fun fact: This is the first film — unless I've been misinformed! — where the term "living dead" is first uttered). I wanted to use a close-up of Lugosi's eyes (a homage to the close-ups of Christopher Lee's in his own role as Dracula). The client requested the addition of Legendre's spellbinding hand configuration, which is why it appears a little cramped.

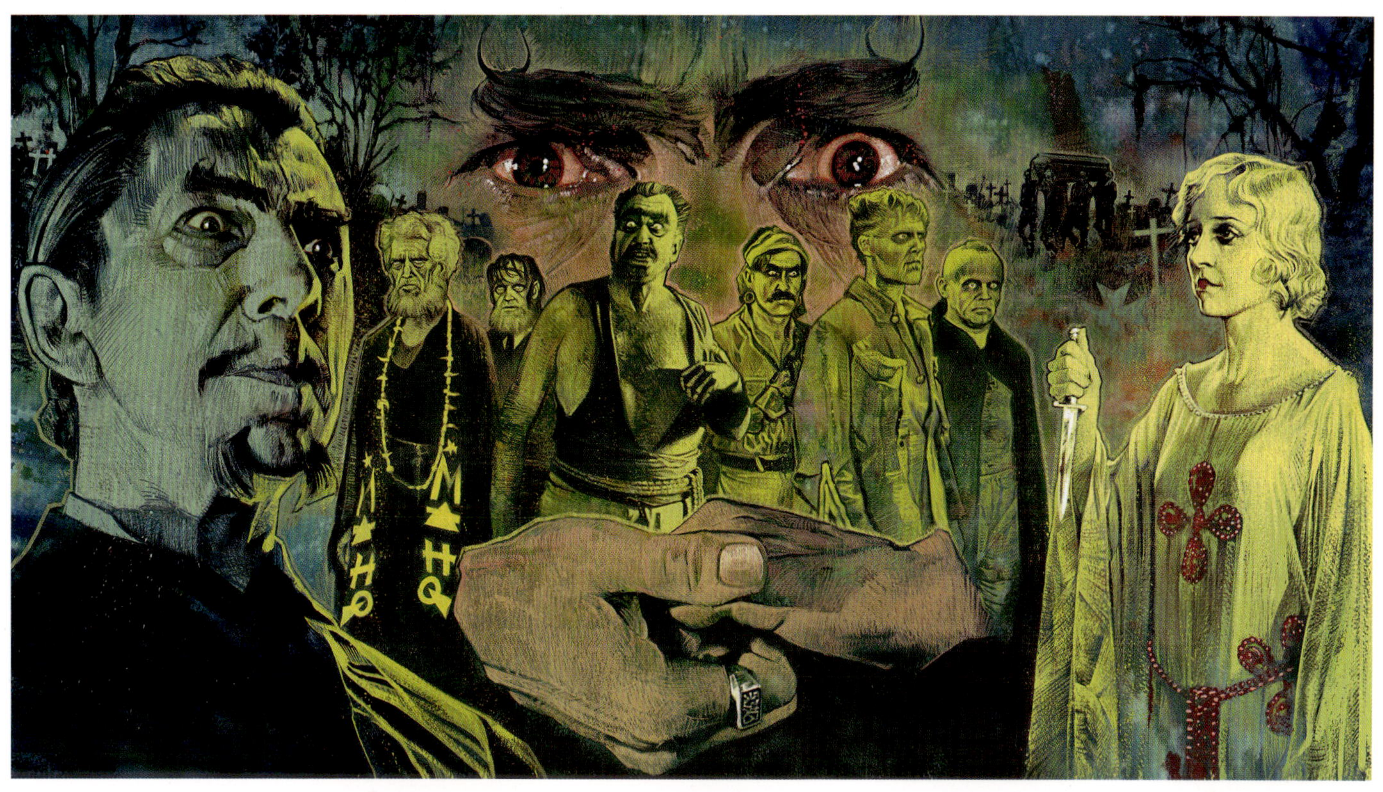

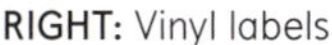
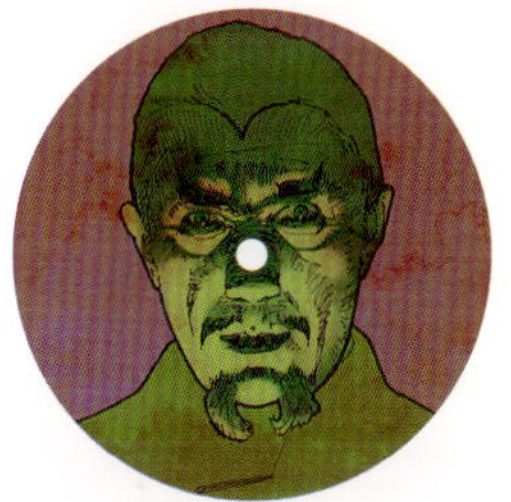
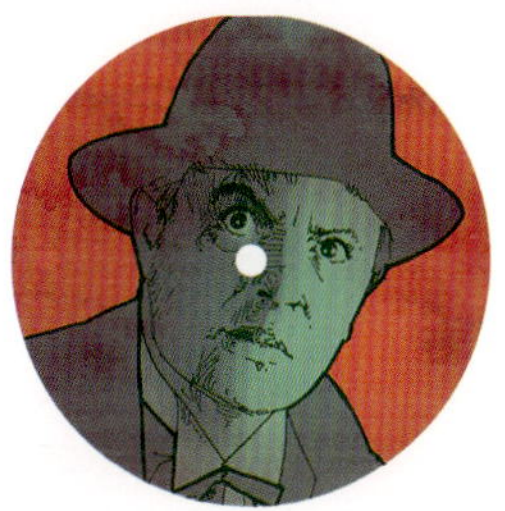
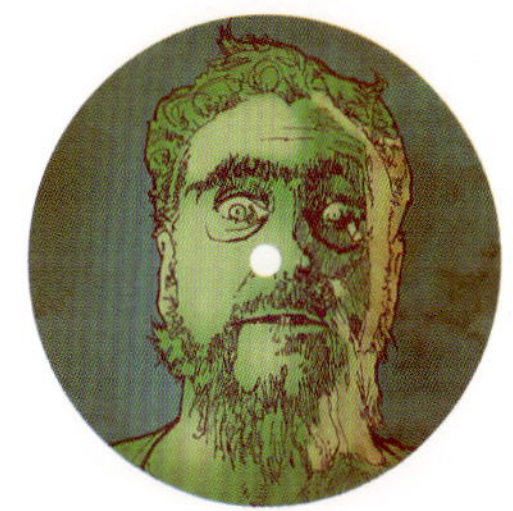
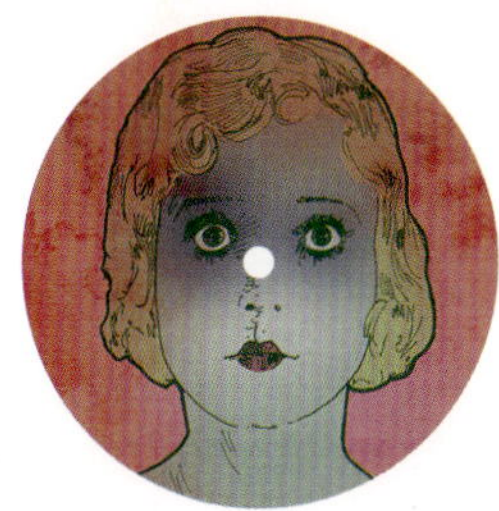

RIGHT: Vinyl labels.

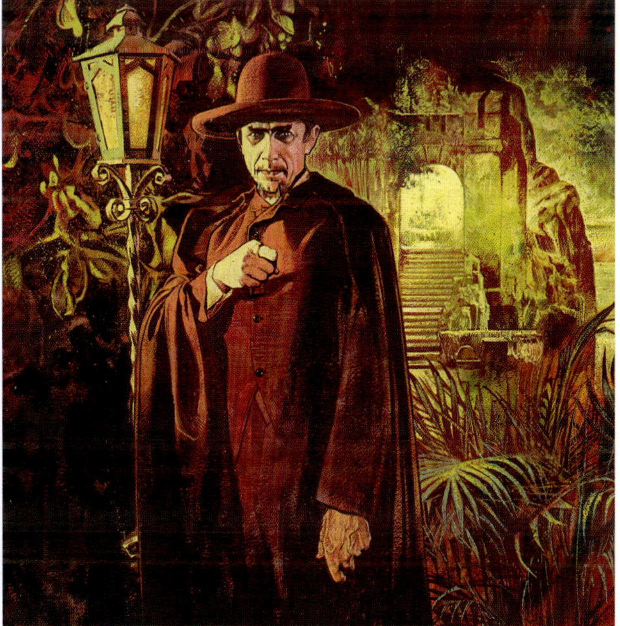

LEFT: *White Zombie* (2021), Waxwork Records; LP cover.

My reverse cover was inspired by the James Bama painted box artworks for the Aurora Monster hobby kits of the 1960s. Like many Monster Kids of my generation, the series of hobby kits were our introduction to the "'classic monsters". The first I owned was the Dracula figure. The box art was superior to the model within. Interestingly, the image of Bela Lugosi that was Bama's reference source was not from the 1931 *Dracula* but the later comedy-horror *Abbott and Costello Meet Frankenstein* (1948).

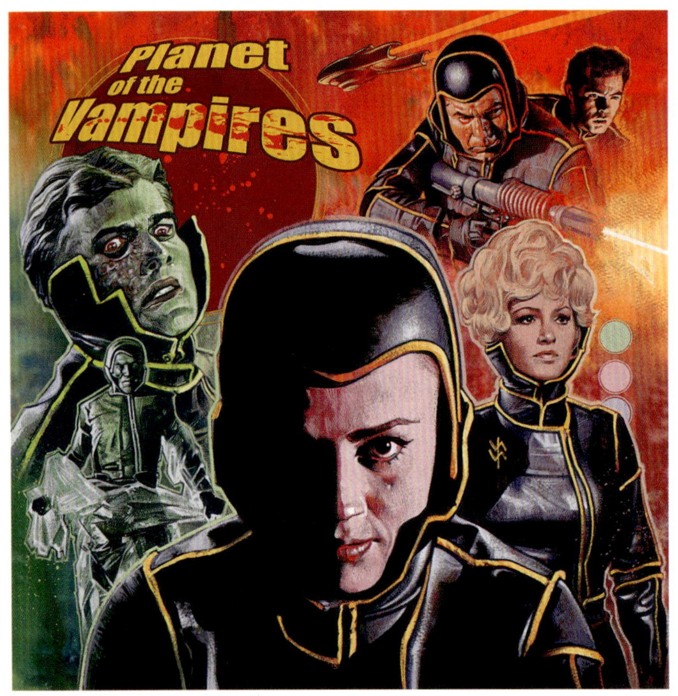

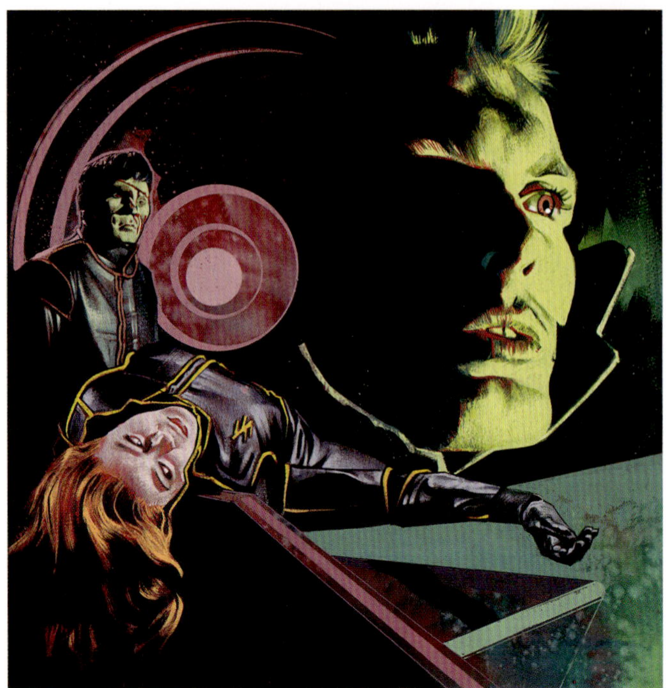

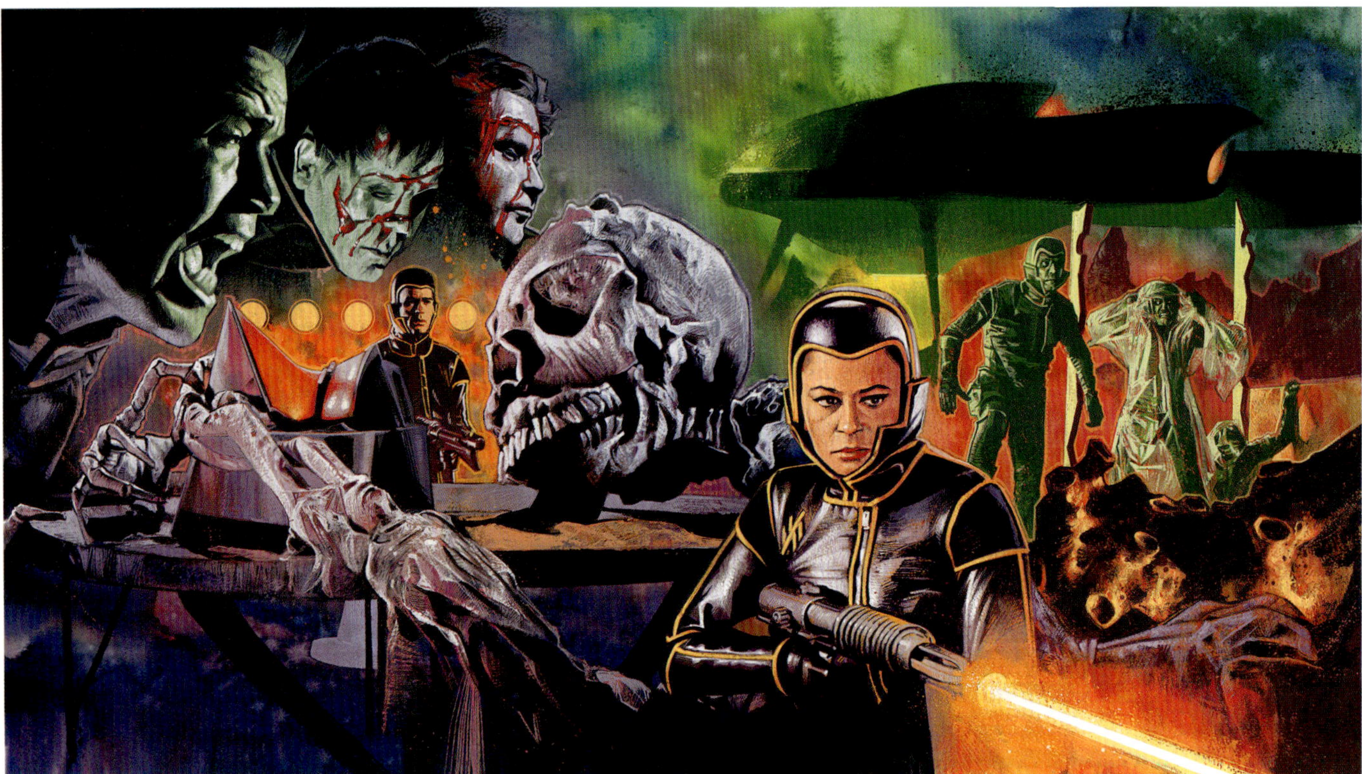

ABOVE LEFT: *Planet of the Vampires* (2022), Mondo; LP front cover.

This soundtrack LP allowed me to use all four panels (two being the centre-fold) to explore the rich imagery of this influential Italian sci-fi film directed by Mario Bava in 1965 — it was filmed with lurid colour palettes that seemed to echo my own. With clear influences on Ridley Scott's *Alien* (1979), I used some of the filmic references within the layout. I also hoped to give it a flavour of classic B-movie posters and ramp up the vampire/zombie elements.

ABOVE RIGHT: *Planet of the Vampires* (2022), Mondo; LP back cover.

The set design occasionally reminded me of the 1956 film *Forbidden Planet*. In constructing my layout, I was particularly struck by a scene that used concentric circles and used this as a pivot for the imagery.

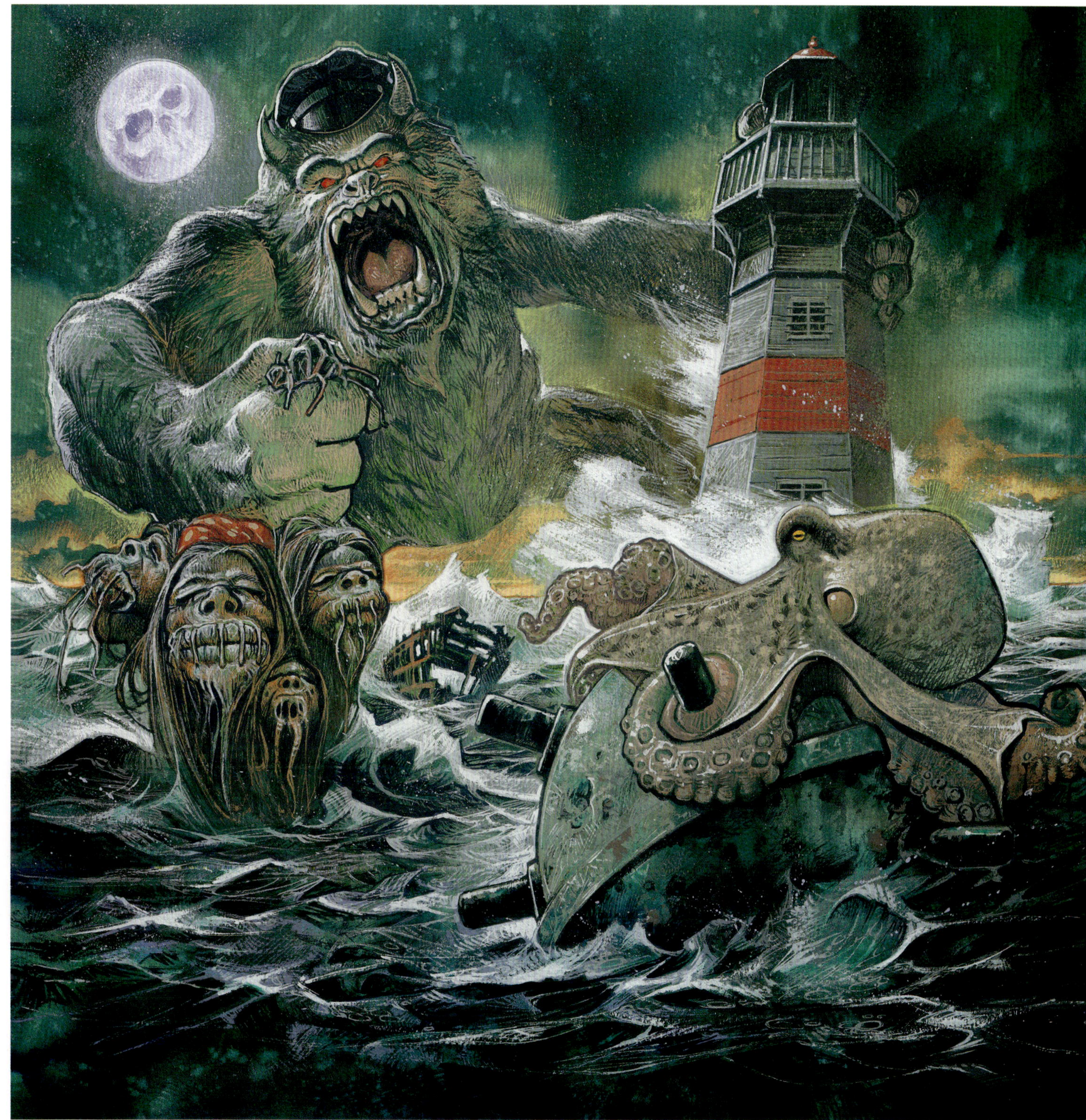

OPPOSITE BOTTOM:
Planet of the Vampires (2022), Mondo; LP cover gatefold.

The extended format allowed me to focus on the fossilised alien creature, often considered to have influenced the design of the "navigator" in *Alien*.

ABOVE: *Sea Savage* (2020), Prosthetic Records LLC; LP cover.

My third LP cover for the thrash metal band Gama Bomb, *Sea Savage* features their Yeti-creature mascot "Snowy" in a seafaring environment. My brief requested a giant Snowy, shrunken heads, and a shipwreck. The rest I constructed using my imagination and sourced images.

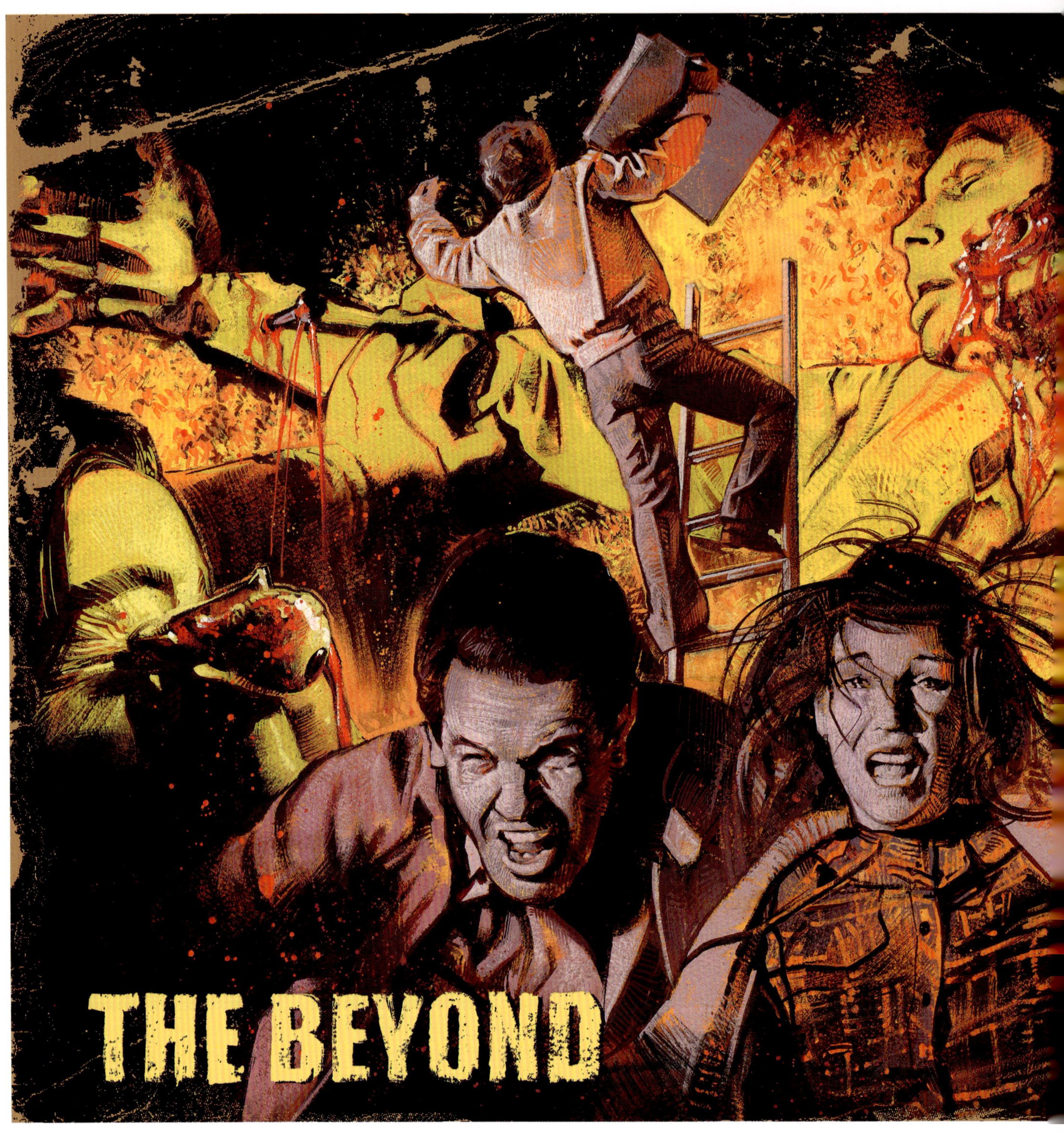

ABOVE: *The Beyond* (2019), Demon Records; LP gatefold.

The first of this trilogy of films that I recall seeing — the scenes of graphic horror have made it legendary in video history, alongside the director's other celebrated film, *Zombie Flesh Eaters*. It's packed with images that are familiar to genre fans. I retained some of them but also added some less well-represented elements. It seemed appropriate to differentiate them with individual colour themes in each of the three panels.

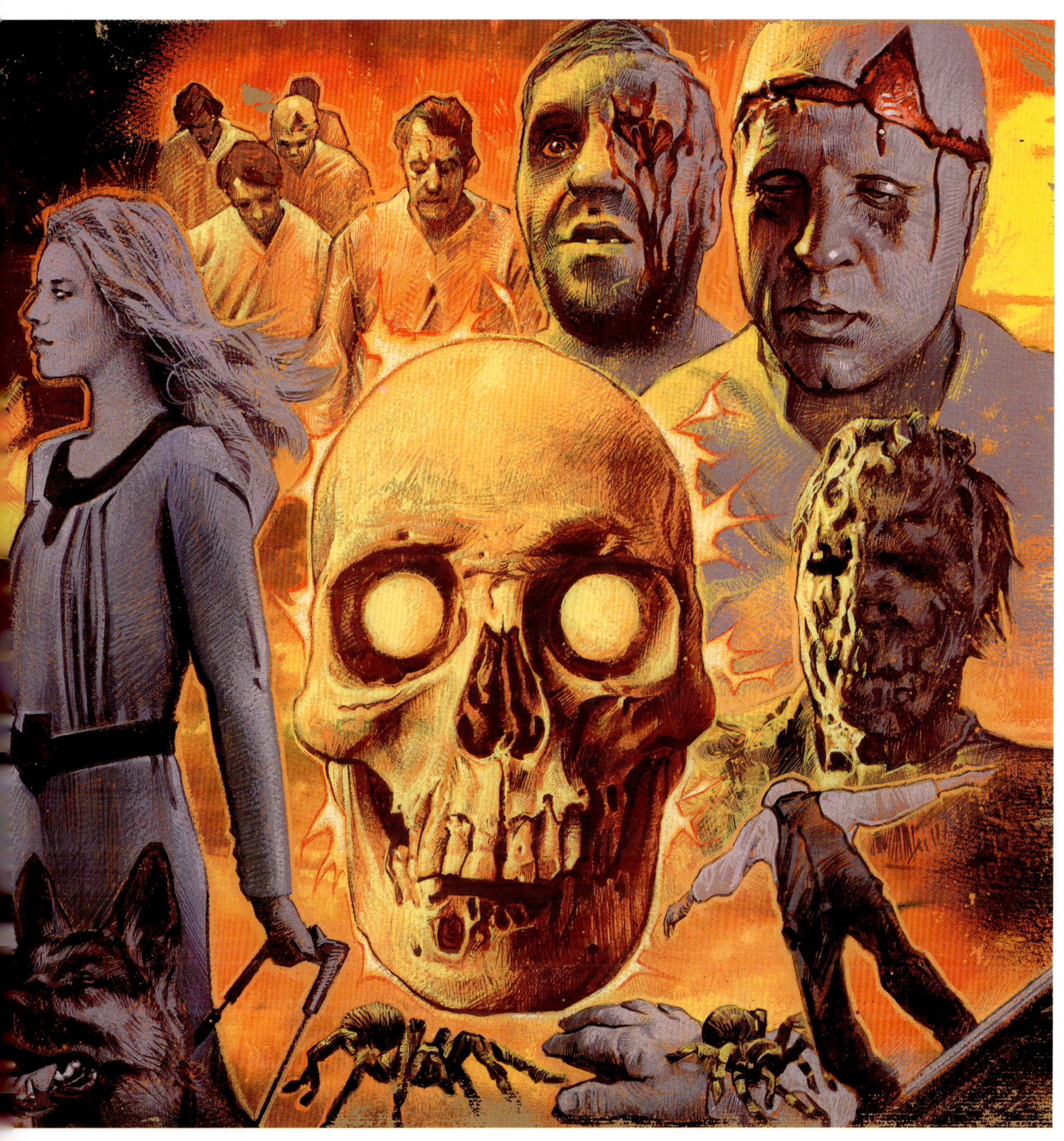

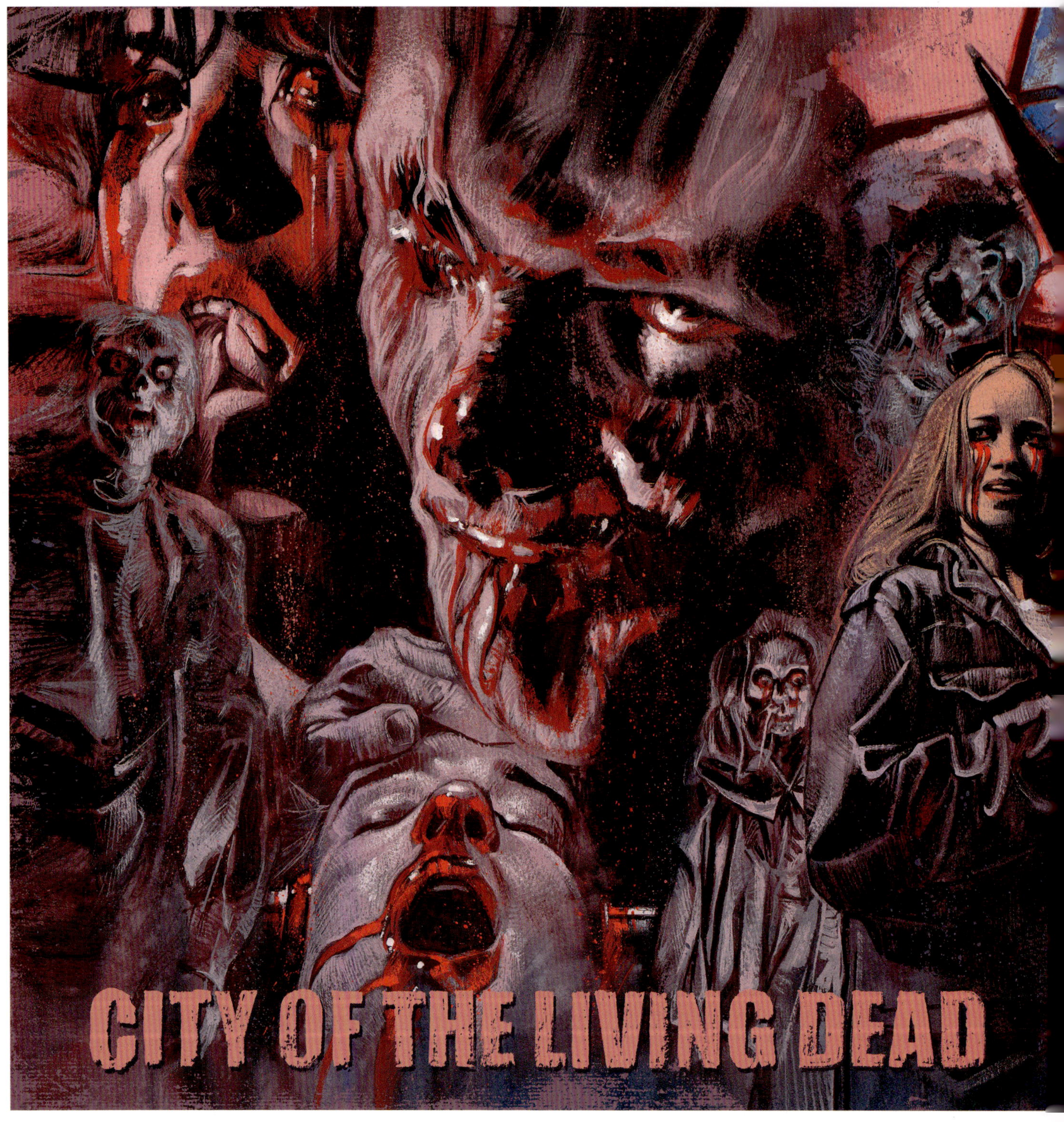

ABOVE: *City of the Living Dead* (2019), Demon Records; LP gatefold.

Elements from the film form the basic layout here, mostly from screen grabs of an unrestored DVD (making sharp images almost impossible to capture). My reference material was a mix of screen grabs and internet searches. This, like its two companions, uses my own photography of a skull in my personal collection.

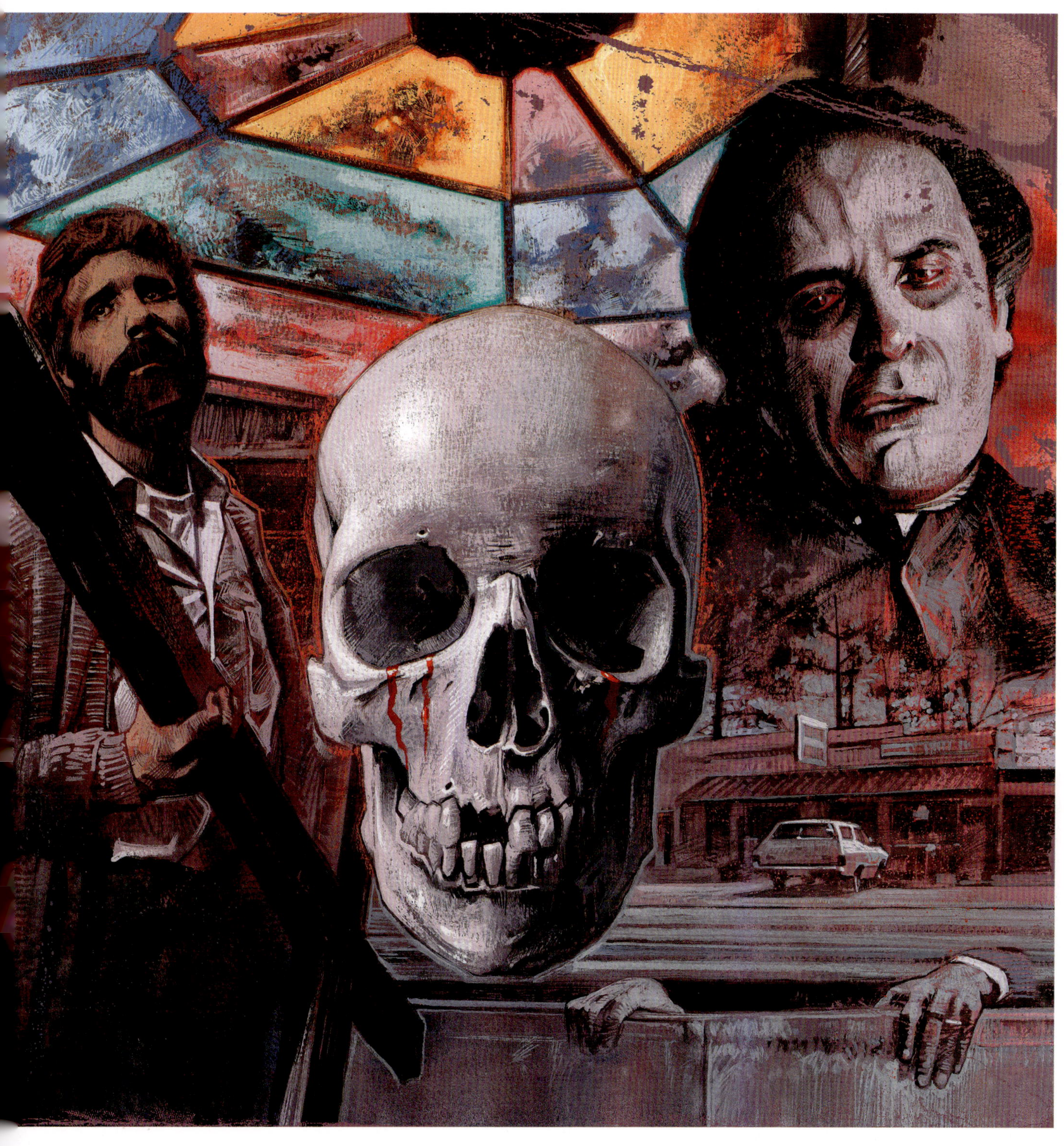

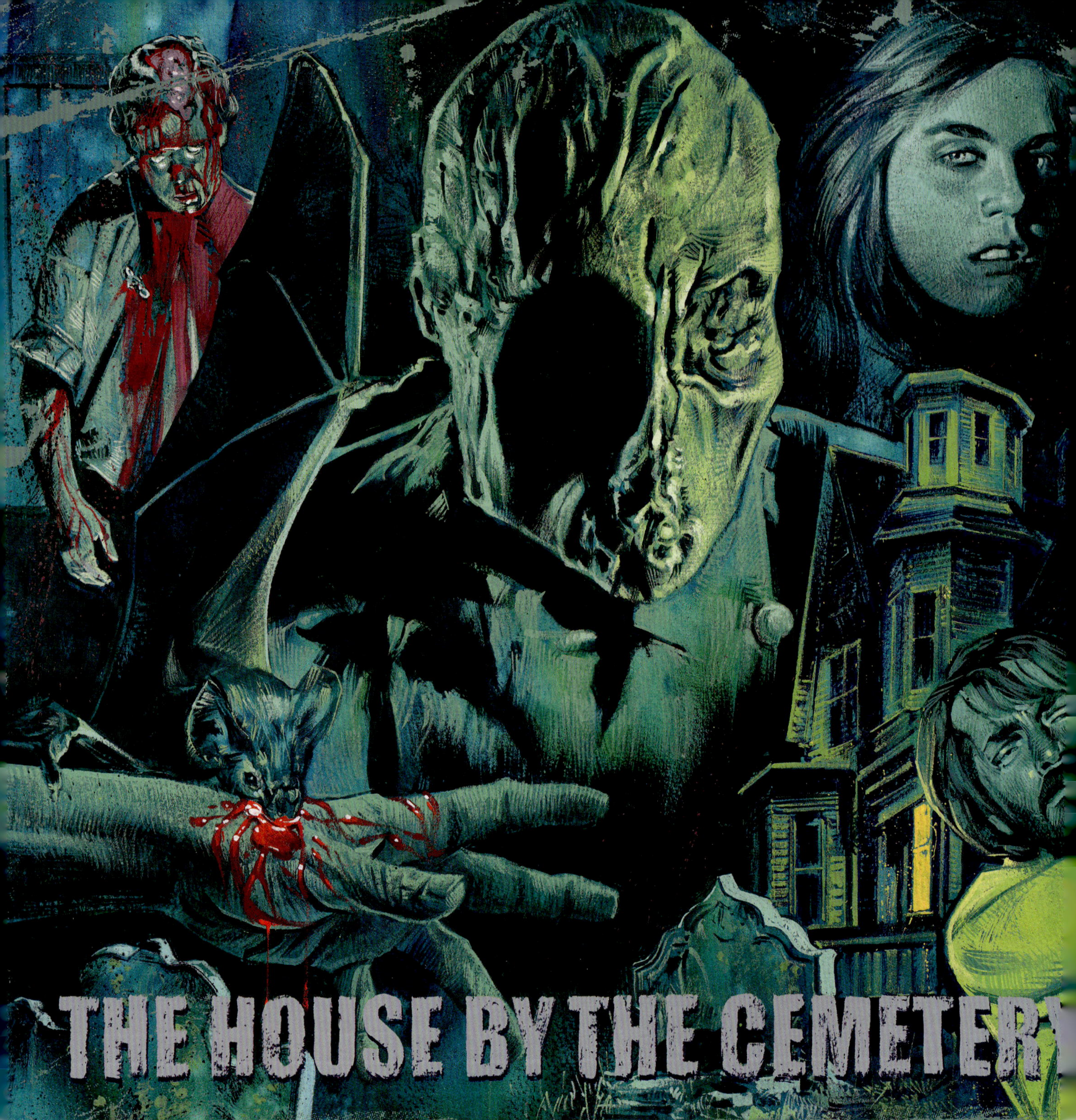

ABOVE: *The House by the Cemetery* (2019), Demon Records; LP gatefold.

One of my first commissions from Death Waltz records several years ago was an LP cover for the soundtrack of this film. This gatefold offered greater scope for incorporating more imagery. For each of the three films in this trilogy, I decided to add a skull in the same layout location — to create a sense of continuity — but with a difference in the eyes that would relate to the individual film. Each skull uses a different reference, so that they're not the same build.

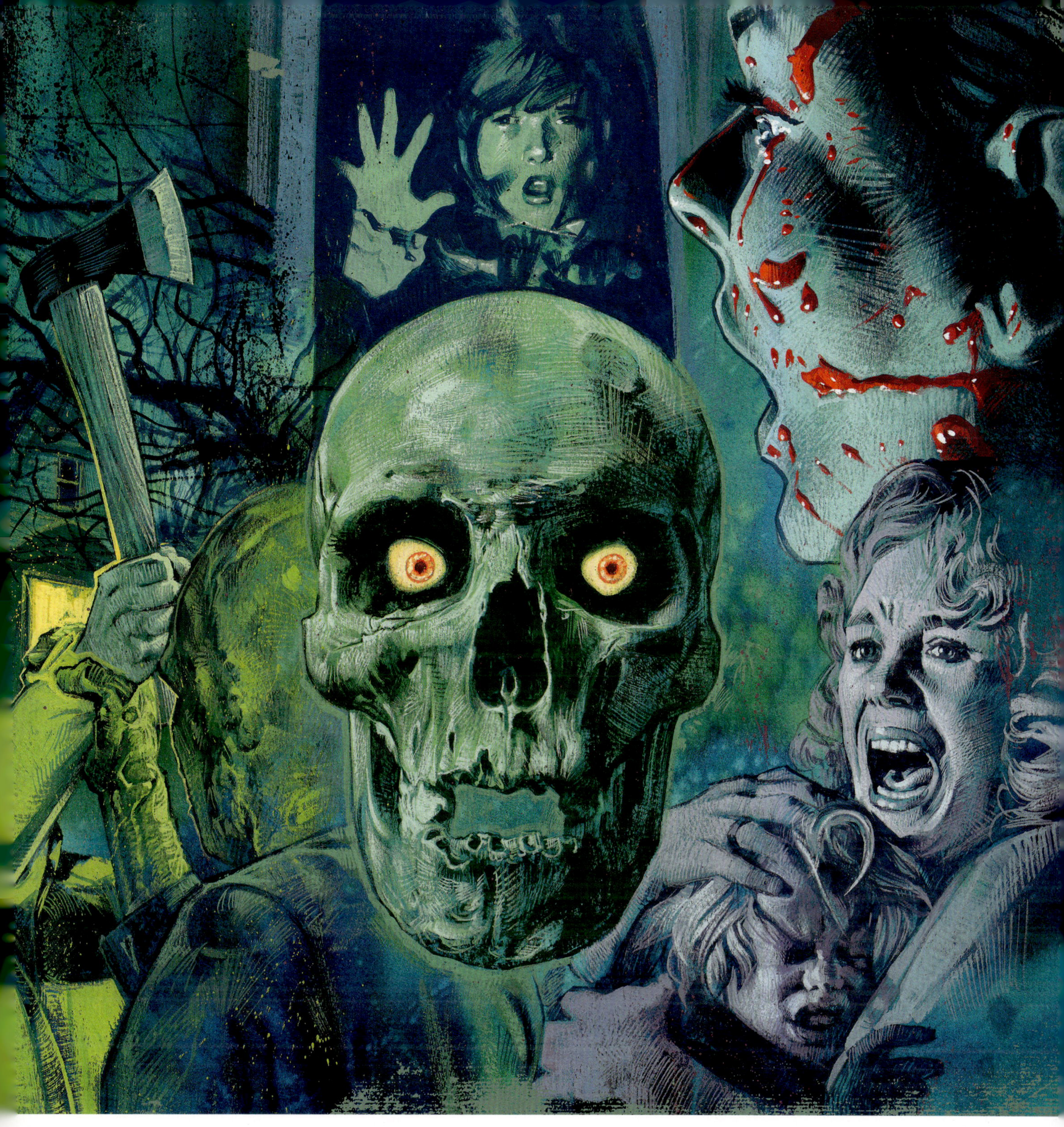

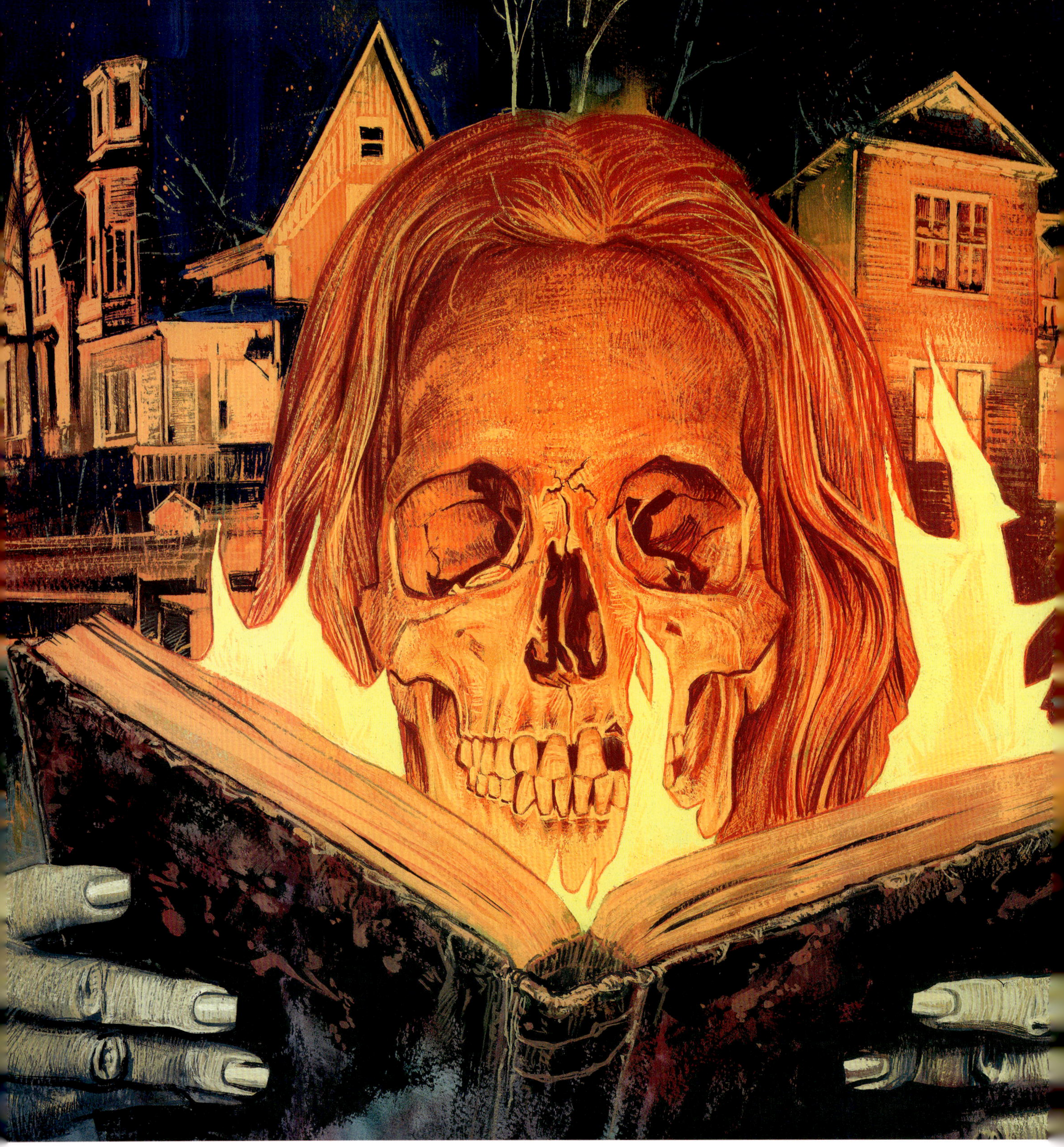

ABOVE: *The Gates of Hell Trilogy* (front panel) (2019),
Demon Records; LP cover.

Each of the soundtracks had already been available in vinyl or CD form. I painted a "trilogy" cover for the Italian company Beat Records in 2017. This LP set was designed to present the recordings in coloured vinyl as a collector's edition, with additional notes and new artwork in book form. I created all the graphics as well as the illustrations.

My cover is non-specific, but the book element is important because a common thread within the plot references the mysterious *Book of Eibon* (much like H.P. Lovecraft's *The Necronomicon*). Thus, the entire presentation takes the form of a book, with the cover representing its deadly spell.

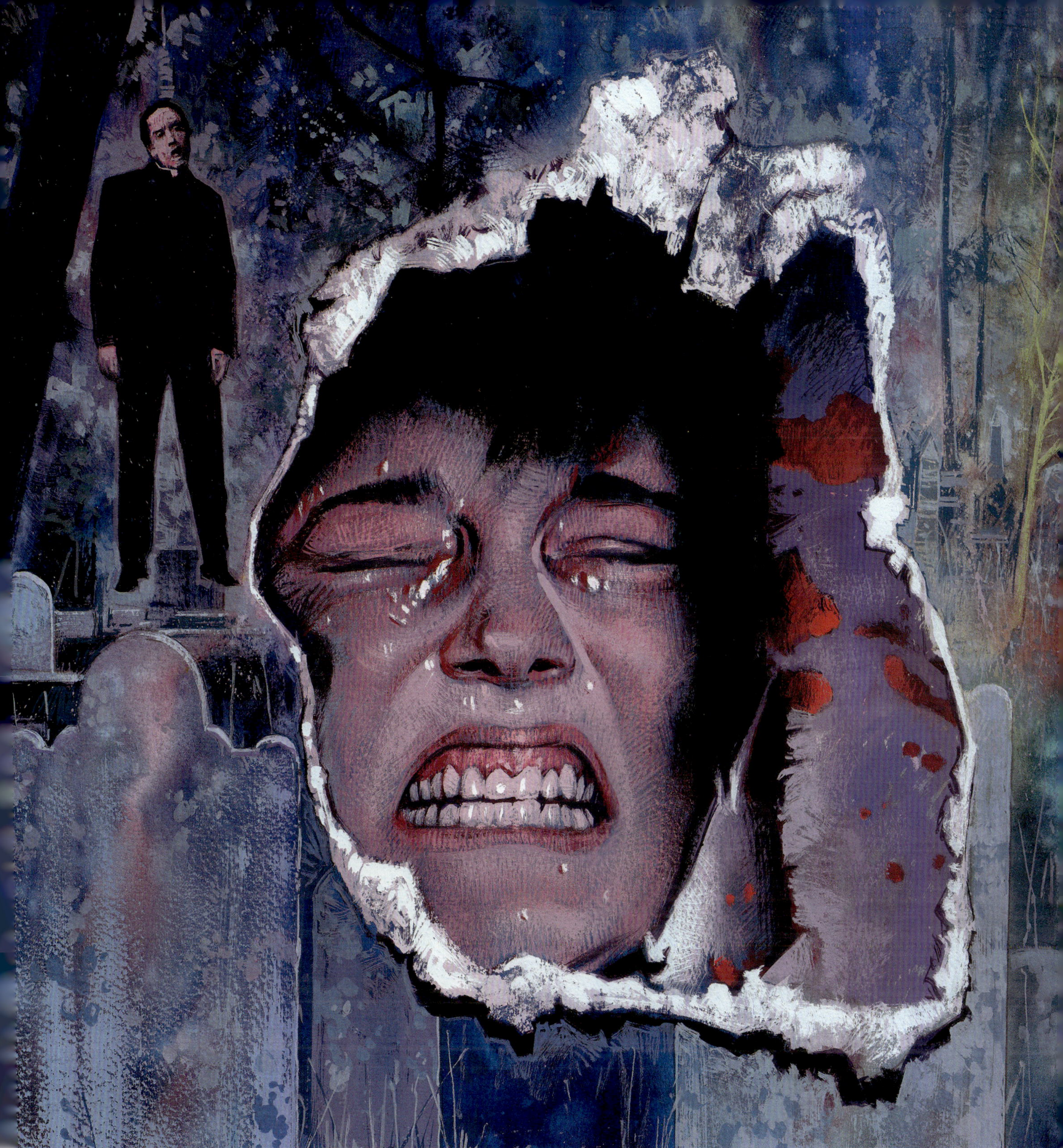

ABOVE: *The Gates of Hell Trilogy* (back cover) (2019),
Demon Records; LP cover.

In a colour contrast to the front panel, I also thought it would be
interesting to make the surface of the cover become the lid of the coffin,
wherein a pivotal scene, a premature burial, is discovered. With religious
rites in mind, the hanging priest seemed to be the perfect addition.

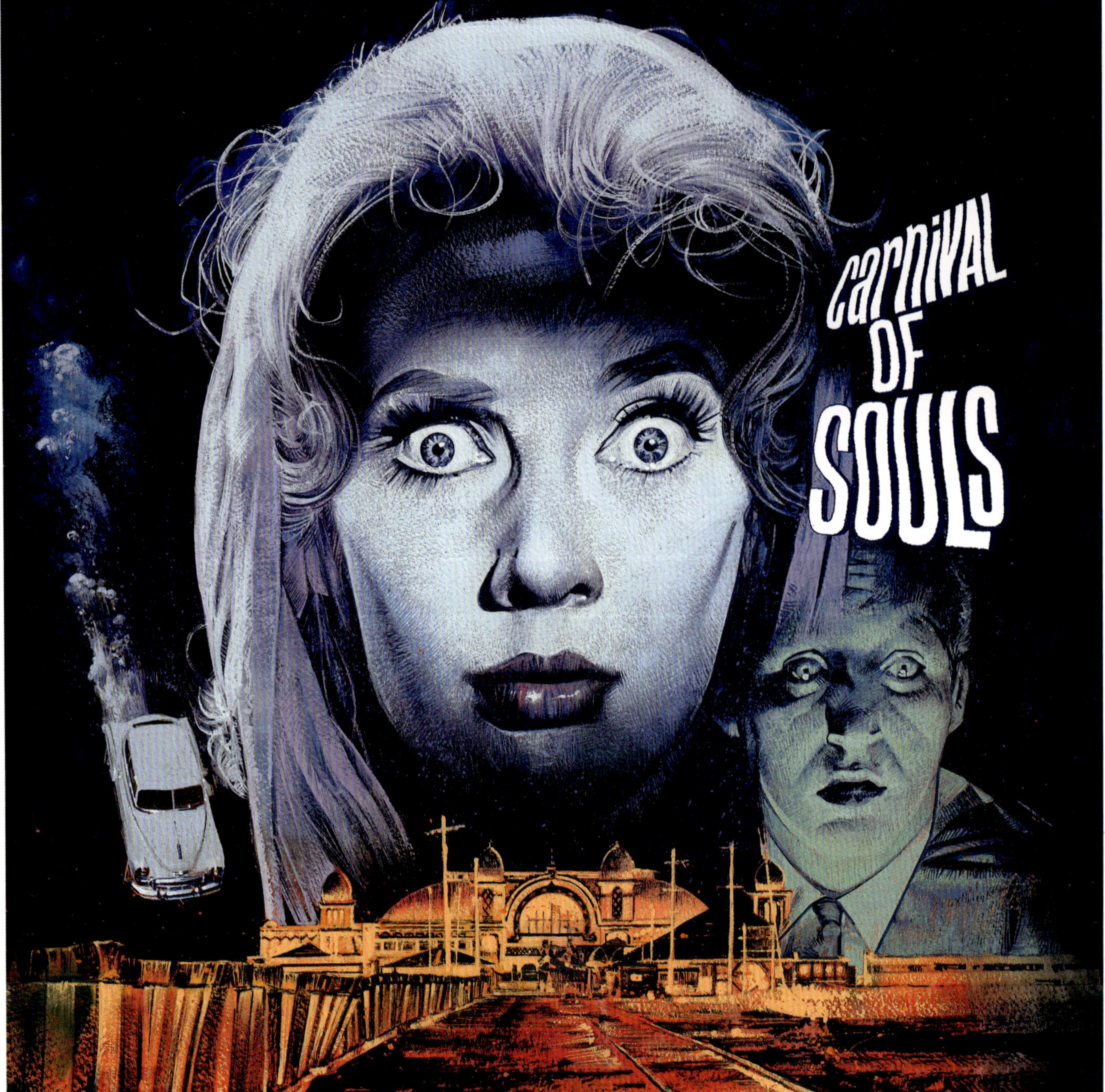

ABOVE: *Carnival of Souls* (2021), Waxwork Records; LP front cover.

The black and white film *Carnival of Souls* (1962), often rated as one of the "greatest horror films ever made", has been cited as an influence on George A Romero and David Lynch. Filled with surreal images, its haunting atmosphere and use of location offered many possibilities for my artwork. I'd initially chosen to use the palette of a colour negative, predominantly blue and orange. Whilst this palette remains on the cover, my client requested that the orange hues be removed from the other panels, which required some repainting.

OPPOSITE TOP: LP gatefold.

I used the extended format of the gatefold to add narrative elements. The wild-eyed expression of the film's focus, actor Candace Hilligoss (playing Mary Henry), is pitted against her landlady and the unwanted attention of another tenant. Mary Henry is a gifted organist, and there's a significant scene where she auditions at a church.

OPPOSITE BOTTOM LEFT: LP back cover.

A key scene depicts the ghostly haunters of the pavilion submerged to the neck in water. This is a composite of several shots from the film. I sourced a historical image of the pavilion for the best possible reference for the backdrop. The filming of *Carnival of Souls* took place in Salt Lake City, Utah, USA and made use of the astounding Saltair Pavillion. An early example of Moorish Revival architecture built in 1893, it had been subjected to a number of disastrous fires and reconstructions, falling into disuse and ruin after 1958, and as such, it provided the perfect backdrop for the film! A third incarnation of the building, Saltair III, is now a music venue. (Fun fact from Wikipedia: A 1960s photo of Saltair II was featured on the cover of the bootleg Beach Boys album *Unsurpassed Masters, Vol. 19*.)

OPPOSITE BOTTOM RIGHT: Bonus insert.

A bonus artwork insert has been a feature of the Waxwork Records releases. In this instance, the client requested I depict a stark moment from the film, retaining a monochrome colour theme.

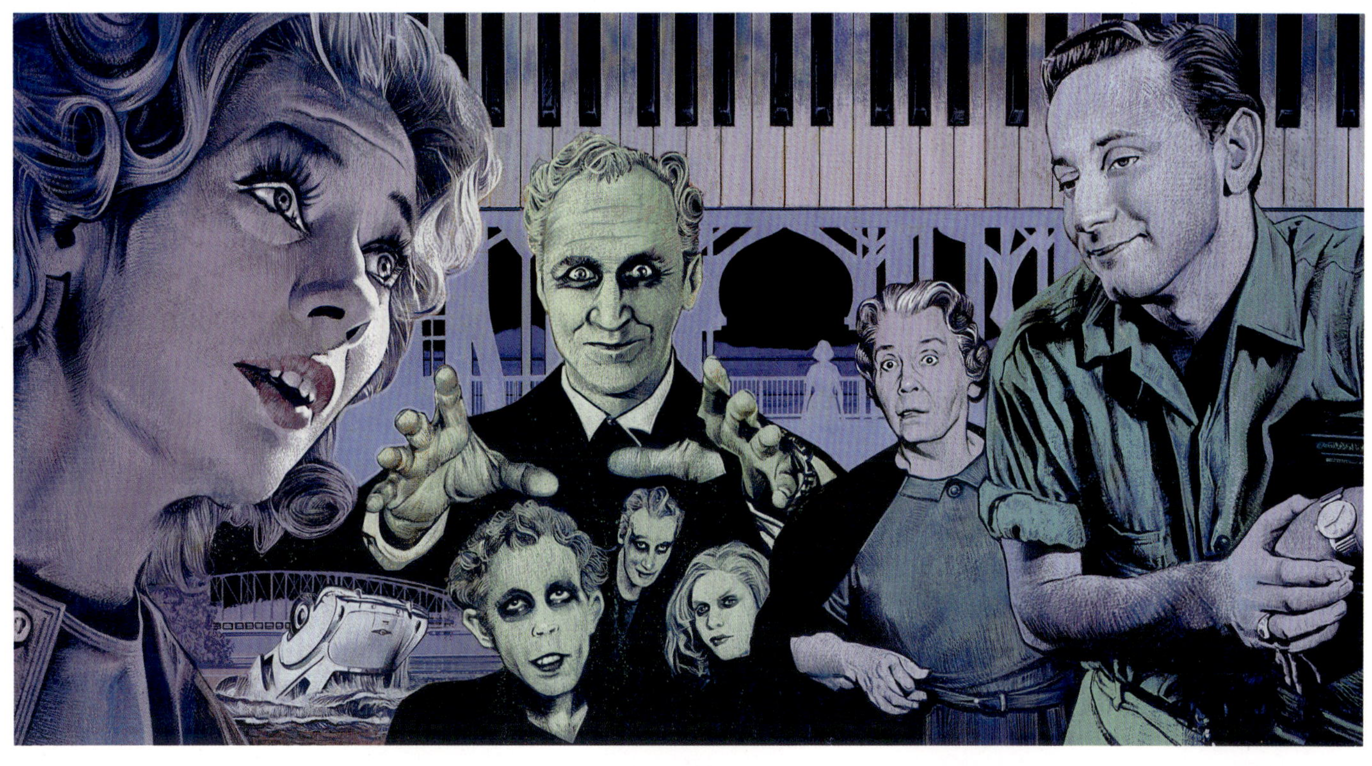

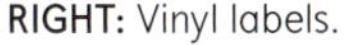
RIGHT: Vinyl labels.

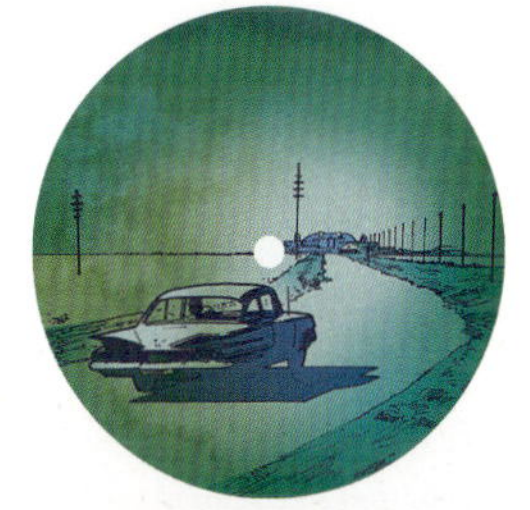
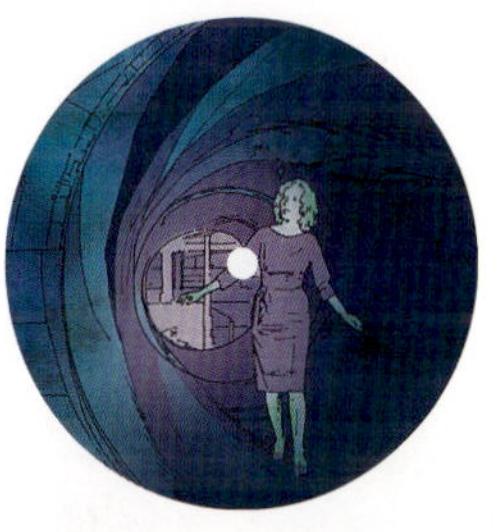
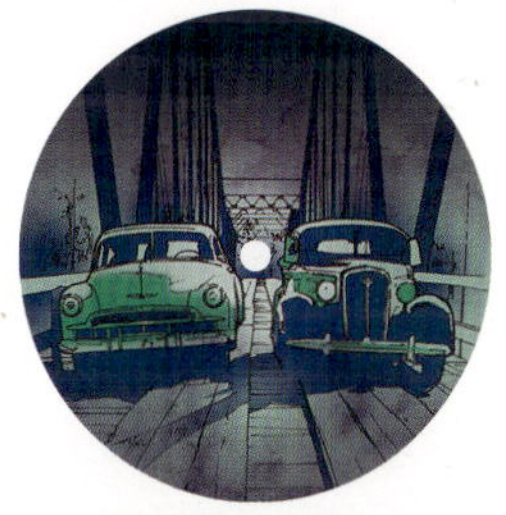
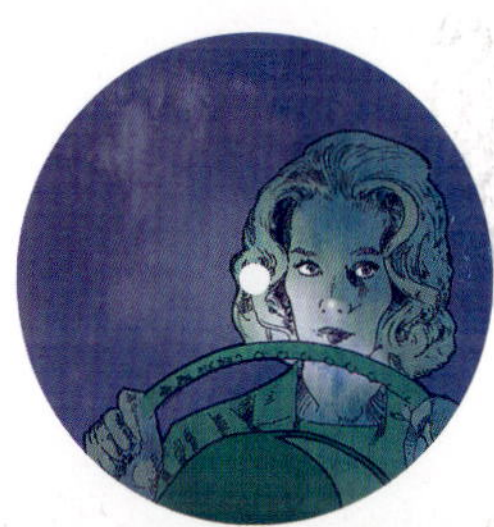

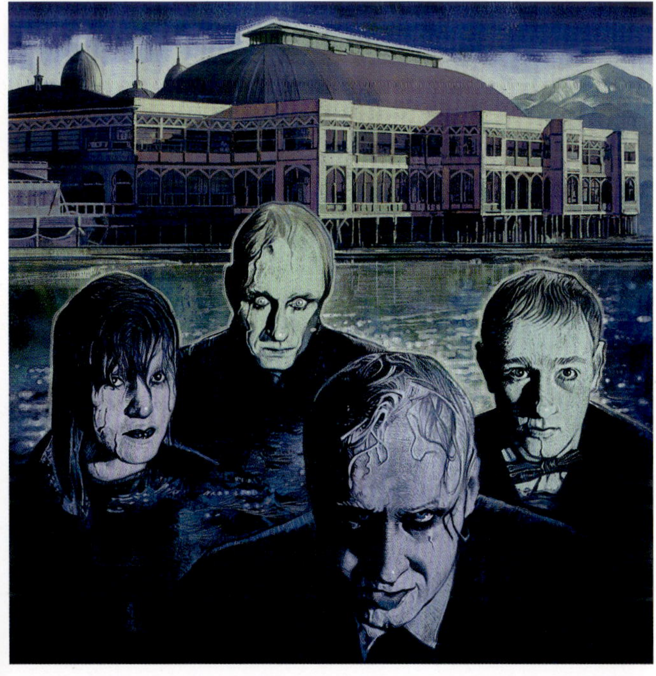

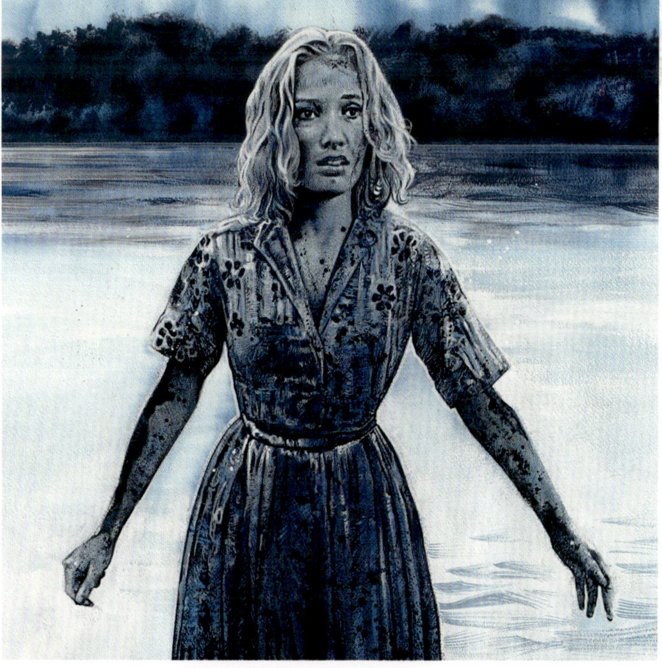

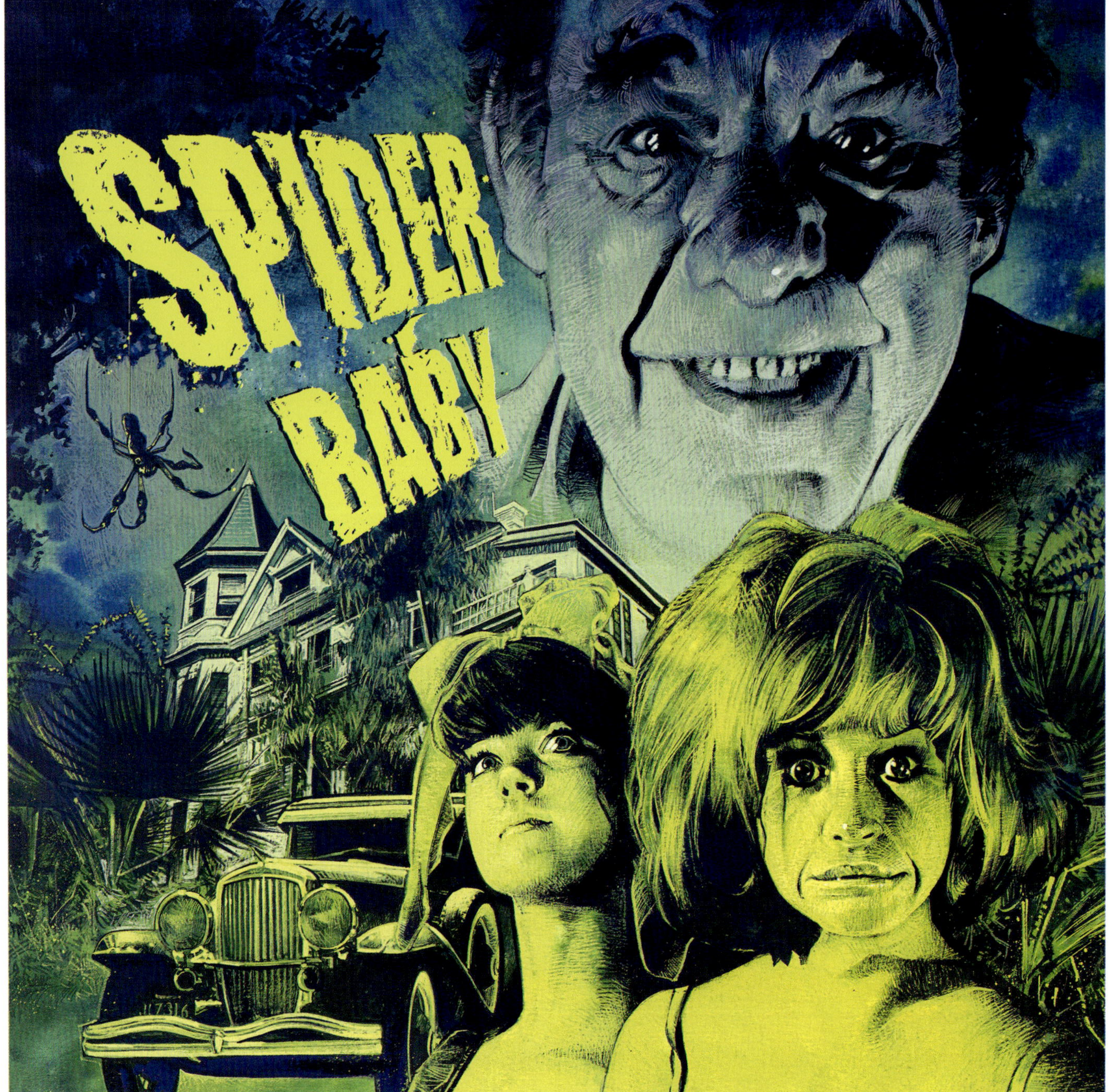

ABOVE: *Spider Baby* (2021), Waxwork Records; LP front cover.

In 2013, I painted a Blu-ray cover for Arrow Films for this title. I loved the film, so I was thrilled to be able to revisit the subject with another decade of experience to my name. The cover came to me in a dream (as do many). I just needed to try my best to represent that vision.

A monochrome film, it nevertheless is suggestive of wild colours that might be associated with the period in which it was made, 1967. As one of Lon Chaney Jr's last films, a link to the old Universal monster movies, it seemed respectful to give him prominence on the cover. With so many images to choose from, I tried to be concise and stick to the two sisters and a setting, although the car was too beautiful to resist. I wanted to create the look of the "golden age of Hollywood" but with an ironic twist.

OPPOSITE TOP: LP gatefold.

I used the gatefold panels to explore the horrors within, like opening the door to see what's behind, and then wishing you hadn't! Another opportunity to add more of the cast.

OPPOSITE BOTTOM LEFT: LP back cover.

The reverse of the sleeve allowed me to add more characters to build up the cast and add intrigue. When I first sent the art to the client, they expressed surprise and concern that I'd abandoned the front cover colours. I explained that the cover was an exterior setting, whilst the back was the gloomy interior — this was acceptable.

OPPOSITE BOTTOM RIGHT: LP bonus insert.

This was the first of my Waxwork Records commissions. The idea of an insert wasn't discussed, but I did suggest a jigsaw puzzle as an extra item to add value to the soundtrack (there's a scene where the two sisters are attempting to complete a jigsaw). The idea wasn't realised, but the art was made, thus becoming a bonus insert. In a further homage to Universal monster movies, I took the poster for the 1931 *Dracula* as my inspiration, the spider web being a perfect match for the film.

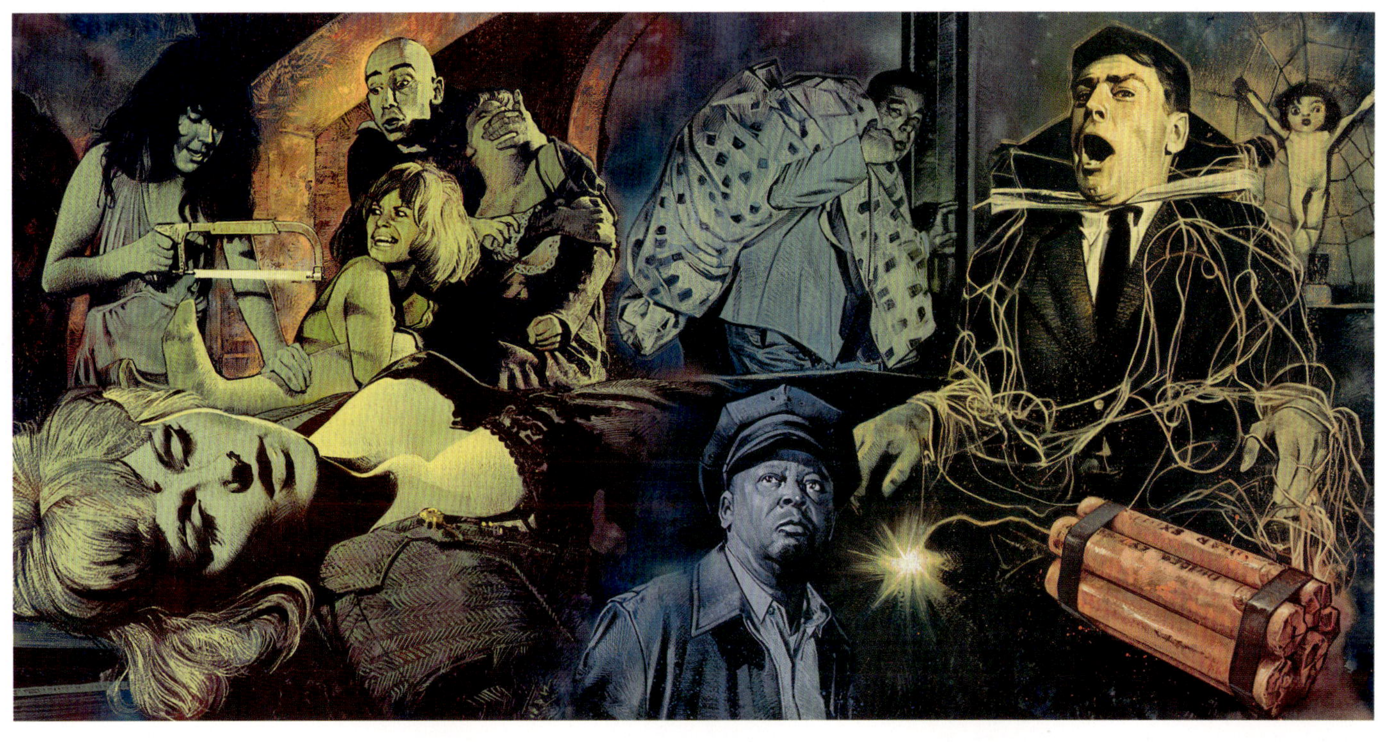

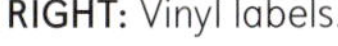
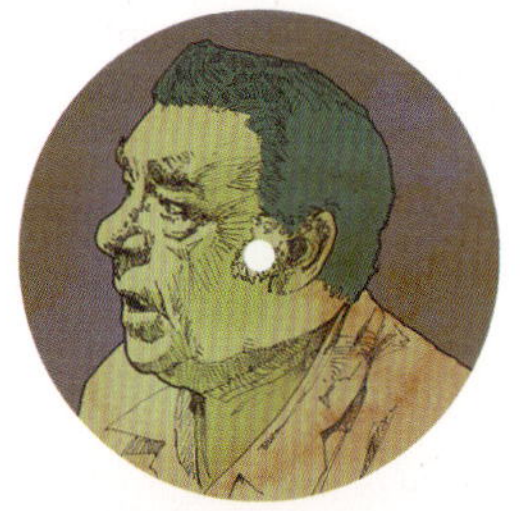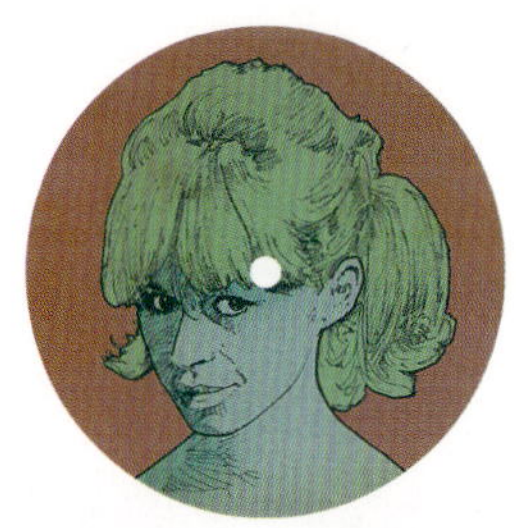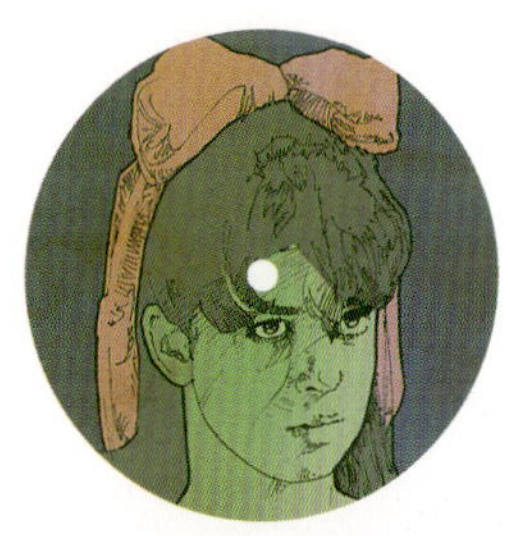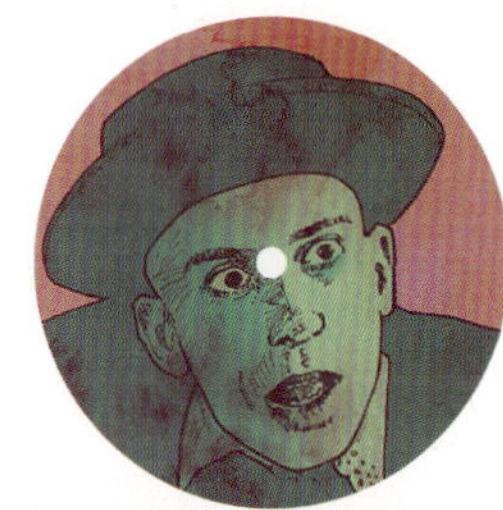

RIGHT: Vinyl labels.

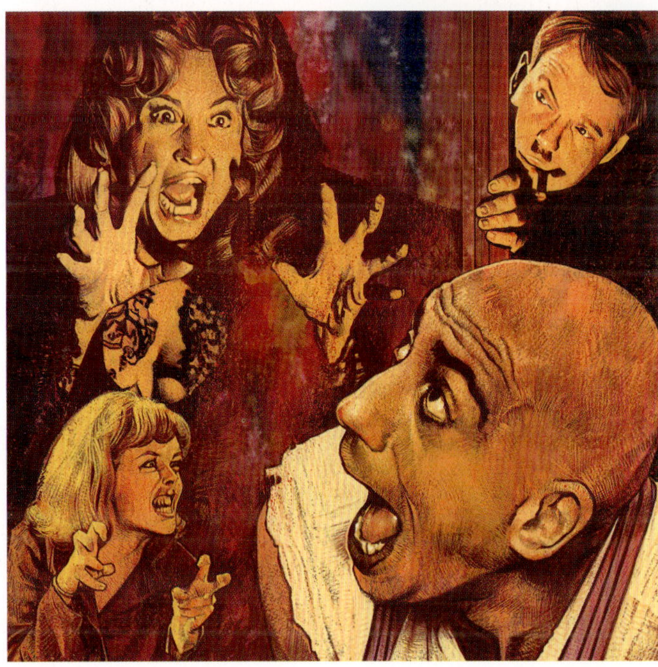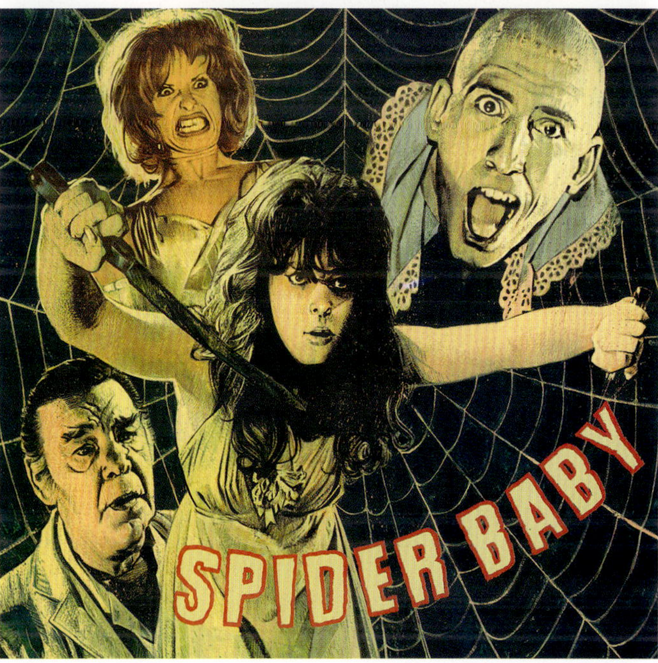

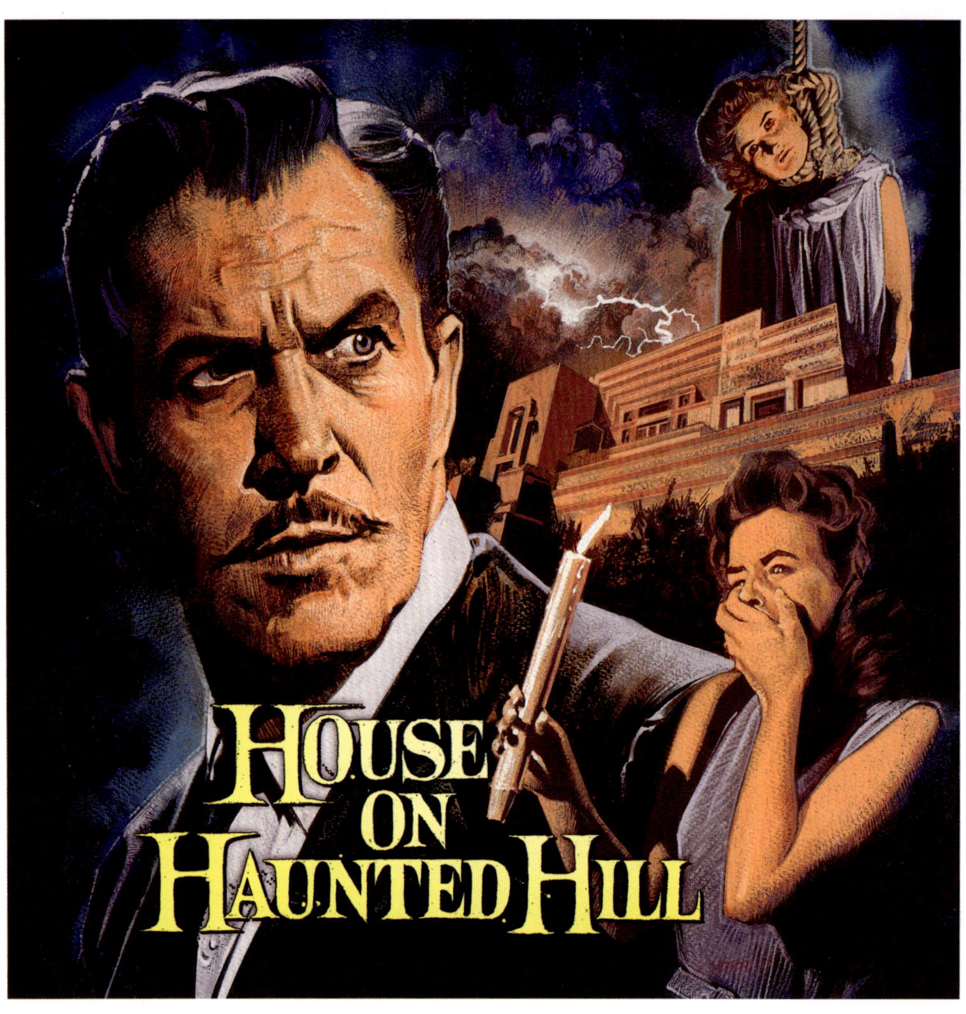

This classic 1959 William Castle film
starring Vincent Price remains a
favourite of the period, embodying
all the tropes of a haunted house film.
My cover would inevitably be a portrait
of the star, but adding a location and
secondary elements to suggest a film
poster. As the film was black and white,
I kept a limited palette suggestive of
hand-tinted photographs.

BELOW LEFT: LP back cover.

The sleeve's reverse was intended to
suggest the actual reverse of the cover
image. The building (Ennis House in Los
Feliz, California, designed by Frank Lloyd
Wright, built in 1924) is seen from the
back elevation on my front cover, but
here from the front roadside elevation
(as seen in the film). The hanging figure
is also seen from the reverse angle.
I added additional characters and a key
plot element to complete the layout but
left space for the track listings.

BELOW RIGHT: Bonus insert.

As a standalone image, this is almost
an alternative film poster. No skeleton
holds a gun in the film; it's simply
emblematic. A key shock moment
is added for extra fright!

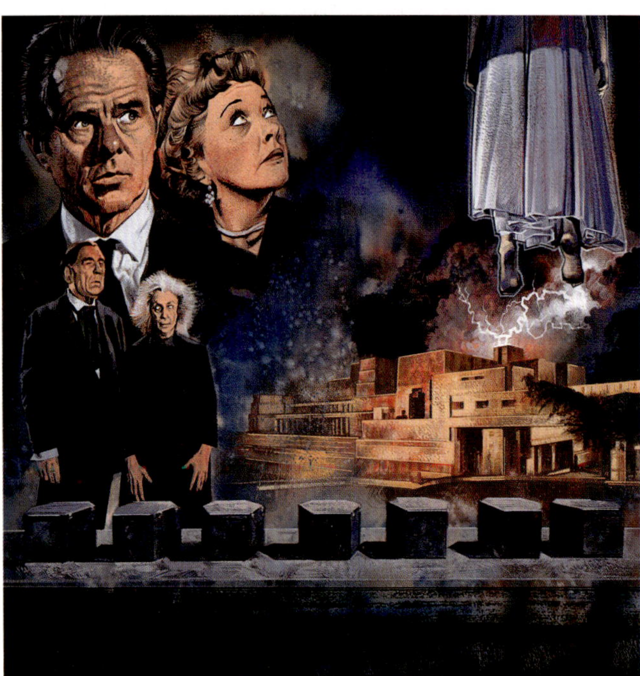

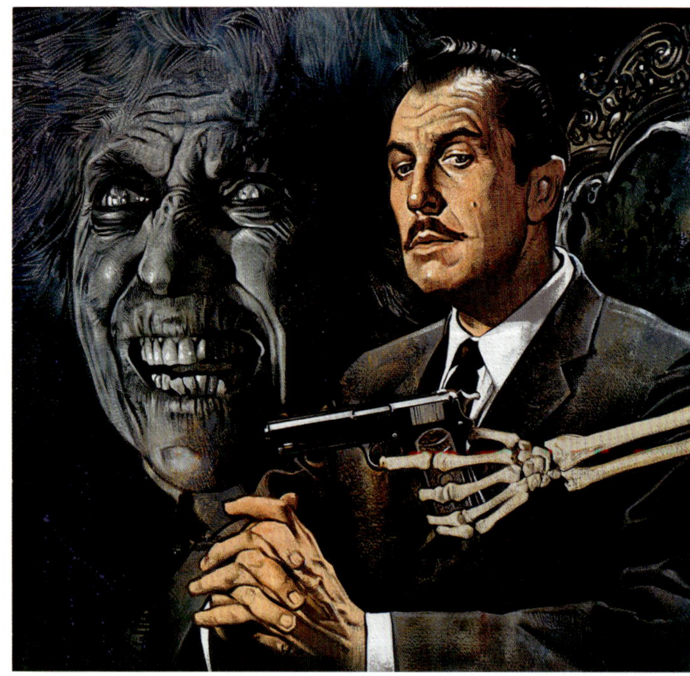

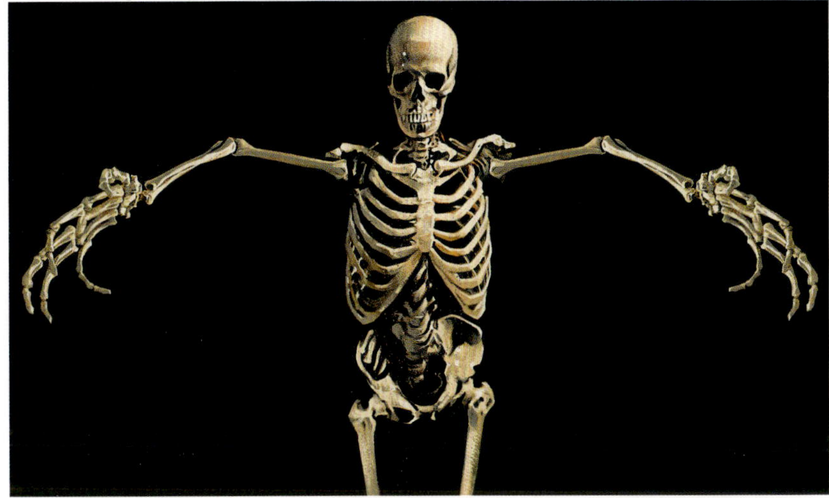

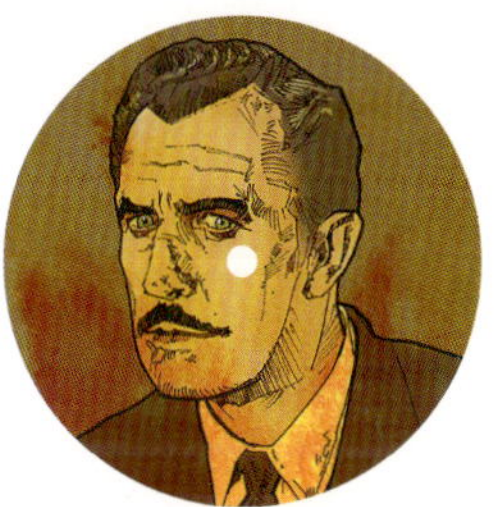
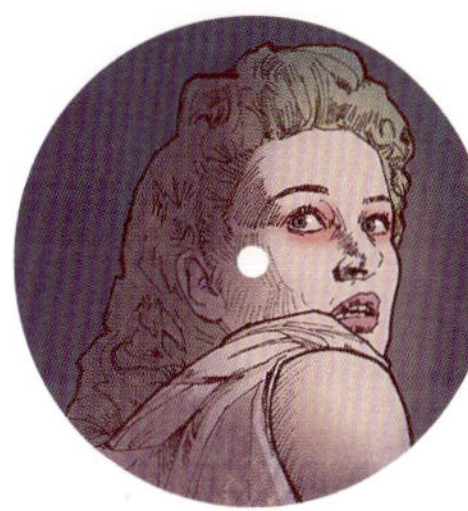
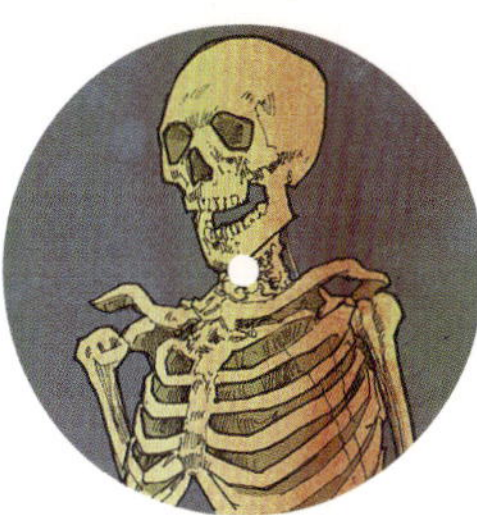
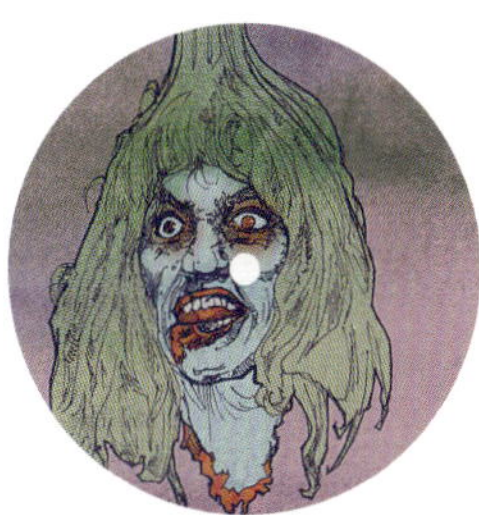

LEFT: Vinyl labels.

BELOW: LP gatefold.

The film was released with a gimmick (a well-known William Castle ploy, intended to generate publicity), in this instance "Emer- go", in which a prop skeleton is "floated" above the audience at a moment to match a climactic scene in the film. Within the plot, a skeleton is puppeteered by the Vincent Price character to scare his unfaithful wife into a vat of acid, from which the skeleton had emerged. I suggested creating a pop-up skeleton as a homage to "Emer- go". This is why there's a separate artwork for the skeleton. (At the time of writing, no final product was available to photograph for this book).

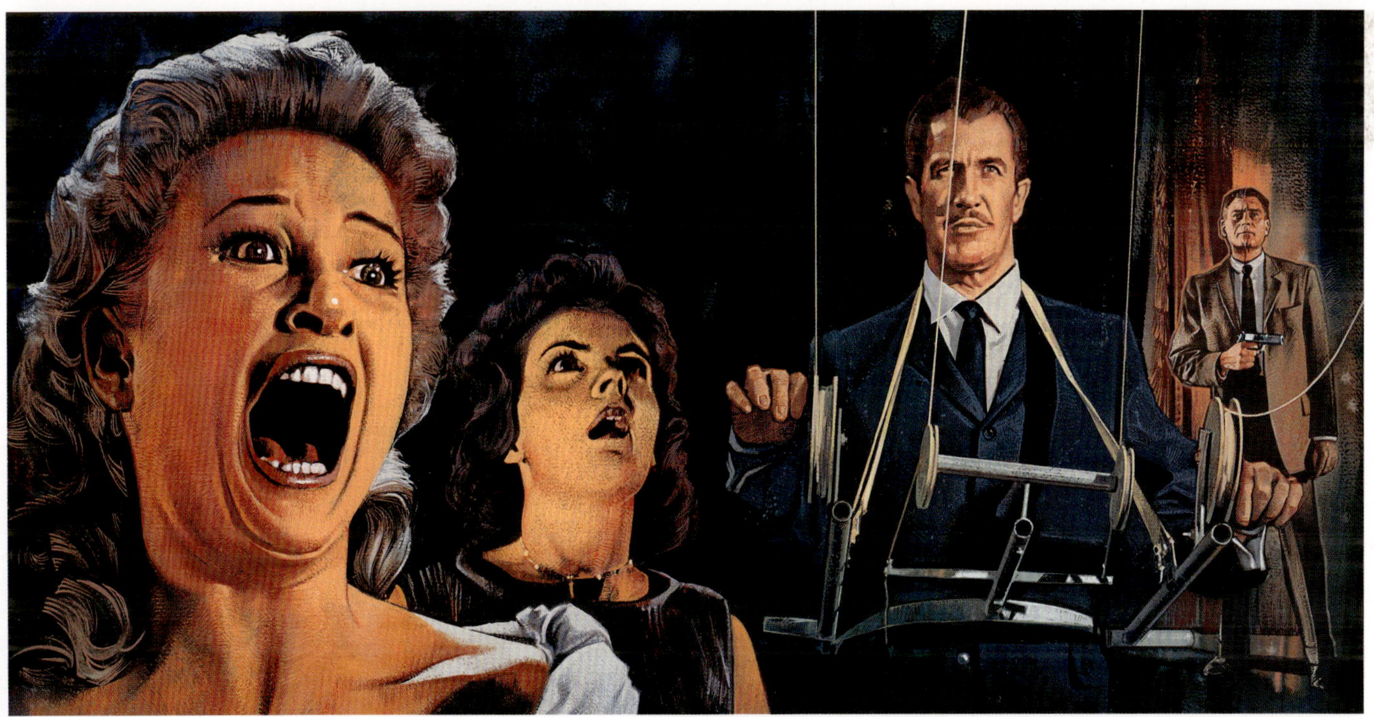

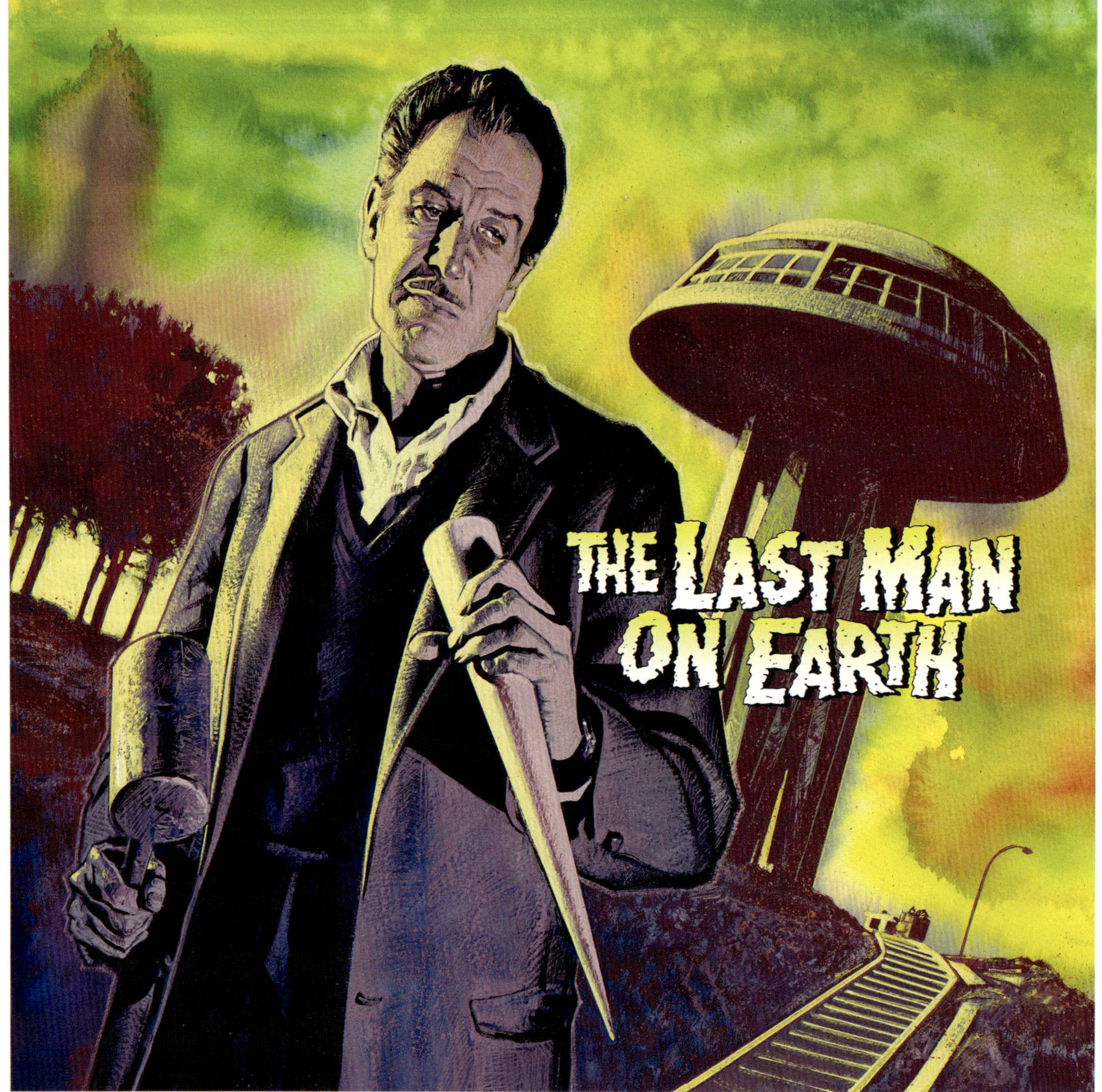

ABOVE: *The Last Man on Earth* (2022), Waxwork Records; LP front cover.

Because the focus of the film is the solitude of the central character, I felt it was essential to retain the image of Vincent Price with little else. However, the location is so unusual that I thought its inclusion was too good an opportunity to miss. The added prop indicates the nature of the story. Once again, the film (1964) is monochrome, so I chose a limited palette.

OPPOSITE TOP LEFT: LP back cover.

I used the reverse panel to add some context and help build the narrative. Dr Robert Morgan (Vincent Price) is researching a deadly virus that has become a pandemic. Also depicted, his colleague falls victim to the virus, from which Morgan is apparently immune. Given that this commission came at the time of a real-life pandemic, the subject was closer to home than would otherwise be comfortable!

OPPOSITE TOP RIGHT: LP bonus insert.

Morgan is horrified when his wife returns from the dead, drawn to the living past of a residual memory. The vampire theme is explored with the mirrors and garlic, which repel the undead (their effective death requires a stake through the heart). In this panel, Morgan's character is menaced by a reflection of his returned wife. I'd initially hoped to convince the client to print the art onto mirror board, where the reflection would be whoever held the print; sadly, that didn't come to pass.

OPPOSITE BOTTOM: LP gatefold.

I kept the horror elements for the gatefold. Despite Morgan's solitude, his life is crowded with the victims of the virus. Although they're displaying vampiric symptoms, the undead are far more akin to the zombies that first appear in George A Romero's "Living Dead' films. *The Last Man on Earth* is an acknowledged influence on *The Night of the Living Dead*, made in 1968, which is also the year in which the 1964 *The Last Man on Earth* is set!

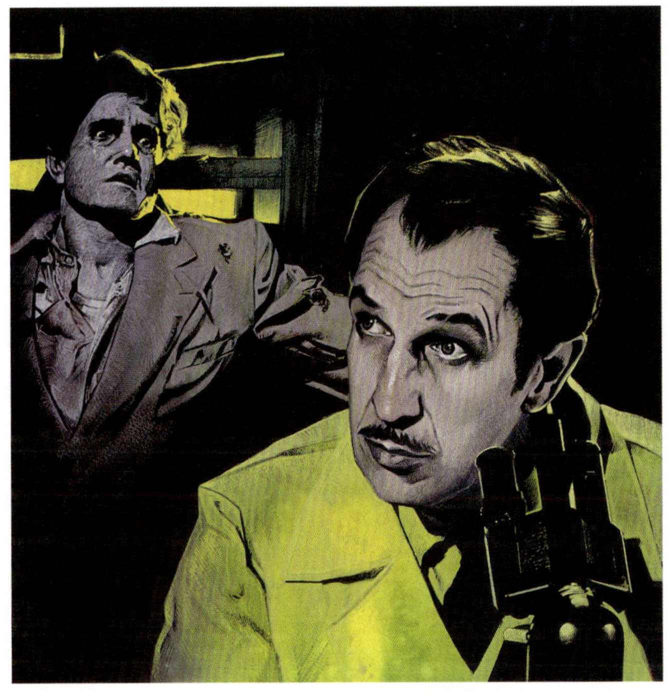
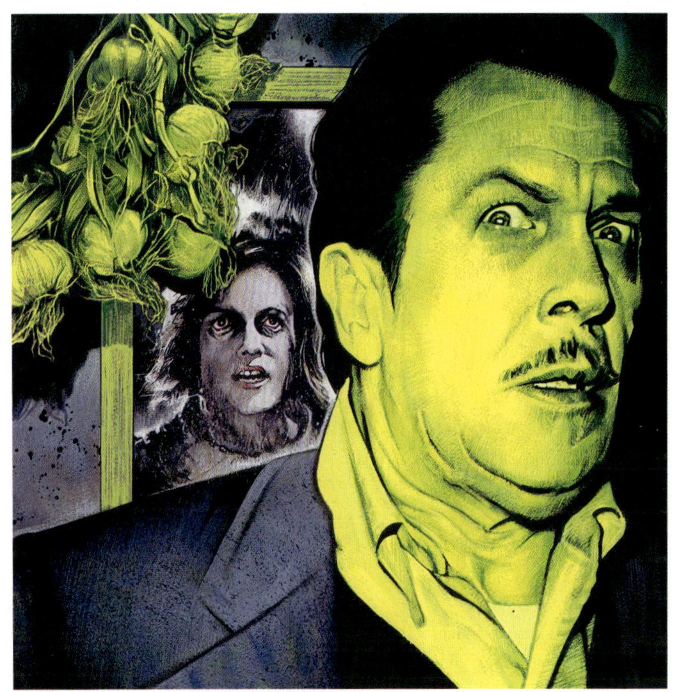

RIGHT: Vinyl labels.

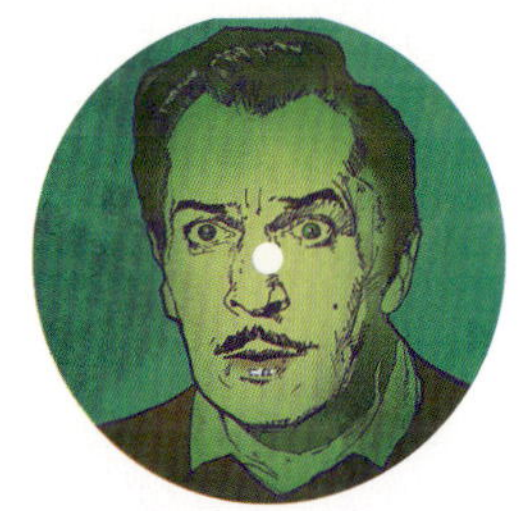
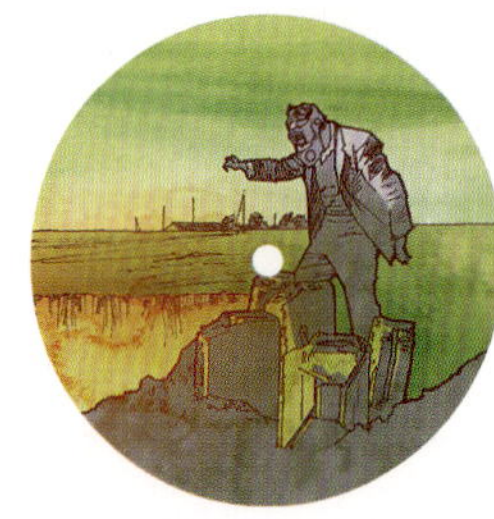
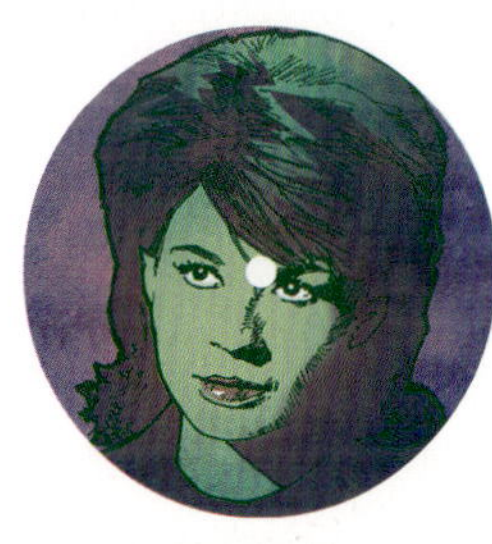
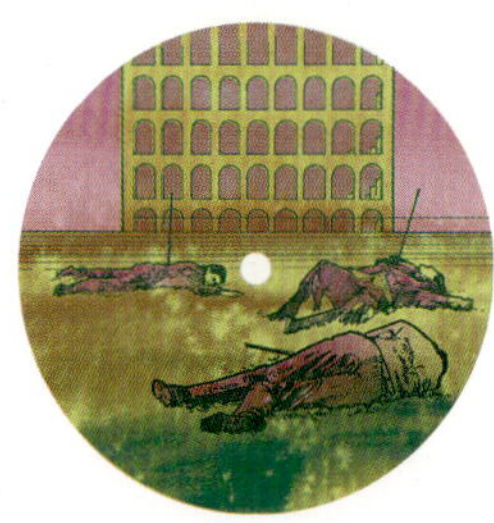

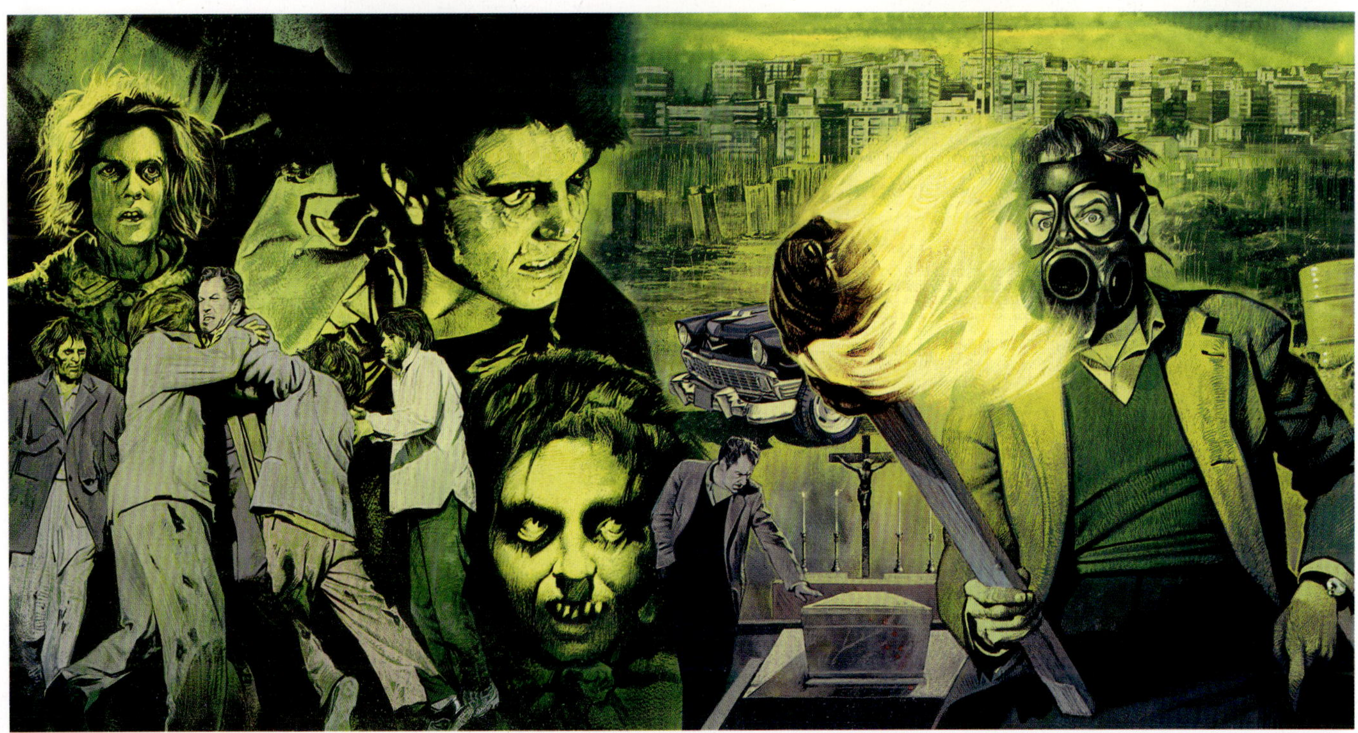

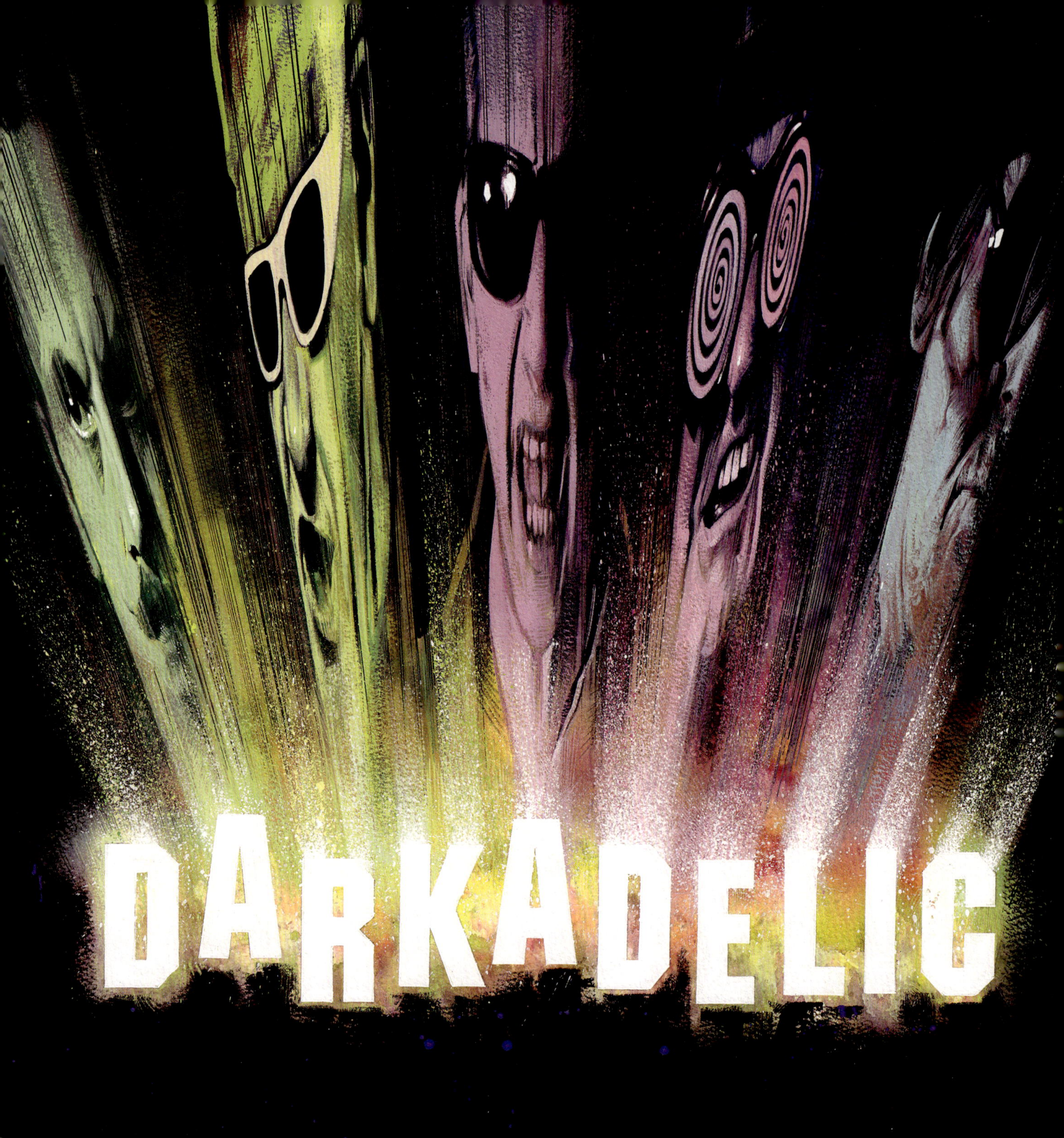

ABOVE: *Darkadelic* (2022), Edel Music & Entertainment; LP cover.

The 2023 album from UK pioneer Punk band The Damned. An artist rarely gets to paint an LP cover for a favourite band, but I was fortunate to be one of those artists. I was drafted in by the band's singer, Dave Vanian, after his lack of faith in the cover that was already being developed prompted a rethink. This was a last-minute, urgent commission, but I'd already begun my thought process after an initial phone call, so by the time we met, I was already prepared with a concept. The title styling had already been developed, a reworking of the well-known Hollywood sign, but Vanian liked the idea of light emanating from the letters, much in the way light is burning through on the title for John Carpenter's *The Thing*. I thought it would be interesting, in another film reference (by coincidence, also John Carpenter), to re-create the look of the images distorted as they're cast from the light source in the poster for *In the Mouth of Madness* (in that instance, the light source is a book). Using screen grabs from the band's new promotional video, I generated a simple Photoshop visual, which was approved for the final painted version. The colours echo that of the promotional video, which uses psychedelic elements, images from which appear on the rest of the sleeve.

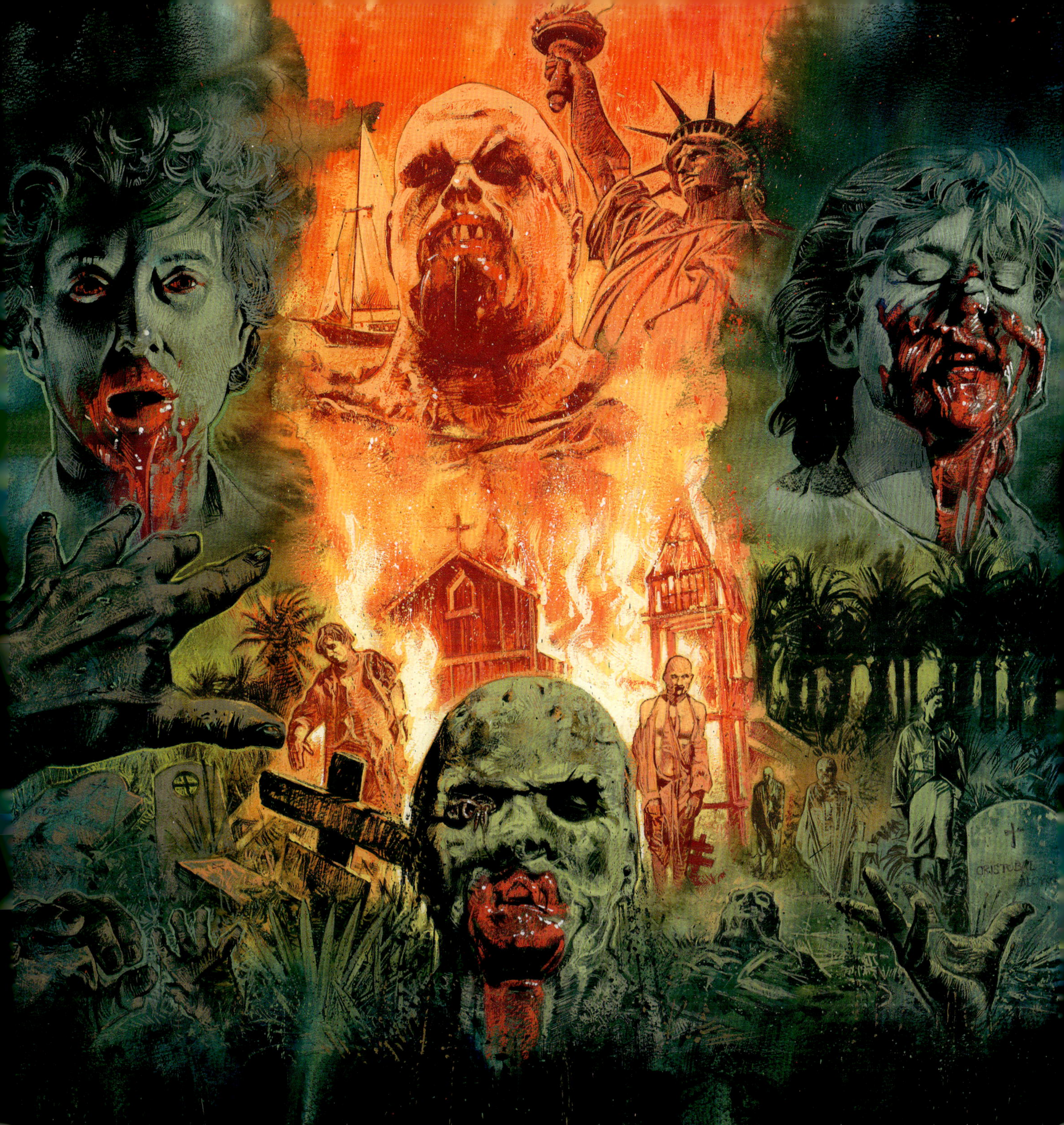

ABOVE: *Zombie Flesh Eaters* (2019), Beat Records; LP cover.

An earlier soundtrack cover painting (for Death Waltz Records, later used by Arrow Video) already existed, so I had to find new inspiration for this cover. I liked the opening sequence set in New York, where the Statue of Liberty (by tradition welcoming the world — how times have changed!) unwittingly welcomes the zombie virus onto American shores. Surrounding this vision are the horrors from the source of the outbreak. It was painted a few months before a real virus arrived on the shores of the US!

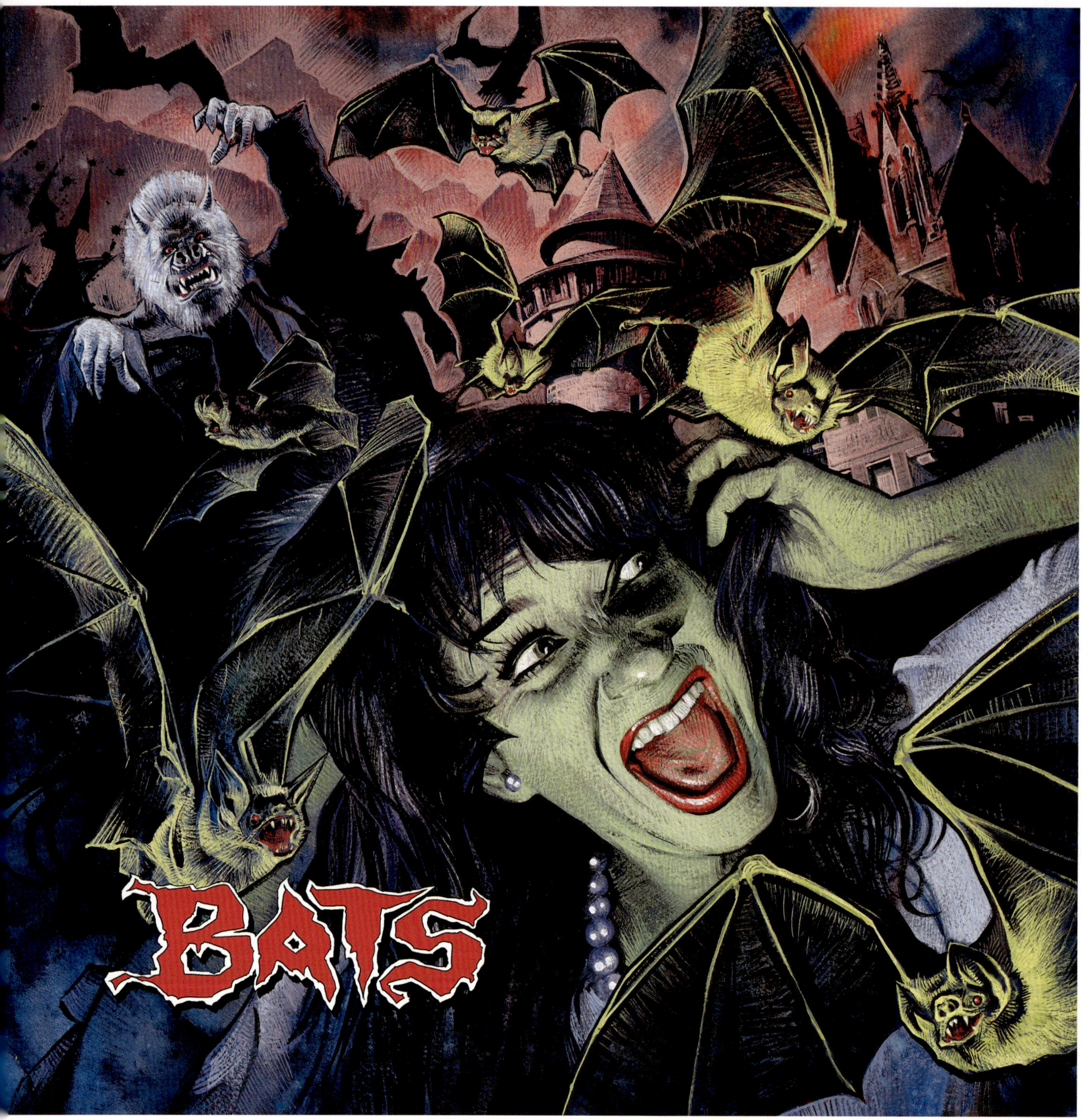

ABOVE: *Bats* (2022), Prosthetic Records LLC; LP cover.

Painted for the thrash metal band Gama Bomb, this is the fourth cover they've commissioned from me. The brief required a Hammer horror theme: castle, mountains, a vampire version of their mascot (a Yeti-type creature called "Snowy"), and a female menaced by bats (which has to emanate from Snowy's cloak). My castle reference is from one of my own travel photographs. A staged photo of someone connected to the band was supplied at my request, and the bat reference came from sourced images. I painted a logo to emulate the title style of the 1960 Hammer film *The Brides of Dracula*.

DEDICATIONS

This volume is dedicated to the memories of recently departed friends:

Dr Charlie Allbright, a fiercely intelligent genre champion.

*Alison Brown, who provided the kindest welcome at
The Cartoon Museum and was always joyous company.*

*Paul Danquah, an amazingly creative man who had decades
of inspirational work ahead, had he not been cruelly taken.*

*Jordan Mooney, the warmest and bravest of souls,
completely independent and terrifyingly free of conformity.*

*Christopher Fowler, the horror genre has been a cathartic platform
for many of us expressing our fears and observations, and Chris knew this well.
But he also understood the joy of humour — and laughter was a constant part
of the life we all shared. That is how I will remember him.*

*Marcus Campbell Sinclair, entrepreneur and man-about-town
— he was always treasured company.*

Jean Scott, my aunt.

ACKNOWLEDGEMENTS

*My thanks go to my extended family and the friends and clients
who have been so supportive in my life and work.*

*I thank the horror community, which has always been a port in troubled seas
—with a special nod to the Gentlemen (and Cads) of Horror:
you know who you are!*

My thanks to Belle and Yak, who brought this volume to print.

*I owe a special gratitude to my guest contributors, Howard Berger,
Sam Irvin, Greg Nicotero, Reece Shearsmith, and Rob Zombie,
each of whom took time out from their busy schedules
to support this book.*

For Monster Kids of all ages!

ALSO AVAILABLE FROM KORERO PRESS

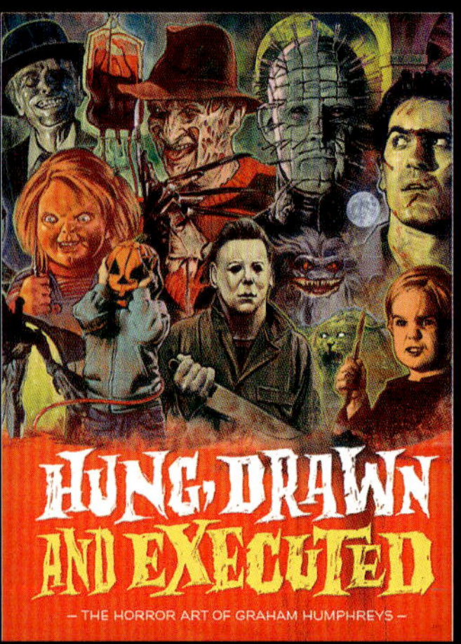

Hung, Drawn and Executed
The Horror Art of Graham Humphreys

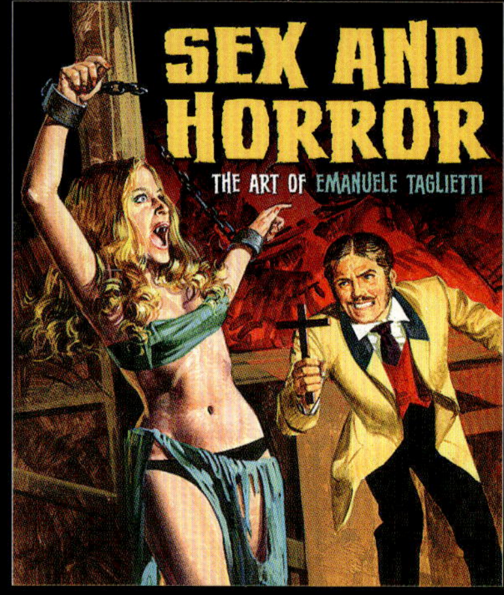

Sex and Horror Volume 1
The Art of Emanuele Taglietti

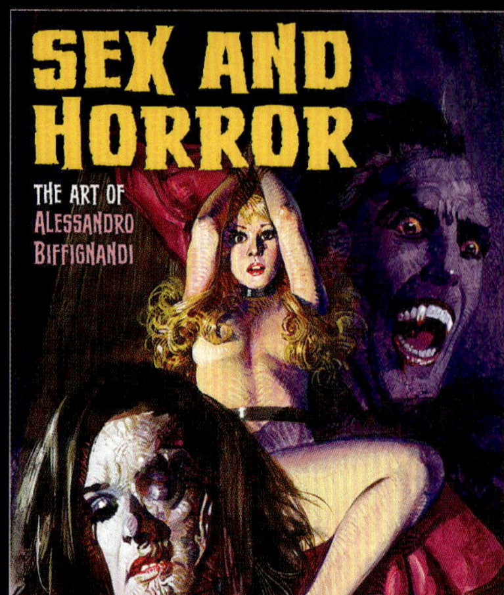

Sex and Horror Volume 2
The Art of Alessandro Biffignandi

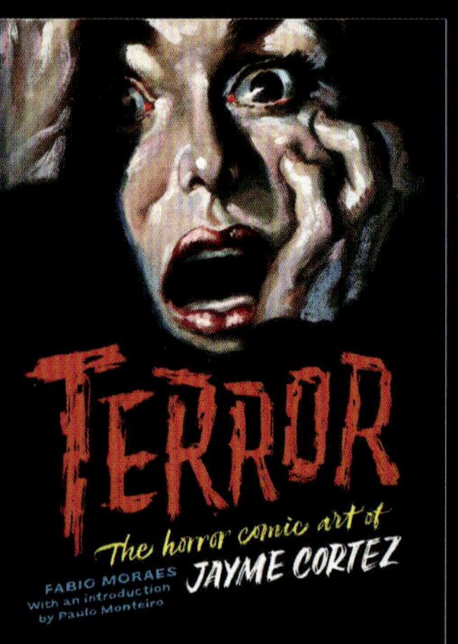

Terror: The Horror Comic Art
of Jayme Cortez, Volume 1

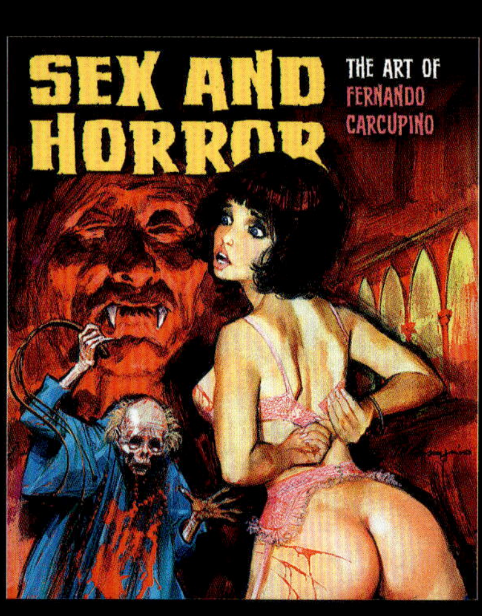

Sex and Horror Volume 3
The Art of Fernando Carcupino

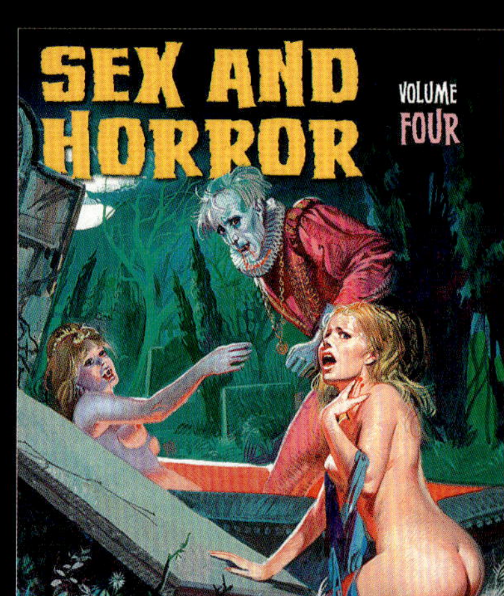

Sex and Horror Volume 4

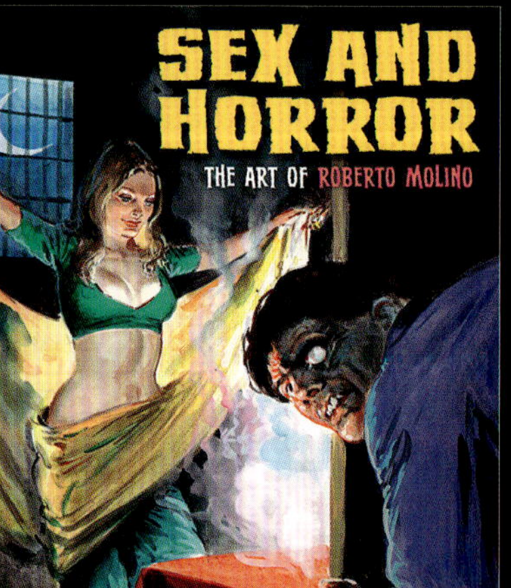

Sex and Horror Volume 5
The Art of Roberto Molinio

For news of new releases, events and offers we recommend you sign up for our newsletter and follow us on social media @koreropress. Our books can be found in traditional bricks and mortar bookshops, or purchased directly from our website and elsewhere online.

www.koreropress.com

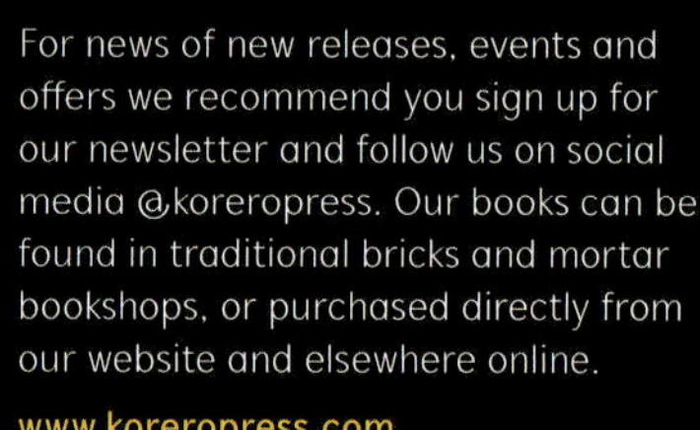

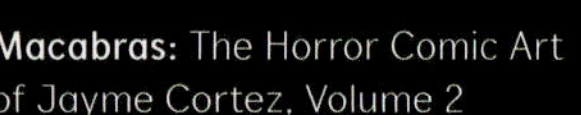

Macabras: The Horror Comic Art
of Jayme Cortez, Volume 2